THE GLOBAL
ENVIRONMENT

D

THE GLOBAL ENVIRONMENT

INSTITUTIONS, LAW, AND POLICY

Edited by

Norman J. Vig
Carleton College

Regina S. Axelrod
Adelphi University

A Division of Congressional Quarterly Inc.
Washington, D.C.

Library of Congress Cataloging-in-Publication Data

The global environment : institutions, law, and policy / Norman J.
  Vig, Regina S. Axelrod, editors.
     p.   cm.
  Includes bibliographical references and index.
  ISBN 1-56802-368-5 (paper). -- ISBN 1-56802-380-4 (hard)
    1. Environmental law. International. 2. Environmental policy.
I. Vig, Norman J. II. Axelrod, Regina S.
K3585.4.G58   1999
341.7'62--dc21   98-56516

For
Carol
Lenny and Gregg

Contents

III. International Environmental Policies and Implementation

IV. Sustainable Development: National Cases and Controversies

Preface

This volume is designed to meet the need for an authoritative assessment of the state of international environmental institutions, laws, and policies at the end of the twentieth century. Although there are numerous texts in individual disciplinary fields, we have brought together a collection of new articles by distinguished American and European scholars who span the traditional boundaries between political science, international relations, international law, policy studies, and comparative politics. We believe that only by integrating the perspectives of diverse fields can we begin to address the enormous complexities of global environmental problems in the next century.

The introductory chapter explains some of the most important concepts derived from these fields for the study of international environmental law and policy. These include basic perspectives on international cooperation drawn from international relations theory, the nature of international institutions and policy regimes, fundamental principles of international law, and the concept of sustainable development. The next three sections of the book focus on the development of international environmental institutions, laws, and policies, respectively. The fourth section presents case studies of policies and projects within individual states that have significant international repercussions. Linkages between national and international actors, as well as between official institutions and nongovernmental organizations, are discussed throughout the book.

In one sense, all serious environmental threats are now international in scope, since nearly all forms of pollution, use of resources, and destabilization of natural ecosystems have implications for the sustainability of life as we know it. Global biogeochemical cycles circulate materials and energy throughout the planetary biosphere, and losses of Earth's inherited biodiversity and mineral resources are irreversible. The consumption of resources by one country or group of people ultimately affects the life chances of other—and much larger—segments of the human population, including all those in future generations.

The nations of the world have begun to deal with many of the most obvious environmental threats over the past century, particularly since the twin imperatives of ecological sustainability and development of the world's poorest economies were put on the global agenda at the Stockholm Conference on the Human Environment in 1972. The concept of "sustainable development" articulated in the 1987 report of the World Commission on Environment and Development (the Brundtland Commission), and the United Nations Conference on Environment and Development held in Rio de Janeiro in 1992, have established a broad intellectual framework and agenda for action by the international community in the coming decades. More than one thousand international environmental agreements already exist.

Despite this hopeful progress, the prospects for attaining the levels of international cooperation necessary to manage the impacts of humans on the natural life-support systems of the planet remain grim. The authors of this book have all been asked to evaluate initial steps toward strengthening international policies and institutions to achieve the goals of sustainable development set out in 1992. Although some advances are documented, the record of the 1990s is not encouraging, and some contributors to this volume question whether there is sufficient political will at the close of the decade to make any substantial progress. The declining leadership of the United States in international environmental policymaking is discussed by several authors, particularly Robert L. Paarlberg in Chapter 11.

Disagreements over the meaning of sustainable development as well as problems in implementing environmental policies are evident throughout this book. Several contributors note the persistence of deep cleavages among "developed," "developing," and "transitional" states in various regions of the world. The raging conflict over exclusion of developing countries from the binding provisions on greenhouse gas emissions of the Kyoto Protocol negotiated in December 1997 is only the latest manifestation of this political chasm. Projects such as expansion of nuclear power in the Czech Republic (Chapter 13) and construction of the Three Gorges dam in China (Chapter 14) raise profound questions about the tradeoffs that may be required to achieve sustainable development and about the role of international financial interests in promoting incompatible forms of development.

We hope this book will be useful as a text in college and university courses as well as of interest to a broad range of scholars, professionals, and citizens who are concerned about the state of the global environment. It is intended to be a companion volume to *Environmental Policy in the 1990s,* edited by Norman J. Vig and Michael E. Kraft, a new fourth edition of which will be published by CQ Press in August 1999 as *Environmental Policy: New Directions for the Twenty-first Century.*

We wish to acknowledge the support of our colleagues and staff at Carleton College and Adelphi University, without which we would not have been able to complete this project. Norman J. Vig extends special thanks also to Michael Faure for providing workspace and assistance at the Institute for Transnational Legal Research at Maastricht University and to Marvin S. Soroos for advice and counsel on the manuscript. Regina S. Axelrod owes thanks to the National Science Foundation for a grant (SBR-9708180) that allowed her to study nuclear power development in the Czech Republic, to colleagues at Charles University, Prague, and to many anonymous officials there and at Directorate-General XI of the European Commission, who expedited her research. She also extends special gratitude to her long-suffering secretary, Pat Koslowski. Finally, both express their appreciation to Brenda Carter and Gwenda Larsen of CQ Press for their encouragement and advice, and to Joanne Ainsworth, Carolyn Goldinger, and Talia Greenberg for their editorial assistance. Any remaining errors are, of course, the authors' responsibility.

Norman J. Vig
Regina S. Axelrod

Contributors

Regina S. Axelrod is professor of political science and chair of the Political Science Department at Adelphi University. She has published numerous articles and books on environmental and energy policy in the United States and the European Union, including *Environment, Energy, Public Policy: Toward a Rational Future* (1981) and *Conflict Between Energy and Urban Environment* (1982). She has lectured at Charles University, Prague, and the University of Budapest on nuclear power and the transition to democracy and is an academic associate of the Atlantic Council and past president of the New York Political Science Association.

Gary C. Bryner is professor of political science and director of the Public Policy Program at Brigham Young University. He teaches courses on natural resource policy, environmental regulation, and international development. He is author of *Blue Skies, Green Politics: The Clean Air Act of 1990 and Its Implementation*, 2d ed. (1995) and *From Promise to Performance: Achieving Global Environmental Goals* (1997).

Daniel C. Esty is director of the Yale Center for Environmental Law and Policy and is professor at the Yale Law School and the Yale School of Forestry and Environmental Studies. He formerly served at the Environmental Protection Agency as special assistant to the administrator, as deputy chief of staff, and as deputy assistant administrator for policy. He is author or editor of a number of articles and three books on trade and the environment, including *Greening the GATT: Trade, Environment, and the Future* (1994) and *Sustaining the Asia Pacific Miracle: Environmental Protection and Economic Integration* (1997).

Michael Faure is professor of comparative and international environmental law at Maastricht University, the Netherlands. He is academic director of the Maastricht Institute for Transnational Legal Research (METRO). He has published widely in the area of environmental law and economics, environmental liability and insurance, and environmental criminal law. With Jürgen Lefevere he has written articles on the issue of environmental federalism within the European Union.

Jürgen Lefevere is staff lawyer at the Foundation for International Environmental Law and Development (FIELD) in London. Although his main area of expertise is European Community environmental law, he also works and publishes in various other fields of environmental law, including

Dutch, English, Spanish, and international environmental law. He is currently completing a book on the implementation of EU environmental law in the Netherlands, the United Kingdom, and Spain. He is also coauthor of the European Environmental Law homepage (*http://www.eel.nl*).

Duncan Liefferink is senior consultant in European and international environmental policy with Deloitte and Touche Environment in the Netherlands. Among other works, he is author of *Environment and the Nation State: The Netherlands, the European Union and Acid Rain* (1996) and coeditor of *European Environmental Policy: the Pioneers* (1997) and *The Innovation of EU Environmental Policy* (1997). He is coeditor of the Issues in Environmental Politics series published by Manchester University Press.

John McCormick is associate professor of political science at the Indianapolis campus of Indiana University, where he specializes in comparative politics, environmental policy, and the politics of the European Union. During the early 1980s he worked for two London-based environmental NGOs, the World Wildlife Fund and the International Institute for Environment and Development. He is author of *The Global Environmental Movement*, 2d ed. (1995) and *Acid Earth: The Politics of Acid Pollution*, 3d ed. (1997), and is currently working on a study of the environmental policy of the European Union.

Richard O. Miller is coordinator of international programs in the Office of Surface Mining Reclamation and Enforcement, U.S. Department of the Interior. He previously served as chief of the Planning and Analysis Staff of OSMRE and as a policy analyst in the Bureau of Land Management. He has also taught at the School of Business and Public Administration, California State University at Bakersfield, and at the Department of Political Science, University of Nevada, Las Vegas. He has written numerous articles on natural resource management and surface mining and is currently conducting a comparative study of environmental regulation in developing countries.

Michael R. Molitor is senior researcher at the Center for Environmental Research and Training at the University of California, San Diego. He has held academic appointments at the University of California, Berkeley, Stanford Law School, Carleton College, and Columbia University. His current work examines the issues that lie at the science-policy interface of the United Nations climate change negotiations. He has served in the UN Secretariat and participated in the Third United Nations Conference on the Law of the Sea as a congressional staff delegate. He is the editor of *International Environmental Law: Primary Materials* (1991).

Robert L. Paarlberg is professor of political science at Wellesley College and an associate at the Weatherhead Center for International Affairs at Harvard University. He specializes in the areas of international agricultural policy, international environmental policy, and U.S. foreign economic policy. His most recent books are *Leadership Abroad Begins at Home: U.S. Foreign Economic Policy After the Cold War* (1995), *Countrysides at Risk: A Political Geography of Sustainable Agriculture* (1994), and *Policy Reform in American Agriculture* (forthcoming). He has also been a consultant to numerous national and international agencies and has frequently testified before Congress on agricultural and trade policy.

Philippe Sands is reader in international law, University of London, School of Oriental and African Studies, and director of studies at the Foundation for International Law and Development, London University. He served as legal adviser on the delegation of St. Lucia during the negotiations on the climate change convention and at the UN Conference on Environment and Development and as legal counsel in several of the cases mentioned in his chapter.

Marvin S. Soroos is professor of political science and public administration at North Carolina State University, where he teaches global environmental law and policy. He is author of *Beyond Sovereignty: The Challenge of Global Policy* (1986) and *The Endangered Atmosphere: Preserving a Global Commons* (1997) and coauthor of *The Environment in the Global Arena: Actors, Values, Politics, and Futures* (1985). He has chaired the Environmental Studies Section of the International Studies Association.

Lawrence R. Sullivan is associate professor of political science at Adelphi University and a research associate at the East Asian Institute, Columbia University. He has also taught at Wellesley College, Miami University, and the University of Michigan, Ann Arbor. He is coeditor and cotranslator of *Dai Qing, The River Dragon Has Come! The Three Gorges Dam and the Fate of the Yangtze River and Its People* (1997), coauthor of *Historical Dictionary of the People's Republic of China* (1997), and editor and translator of numerous other books and articles on China.

Norman J. Vig is professor of political science and the Winifred and Atherton Bean Professor of Science, Technology, and Society at Carleton College, where he has taught since 1966. He is author of *Science and Technology in British Politics* (1968) and coeditor and coauthor of several books on comparative politics, political economy, environmental policy, and science and technology policy, including *Environmental Policy: New Directions for the Twenty-first Century*, 4th ed., and *Parliaments and Technology: the Development of Technology Assessment in Europe* (both forthcoming).

Edith Brown Weiss is Francis Cabell Brown Professor of International Law at Georgetown University Law Center. She served as president of the American Society of International Law from 1995 to 1996 and is a member of the board of editors of the *American Journal of International Law* and other scholarly journals. In 1990 and 1992 she was associate general counsel for international law at the U.S. Environmental Protection Agency. Among many other works, she has written *In Fairness to Future Generations* (1989) and is coauthor of *Engaging Countries: Strengthening Compliance with International Environmental Accords* (1998) and *International Environmental Law and Policy* (1998). She has received many awards, including the Elizabeth Haub Prize from the Free University of Brussels, the 1990 Certificate of Merit from the American Society of International Law, and the Harold and Margaret Sprout Award from the International Studies Association.

1

Introduction: Governing the
International Environment

Norman J. Vig

As the twentieth century draws to a close, the earth's physical and biological systems are under unprecedented strain. The human population will reach 6 billion in early 1999 and is projected to increase to 9.4 billion by the middle of the next century. The United Nations estimates that one-third of the world's people live in countries with moderate to high shortages of freshwater and that this percentage could double by 2025. Many of the world's largest cities are increasingly choked by pollution. As carbon dioxide and other greenhouse gases build in the atmosphere, the surface temperature of the earth has reached the highest level since reliable measurements have been taken; at this writing it appears that 1998 will set a new record, following previous records in 1990, 1995, and 1997. The biological diversity of the planet is also under heavy stress. Scientists believe that a mass extinction of plants and animals is under way and predict that as many as 20 percent of all species could disappear within thirty years. According to one study published in 1998, at least one in eight plant species in the world—and nearly one in three in the United States—is already threatened by extinction. Without question, the human impact on the biosphere will be one of the most critical issues of the twenty-first century.[1]

Threats to the earth's flora and fauna, water systems, and atmosphere have been recognized by scientists and conservationists for more than a century, but it is only in the past three decades that nations have begun to address these issues on a global scale. The 1972 United Nations Conference on the Human Environment in Stockholm, Sweden, attended by 113 states, marked the beginning of organized international efforts to devise a comprehensive agenda to safeguard the environment while also promoting economic development.[2] Although no binding treaties were adopted at Stockholm, the United Nations Environment Programme (UNEP) was established, creating a permanent forum for monitoring global environmental trends, convening international meetings and conferences, and negotiating international agreements. Among its most important achievements were the Vienna Convention for the Protection of the Ozone Layer in 1985 and the binding Montreal Protocol on Substances That Deplete the Ozone Layer in 1987.[3] In 1987 the World Commission on Environment and Development (known as the "Brundtland Commission" after its chair, the former Norwegian prime minister Gro Harlem Brundtland) also issued its historic report, *Our Common Future*, calling for a new era of "sustainable development."[4] To begin implementing this strategy, the UN Conference on Environment and Development (UNCED), or "Earth Summit," was convened in Rio de Janeiro, Brazil, in June 1992. The conference produced major international treaties on climate change and biodiversity, as well as two declarations of principle and a lengthy action program (Agenda 21) for implementing sustainable development throughout the world.[5] Most recently, in December 1997, more than 150 states met in Kyoto, Japan, to negotiate the first binding obligations to reduce greenhouse gases in the atmosphere by 2008–2012.[6]

These are only a few of the highlights of diplomatic activity to protect the earth's environment. There are now hundreds of other bilateral, regional, and global international agreements; Edith Brown Weiss (Chapter 5) estimates that there are more than 1,000 legal instruments with environmental provisions among 33,000 international agreements registered with the United Nations. These agreements have resulted in the rapid growth of international environmental institutions to deal with environmental problems, and they have expanded the role of other intergovernmental organizations (IGOs) in environmental matters. Some of these are formal IGOs that carry out the wishes of member states, but many more are private or nongovernmental organizations (NGOs) such as environmental groups and private business or trade associations. Indeed, many scholars have argued that a new "global civil society" has come into being that increasingly shapes the agenda and activities of official diplomatic actors.

This book presents an overview of the development of international environmental institutions, law, and policies and attempts to assess their adequacy at the end of the century. The authors analyze developments since World War II, with special emphasis on trends since the historic Earth Summit of 1992. The United Nations General Assembly itself convened a special session in June 1997 to assess progress in implementing the Rio agenda. The consensus at that "Rio + 5" meeting in New York was pessimistic, even despairing, about meeting the goals set out in 1992: no clearer definition of sustainable development could be achieved, and it appeared that nations and leaders had lost their enthusiasm for the entire UNCED project.[7] The contributors to this volume share some of this pessimism but take a longer view in evaluating the new environmental regimes that are emerging.

While cooperation among nation-states is obviously necessary to address many transboundary and common property problems, virtually all policies must be implemented at the national or local level. There are no international governments, laws, or courts that can enforce binding decisions on sovereign nations (with the partial exception of the European Union, as explained later in this volume). But equally important, actions taken by individual states (or by actors within individual countries) can have major international implications. For example, states may engage in activities that cause transboundary pollution, seriously deplete scarce resources or biodiversity, or threaten the atmosphere or other parts of the "global commons." Multinational corporations and international financial institutions may also be deeply involved in such "national" projects. The growing interaction between national and international actors and levels of governance is thus an increasingly important aspect of international environmental policy. Part IV of this book focuses on a variety of responses within individual states that may or may not promote global sustainable development.

The next two sections of this chapter provide a brief overview of the theoretical context for studying international environmental governance. The first of these summarizes the most important perspectives from international relations theory relevant to the emergence of international environmental institutions and law. The second section discusses the concept of "sustainable development," which has become the dominant ideological framework for global environmental policies in the 1990s. The third section of the chapter outlines the organization and contents of the book, briefly discussing each of the four parts: (I) international environmental *institutions*, (II) international environmental *law*, (III) international environmental *policies*, and (IV) *national case studies* in sustainable development. A short conclusion then summarizes some of the themes of the book.

International Relations, Regimes, and Governance

There is a large body of international relations theory applicable to the development of international environmental institutions and agreements.[8] The study of international relations has traditionally been dominated by two broad theoretical schools: realism and liberalism. "Realists" (or "neorealists") view the world as an anarchic collection of sovereign nation-states, each of which is a unitary actor in pursuing its unique national interests. These interests are largely defined in terms of relative power and security as compared with other states. In this perspective, nation-states do not cooperate with each other unless it is clearly in their self-interest to do so, and cooperative behavior will continue only as long as the parties perceive this condition to be met. International laws and institutions are thus essentially instruments for promoting or defending national interests and have little or no independent effect on the behavior of nations. Indeed, they can usually function only if strong or "hegemonic" states maintain them and enforce their decisions against weaker members or other states (for example, actions by the United Nations Security Council). The potential for international cooperation is therefore limited, and international laws and institutions are likely to be fragile and impermanent.[9]

This anarchic, state-centered perspective has been increasingly challenged in recent decades by a variety of "liberals," "neoliberals," and "liberal institutionalists." While most of these theorists concede that states are the primary actors on the international level, they hold that the traditional view of state sovereignty and unitary interest cannot explain the steady growth of international cooperation or the persistence of many specialized international institutions in the contemporary world. Although there are many strands of thinking, most liberal theorists hold that states are interdependent and in fact have many common interests that lead them to cooperate; moreover, they believe that international institutions not only serve these common interests but create further incentives for cooperation.[10] In other words, institutions matter, and they influence the preferences and behavior of states by allowing them to improve collective welfare outcomes by cooperating. Whereas realists focus on *relative* status gains (especially regarding military security), liberals tend to emphasize *absolute* benefits (especially mutual economic gains) made possible by international agreements and institutions that solve collective action problems.

The proliferation of international treaties and agreements to address many new kinds of problems has led many scholars to turn to the concept of *international regimes* in the past twenty years.[11] This concept has been defined in various ways, but the most widely cited usage is that of the political scientist Stephen D. Krasner: international regimes are "principles, norms, rules and decision-making procedures around which actor expectations converge in a given issue-area."[12] There are several important aspects of this definition. First, it directs attention to a large variety of functional "regimes" designed to address specific issues, such as global warming or biodiversity loss. Second, it emphasizes the acceptance of substantive principles, norms, rules, and procedures, rather than formal organization and law. Third, it leaves the door open to nonstate actors of all kinds; indeed, "convergence of expectations" involves the development of consensus among a broad range of participants, including political leaders, scientists, and interest groups. Regimes, therefore, reflect the growth of *cognitive* and *normative* understandings that facilitate voluntary cooperation, whether the resulting cooperative arrangements take the form of fully binding legal agreements or not. One can speak of an "ozone regime," a "climate change regime," and so on, providing that states and other parties act in line with mutual expectations and obligations. Finally, since regimes are not equated with static texts or laws, they can evolve over time as knowledge advances or as the parties' expectations change. For example, the 1989 Basel Convention on transboundary shipment of hazardous wastes evolved within a few years from a weak regime requiring "informed consent" by receiving nations into a strong regime banning virtually all export of hazardous wastes from developed to developing countries. Much of regime theory has focused on the conditions under which cooperative regimes come into being, are maintained, and change over time.

One approach to explaining such conditions that has been rapidly gaining attention is "cognitive" theory. This branch of theory stresses the importance of knowledge and learning, especially the growth of new scientific knowledge, as a driving force for international cooperation. One leading scholar, Peter Haas, has argued that such knowledge gives rise to "epistemic communities" of experts that are essentially transnational in nature; that is, they owe their allegiance to universally disseminated research findings or ideas that generate common understandings of problems and potential solutions.[13] From this perspective, new scientific knowledge about the physical and ecological processes of the earth has been an especially important factor in motivating cooperation among nations to solve problems such as species extinction, stratospheric ozone depletion, and global warming.[14] The resulting learning process affects other intellectual realms as well; for example, concepts of ecology and sustainability deriving from the biological sciences now affect our understanding of national security as well as economic development.

Some regime theorists have taken a further step and have begun to speak of a global "governance" system comprised of an increasingly dense and interactive network of international regimes.[15] "Governance" in this sense does not presuppose a central "government"; rather, that coordination of action can occur through many different institutions, including private social and economic systems and nongovernmental organizations, as well as a variety of governmental institutions at different levels, including IGOs. This concept often presupposes some kind of global "civil society" or decentralized network of autonomous social institutions that represent citizens and organized interests and engage in cooperative actions to achieve broad goals such as sustainable development. Increased communication and exchange of information among individuals and groups (not just experts) around the world through the Internet and other means can magnify the impact of such civic action to the point where common ideas and values begin to influence the actions of governments throughout the world from the bottom up (while also undermining the authority of national governments).[16]

This brief discussion should highlight the fact that whatever one's basic theoretical perspective, the development of international environmental cooperation has become one of the most fruitful and dynamic fields of international relations scholarship in the past decade. Although there is no consensus among scholars as to the nature of the world system or the autonomy and durability of current international environmental institutions, laws, and policies, it is undeniable that the global environment has become a principal concern of political actors as well as scholars throughout the world. From this broader vantage point, the halting and confused human response to gathering evidence of potential ecological catastrophe may be less discouraging than short-term observations suggest.

Sustainable Development

Cutting across theoretical disputes are the realities of world economic and social development. Environmental threats are the product not only of population growth and of ignorant or careless individual actions; they are deeply embedded in our religious, cultural, economic, and social systems. Perhaps the most obvious realities are that these systems are highly fragmented and differentiated and that global economic development is grossly uneven. The gap between the rich and the poor nations of the world is enormous and continues to grow. This difference among nations at various stages and levels of development has profound implications for the global environment. As has been recognized at least since the Stockholm conference, the needs and agendas of developed nations (the "North") and developing countries (the "South") are fundamentally different, making it difficult to reach consensus on international policies that benefit all parties.[17] Essentially, while the North gives substantial attention to "environmental" issues that threaten ecological stability, the South has placed greater emphasis on immediate needs for economic growth to raise standards of living. Indeed, developing countries threatened to boycott the Stockholm conference out of fears that environmental protection was a plot by the North to limit their development—a concern that still echoes through all international negotiations.[18]

The North-South division raises fundamental issues of international equity.[19] Developing countries rightly argue that the developed countries have benefited from environmental exploitation in the past and are responsible for most of the world's pollution and resource depletion, including that leading to ozone depletion and climate change; therefore it is primarily their responsibility to deal with these problems. Furthermore, they are not willing to foreclose opportunities for economic growth that would permanently lock them into poverty and dependency while the peoples of the North engage in profligate consumption. Representatives of developing countries (organized as the Group of 77 in the United Nations since 1964, but now actually including some 155 states) thus usually condition their willingness to participate in international environmental treaties and agreements on concessions from the North, such as guarantees of special funding and transfer of technologies to enable them to reduce their impact on the environment while increasing economic growth.

Another fundamental dimension of global environmental protection concerns intertemporal, or intergenerational, equity. That is, policies must consider not only the needs of the present generation but those of the future. There are many aspects of this obligation, but in her chapter Edith Brown Weiss defines three essential principles: (1) each generation should be required to conserve the diversity of the resource base so that it does not unduly restrict the options available to future generations; (2) each generation should maintain the planet's overall quality so that it is bequeathed in no worse condition than received; and (3) members of every generation should have comparable rights of access to the legacy of past generations and should conserve this access for future generations. The latter principle implies a degree of intragenerational equity as a condition for intergenerational equity; that is, no group should either be denied a right to present environmental resources or be asked to bear a disproportionate share of environmental burdens (a principle often referred to as *environmental justice*).

The concept of sustainable development was born of these concerns. First set out in *World Conservation Strategy*, published by the International Union for the Conservation of Nature (IUCN) in cooperation with the World Wildlife Fund and UNEP in 1980, the concept was popularized in the Brundtland Report of 1987. The famous definition of sustainable development is from this report: "Sustainable development is development that meets the needs of the present without compromising the ability of future generations to meet their own needs." This was immediately followed by the statement that two key concepts were embedded within it: "the concept of 'needs,' in particular the essential needs of the world's poor, to which over-riding priority should be given"; and "the idea of limitations imposed by the state of technology and social organization on the environment's ability to meet present and future needs."[20]

Several elements in this definition are critical for an understanding of sustainable development. First, the concept clearly represents an attempt to bridge the concerns and interests of developed and developing nations, but it applies to both (that is, industrial as well as less-developed countries must change their production and consumption patterns). Second, it attempts to reconcile economic growth and environmental protection rather than viewing them as tradeoffs; indeed, the Brundtland Report argues that nei-ther is possible without the other. Third, the concept is strongly anthro-pocentric. It starts from the premise that human needs must be met in order to address environmental problems. Thus, improvement in the living condi-tions in poor countries, and especially of women and marginal social and economic groups, is an essential precondition for ecological preservation. Fourth, the limits to growth are not ultimately physical or biological but social and technological; it is assumed that environmental problems can be solved. Finally, the concept is extremely general, lacking in specific content as to how sustainable development is to be attained or who is responsible for achieving it. This vagueness was deliberate: it allows the idea to be adopted by virtually everyone as a way of bringing people together to seek common ground. In this formulation it is clearly a political and social construct, not a scientific concept or blueprint.[21]

There are numerous other definitions of sustainable development; indeed, by one count there are at least seventy in circulation.[22] These formu-lations reflect the different values and priorities of the holders. For example, in 1991 the IUCN published a sequel to *World Conservation Strategy* entitled *Caring for the Earth*, which put more emphasis back on ecological limits: sus-tainable development was defined as "improving the quality of human life while living within the carrying capacity of supporting ecosystems." The more general idea of "sustainability" has also been the subject of considerable controversy; *Caring for the Earth* defines it simply as "a characteristic of a process or state that can be maintained indefinitely."[23]

Scholars have tried to sort out the many meanings and implications of these ideas. From the beginning it was clear that there were stronger and weaker ideologies of sustainable development, ranging from marginal requirements for "greening" industrial development to calls for radical social-political change to bring human actions into harmony with ecocentric values. Table 1-1 presents one effort by a group of European scholars to summarize these variants in the form of a "ladder" extending from the traditional (cur-

Table 1-1 The Ladder of Sustainable Development in Advanced Industrial Societies

Approach to sustainable development	Role of economy and nature of growth	Geograph-ical focus	Nature	Policies and sectoral integration	Technology	Institutions	Policy instruments and tools	Redistri-bution	Civil society	Philosophy
"Ideal Model" of sustainable development	Right liveli-hood; meeting needs not wants; changes in patterns and levels of production and con-sumption	Bioregion-alism; extensive local self-sufficiency	Promoting and pro-tecting bio-diversity	Holistic intersectoral integration	Labour-intensive appropriate technology	Decentral-ization of political, legal, social and eco-nomic insti-tutions	Full range of policy tools; sophisticated use of indi-cators ex-tending to social di-mensions	Inter- and intra-gener-ational equity	Bottom-up community structures and control. New ap-proach to valuing work	Ecocentric/biocentric
Strong sustainable development	Environ-mentally regulated market; changes in patterns of production and con-sumption	Heightened local eco-nomic self-sufficiency, promoted in the context of global markets	Environ-mental man-agement and protection	Environ-mental policy inte-gration across sec-tors	Clean technology; product life-cycle manage-ment; mixed labour- and capital-intensive technology	Some restructuring of institu-tions	Advanced use of sus-tainability indicators; wide range of policy tools	Strength-ened redis-tribution policy	Open-ended dialogue and envisioning	

Weak sustainable development	Market-reliant environmental policy; changes in patterns of consumption	Initial moves to locate economic self-sufficiency; minor initiatives to alleviate the power of global markets	Replacing finite resources with capital; exploitation of renewable resources	Sector-driven approach	End-of-pipe technical solutions; mixed labour- and capital-intensive technology	Minimal amendments to institutions	Token use of environmental indicators; limited range of market-led policy tools	Equity a marginal issue	Top-down initiatives; limited state-environmental movements dialogue	Anthropocentric
Treadmill	Exponential growth	Global markets and global economy	Resource exploitation	No change	Capital-intensive production technologies; progressive automation	No change	Conventional accounting	Equity not an issue	Very limited dialogue between the state and environmental movements	

Source: Susan Baker, Maria Kousis, Dick Richardson, and Stephen Young, *The Politics of Sustainable Development* (London: Routledge, 1997), 9.

rently predominant) concept of unlimited economic growth ("Treadmill") to "weak," "strong," and "ideal" versions of sustainable development.

Whatever the conceptual and ideological differences below the surface, there have been numerous attempts to translate sustainable development into policy initiatives. The most important political effort to do so occurred at the UN Conference on Environment and Development in 1992. UNCED produced both a general declaration of principles (Rio Declaration on Environment and Development) and Agenda 21, a massive effort to define strategies and policies for implementing sustainable development. Governments throughout the world pledged to formulate sustainable development plans and programs, and a new Commission on Sustainable Development was established by the UN General Assembly to monitor these commitments. Many other regional, national, and local organizations have adopted the principles and goals of sustainable development since 1992, including the European Union. Organizations such as UNEP, the IUCN-World Conservation Union, the World Bank, the Organisation for Economic Cooperation and Development, and the U.S. National Academy of Sciences have also been actively working to identify specific empirical "indicators" for measuring progress toward sustainable development.[24]

Most of the chapters in this book discuss efforts to incorporate the idea of sustainable development into international environmental institutions, treaties, and policies in the 1990s (see especially Chapters 2, 4, 6, 8, and 12–15). Chapter 8 focuses specifically on the difficulties of implementing Agenda 21 on a global scale. The case studies in Part IV evaluate particular national policies from this perspective, further illustrating the obstacles to realizing sustainable development in both North and South.

Overview of the Book

This section outlines the main themes and concepts of the four parts of the book and briefly summarizes each of the individual contributions.

International Environmental Institutions

International political institutions have traditionally been regarded as weak and fragile, especially by the realist school of international relations. Students of international environmental regimes have been somewhat more optimistic in light of the proliferation of environmental treaties and agreements since 1972 and the enhanced role of United Nations and European Community institutions in environmental policymaking. Some new institutions—such as the Global Environment Facility and the Commission for Sustainable Development—have been created in the 1990s, while many existing institutions—such as the World Bank and the United Nations Development Programme—have taken on new environmental obligations.[25] Both the Brundtland Report and Agenda 21 emphasized the importance of strengthening environmental institutions at both national and international levels. An entire chapter (38) of Agenda 21 was devoted to strengthening and coordinating the various components of the UN system, while another (27) called for enhancing the role of nongovernmental organizations (NGOs) in all aspects of sustainable development.

The term *institutions* has been used differently by international theorists. Some limit the term to formal organizations that have defined memberships, offices, staffs, and other tangible facilities. Others use the term to cover almost any regularized pattern of interaction or behavior, whether formally organized or not. Some tend to equate international institutions with "regimes," while others draw sharp distinctions between organizations and regimes.[26] For our purposes, the term *institutions* will refer to both formal intergovernmental organizations (IGOs) and international nongovernmental organizations (INGOs) that play a role in the establishment, maintenance, and implementation of environmental policy regimes. Regimes are arrangements for cooperation in specific areas of international law or policy that include all relevant actors—member states, international organizations and officials, and unofficial participants such as INGOs and groups of experts— together with the various relevant documents such as treaties, conventions, or declarations that establish the rules and expectations. The degree of formal legal obligation involved in regimes varies greatly, but there are usually some binding requirements.

International environmental organizations take many forms. Some of the oldest, like European river basin commissions or the International Joint Commission formed by the United States and Canada in 1909 to preserve the Great Lakes, are bilateral or multilateral bodies created to encourage cooperation in managing a shared resource. Some, like the International Whaling Commission (1946) and International Tropical Timber Organization (1987), concern the worldwide harvesting and trade of specific categories of living resources, while others protect "common pool" resources such as Antarctica and the high seas that are beyond national jurisdictions. The International Maritime Organization (1982) regulates shipping to reduce pollution both as a result of normal operations and accidents. Still others, like the World Meteorological Organization (1950), conduct scientific research and monitor environmental change on a global scale. Finally, many are essentially ad hoc organizations, such as the Conferences of Parties (COPs) that are created to monitor and develop detailed protocols to treaties and conventions.

Most of these international bodies are intergovernmental organizations, meaning that they are created by member states and are accountable to them. In most cases member states are formally equal in governing (though not financing) these institutions, but in some (notably the World Bank and the International Monetary Fund) weighted voting procedures are used that reflect donor contributions. This has become a contentious issue in recent negotiations over multilateral funding mechanisms to channel special economic assistance to the South. The Global Environment Facility, which provides funding primarily for implementation of the climate change and biodiversity conventions in developing countries, was restructured after 1992 to give recipient countries more influence in financial decisions.

How effective have these formal organizations been? Have they been strengthened significantly since the Rio conference? Are they sufficiently strong and resilient at the turn of the century to handle the growing array of global environmental problems?

In Chapter 2, Marvin S. Soroos looks at the evolution of global institutions since the Stockholm era and focuses on the record and current state of five principal IGOs: the United Nations General Assembly, the United Nations Environment Programme, the UN Commission on Sustainable Development (CSD), the Global Environment Facility (GEF), and the World Bank. Overall, he finds substantial accomplishments in regard to focusing worldwide attention on environmental problems; framing new principles, policies, and laws; facilitating international treaties and agreements; coordinating environmental monitoring and promoting scientific research; and providing modest technical and financial support for sustainable development projects. But the picture is a very mixed one at the end of the 1990s. The new institutions, GEF and CSD, have gotten off to a slow start in promoting sustainable development. The UN General Assembly and UNEP have lost the support of a number of key governments since 1992, notably that of the United States (see Chapter 11); indeed, UNEP appeared on the brink of collapse in 1997–1998. And while the World Bank has made considerable efforts to develop environmentally sensitive loan policies, it continues to support many destructive projects and it is doubtful whether, on balance, it can be said to be furthering sustainable development. Overall, despite great progress since the 1960s, it appears that the state of critical environmental IGOs has deteriorated rather than improved in the post-Rio period. Soroos suggests that a new central UN agency such as an Environmental Security Council may be needed to deal effectively with coming problems, but he doubts that agreement could be reached on creating such an institution. The alternative is to strengthen existing institutions and improve coordination between them.

In Chapter 3, John McCormick also reviews the basic functions and performance of IGOs and finds them wanting. He argues that the failure of the nation-state system since World War II—including its dependent environmental organizations—has led to the rapid rise of local, national, and international nongovernmental organizations to fill the vacuum. These groups, ranging from thousands of local grassroots organizations to large federations of national organizations such as the International Union for Conservation of Nature and the World Wide Fund for Nature, play an increasingly important role in setting the environmental agenda, participating in negotiations that create environmental regimes, and monitoring the implementation of treaties and agreements and environmental conditions generally. NGOs are now essential actors in international environmental regimes whether they have official status or not. Collectively, McCormick and others argue, they provide the backbone of an emerging global civil society in which the loyalties of individuals transcend national boundaries.

This does not mean that NGOs or INGOs are homogeneous in their beliefs, goals, or methods. McCormick distinguishes several different philosophies of environmentalism, as well as basic differences between groups in developing and developed countries and among different socio-economic groups. Focusing on some of the larger INGOs, he provides numerous examples of how they carry out different functions and specialize in different issue areas. They also collaborate with each other and with IGOs in various campaigns, often forming broad international alliances (for example, to save tropical rain forests and endangered species). However, they are also handicapped by the lack of any central environmental authority on the international level, by the consequent need to influence a large number of national governments, by the power of countervailing interest groups, and by the weakness of international legal enforcement.[27]

The role of NGOs is thus limited by the state of IGOs and of the inter-national system generally. One important issue is how much access these groups are allowed to information and to the internal decision processes of IGOs and their subsidiary organizations (such as panels of experts). This is generally framed as an issue of *transparency;* that is, the degree of "openness" of the operations of international agencies. The overall trend noted by many scholars is toward greater access and transparency in international relations, but some important IGOs remain exceptions. In particular, the new World Trade Organization (WTO), which makes decisions on the legality of trade barriers under the General Agreement on Tariffs and Trade (GATT) that may conflict with environmental protections, has remained closed to NGOs and unresponsive to environmental concerns (see Chapter 9).

One international organization stands out for having made the greatest progress in transcending the limits of state sovereignty—the European Union. Initially created by the Treaty of Rome in 1957 as a "common market" of six European nations, it now has fifteen members and is poised to expand to much of central and eastern Europe. Although still in many respects an intergovernmental organization, since final decisions are made by the Council of Ministers representing member states, the EU also has many supranational attributes; that is, under the various treaty revisions since 1957 the member states have gradually pooled a substantial degree of sovereignty. While the principal goal of the EU remains economic integration to create a "single economic market," the Union has also established a vast array of common environmental policies that now largely govern environmental pro-tection in the individual member states. The EU has also become a principal actor in international environmental diplomacy, leading the way, for example, in pushing for a stronger climate change regime.

Chapter 4, by Regina S. Axelrod and Norman J. Vig, describes the unique structure and evolution of the EU (which incorporates the European Community) and analyzes policy developments since 1992 (the date of the critical Maastricht EU treaty revisions as well as the Rio conference). While generally optimistic, the authors note a significant shift in governance strategy in response to the more prominent position given to the principle of "subsidiarity" in the Maastricht Treaty. Subsidiarity holds that the EU should act only "if and in so far as the objectives of the proposed action cannot be sufficiently achieved by the member states." As a result the EU has been less willing to initiate new legislation since 1992, and most of the new laws that have been enacted now take the form of "framework directives" that set general sustainability goals but allow states greater freedom to define specific implementation strategies. Thus, although the EU has strongly endorsed the general principles of sustainable development in its Fifth Environmental Action Programme, it is questionable whether these goals will be met in many countries. The chapter concludes that despite great progress, the EU faces major institutional challenges in improving policy implementation and enforcement, devising new and more efficient policy instruments, and in managing the enlargement to transitional central and eastern European states without weakening or reversing gains that have been made in the past.

International Environmental Law

Law is the traditional instrument for implementing public decisions. International law differs from domestic law mainly in that there is no legislature and no sovereign authority to enforce compliance. Although there are international courts and tribunals of various kinds—including the International Court of Justice, or "World Court," and the European Court of Justice—they are ultimately dependent on national governments to carry out their decisions. International law differs from domestic law also in that it generally applies only to states, not individuals (there are exceptions for war crimes and certain other aspects of human rights law). International law has several sources, including norms that are recognized as binding and honored through state practice, known as customary law; general principles of law that are widely recognized in national legal systems; and, most important, treaties, conventions, and other formal agreements that are signed and ratified by states. International organizations established by treaty can also make further international law through secondary legislation. It should be noted that treaty law is binding only on the parties (signatories), whereas general principles of law and customary law are considered obligatory for all nations.[28]

The study of international law and the study of political science have traditionally been separate domains, but this is beginning to change. At least among some legal scholars and international relations theorists, there is growing convergence of analytical perspectives around the concept of international regimes.[29] Essentially, political scientists are becoming more appreciative of the importance of formal legal structures, while students of international law are recognizing the interrelatedness of law with political and economic processes. International regimes can be seen as combining these elements in building consensus on "principles, norms, rules, and decision-making procedures," with legal rules and protocols forming a part but not all of the overall regime structure.[30] The evolution of broad framework conventions into increasingly detailed binding agreements in the form of protocols can then be understood as part of the overall regime formation process.

As noted earlier, there has been a rapid growth of international environmental law in the past three decades as a result of the many treaties and conventions that have been negotiated. Some nonbinding statements of principle adopted by international institutions or conferences (a form of "soft law") have also come to be recognized and observed by states to the point where they are considered expressions of customary law. Perhaps the most important is Principle 21 of the Stockholm Declaration, which reads:

> States have, in accordance with the Charter of the United Nations and the principles of international law, the sovereign right to exploit their own resources pursuant to their own environmental policies, and the responsibility to ensure that activities within their jurisdiction or control do not cause damage to the environment of other States or of areas beyond the limits of national jurisdiction.

This formulation, which attempts to balance the principle of territorial sovereignty with the obligation not knowingly to impair the rights of others, can be traced back to Roman law doctrine limiting sovereignty (*sic utere tuo ut alienum non laedas*).[31] It underlies all modern law governing transboundary pollution and use of common resources, including the landmark *Trail Smelter* decision of 1941 in which an arbitration tribunal awarded damages to the United States for air pollution originating in Canada.[32] In the context of recent conventions on such matters as biodiversity and climate change, Principle 21 raises acute questions about the global consequences of national activities such as destruction of rain forests and emission of greenhouse gases.

Fearing that Principle 21 might be used to limit their growth, developing nations were instrumental in drafting a new Principle 2 of the Rio Declaration which inserted the words "and developmental" after "environmental" in the first clause of Principle 21, thus implying that economic development policies as well as environmental policies should guide resource exploitation.[33] The Rio Declaration and Agenda 21 refer to "the international law on sustainable development" rather than "international environmental law" for the same reason. However, other emerging principles of international law—such as the "precautionary principle," which holds that when environmental threats are potentially severe, actions should be taken even in the absence of scientific certainty—are also cited in the Rio Declaration and are incorporated into recent treaties such as the Framework Convention on Climate Change.

Two chapters in Part II discuss the growing volume and importance of international environmental law. Edith Brown Weiss sets the stage in Chapter 5 with an overview of the changing structure of the entire international political and legal system. She begins by noting that the conventional concept of unitary sovereign states no longer describes reality. The world is simultaneously becoming more integrated at the elite level and more fragmented at the local community level. New forms of communication have created new transnational elites and organizations of all kinds, while at the same time intensifying awareness of differences among peoples and cultures. As the world becomes less hierarchical, international law becomes increasingly important in providing the "normative framework and the procedures for coordinating behavior, controlling conflict, facilitating cooperation, and achieving values."

But there are also fundamental changes in the structure and processes of international law. Traditional distinctions between international and domestic law, and between public and private law, are rapidly breaking down. Indeed, much of current international environmental law is being created through private international agreements that set product and process standards and define environmental management practices throughout the world. Legally nonbinding voluntary agreements are becoming increasingly important as more nongovernmental actors participate in the definition and implementation of soft law norms. At the same time, the substance of public international law increasingly reflects concern with moral issues such as human rights and intergenerational equity and extends to many areas heretofore considered private. The resulting legal structure is exceedingly complex, raising a host of new questions about its consistency and manageability, as well as about the accountability of the many new transnational nonstate actors involved.

Philippe Sands provides a more detailed history of the development of international environmental law and principles in Chapter 6. He points out that prior to the establishment of the United Nations in 1945, there was no international forum in which to raise international environmental issues. Although the UN Charter does not explicitly mention the environment or conservation of resources, the UN convened its first environmental conference in 1949 and hosted many negotiations prior to the Stockholm conference in 1972. Most of the current environmental treaties were signed in the two decades between 1972 and 1992, and recent decisions of the International Court of Justice confirm that the environment is now considered within the mainstream of international law. Sands discusses the most important emerging principles of environmental law and summarizes the development of international legal standards in six broad fields: protection of flora and fauna, the marine environment, freshwater resources, air quality, waste management, and hazardous substances. He concludes that enforcement of this body of international law will be the most critical issue in the next phase of its development, suggesting that international judicial and quasi-judicial bodies will have to play a much stronger role than heretofore.

There are several recent studies on environmental treaty compliance and implementation.[34] Chapter 7, by Michael Faure and Jürgen Lefevere, reviews some of this literature and focuses on the changing theory and practice of compliance. First, the authors distinguish between treaty compliance, implementation, enforcement, and effectiveness. Whereas *compliance* refers to the extent to which the behavior of states conforms to the rules set out in a treaty, *implementation* involves specific actions taken by states within their own legal systems to make a treaty operative; *enforcement* denotes measures to force state compliance and implementation; and *effectiveness* focuses on whether the objectives of the treaty are actually achieved. Compliance does not guarantee effectiveness but is usually a necessary condition unless the treaty itself is so weak that compliance requires no changes in behavior.

Traditionally, international agreements have included some dispute settlement procedures or other provisions for invoking legal, economic, or political sanctions against noncompliant parties, but in practice such sanctions have rarely been enforced and are seldom effective in achieving treaty objectives. Faure and Lefevere discuss the many factors that can affect rates of compliance, including the number of parties involved, the capacities of national governments, the strength of NGOs, and the nature of the substantive provisions (primary rules) written into the treaties themselves. They show how there has been a shift from the traditional enforcement approach to a managerial approach in some recent environmental agreements such as the Montreal Protocol on ozone-depleting substances. These new "comprehensive noncompliance response" systems put more emphasis on improving information and reporting systems and inducing compliance through negotiation and incentives than on threats of punishment. The authors suggest that such nonadversarial methods can improve environmental performance.

International Environmental Policy

International policies are "joint responses to common problems that two or more national governments work out with one another, often with the active participation of IGOs and INGOs."[35] As such, international policies may or may not take the form of international law (norms or agreements that are binding on states). In the field of international environmental policy, they range from broad policy declarations and informal agreements to highly articulated conventions and treaties. They can apply to private parties as well as to states (for example, regulations concerning commerce in hazardous materials), and they may or may not be implemented by governments. It is becoming increasingly common to speak of "policy regimes" when a large number of countries are involved in ongoing policy negotiations regarding a particular issue or problem.

The range of international environmental policies currently in force is vast, covering protection of endangered plants and animals; protection against transboundary pollution of air, water, and soil; protection of the atmosphere against acidification, ozone depletion, and climate change; protection of the oceans against oil spills and the dumping of radioactive and other hazardous materials; conservation of fisheries; protection against trade in dangerous chemicals, pesticides, and hazardous wastes; measures to combat desertification; and protection of Antarctica. In addition to these specific policy regimes, new policies are also emerging for consideration of environmental protection under the rules of international trade, and for promoting sustainable development initiatives pursuant to Agenda 21.[36]

One critical aspect of sustainable development recommended in the Brundtland Report and in the Rio documents is the need for *policy integration*. Environmental policy should no longer be considered as a separate policy sector but should be incorporated into all other policymaking as well. This is becoming especially important in areas such as energy, transportation, agriculture, employment, trade, and tourism. The Amsterdam Treaty of the European Union requires that environmental protection be integrated into all EU policies and activities, but even the EU is having a difficult time making this a reality. The European Commission is divided up into twenty-three directorates, each with different policy responsibilities; and at the national level separate bureaucracies and their constituencies usually fight to maintain control of their specific sectors.

In Chapter 8, Gary Bryner examines worldwide efforts to implement sustainable development policies pursuant to Agenda 21. After summarizing the goals and detailed contents of the document itself, he asks whether there was any progress toward realizing them in the five years after 1992. Citing a wide array of empirical indicators, he finds little if any evidence of a transition toward sustainability; indeed, for much of the developing world social and economic conditions have continued to deteriorate. Part of the problem is that developed countries have failed to provide the financial assistance recognized as essential at Rio (overseas development aid has actually declined). But the problems are so deeply embedded in social, economic, and cultural systems that it is difficult to see how current international institutions can address them. Bryner's analysis largely supports the UN General Assembly's pessimistic review at "Earth Summit II" in 1997. He also looks in some detail at why the United States has responded so weakly to the idea of sustainable development, though he finds some bright spots in initiatives at the local level. Overall, he concludes that we need to rethink many of our fundamental concepts of economic development and international trade, reverse current economic policies that subsidize unsustainable resource use, and strengthen and coordinate international institutional efforts if any substantial progress is to be made toward realizing the basic goals of Agenda 21.

Daniel C. Esty, in Chapter 9, takes a somewhat more optimistic view of the potentials for balancing international trade and environmental protection. He carefully analyzes the concerns of environmentalists that liberalized trade and increasing competitive pressures will undermine existing environmental protections and magnify environmental stress, and then he summarizes the counterarguments of free trade advocates. The North American Free Trade Agreement (NAFTA) between the United States, Mexico, and Canada was the first such agreement to integrate environmental and trade policy. Esty evaluates the Environmental Side Agreement to NAFTA in some detail, generally finding it a more successful effort to balance economic and environmental goals than many critics have suggested.[37] Still, little progress has been made toward building environmental considerations into the new international trade rules being negotiated under the GATT and its implementing agency, the WTO. Indeed, several recent WTO panel rulings have found environmental restrictions to be illegal barriers to trade, despite protests by the United States and other nations. Esty concludes that the WTO needs reform—especially to increase transparency and access by NGOs—and that current efforts by Congress to exclude environmental safeguards from the proposed Free Trade Agreement of the Americas are doomed to failure.

The final two chapters in Part III address perhaps the most important and contentious environmental policy issue facing the world community: the problem of climate change and especially the Kyoto Protocol of 1997. In Chapter 10, Michael R. Molitor traces the origins and development of international negotiations to stabilize greenhouse gas concentrations in the atmosphere. After explaining some essential elements of atmospheric science, he discusses efforts by the Intergovernmental Panel on Climate Change and other bodies to build scientific consensus on the human impacts on the climate system and the potential consequences of climate change for humankind. While science cannot yet provide definitive answers, enough political consensus emerged to pass the Framework Convention on Climate Change and subsequent Kyoto Protocol, setting binding limits on greenhouse gas emissions. Molitor discusses the issues and negotiations leading up to Kyoto, the events in Kyoto, and the provisions of the resulting agreement in considerable detail.[38]

Chapter 11, by Robert L. Paarlberg, makes it abundantly clear that no consensus exists within the U.S. government on the matter of climate change. He compares opposition (especially in Congress) to the Kyoto Protocol and the Convention on Biological Diversity (CBD) with American support for previous international agreements such as the Montreal Protocol, and asks why the United States has become such a laggard in international environmental diplomacy in the 1990s. Although the reasons for failure to ratify the CBD—despite the support of the Clinton administration, industry, and most environmental NGOs—are numerous, it appears that sheer ideological partisanship in the Senate has played a major role. Opposition to the climate change agreements is another matter entirely. Climate change itself presents far more complex and pervasive policy issues. Moreover, opposition to both domestic energy taxes and to binding international agreements to limit greenhouse gas emissions has essentially been nonpartisan: the Senate passed a resolution in July 1997 by a 95-0 vote opposing any climate treaty that did not impose limits on developing countries and that might hurt the U.S. economy. Looking more deeply, Paarlberg finds that none of the factors that facilitated ratification of the Montreal Protocol are present in the battle over climate change. He thus sees little hope for the binding emissions approach adopted at Kyoto, and suggests that the United States might best reassert a leadership role through unilateral actions such as passage of a revenue-neutral tax on fossil fuels.

Sustainable Development: National Cases and Controversies

Since the concept of sustainable development is broad and has quite different meanings when translated into different languages, it is difficult to evaluate national policies in terms of specific criteria or indicators of sustainability.[39] Some nations such as New Zealand and the Netherlands have adopted far-reaching sustainable development plans and programs, whereas others have dealt with sustainability issues in piecemeal and ad hoc fashion if at all.[40] But apart from rhetorical justification of selected measures under the sustainable development label, many policies and projects at the national and local levels do in fact have major implications for sustainability. Decisions about energy supply or land use within a given country can impact other nations or the entire global system; this is especially true of very large nations such as China, Brazil, and the United States. Major projects within countries (even small states) also attract capital and technical support from international banks and corporations, thus involving the international community in what may appear to be local developments. It is important to study these linkages between national and international action as part of global environmental policy.[41]

One aspect of sustainable development that has not been emphasized sufficiently is the role of political participation. Principle 10 of the Rio Declaration states:

> Environmental issues are best handled with the participation of all concerned citizens, at the relevant level. At the national level, each individual shall have appropriate access to information concerning the environment that is held by public authorities, including information on hazardous materials and activities in their communities, and the opportunity to participate in decision-making processes. States shall facilitate and encourage public awareness and participation by making information widely available. Effective access to judicial and administrative proceedings, including redress and remedy, shall be provided.

Women, youth, indigenous peoples, and local communities are singled out as having an indispensable role to play (Principles 20-22). According to this philosophy, sustainable development cannot be achieved without grassroots participation and empowerment.

The nature of domestic political processes is therefore an important variable in environmental policymaking. Nations with strong democratic traditions, especially at the local level, are more likely to enact strong environmental protections. This raises intriguing questions about the potential for sustainable development in authoritarian states and transitional democracies such as those of eastern Europe. The cases presented in Part IV cover a variety of countries at different levels of economic development that have political systems ranging from strong democracy (Netherlands), to transitional democracy (Czech Republic), to what can perhaps best be thought of as modernizing authoritarian regimes (China and Indonesia).

The Netherlands gained worldwide recognition in 1989 when it adopted a National Environmental Policy Plan (NEPP) that soon became a kind of blueprint for national sustainability planning as well as an inspiration for the Rio conference and the European Union's Fifth Environmental Action Programme. Duncan Liefferink traces the origins, development, implementation, and "export" of this plan in Chapter 12. He shows that the NEPP was deeply rooted in Dutch traditions of consensual policymaking and in earlier environmental policies and planning processes. But it also involved an unprecedented attempt to integrate environmental planning into all policy sectors, based on a comprehensive analysis of the sources of pollution and other forms of environmental degradation. Targets were set for reducing environmental impacts in eight broad areas by the year 2000. The breadth of the approach, coupled with the introduction of new policy instruments such as voluntary industry agreements (covenants) and new procedures for local and regional planning, make the Dutch system unique.[42] But how effective has it been in practice? Liefferink presents the most recent data from the third version of NEPP (1998) and other documents, indicating significant but by no means complete success in achieving the plan's original goals (especially regarding energy and agriculture). Nevertheless, he argues that the Dutch approach is an example of an emerging paradigm of "ecological modernization" that relies on advanced technology and extensive consultation and partnership rather than heavy-handed regulation to achieve environmental goals. Whether this approach will bring about enough changes in the structure of production and in consumer behavior to achieve long-term sustainability—or whether it has already reached its limits—remains to be seen, but it represents perhaps the most remarkable national effort thus far.

Despite numerous efforts to export the Dutch model, other countries in Europe and elsewhere may lack the cultural and institutional requisites to make collaborative planning and "shared responsibility" of this kind work. Ironically, this may be the case in the former socialist countries of central and eastern Europe that are in the process of transition to democracy and market economies.[43] Regina Axelrod discusses one fascinating example in Chapter 13: the political controversy surrounding the Temelin nuclear power plant in the Czech Republic. Western governments, banks, and corporations, as well as various IGOs, are involved in upgrading Soviet-designed nuclear power reactors such as Temelin in the central and eastern European countries to ensure their safety (many are similar in design to those at Chernobyl) and to provide alternative sources of energy to dirty coal-fired plants. However, as Axelrod explains, many serious technical and environmental problems raise questions about the wisdom of this strategy and have led to protests both inside and outside the Czech Republic. She looks at the project in the broader context of sustainable development and the evolution of Czech democracy and society since 1989. Essentially she finds a disturbing rejection of sustainable development policies by Czech governments since 1992, accompanied by an exclusion of environmental NGOs and the reassertion of state bureaucratic and technocratic methods of decision making. It does not appear that Czech citizens have either access to information or opportunities to participate in what are regarded as technical areas of regulation. This raises profound questions about both the democratization process and the priority being given to sustainability issues in the rush to marketization.

Many of the same kinds of issues arise in the case of China, as Lawrence R. Sullivan shows in his analysis of the Three Gorges Dam project in Chapter 14. Although China has embraced the idea of sustainable development, and hydroelectric power is a form of renewable energy, Sullivan argues that the enormous Three Gorges project violates the basic principles of sustainable development by failing to consider the needs of the local population, which will be the most directly affected. In particular, the displacement of 1.3 million to 1.9 million people is likely to result in severe economic losses for the relocatees and unsustainable land-use practices in the relocation areas. Despite such concerns, the Chinese government has not allowed any local input into planning of the dam and has actively suppressed debate and dissent. Sullivan concludes that "[i]f sustainable development means a concern for maintaining the integrity of ecological systems and involving the local population that will be affected in a process that meets their social and economic needs, the Three Gorges Dam does not qualify."

The weakness of civil society and the absence of effective political participation are major barriers to sustainable development in much of the developing world, but the capacity of government bureaucracies effectively to implement new environmental policies is another important variable. The final chapter of the book, by Richard O. Miller, takes up the case of mining regulation in Indonesia. Although known mostly for its destructive forestry practices,[44] Indonesia, like many other developing countries, has an extensive set of environmental laws and regulations on the books. Indeed, Miller finds Indonesian legislation requiring environmental impact assessments, mined land restoration, and polluter liability to be comparable to policies in developed countries. The extent to which such policies are implemented and enforced is another matter. Indonesian culture favors a consensual rather than adversarial style of regulation, which can facilitate industry cooperation but can also make legal enforcement difficult. While large multinational companies usually follow accepted environmental management practices, many state-owned and smaller or illegal operations do not. A "race to the bottom" is possible as competition for mineral rights grows and mining is increasingly seen as a means of "sustaining development" rather than as an ultimately unsustainable process for exploiting nonrenewable resources that must be managed with the utmost care to protect other sustainable development options.

The Uncertain Future

The contributions to this book convey a very mixed and sobering message. While great progress was made between the Stockholm and Rio conferences in establishing international environmental institutions, laws, and policies to address problems such as marine pollution and depletion of the ozone layer, it appears that advancement of the global environmental agenda has faltered since 1992. The concept of sustainable development turned out to be enormously complex and difficult to implement in the decade after its introduction by the Brundtland Commission. Its most basic requirements for raising the living standards of the world's poor have not been met, nor can it be said that environmental concerns are being effectively integrated into all sectors of economic and social development. Nor does the political will appear to exist to address the preeminent global environmental problem, climate change. Most international agencies, including the United Nations Environment Programme, Global Environment Facility, and Commission on Sustainable Development, are inadequately financed and torn by North-South divisions and other ideological conflicts. With the exception of the European Union and certain specific policy regimes, international environmental governance remains weak. National governments also vary greatly in their interpretation of, and commitment to, the idea of sustainable development, but few have given high priority to environmental sustainability in the post-Rio period. Most disappointingly, perhaps, the United States has abdicated what leadership it could previously claim in international environmental diplomacy. Conversely, local governments, private organizations, and a host of NGOs have become more important actors in defining the environmental norms of civil society.

Overall, the last decade of the first "environmental century" has been a period of consolidation and uncertainty for environmental policy, combined with an overriding preoccupation with trade liberalization and globalization of economic activity. Whether this rapid growth in economic integration, fueled by a rising global population and consumption level, will prove compatible with the integrity of the earth's ecological systems remains to be seen. What can be said is that international environmental governance will demand a great deal more attention in the new century.

Notes

1. World Resources Institute et al., *World Resources 1998-99* (New York: Oxford University Press, 1998), 141, 188-189; World Resources Institute et al., *World Resources 1996-97: The Urban Environment* (New York: Oxford University Press, 1996); William K. Stevens, "Ever-so-Slight Rise in Temperatures Led to a Record High in 1997," *New York Times,* January 8, 1998; *Greenwire,* July 8, 1998. July 1998 was the hottest month ever recorded. William K. Stevens, "One in Every 8 Plant Species Is Imperiled, a Survey Finds," *New York Times,* April 9, 1998.
2. Lynton K. Caldwell, *International Environmental Policy,* 3d ed. (Durham: Duke University Press, 1996).
3. See esp. Richard Elliot Benedick, *Ozone Diplomacy* (Cambridge: Harvard University Press, 1991).
4. World Commission on Environment and Development (WCED), *Our Common Future* (New York: Oxford University Press, 1987).
5. Stanley P. Johnson, *The Earth Summit: The United Nations Conference on Environment and Development (UNCED)* (London: Graham and Trotman, 1993); Michel Grubb et al., *The Earth Summit Agreements: A Guide and Assessment* (London: Earthscan, 1993);

United Nations, *Agenda 21: Programme of Action for Sustainable Development*, 1993, E.93.I.11.

6. William K. Stevens, "Tentative Accord Is Reached to Cut Greenhouse Gases," *New York Times*, December 11, 1997; "Despite Pact, Gases Will Keep Rising," *New York Times*, December 12, 1997.

7. Barbara Crosette, "Half-Hearted Global Warming Conference Closes Gloomily," *New York Times*, June 28, 1997; William K. Stevens, "5 Years After Environmental Summit in Rio, Little Progress," *New York Times*, June 17, 1997. For the official report and commentary, see Derek Osborn and Tom Bigg, *Earth Summit II: Outcomes and Analyses* (London: Earthscan, 1998).

8. See, for example, Andreas Hasenclever, Peter Mayer, and Volker Rittberger, *Theories of International Regimes* (Cambridge: Cambridge University Press, 1997); and Ian H. Rowlands, *The Politics of Global Atmospheric Change* (Manchester, England: Manchester University Press, 1995).

9. For a recent statement of this position, see John J. Mearsheimer, "The False Promise of International Institutions," *International Security* 19 (1995): 5–49. Classic realist texts include Hans J. Morgenthau, *Politics among Nations: The Struggle for Power and Peace*, 5th ed. (New York: Knopf, 1978), and Kenneth N. Waltz, *Theory of International Politics* (New York: Random House, 1979).

10. For a standard text, see Robert O. Keohane and Joseph S. Nye, *Power and Interdependence: World Politics in Transition* (Boston: Little, Brown, 1977).

11. See esp. Oran R. Young, *International Cooperation: Building Regimes for Natural Resources and the Environment* (Ithaca, N.Y.: Cornell University Press, 1989); and Oran R. Young and Gail Osherenko, *Polar Politics: Creating International Environmental Regimes* (Ithaca, N.Y.: Cornell University Press, 1993).

12. Stephen D. Krasner, ed., *International Regimes* (Ithaca, N.Y.: Cornell University Press, 1983), 1. See also Stephan Haggard and Beth A. Simmons, "Theories of International Regimes," *International Organization* 41 (summer 1987): 491–517.

13. Peter M. Haas, *Saving the Mediterranean* (New York: Columbia University Press, 1990); and Haas, "Introduction: Epistemic Communities and International Policy Coordination," in *Knowledge, Power, and International Policy Coordination*, special issue, *International Organization* 46 (winter 1992): 1–36.

14. See Karen T. Litfin, *Ozone Discourses: Science and Politics in Global Environmental Cooperation* (New York: Columbia University Press, 1994).

15. Oran R. Young, ed., *Global Governance: Drawing Insights from the Environmental Experience* (Cambridge: MIT Press, 1997); Oran R. Young, George J. Demko, and Kilaparti Ramakrishna, *Global Environmental Change and International Governance* (Hanover, N.H.: University Press of New England, 1996); and Paul F. Diehl, ed., *The Politics of Global Governance* (Boulder, Colo.: Rienner, 1997).

16. See, for example, Ronnie D. Lipschutz, with Judith Mayer, *Global Civil Society and Global Environmental Governance* (Albany: State University of New York Press, 1996); and Margaret E. Keck and Kathryn Sikkink, *Activists beyond Borders: Advocacy Networks in International Politics* (Ithaca, N.Y.: Cornell University Press, 1998).

17. Marian A. L. Miller, *The Third World in Global Environmental Politics* (Boulder, Colo.: Rienner, 1995); Colin Sage, "The Scope for North-South Cooperation," in *Environmental Policy in an International Context: Prospects for Environmental Change*, ed. Andrew Blowers and Pieter Glasbergen (London: Arnold, 1996).

18. On the conflict preceding the Stockholm conference, see Caldwell, *International Environmental Policy*, 57–62.

19. See, for example, John Lemons and Donald A. Brown, eds., *Sustainable Development: Science, Ethics, and Public Policy* (Dordrecht: Kluwer Academic Publishers, 1995); and Ian H. Rowlands, "International Fairness and Justice in Addressing Global Climate Change," *Environmental Politics* 6 (autumn 1997): 1–30.

20. WCED, *Our Common Future*, 43.

21. For an excellent collection of essays, see Susan Baker, Maria Kousis, Dick Richardson, and Stephen Young, eds., *The Politics of Sustainable Development* (London: Routledge, 1997).
22. Thaddeus C. Trzyna, ed., *A Sustainable World: Defining and Measuring Sustainable Development* (Sacramento: California Institute of Public Affairs, 1995), 23 n. 1.
23. Ibid., 15.
24. Some of these are discussed in Trzyna, *Sustainable World.*
25. For recent surveys and attempts to judge the effectiveness of international environmental institutions, see Peter M. Haas, Robert O. Keohane, and Marc A. Levy, eds., *Institutions for the Earth* (Cambridge: MIT Press, 1993); Jacob Werksman, ed., *Greening International Institutions* (London: Earthscan, 1996); and Robert O. Keohane and Marc A. Levy, eds., *Institutions for Environmental Aid* (Cambridge: MIT Press, 1996).
26. Young, *Global Governance,* 19; Friedrich Kratochwil and John Gerard Ruggie, "International Organization: The State of the Art," in Diehl, *Politics of Global Governance.*
27. See Thomas Princen and Matthias Finger, *Environmental NGOs in World Politics* (London: Routledge, 1994); Paul Wapner, *Environmental Activism and World Politics* (Albany: State University of New York Press, 1996); and Keck and Sikkink, *Activists beyond Borders.*
28. If treaties are ratified by a large number of states, they may take on the stature of customary law. For authoritative texts, see Patricia W. Birnie and Alan E. Boyle, *International Law and the Environment* (New York: Oxford University Press, 1992); and Philippe Sands, *Principles of International Environmental Law,* vol. 1, *Frameworks, Standards, and Implementation* (Manchester, England: University of Manchester Press, 1995).
29. See Lynne M. Jurgielewicz, *Global Environmental Change and International Law* (Lanham, Md.: University Press of America, 1996), chap. 3.
30. Krasner, *International Regimes,* 6.
31. Gunther Handl, "Territorial Sovereignty and the Problem of Transnational Pollution," *American Journal of International Law* 69 (1975). For a history of the drafting of Principle 21, see Louis Sohn, "The Stockholm Declaration on the Human Environment," *Harvard International Law Journal* 14 (1973). Both articles are excerpted in Anthony D'Amato and Kirsten Engel, eds., *International Environmental Law Anthology* (Cincinnati: Anderson, 1996), 93–99 and 17–21, respectively.
32. See Caldwell, *International Environmental Policy,* 151; Jurgielewicz, *Global Environmental Change and International Law,* 53.
33. Jurgielewicz, *Global Environmental Change and International Law,* 55–56.
34. See David G. Victor, Kal Raustiala, and Eugene B. Skolnikoff, eds., *The Implementation and Effectiveness of International Environmental Commitments: Theory and Practice* (Cambridge: MIT Press, 1998); and Edith Brown Weiss and Harold K. Jacobson, *Engaging Countries: Strengthening Compliance with International Environmental Accords* (forthcoming).
35. Marvin S. Soroos, *Beyond Sovereignty: the Challenge of Global Policy* (Columbia: University of South Carolina Press, 1986), 20.
36. For comprehensive surveys, see Caldwell, *International Environmental Policy;* Sands, *Principles of International Environmental Law;* and Gareth Porter and Janet Welsh Brown, *Global Environmental Politics,* 2d ed. (Boulder, Colo.: Westview, 1996).
37. See John J. Audley, *Green Politics and Global Trade: NAFTA and the Future of Environmental Politics* (Washington, D.C.: Georgetown University Press, 1997); and Jerry Mander and Edward Goldsmith, eds., *The Case against the Global Economy* (San Francisco: Sierra Club, 1996).
38. For additional background, see esp. Rowlands, *Politics of Global Atmospheric Change;* Matthew Paterson, *Global Warming and Global Politics* (London: Routledge, 1996); and Gunnar Fermann, ed., *International Politics of Climate Change: Key Issues and Critical Actors* (Oslo: Scandinavian University Press, 1997).

39. For a comparison of European language translations, see Nigel Haigh, "'Sustainable Development' in the European Union Treaties," *International Environmental Affairs* 8 (winter 1996): 87–91.

40. Huey D. Johnson, *Green Plans: Greenprint for Sustainability* (Lincoln: University of Nebraska Press, 1995). See also Tim O'Riordan and Heather Voisey, eds., *Sustainable Development in Western Europe: Coming to Terms with Agenda 21,* special issue, *Environmental Politics* 6 (spring 1997).

41. For some good examples, see Miranda A. Schreurs and Elizabeth A. Economy, eds., *The Internationalization of Environmental Protection* (Cambridge: Cambridge University Press, 1997).

42. On the broader significance of this approach, see Albert Weale, *The New Politics of Pollution* (Manchester, England: Manchester University Press, 1992), esp. chaps. 4 and 5.

43. For a survey of recent developments in this region, see Susan Baker and Petr Jehlicka, eds., *Dilemmas of Transition: The Environment, Democracy, and Economic Reform in East Central Europe,* special issue, *Environmental Politics* 7 (spring 1998).

44. See, for example, Charles Victor Barber, "Forest Resource Scarcity and Social Conflict in Indonesia," *Environment* 40 (May 1998).

PART I. INTERNATIONAL INSTITUTIONS AND REGIMES

2

Global Institutions and the Environment: An Evolutionary Perspective

Marvin S. Soroos

The last half of the twentieth century has seen a significant rise in the impacts of humanity on the natural environment. This trend is attributable in part to a burgeoning of the world's population from approximately 2.5 billion in 1950 to nearly 6 billion currently, with most of the increase taking place in Africa, Asia, and Latin America. Over the same period, the world's economy has grown sixfold (in constant dollars) and trade by a factor of fifteen.[1] The global push to industrialize and enhance living standards has devoured immense amounts of natural resources and released huge quantities of pollutants into the environment. Global food production has kept pace with population growth, which has been made possible by converting large expanses of land to agriculture; substantially increasing consumption of water, energy, fertilizers, and pesticides; and intensively harvesting marine fisheries. With the growing magnitude of human activities, environmental degradation, which was once largely localized within the borders of states, has increasingly taken on transnational, regional, and even global proportions. Scientists warn that human beings have become the agents of fundamental alterations of the Earth system resulting from such developments as the depletion of the stratospheric ozone layer, global climate change, and loss of biological diversity.[2]

The world's political system has also undergone a major transformation over the past several decades. The dissolution of the far-flung colonial empires of Britain, France, the Netherlands, Belgium, and Portugal has more than tripled the number of independent states participating in the international arena since the end of the Second World War; all claim the sovereign right to decide on the use of natural resources located within their boundaries. Within the past decade, the collapse of the Soviet empire and the state of Yugoslavia led to the addition of nearly a score of new states in eastern Europe and Central Asia, bringing the membership of the United Nations by 1997 to 185, from its 51 charter members in 1945. This fragmentation of political authority among such a large number of independent states, having diverse interests and a reluctance to relinquish authority over their natural resources, has significantly complicated the task of achieving international cooperation on responding to regional and global environmental problems.

The centrifugal tendencies of the nation-state system are being coun-teracted to some extent by the emergence and maturation of international regimes, which provide a measure of "international governance" for addressing numerous environmental problems.[3] The term *international regimes* has been widely used to refer to the combination of international institutions, customary norms and principles, and formal treaty commit-ments that guide the behavior of states related to a specific subject, problem, or region.[4] For example, there are international regimes for preserving bio-logical diversity, reducing transboundary air pollution in Europe, and man-aging uses of outer space.

International institutions have played a fundamental role in the cre-ation, development, and operation of international environmental regimes. They include not only the global intergovernmental organizations (IGOs) of the United Nations system, but also regional ones, such as the European Union and the Organization of African Unity. Most of these IGOs were not established expressly to address environmental problems, but over time such problems were added to their agendas as ecological concerns arose. A rela-tively small number of IGOs have been created with responsibilities that are primarily or exclusively environmental, the most notable example being the United Nations Environment Programme (UNEP).

The work of these international institutions has been complemented by a rise in the numbers and influence of nongovernmental organizations (NGOs), including scientific associations, such as the International Council of Scientific Unions (ICSU), and numerous environmental advocacy organi-zations, such as Greenpeace and the World Wildlife Fund. Collectively, NGOs have been described as an "international civil society" in view of the role that they play in drawing together people and groups from multiple countries around a common interest or cause.[5]

This chapter reviews the roles that global institutions have been playing in addressing threats to the environment posed by human activities. It begins with a historical overview of the subject with emphasis on how other issues—in particular the quest by a growing bloc of developing countries for economic development and equity—have shaped the response of global institutions to environmental problems. The chapter then presents case studies of five global institutions that are key players in addressing environmental concerns. The concluding section asks whether these and other international institutions are adequate to the challenge of responding to the increasingly ominous array of environmental threats and considers alternative forms of global environ-mental governance that may be more effective in addressing these threats.

Historical Perspective

The evolution of environmental issues on the agendas of international institutions can be better understood by dividing the postwar period into three periods defined by two major landmark meetings—the United Nations Conference on the Human Environment, which was convened in Stockholm in June 1972, and the United Nations Conference on Environment and Development, otherwise known as the Earth Summit, which was held in Rio de Janeiro in June 1992. The first, or *pre-Stockholm era*, extends to 1968, the year in which the UN General Assembly adopted a resolution to convene the Stockholm conference four years later. The second, or the *Stockholm era*, spans two decades, from 1968 to 1987. It encompasses the 1972 Stockholm conference, including the extensive array of preparatory meetings in the years preceding it, as well as the implementation of its recommendations over the following decade. The third, or *Rio de Janeiro era*, commences in 1987 with the release of the influential report of the Brundtland Commission (see Chapter 1), entitled *Our Common Future*,[6] which set the stage for the Earth Summit in 1992. The Rio de Janeiro period continues through the summit and follow-up efforts to implement the summit's lengthy and elaborate plan of action entitled Agenda 21.[7]

The Pre-Stockholm Era (Prior to 1968)

International institutions have addressed specific environmental problems for more than a century. International commissions for the Rhine and Danube Rivers were formed during the nineteenth century to foster cooperation among the riparian states on matters such as navigation, hydrology, flood control, and pollution.[8] The International Meteorological Organization was established in 1872 to standardize and coordinate the collection of meteorological data to improve weather forecasts. The organization was the predecessor of the World Meteorological Organization (WMO), a UN specialized agency founded in 1950 that has been a key actor in the development of scientific knowledge on the atmosphere and global climate change.[9] The International Joint Commission, formed by the United States and Canada in 1909, has a long history of resolving transboundary environmental issues that have arisen between the two countries, especially those pertaining to the lakes and river systems along their 3,000-mile shared border.[10]

There was very little consciousness of environmental problems when the UN was established immediately after the Second World War.[11] Thus, even though the new organization was given a significantly broader mission than that of the League of Nations, especially on economic, social, and humanitarian matters, no mention was made of the natural environment in the UN charter. In the following decades, a growing number of specific environmental problems were taken on by existing IGOs, including the WMO and other semiautonomous specialized agencies loosely coordinated by the United Nations Economic and Social Council. For example, the Food and Agriculture Organization, which is concerned with relationships between food production and the environment, has facilitated the founding of a score of international fishery commissions to conserve marine fish stocks. The World Health Organization has investigated the impacts of air and water pollution on human health, while the International Labor Organization has sought to protect workers from environmental perils, such as dust and pesticides. The International Maritime Organization has sponsored a series of international agreements dating back to 1954 that were designed to regulate pollution of the oceans from vessels, especially oil tankers. The International Atomic Energy Agency has sought to prevent radioactive contamination from nuclear power plants. The United Nations Educational, Scientific and Cultural Organization (UNESCO) has supported research on environmentally related matters, including the Man and the Biosphere Program. The International Whaling Commission was established in 1946 to regulate the harvesting of whales because stocks of major whale species were becoming seriously depleted.[12]

What international attention was given to environmental issues through the 1960s was directed primarily toward rather narrowly defined ecological problems, such as the prevention of certain types of pollution or the conservation of specific species of wildlife. No major international organizations existed whose primary mission was broadly environmental, in contrast to the economic realm, in which the three powerful Bretton Woods institutions—the World Bank, the International Monetary Fund (IMF), and the General Agreement on Tariffs and Trade (GATT)—shaped the development of an increasingly integrated world economy. The existing forms of international environmental governance were rudimentary and fragmented across many largely independent IGOs, for whom environmental issues were secondary to their central missions in sectors such as transport, labor, weather, health, resources, energy, and science. This decentralized, sectoral approach to international environmental problems had become well entrenched during the pre-Stockholm era and has proven difficult to change even in the face of compelling arguments for a more integrated and coordinated approach to the environment.

The Stockholm Era (1968–1987)

A wave of public concern about the environment led by NGOs in Europe and North America began building during the late 1960s and peaked during the early 1970s. Among the specific problems receiving attention were the dispersion of DDT and other toxic substances through ecosystems, radioactive contamination from the aboveground testing of nuclear weapons, and damage to forests and aquatic life from acid deposition. The immense oil spill from the grounding of the supertanker *Torrey Canyon* in the English Channel in 1967 was described by the political scientist Richard Falk as the "Hiroshima of the environmental age."[13] The devastating effect of warfare on the environment in Vietnam became a contentious issue at the Stockholm conference, during which Sweden introduced the term *ecocide* in referring to American use of tactics such as defoliation and land clearing to deny guerrillas the cover of the jungle canopy.

More significantly, however, this era saw a growing tendency to view the environment in a holistic way. This perspective had its origins in the International Geophysical Year of 1957–1958, an eighteen-month global scientific project sponsored by ICSU, which added considerable new scientific knowledge about the vast areas of the planet, including Antarctica, the oceans, and outer space.[14] This holistic perspective was also inspired by pictures from the moon and orbiting satellites showing the planet Earth as a fragile sphere drifting through the dark vastness of space, an image that prompted Barbara Ward to coin the phrase "spaceship Earth."[15] By the latter 1960s there was a growing uneasiness about the prospect that exponential population growth and booming industrial development would rapidly deplete the planet's natural resources and severely degrade its environment.[16] This possibility was systematically explored in the influential and controversial book *The Limits to Growth,* which projected an apocalyptic end to growth in population and industrial production within 100 years unless decisive steps were taken to moderate these trends.[17]

Revelations that the increasingly serious problem of acidification in southern Scandinavia was being caused by pollutants from as far away as the British Isles and continental Europe prompted Sweden to propose the United Nations Conference on the Human Environment that was held in Stockholm in 1972. The Stockholm conference, which was significant for placing the environment as a whole on the UN's agenda on a continuing basis, adopted a Declaration of Principles to guide the development of international environmental policy and an ambitious action program containing numerous concrete proposals for strengthening the role of the UN in the ecological field. Later in the same year, the UN General Assembly adopted a resolution establishing the United Nations Environment Programme, which was to be a focal point for UN programs on the environment. The new organization, to be headquartered in Nairobi, was charged with catalyzing and coordinating environmental activities and programs within international organizations and member states, rather than serving as a large operating agency that would carry out its own programs.[18]

The Stockholm conference became the prototype for a spate of major world conferences, sometimes referred to as "global town meetings," which focused worldwide attention on major international issues. Among those on environmentally related subjects were the World Population Conference in Bucharest in 1974, the World Food Conference in Rome in 1974, the United Nations Conference on Human Settlements in Vancouver in 1976, the United Nations Water Conference in Mar del Plata (Argentina) in 1977, and the United Nations Conference on Desertification in Nairobi in 1977. In each case, a series of preparatory meetings was held to draft official documents, typically a declaration of principles and a plan of action, that were revised and adopted at the conference itself. The governments of most nations were represented at these world conferences along with the UN agencies and other intergovernmental organizations that had a specific interest in the problem being addressed. Nongovernmental organizations, some of which were given limited opportunities to participate in the official governmental meetings, organized simultaneous public forums of their own that often had even more interesting exchanges of ideas on the problems and solutions being considered.[19]

The surge in environmental concern during the Stockholm era came primarily from the industrial nations, which had begun establishing environmental ministries, departments, or agencies (such as the U.S. Environmental Protection Agency) to address domestic problems such as air and water pollution. Developing countries were skeptical of the new environmental agenda because for them economic development and alleviation of poverty were much more pressing priorities. They were also concerned that the perception that Earth's resources are finite and rapidly being depleted and degraded, as suggested by the book *The Limits to Growth*, would become a rationale for denying them their right to develop high-consumption technologies. Moreover, by the time of the Stockholm conference, the developing countries were actively pressing their demands for a "new international economic order" that would entail significant reforms in the major global economic institutions. The developing countries refused to enter into a meaningful dialogue on the ecological issues of concern to the industrial countries without strong assurances that international environmental initiatives would not be undertaken at the expense of their legitimate aspirations for development. The decision to locate the headquarters of UNEP in Nairobi, the first major global UN agency to be based in a developing country, was another concession to the concerns of developing countries that the new organization might be prejudicial to their interests.[20]

The divergence of views between North and South was especially pronounced on the emotionally laden issue of population growth. The North looked upon the rapidly swelling populations of developing countries as an important driver of the looming environmental crisis. The South argued in response that the lavish lifestyles of the "overdeveloped" countries were more degrading to the global environment than population growth. It was even intimated in some circles that northern efforts to constrain population growth in the developing countries were part of a poorly disguised strategy for maintaining the North's global dominance. It is significant that world population growth was given little consideration in the context of other environmental issues either at Stockholm in 1972 or at Rio de Janeiro in 1992. Furthermore, when population was the focus of the World Population Conference in Bucharest in 1974, discussions centered upon economic and social issues, including the status of women. The declaration adopted at the Bucharest conference reaffirmed the principle that population policies were a matter for states to decide for themselves.[21]

The initial wave of international environmental concern that peaked about the time of the Stockholm conference dissipated by the late 1970s; this change was reflected in a declining number of relevant world conferences. Despite its limited funding, UNEP made remarkable progress in implementing key parts of the action plan adopted at Stockholm. Several of the UN specialized agencies took on additional environmental projects. In many cases they worked in partnership with one another, UNEP, and even some NGOs, such as the International Union for the Conservation of Nature and Natural Resources. Nevertheless, the response of the UN system to environmental problems continued to be fragmented and largely uncoordinated. Furthermore, international efforts in the realms of environment and economic development proceeded largely on separate institutional tracks, despite the efforts of developing countries to link the two overarching priorities.

The Rio de Janeiro Era (1987 to the Present)

A second major wave of international environmental concern arose during the latter 1980s and reached a climax at the time of the Earth Summit in Rio de Janeiro in 1992. The problems receiving most attention during this second wave were depletion of the stratospheric ozone layer, climate change, rapid shrinkage of tropical rain forests, the loss of biological diversity, the spread of deserts, and the decline of marine fisheries. The term *global change* was widely adopted in the scientific community to suggest that human activities had the potential for permanently altering the functioning of the Earth system, a perspective that has guided the International Geosphere-Biosphere Program, a continuing global scientific research effort initiated in 1986 by ICSU in the tradition of the International Geophysical Year of 1957–1958.[22]

The Rio de Janeiro era also saw significant shifts in the responses by international institutions to environmental problems. The first was a move to adapt international environmental initiatives to the aspirations of the South for economic development and equity, with the overarching challenge being the pursuit of "sustainable development." This reorientation of UN environmental programs was proposed by a group of twenty-two notable international figures from all geographical regions, which was chaired by the Norwegian prime minister Gro Harlem Brundtland. The group, formally named the World Commission on Environment and Development but known widely as the Brundtland Commission, was created as a response to the continuing misgivings of the developing countries about the direction of the UN environmental programs. Southern governments were also frustrated with the slow pace of economic development during the 1980s and the resistance of the North to implementing the economic reforms contained in proposals by developing countries for a new international economic order. These reforms were acknowledged by the Charter on the Economic Rights and Duties of States, which was adopted by the UN General Assembly in 1974.[23] The Brundtland Commission's report, *Our Common Future,* was notable for recognizing that poverty and underdevelopment in developing countries were important causes of environmental degradation. The report argued persuasively that environmental priorities could not be achieved without at the same time reducing poverty through sustainable economic growth in the developing countries and addressing inequities between rich and poor countries in the consumption of the planet's limited resources.[24]

The report of the Brundtland Commission (see Chapter 1) provided the intellectual framework for the conference held in Rio de Janeiro in June 1992, on the twentieth anniversary of the landmark Stockholm conference.

The conference, which became known as the Earth Summit because of the attendance of 116 heads of state, the largest assemblage of world leaders to that date, testified to the rise of the environment in the constellation of global issues before the United Nations. The gathering adopted a revised set of principles and the plan of action called Agenda 21, as well as major international treaties on climate change and biological diversity and a statement of forest principles. The UN General Assembly followed up by creating the Commission on Sustainable Development (CSD) to implement Agenda 21, rather than assigning this responsibility to UNEP. UNEP was viewed as being too narrowly focused on environmental problems to carry out the broad range of proposals adopted at the Rio de Janeiro conference. The CSD began meeting in 1993 and since then has devoted much of its attention to reviewing the reports submitted by states on steps they have taken to implement Agenda 21. The commission's impact has been severely limited because governments have given it neither the authority to make binding decisions nor the financial resources to provide substantial funding for sustainable development.

The Earth Summit was only one of several major world conferences held during the 1990s in which environmental issues were discussed within the context of a "people centered" emphasis of the United Nations. These included the World Conference on Human Rights in Vienna in 1993, the United Nations Conference on Population and Development in Cairo in September 1994, the World Summit on Social Development in Copenhagen in March 1995, and the Fourth World Conference on Women in Beijing in September 1995.[25] These conferences are also notable for the heightened involvement of NGOs at all stages, from the preparatory meetings through the implementation of the action programs that were adopted.

A secondary shift taking place during the Rio de Janeiro era was a campaign spearheaded by environmental NGOs to "green" the major global economic institutions, in particular the International Monetary Fund, the General Agreement on Tariffs and Trade, and the World Bank. All three have been targets of strong criticism for not being sufficiently sensitive to the environmental consequences of their policies and loan programs. As a condition for loans to developing countries burdened by excessive foreign debt, the IMF has pressured recipient countries to take steps to reduce trade imbalances by substantially increasing exports. Often this can be accomplished only by accelerating the exploitation of natural resources such as by introducing single-product cash crop agriculture, clear-cutting tropical forests for wood exports, and overgrazing cattle for export. All these options carry with them substantial environmental costs.[26] The GATT, which was transformed into the World Trade Organization in 1995, has been criticized for not allowing states to use trade restrictions as a means of enforcing both national and international environmental laws. A case in point is a ruling against a national regulation of the United States barring the import of tuna harvested with nets that entrap and kill dolphins that accompany schools of tuna.[27] The World Bank has been criticized for funding large resource development and infrastructure projects, such as hydroelectric dams, in developing countries that have had catastrophic environmental consequences. These three so-called Bretton Woods institutions, in particular the World Bank, have taken steps to become more responsive to environmental concerns, but not to the satisfaction of environmental advocacy groups. Reforming them is likely to become an increasingly salient issue as they continue to expand their roles in guiding the world economy following the collapse of world communism.

Major Global Institutions

This section profiles five global institutions from among many whose activities have a significant bearing on the environment. The UN General Assembly is not only the arena in which numerous environmental issues are first raised, but it is also the body that instigates and reviews the response to them by the UN family of organizations, including the specialized agencies. The United Nations Environment Programme and the Commission on Sustainable Development are, respectively, the principal institutional products of the Stockholm and Rio de Janeiro conferences. The Global Environment Facility has become a key instrument for dispersing funding for environmental projects in developing countries. Finally, the World Bank is a major global economic institution that has been seeking to "green" its image in response to strong criticism for its failure to take environmental consequences into account in funding large-scale development projects.

United Nations General Assembly

The General Assembly is the only one of the six principal organs of the United Nations that has universal membership of all states. Since 1945 it has been the central meeting place of the international community in which a broad range of issues are raised, discussed, and debated. The institution has been known as the world's preeminent "debating society" because it provided the most visible international forum for the clashing views between East and West during the cold war and also because of the often contentious "North-South dialogue" between the industrial and developing countries. The General Assembly is, however, much more than an arena for airing conflicting perspectives. Although the organ lacks the authority to make decisions that bind its members, it has played a key role in framing and implementing international strategies for addressing a wide array of problems, including numerous environmental ones.

To cope more effectively with the growing number of issues competing for limited time at its regularly scheduled sessions, the General Assembly began in the 1970s to convene major world gatherings—including the Stockholm conference, the Earth Summit, and others mentioned previously—to focus worldwide attention on a newly emerging or neglected issue or periodically to review and redirect international efforts to address a previously existing problem. To the casual observer, these conferences often appeared to be extravagant media events that only temporarily heightened interest in a given issue. The importance of these meetings cannot, however, be fully appreciated without viewing each of them as the most visible event in a much longer process that includes preparatory meetings that draft the documents to be approved at the conference. Consideration must also be given to efforts undertaken both by governments and by international organization secretariats after the conferences to monitor the implementation of their recommendations continually and to review the progress that has been made periodically. Ultimately, the significance of any given global conference should be judged by the new institutions that are created, the programs that are launched or expanded, the international treaties and policies that are adopted, and, ultimately, by the eventual impacts of all these initiatives.[28]

The General Assembly has played a significant role in the development of international environmental law and policy. Declarations of principles, adopted at either regular or special sessions of the General Assembly or at the world conferences it sponsors, have become the foundations for international legal regimes, an example being the Declaration of Principles Governing the Seabed Beyond the Limits of National Jurisdiction of 1970. The Declaration on the Human Environment produced by the 1972 Stockholm conference was originally considered to be a nonbinding statement of principles. However, some of the specific articles contained in the declaration have been cited so frequently that they are now widely viewed as expressions of international customary law, which is binding on all countries. The General Assembly also facilitates the creation of international treaty law by sponsoring negotiating sessions; notable examples are the three United Nations Law of the Sea conferences of 1958, 1960, and 1973–1982, the third of which culminated in the signing of the comprehensive Convention on the Law of the Sea. The General Assembly sponsored negotiations that drafted the 1992 Framework Convention on Climate Change and a 1995 treaty on the conservation of straddling and highly migratory fish stocks. In addition, the General Assembly has adopted numerous resolutions setting forth nonbinding regulations and standards, which are commonly referred to as "soft law" (see Chapter 6). For example, a 1992 resolution calls for a moratorium on large-scale drift-net fishing on the high seas, a practice that had taken a heavy toll on marine life.[29]

The General Assembly plays a role in environmental problems by delegating tasks and responsibilities to other institutions. It has been a primary creator of new IGOs, including those with key environmental responsibilities, such as the United Nations Environment Programme, the Global Environment Facility, and the Commission on Sustainable Development. The General Assembly has also convened independent panels of prominent international political figures and experts to investigate and make recommendations on how to tackle major international problems; examples are the Brandt Commission on international development issues and the Brundtland Commission mentioned earlier.[30] The General Assembly frequently calls upon existing international organizations to assume additional environmental responsibilities. A 1961 General Assembly resolution, for example, called upon the WMO to develop an improved global weather monitoring and reporting system that would take advantage of technological advancements in the fields of satellites, computers, and telecommunications. A 1962 resolution proposed that the WMO undertake the Global Atmospheric Research Program; it did so from 1967 to 1981, significantly increasing knowledge about atmospheric processes. Collectively, these programs have provided data and knowledge that have been critical to understanding the prospects for human-induced climate change.[31]

The General Assembly has been the arena of choice for developing countries both because of the universality of its membership and because each country has one vote regardless of economic or population size, level of development, or contributions to the United Nations budget. Thus, it has been possible for the far more numerous developing countries to dictate the Assembly's agenda and, through their caucusing coalition known as the Group of 77, to routinely pass resolutions of interest to them by overwhelming majorities. In the 1970s the General Assembly was the arena in which the developing countries pushed their proposals for a "New International Economic Order" (NIEO). These proposals were elaborated in several General Assembly resolutions, most notably the Charter on the Economic Rights and Duties of States, which was adopted by a vote of 120–3 in 1974.[32] In the 1980s, the General Assembly became the forum that oversaw the merging of the environmental and development agendas within the goal of sustainable development. Developing countries have been repeatedly frustrated, however, that their dominance in agenda setting and voting in the General Assembly has had limited results, especially in implementing the NIEO, because the body's resolutions are not binding on the developed countries whose cooperation is needed to implement them. The industrial countries have preferred to take up such issues in the IMF and World Bank, where they hold the majority of votes, because voting is weighted according to the size of a government's voluntary financial contribution.

The United Nations Environment Programme

None of the UN agencies existing in 1972 was prepared to take primary responsibility for implementing the action plan adopted at the Stockholm conference. Thus, the General Assembly created UNEP to become the institutional focus for environmental activities within the UN system. To keep the new organization from competing directly with well-established specialized agencies such as the Food and Agriculture Organization and the World Meteorological Organization, which had previously assumed some environmentally related functions, UNEP's role was to be limited primarily to catalyzing and coordinating environmental programs both by nations and other international organizations. In keeping with this limited mission, UNEP was given a very small staff and budget, and its headquarters were located in

Nairobi, far from the principal centers of UN activity, in particular, New York, Geneva, and Vienna.

With strong, effective leadership from its first two executive directors, Maurice Strong of Canada and Mostafa Tolba of Egypt, UNEP was remarkably successful in using its modest resources to carry out the mission set forth for it at the Stockholm conference. The organization has done much to gather, compile, and disseminate a variety of environmentally relevant information through the components of its Earthwatch program. Among these are the Global Environmental Monitoring Systems (GEMS), which coordinate numerous satellite- , Earth- , and ocean-monitoring networks supervised by other UN agencies that collect data on environmental variables such as climate, land cover, and air and water pollution. UNEP's International Registry of Toxic Chemicals (IRTC) is a repository of information on the environmental and health effects of numerous widely used chemical substances. INFOTERRA is a referral system available to those seeking information on how environmental problems are being dealt with around the world. Finally, UNEP's Global Resource Information Database (GRID) integrates environmental data for geographical units ranging from local to global levels in forms that are useful to planners and policymakers.[33]

UNEP has also been notably successful in stimulating the development of international environmental law and policy. In the mid-1970s UNEP launched its Regional Seas Programme by bringing together the diverse and conflict-prone states bordering the Mediterranean Sea to adopt a series of intergovernmental agreements. These agreements were to cut back on the flow of both vessel and land-based sources of pollution that were contaminating their common body of water.[34] What is known as the Mediterranean Blue Plan became the prototype for similar projects that address the environmental problems of other regional seas, including the Black Sea, the Red Sea, the Caribbean, the Persian Gulf, the West and Central African seas, the South Pacific, and the East Asian seas, which now collectively involve more than 140 coastal states.[35]

In 1981 the Governing Council of UNEP adopted an ambitious plan for the development of international environmental law known as the Montevideo Programme. The plan established three priorities: prevention of marine pollution from land-based sources, protection of the stratospheric ozone layer, and the handling and disposal of toxic wastes. Efforts directed toward stemming the flow of chlorofluorocarbons (CFCs) and other ozone-depleting substances into the atmosphere led to the adoption of the 1985 Vienna Convention on Protecting the Ozone Layer and two years later to the famous Montreal Protocol on Substances That Deplete the Ozone Layer. The latter document was amended in 1990, 1992, and 1995 to control additional substances that threaten the ozone layer, to make the phase-outs complete, and to shorten deadlines. The Montreal Protocol as amended has been a timely and comprehensive, precautionary response to the threat of ozone depletion and arguably the most significant accomplishment thus far in the development of international environmental law.

UNEP also sponsored negotiations to regulate what had become a significant trade in hazardous waste substances, especially from industrial nations to developing countries, which in many cases were unprepared to dispose of them safely. The negotiations led to the 1989 Basel Convention, which provides that such trade may take place only after the government of the recipient country has been informed of a proposed transfer of hazardous waste substances and gives its approval. The conventions and protocols on the ozone layer and the treaty on trade in toxic wastes are but two of UNEP's notable legal achievements. These and other UNEP-brokered agreements have contributed to making the environment one of the most dynamic growth areas of international law over the past two decades.[36]

Since its establishment, UNEP has been sensitive to development issues and continues to be the only global UN agency whose headquarters are in a developing country. Furthermore, in 1982 UNEP's Governing Council proposed what became the Brundtland Commission to delve into the relationship between environment and development. Nevertheless, UNEP's role came under challenge as the environmental agenda of the United Nations was redirected toward the pursuit of sustainable development during preparations for the Rio de Janeiro Earth Summit. Developing countries looked upon UNEP as being overly attentive to the concerns of the industrial countries with global environmental problems, such as stratospheric ozone depletion and human-induced climate change, and not sufficiently responsive to environmental problems that beset developing countries, such as desertification and land erosion, or to their aspirations for economic development. Thus, the General Assembly created a special negotiating committee for the climate change negotiations beginning in 1991, rather than assigning them to UNEP, even though UNEP had had a decade-long involvement with the issue. It has been a cosponsor of the Intergovernmental Panel on Climate Change and was notably successful in facilitating the agreements to protect the ozone layer and the stratospheric ozone layer. Moreover, rather than placing UNEP in charge of implementing the Earth Summit's Agenda 21, the General Assembly created a new body, the Commission on Sustainable Development, to undertake this responsibility even against a background of strong pressure from the United States and other industrial countries for the UN to streamline its operations.[37]

The creation of the CSD, described further in the next section, has made it possible for UNEP to concentrate on its original mission of being the environmental conscience within the United Nations system. Agenda 21 called on UNEP to continue its role as both a coordinator and a catalyst of environmental activities within the UN system, to further develop the various components of the Earthwatch program, and to facilitate the drafting and negotiation of environmental treaties.[38] Nevertheless, UNEP has been a subject of considerable controversy between industrial and developing countries in recent years that has threatened its future. The conflict came to a head in the spring of 1997, when the United States, the United Kingdom, and Spain threatened to withhold funds for the organization until reforms were made to strengthen the role of environmental ministers in determining UNEP's policies while weakening the power of Nairobi-based diplomats who reflected the interests of developing countries.[39] Amid continuing complaints that UNEP had lost its way, its executive director, Elizabeth Dowdeswell of Canada, declined to seek a second five-year term and was replaced in 1998 by Klaus Töpfer of Germany.

The Commission on Sustainable Development

The General Assembly adopted a resolution in December 1992 providing for the establishment of a Commission on Sustainable Development. The new body would monitor and facilitate efforts to implement the diverse goals and recommendations of the Earth Summit, in particular the Declaration on the Environment and Development, or Agenda 21, and the Statement of Forest Principles. It would comprise representatives from fifty-three member states of the United Nations elected to staggered three-year terms. While CSD would report directly to the UN Economic and Social Council, it would also make recommendations directly to the General Assembly. CSD's headquarters would be located in New York, where the commission would convene annual meetings. Lacking both the power to make binding decisions and its own financial resources to fund programs, CSD's charge was to further the recommendations of the Earth Summit by promoting dialogue and encouraging partnerships among governments, UN agencies, the NGO community, and the numerous groups identified in Agenda 21, such as women, youth, indigenous peoples, workers, and business and industry.[40]

Beginning with its first session in June 1993, the CSD has provided a forum for the discussion of a wide range of issues related to sustainable development. In view of the breadth of subjects covered by Agenda 21, the commission set up a multiyear schedule that focused attention on three or four environmental problems each year—health, human settlements, fresh water, and hazardous wastes in 1994; land, desertification, forests, and biological diversity in 1995; and the atmosphere, oceans, and all kinds of seas in 1996. Certain cross-sectoral issues appear on the agenda each year, such as trade and the environment, poverty, population dynamics, financial resources, and the transfer of environmentally sound technologies. Member governments and the United Nations have convened additional conferences between the annual sessions of the CSD to focus attention on subjects such as chemical safety, drinking water and environmental sanitation, and the transfer of technologies to replace lead in gasoline. In 1995 the CSD established the Intergovernmental Panel on Forests with a two-year lease to make proposals for carrying out provisions of Agenda 21 pertaining to forests and the Statement of Forest Principles.[41]

The CSD was also charged with monitoring the progress made by both industrial and developing countries to implement provisions of Agenda 21. However, industrial countries have been reluctant to institute a procedure that might generate embarrassing criticisms of their performance, while developing countries have been leery of a reporting system that could become the basis for imposing environmental conditions for economic assistance. At the Earth Summit and its preparatory meetings, developing countries rallied behind the slogan "additionality, not conditionality." Thus, states are asked, but not required, to submit annual reports to the CSD explaining what they are doing to further sustainable development. As would be expected, few such reports were submitted in the early years of the CSD, in part because governments had numerous reports to prepare on other subjects. Furthermore, the CSD has needed time to develop a format for these reports and to establish procedures for reviewing them and providing feedback. The year 2000 is the target date for articulating a set of internationally accepted indicators of sustainable development that can be used to track the progress that has been made more systematically.[42]

The CSD has proven to be a lively and open forum for continuing discussions among governments, international organizations, and NGOs on how to carry out the plan of action on environment and development set forth in Agenda 21. It has stimulated the creation of sustainable development commissions in at least 117 countries, including a body in the United States led by the vice president, and nearly 2,000 cities in 64 countries have adopted environmental plans. A coalition of 120 corporations from 35 nations has formed the World Business Council for Sustainable Development.[43] Aside from these encouraging organizational developments, however, little progress has been made thus far on implementing key provisions of the documents from the Earth Summit. Such was the conclusion of the General Assembly's Special Session on "Rio Plus Five," held in June 1997 in New York and attended by sixty-five heads of state. If anything, both the environment and development situations around the world seem to have deteriorated further since the Earth Summit because of continued rapid growth of the world's population, substantial increases in consumption of fossil fuels, and the alarming rate at which tropical forests and biological species are disappearing. Developing countries are discouraged by the failure of the industrial nations to follow through on their commitments to increase economic assistance substantially and to facilitate the transfer of environmentally benign technologies.[44] These disturbing trends do not necessarily reflect badly on the efforts of the CSD, which lacks the power and resources to effect substantial change on its own. The problem lies in the failure of governments to follow through on commitments made at Rio de Janeiro and the gulf that continues to exist between North and South on the relative priority that should be given to preserving the environment as opposed to economic development and reducing poverty.

The Global Environment Facility

In 1990, at the suggestion of France and Germany, the World Bank took the lead in setting up an experimental program named the Global Environment Facility (GEF), to provide funds on favorable terms to low- and middle-income countries for environmental projects that would have global benefits. At the time, developing countries were insisting that their acceptance of several of the major environmental treaties being promoted by the industrial countries was conditional upon assurances of new and additional sources of international assistance that would be needed to comply with provisions of the treaties. The GEF funds would be targeted at four major environmental priorities: protection of the stratospheric ozone layer, limiting emissions of greenhouse gases, preservation of biological diversity, and protection of international waters. The industrial countries sponsoring the GEF saw it as a way to avoid the inefficiencies of establishing a separate fund for each major environmental treaty.[45] It was hoped that GEF assistance would induce developing countries to embark on projects that would benefit the larger community of nations. Without such assistance, developing countries would have little incentive for allocating their limited resources for environmental projects in view of other compelling national priorities.

The World Bank has shared responsibility for operating the GEF with the United Nations Development Programme (UNDP) and UNEP. The World Bank, which has been the dominant partner, administers the GEF's trust fund and manages the program's application process. The UNDP oversees technical assistance projects and coordinates them with the national environment programs of the recipient countries. UNEP's role has been to provide scientific and technical oversight, as well as guidance in identifying and selecting projects to be funded. To assist in carrying out its responsibility, UNEP established a fifteen-member Scientific and Technical Advisory Panel to provide advice on broad scientific and technical issues. Thus, the GEF is unusual for the ways in which it links a major Bretton Woods economic institution with UN agencies. For the World Bank, the arrangement furthered its objective of greening its image; for the UN programs, it offered the prospect of considerably greater funding than would otherwise have been available to them.

The GEF's first phase, which ran from July 1991 through July 1993, was designed as a trial to see if it could be an effective mechanism for dispersing assistance in support of major environmental treaties. During this period, the GEF allocated $750 million for projects, with global warming and biological diversity projects each receiving approximately 40 percent of the funds, while international waters projects received most of the remaining 20 percent. Very few funds were allocated to protecting the stratospheric ozone layer in view of the existence of a separate multilateral fund linked to the Montreal Protocol. The GEF quickly encountered criticism, especially from NGOs, for rushing into making what were considered to be ill-conceived grants before criteria for awarding them had been established.[46]

The future of the GEF became a North-South issue at the Earth Summit in 1992 in the context of discussion over funding for Agenda 21. To developing countries, the GEF's emphasis on global environmental problems under the leadership of the World Bank reflected the priorities of the industrial countries. It provided no support, however, for tackling the more localized environmental problems considered by developing countries to be more pressing, such as desertification, soil loss, and urban air pollution. The developing countries argued for the creation of a general purpose Green Fund not dominated by the World Bank model of weighted voting, which would support a broader range of the proposals associated with sustainable development. Moreover, their governments were critical of the secretive ways of the World Bank. As the providers of funding for the GEF, the industrial nations insisted on retaining substantial authority over GEF decision making by continuing it under the auspices of the World Bank; they also insisted on keeping the program focused on preserving global commons.[47]

The deadlock over the future of the GEF was finally broken at the Earth Summit, when it was agreed that the GEF should undergo a major restructuring and would be only an interim mechanism for transferring funds to carry out the treaties on climate change and biological diversity that were adopted at the Rio de Janeiro meetings. It took an additional eighteen months of sometimes intense negotiations for seventy-three participating countries to work out the specifics on how to restructure the GEF as a permanent institution. The design for the GEF's second phase was a compromise between the industrial countries' quest for institutional efficiency and the demands of the developing countries for an organization that would be more open and democratic and would balance the interests of the donor and recipient countries. The restructuring provided for two decision-making bodies: an assembly in which all participating countries would be represented, which would meet every three years to review the general policies of the GEF; and a Governing Council that would meet more frequently and be the GEF's primary governing body. Of the thirty-two seats on the council, fourteen were allocated to industrial countries, sixteen to developing countries, and two to the transitional countries of the former Soviet bloc. Decisions of the council would require simultaneous double majorities. One majority must comprise at least 60 percent of the member states, thus protecting the interests of recipient developing countries. The other majority must include the votes of countries that make at least 60 percent of all contributions to the GEF, thus protecting the interests of the major donor countries. The GEF would be the funding mechanism for the climate change and biological diversity treaties, but only on an interim basis. The Conferences of the Parties to each of the two treaties would establish the priorities and eligibility requirements for grants provided in support of each.[48] The industrial countries committed $2 billion to replenish the GEF's trust fund for the period 1994–1997. Nevertheless, developing countries have complained about the general level of funding and the complex application process, which has significantly delayed the awarding of grants.

The GEF has emerged from the turmoil and contentiousness of its initial experimental phase to become a useful complement to other sources of financial assistance for environmental projects in developing countries, including various multilateral funds, UN agencies, regional development banks, nongovernmental organizations, and bilateral assistance programs.[49] Upwards of 160 nations have become members of the GEF and by 1995 more than 113 grants had been provided to 63 developing countries. Funds related to climate change have gone to projects that increase carbon-absorbing forest cover, known as carbon sinks, which encourage energy conservation or to the harnessing of solar and other renewable sources of energy. Grants directed toward promoting biological diversity have gone largely to projects for the protection of habitats, such as the establishment of parks and nature preserves and facilities for ecotourism.[50] The future of the GEF will depend on whether it becomes the permanent mechanism for financial transfers for the climate change and biological diversity regimes. For now it has been a creative solution to the problem of assisting developing countries in becoming partners in maintaining global public goods.

The World Bank

The World Bank, whose official name is the International Bank for Reconstruction and Development (IBRD), was established in 1946 to provide funding for reconstruction of the war-devastated countries of Western Europe. Its initial priority was to rebuild the infrastructure of these countries, such as roads, bridges, dams, water systems, and power plants, which private investors were reluctant to fund. After making a number of such loans, the World Bank shifted its attention to providing loans that would propel the development of African and Asian countries, many of which emerged from colonialism during the late 1950s and 1960s. Over the years, the World Bank has directed its loans mostly toward large infrastructure projects and the exploitation of natural resources, rather than to the development of human capital through programs in such sectors as health and education. Loans provided by the World Bank are normally made directly to governments at interest rates approaching commercial levels. The Bank expects its loans to generate sufficient economic activity to enable the recipient countries to pay them off in a timely way. In 1960 the World Bank opened a "separate window" known as the International Development Agency that would provide loans to the least-developed countries at zero interest and with an extended repayment schedule.

The World Bank has provided nearly $400 billion in loans to developing countries and economic institutions, making it by far the world's largest single source of development assistance. The International Development Agency has provided an additional $100 billion in development loans to the world's poorest countries. While the Bank has done much to facilitate economic development, it has also been one of the most criticized of international institutions for funding numerous ill-conceived projects. Critics attribute the Bank's misjudgments in part to a compulsion to lend the large amounts of capital it has had available to invest. Many of the projects have fallen far short of generating the revenues needed to pay them off. Such projects have thus added to the chronic debt burdens of developing countries, which for many became especially burdensome in the 1980s after dramatic decreases in the world price of oil and other commodities they depend upon for export revenue. Critics also point to the large numbers of people, currently more than two million, who have been displaced without adequate provision being made for their relocation as a result of World Bank projects, in particular the construction of large dams for power generation and irrigation. It is also alleged that World Bank projects tend to benefit those who are already well off in developing societies, while further impoverishing the poorest classes.[51]

The World Bank has drawn especially heavy criticism for its failure to anticipate the ecological impacts in approving projects, including several that are frequently cited for having had especially catastrophic environmental consequences. During the 1980s the Bank provided $500 million to Indonesia to assist in the relocation of 3.5 million peasants from heavily populated Java to the nation's outer islands of Sumatra, Kalimantan, Sulawesi, and West Papua. Unfortunately, the soils of these islands are not suitable for food crop rotations, leaving the settlers few options but to engage in slash-and-burn agriculture, which along with commercial logging has devastated the forests. The World Bank also supported a large population relocation project in Brazil known as Polonoroeste by providing $440 million for the construction of a 1,500-kilometer road deep into the northwestern Amazon state of Rodônia. As in Indonesia, the tropical soils were unsuitable for sustained cultivation and many of the tens of thousands of settlers drawn to the region by government promises of land engaged in slash-and-burn methods of agriculture over an area the size of the United Kingdom. The result has been destroyed forests and displaced indigenous forest dwellers. Large tracts of Amazon forest have also been destroyed by Brazil's Greater Carajas project, which included a large iron-ore mine, a railway, and a deep-water port. To develop the infrastructure for the project the World Bank provided more than $300 million.[52]

Growing concern over global climate change has drawn attention to World Bank projects that have added significantly to anthropogenic greenhouse gas emissions. The Bank has funded numerous projects for oil wells, refineries, coal mines, power stations, and road building, which have led countries to develop economies heavily dependent on fossil fuels. The Bank has been especially supportive of India's coal industry from mining operations to power plants, an example being the $850 million in loans it provided for the notorious Singrauli complex of twelve open pit coal mines and eleven coal-fired power plants. The complex, known as "the inferno," emits 10 million tons of carbon into the atmosphere each year and has denuded a large area that previously was lushly forested and home to indigenous peoples and numerous plant and animal species. China, Indonesia, Pakistan, the Philippines, and Poland are among numerous other countries that have constructed large coal or oil-fired power plants with loans from the World Bank. The destruction of forest cover, such as that caused by the projects in Indonesia and Brazil mentioned above, also contributes significantly to atmospheric greenhouse gas increases both by releasing the carbon contained in the trees when they are burned and by diminishing an important carbon sink provided by ongoing living material and photosynthesis.[53]

In 1987 the incoming World Bank president Barber Conable acknowledged that the Bank had not given sufficient scrutiny to the environmental consequences of the projects that it had funded. To address the problem, Conable created an environment department, which makes policy recommendations and oversees the GEF. In addition, environmental divisions were established for each of the Bank's four regional operational offices—Sub-Saharan Africa, Asia, the Middle East, and Latin America and the Caribbean—which are charged with assessing the environmental impacts of all loan applications. The Bank's annual report for 1992 stressed the importance of the relationship between environment and development in line with the report of the Brundtland Commission and the theme of the Earth Summit at Rio de Janeiro. The Bank played a central role in the creation of the GEF (described in the previous section) and by 1995 had expanded its "green" portfolio to 137 projects in 62 countries amounting to $10 billion in loans. Examples of such green projects are the cleanup of the Komi oil spill in Russia, expanded sewage collection and treatment in Bombay, reduction of industrial pollution in China's Liaoning province, and conservation of wetlands in the Baltic Sea basin. The Bank has also developed a new system for measuring wealth, which takes into account social and economic factors.[54]

Despite these efforts to improve its environmental image, questions persist about whether the World Bank has actually enacted sufficient reforms. It is not apparent that the environmental units and policies are having any meaningful impact on the culture of the organization, which still appears to be oriented toward making new loans with little critical attention to environmental and human impacts. For example, the Bank continued to provide loans for the controversial Sardar Sarovar dam project in India until an independent commission chaired by the former U.S. congressman Bradford Morse issued a report in 1992 that strongly criticized the lending agency for violating its own rules on environmental impact assessment and its standards for the resettlement of displaced peoples.[55] The fiftieth anniversary of the Bretton Woods Conference became the occasion for a campaign by a coalition of more than 200 NGOs that suggested that the World Bank and the IMF in their existing forms may have outlived their usefulness and questioned whether they could be reformed to play more constructive roles in furthering sustainable development.[56] The Bank was continuing to fund projects that collectively may displace as many as two million people, including the Nam Theun Two dam in Laos, which will be the largest hydroelectric project in Southeast Asia.[57] And even as efforts are made to negotiate treaties that would reduce emissions of greenhouse gases, funds provided by the Bank in support of energy efficiency and the development of sustainable energy sources continue to be a very small fraction of the amount loaned for large-scale fossil fuel projects.[58]

Prospects for Change

International institutions have accomplished much over the past several decades toward facilitating cooperation among nations in addressing environmental problems that transcend their borders and affect the global commons. These include the international institutions whose mission is primarily environmental, most notably UNEP and the GEF, as well as numerous other organizations that have taken up environmental problems as part of their broader missions, such as the UN General Assembly and several of the specialized agencies of the United Nations family of organizations. Other major global organizations, such as the three Bretton Woods institutions—the IBRD, the IMF, and the GATT—have adopted reforms in the face of strong criticism for pursuing their economic missions in ways that have further aggravated environmental problems.

Nevertheless, the ecological predicament of humanity appears to be deepening, despite the monitoring networks, scientific research projects, environmental treaties and standards, reporting mechanisms, and funding programs that have been sponsored by these international institutions. While the efforts of international institutions have contributed to solutions to some environmental problems, most conspicuously the preservation of the stratospheric ozone layer, they have been largely ineffective in brokering effective international responses to others, including human-induced climate change, which has become the preeminent ecological problem confronting humanity as it enters the twenty-first century.

The question arises whether international institutions, as presently constituted, possess the capacity to deliver the global collective environmental benefits that they are being asked to provide. In the prevailing anarchical world order, states for the most part cannot be compelled against their will to enter into cooperative arrangements to address international problems. Thus, international agreements are the product of complex and time-consuming negotiations among disparate countries that typically produce weak documents reflecting the lowest common denominator of perceived interests. Each country tends to seek treaties that maximize the responsibilities of other nations while minimizing their own obligations, thus playing the role of "free-rider." The European Union is the one major international institution in which the member governments have relinquished a significant portion of their sovereignty by agreeing to be bound by decisions adopted by voting majorities of the organization's member states.

Concern over impending global ecological crises has prompted proposals for strengthening international institutions. One possible direction would be to establish a strong central organ within the United Nations system, possibly in the form of an Environmental Security Council that would take the place of the Trusteeship Council, which has all but completed its mission of decolonization. Such a body would elevate the environment from being a peripheral, cross-sectoral issue to being one of the core priorities of the United Nations, along with peacekeeping and economic development. Another direction of thought would create institutions with the power to make binding decisions that are needed to effectively address environmental problems. The creation of such institutions was discussed at an international conference attended by leaders from seventeen states convened by the prime ministers of France, Norway, and the Netherlands in The Hague in 1988. The resulting Hague Declaration called for a new or strengthened institution within the United Nations that would have the power to make binding decisions needed to address human-induced climate change and stratospheric ozone depletion. The absence of the United States, the Soviet Union, and China, the world's three leading emitters of carbon dioxide, did not bode well for the implementation of such a proposal.[59]

It is difficult to conceive of circumstances in which states would be willing to relinquish or pool their sovereignty to substantially strengthen global institutions charged with mounting a more effective response to the deepening environmental crisis confronting humanity. If anything, there is growing public disillusionment with global institutions and policies in both industrial and developing countries because of their perceived failure to be responsive to local needs and preferences. The best hope appears to lie in strengthening existing institutions and in enhancing coordination between them. Nongovernmental organizations can be expected to play a significant role in mobilizing support for stronger international policies and programs and monitoring compliance with them. Whether such a decentralized, problem-specific approach to addressing global environmental policies will be adequate to the challenges that lie ahead remains to be seen. Unfortunately, at least for now, there appears to be no viable alternative.

Notes

1. Lester R. Brown, Michael Renner, and Christopher Flavin, *Vital Signs 1998* (Washington, D.C.: Worldwatch Institute, 1998), 75, 77.
2. See Constance Mungall and Digby J. McLaren, eds., *Planet under Stress: The Challenge of Global Change* (New York: Oxford University Press, 1990).
3. See Oran Young, *International Governance: Protecting the Environment in a Stateless Society* (Ithaca, N.Y.: Cornell University Press, 1994); and Lamont C. Hempel, *Environmental Governance: The Global Challenge* (Washington, D.C.: Island Press, 1996).
4. See Stephen D. Krasner, ed., *International Regimes* (Ithaca, N.Y.: Cornell University Press, 1983).
5. See Paul Wapner, *Environmental Activism and World Civic Politics* (Albany: State University of New York Press, 1996), and Ronnie D. Lipschutz, with Judith Mayer, *Global Civil Society and Global Environmental Governance: The Politics of Nature from Place to Planet* (Albany: State University of New York Press, 1996).
6. World Commission on Environment and Development, *Our Common Future* (New York: Oxford University Press, 1987).
7. United Nations, *Agenda 21: Programme of Action for Sustainable Development*, 1993, E.93.I.11.
8. Lynton Keith Caldwell, *International Environmental Policy*, 3d ed. (Durham, N.C.: Duke University Press, 1995), 160–161.

9. See Marvin S. Soroos and Elena Nikitina, "The World Meteorological Organization as a Purveyor of Global Public Goods," in *International Organizations and Environmental Policy*, ed. Robert Bartlett, Priya Kurian, and Madhu Malik (Westport, Conn.: Greenwood Press, 1995), 69–82.

10. See John E. Carroll, *Environmental Diplomacy: An Examination and a Prospective of Canadian–U.S. Transboundary Environmental Relations* (Ann Arbor: University of Michigan Press, 1983).

11. For an overview of perceptions of environmental issues during this era, see John McCormick, *Reclaiming Paradise: The Global Environmental Movement* (Bloomington: Indiana University Press, 1979), 25–46.

12. See Patricia Birnie, "The UN and the Environment," in *United Nations, Divided World: The UN's Roles in International Relations*, 2d ed., ed. Adam Roberts and Benedict Kingsbury (New York: Oxford University Press, 1993), 355–358.

13. Richard A. Falk, *This Endangered Planet: Prospects and Proposals for Human Survival* (New York: Vintage Books, 1971), 284. For an account of accidents involving supertankers see Noël Mostert, *Supership* (New York: Warner Books, 1975).

14. See Wallace W. Atwood Jr., "The International Geophysical Year in Retrospective," *Department of State Bulletin* 40 (1959): 682–89.

15. Barbara Ward, *Spaceship Earth* (New York: Columbia University Press, 1966).

16. An influential book on world population growth was Paul R. Ehrlich's *The Population Bomb* (New York: Ballantine Books, 1968).

17. Donella H. Meadows, Dennis L. Meadows, Jørgen Randers, and William W. Berhrens III, *The Limits to Growth* (New York: Universe Books, 1972). See also the follow-up study by Donella H. Meadows, Dennis L. Meadows, and Jørgen Randers, *Beyond the Limits: Confronting Global Collapse, Envisioning a Sustainable Future* (Post Mills, Vt.: Chelsea Green, 1992).

18. See Caldwell, *International Environmental Policy*, 63–78.

19. See A. LeRoy Bennett, *International Organizations: Principles and Issues*, 3d ed. (Englewood Cliffs, N.J.: Prentice Hall, 1984), 293–323.

20. See Marian A. L. Miller, *The Third World in Global Environmental Politics* (Boulder, Colo.: Rienner, 1995).

21. See Barbara B. Crane, "International Population Institutions: Adaption to a Changing World Order," in *Institutions for the Earth: Sources of Effective International Environmental Protection*, ed. Peter M. Haas, Robert O. Keohane, and Marc A. Levy (Cambridge: MIT Press, 1993), 351–393.

22. Thomas F. Malone, "Mission to Planet Earth: Integrating Studies of Global Change," *Environment* 28 (October 1986): 6–11, 39–42.

23. See Roger D. Hansen, *Beyond the North-South Stalemate* (New York: McGraw-Hill, 1979), and Stephen D. Krasner, *Structural Conflict: The Third World against Global Liberalism* (Berkeley: University of California Press, 1985).

24. See n. 6.

25. See John Tessitore and Susan Woolfson, eds., *A Global Agenda: Issues before the 49th General Assembly of the United Nations* (New York: University Press of America, 1994), 154.

26. Korinna Horta, "The World Bank and the International Monetary Fund," in *Greening International Institutions*, ed. Jacob Werksman (London: Earthscan, 1996), 142–146.

27. See Daniel C. Esty, *Greening the GATT: Trade, Environment, and the Future* (Washington, D.C.: Institute for International Economics, 1994).

28. See Bennett, *International Organizations*.

29. See Blaine Sloan, *United Nations General Assembly Resolutions in Our Changing World* (Ardsley-on-Hudson, N.Y.: Transnational, 1991).

30. Independent Commission on International Development Issues, *North-South: A Programme for Survival* (Cambridge: MIT Press, 1980).

31. See Marvin S. Soroos, *The Endangered Atmosphere: Preserving a Global Commons* (Columbia: University of South Carolina Press, 1997), 58–61.
32. See Marvin S. Soroos, *Beyond Sovereignty: The Challenge of Global Policy* (Columbia: University of South Carolina Press, 1986), 195–226.
33. See Peter M. Haas, "Institutions: United Nations Environment Programme," *Environment* 36 (September 1994): 43–45.
34. See Peter M. Haas, *Saving the Mediterranean: The Politics of International Environmental Cooperation* (New York: Columbia University Press, 1990).
35. "United Nations Environment Programme: Two Decades of Achievement and Challenge," *Our Planet* 4, no. 5 (1992): 9.
36. See Carol Annette Petsonk, "The Role of the United Nations Environment Programme (UNEP) in the Development of International Environmental Law," *American University Journal of International Law and Policy* 5 (1990): 351–391.
37. See Konrad von Moltke, "Why UNEP Matters," in *Green Globe Yearbook 1996*, ed. Helge Ole Bergesen and Georg Parmann (New York: Oxford University Press, 1996), 58–59.
38. Dale Boyd, "UNEP after Rio," *Our Planet* 4, no. 4 (1992): 8–11.
39. Fred Pearce, "Environmental Body Goes to Pieces," *New Scientist*, February 15, 1997, 11.
40. See Chris Mensah, "The United Nations Commission on Sustainable Development," in Werksman, *Greening International Institutions*, 21–37.
41. See Jared Blumenfeld, "Institutions: The United Nations Commission on Sustainable Development," *Environment* 36 (December 1994): 2–33; "Rionewal: Taking Stock," *United Nations Chronicle* 34, no. 2 (1997): 7–11.
42. See Martin Khor, "The Commission on Sustainable Development: Paper Tiger or Agency to Save the Earth?" in *Green Globe Yearbook 1994*, ed. Helge Ole Bergesen and Georg Parmann (New York: Oxford University Press, 1994), 103–113.
43. Jack Epstein, "Summit Finds It's Not Easy Being Green," *Christian Science Monitor*, March 20, 1997, 1, 9.
44. Alexandra Marks, "Rio + 5: Wake-up Call for Earth Cleanup," *Christian Science Monitor*, June 24, 1997, 1, 10–11.
45. "The Global Environmental Facility," *Our Planet* 3, no. 3 (1991): 10–13.
46. See Andrew Jordan, "Paying the Incremental Costs of Global Environmental Protection: The Evolving Role of the GEF," *Environment* 36 (July/August 1994): 12–20, 31–36.
47. David Fairman, "The Global Environment Facility: Haunted by the Shadow of the Future," in *Institutions for Environmental Aid*, ed. Robert O. Keohane and Marc A. Levy (Cambridge: MIT Press, 1996), 57–58. See also Helen Sjöberg, "The Global Environmental Facility," in Werksman, *Greening International Institutions*, 148–162.
48. Fairman, "The Global Environment Facility," 66–69.
49. See Keohane and Levy, *Institutions for Environmental Aid*.
50. Shalendra D. Sharma, "Building Effective International Environmental Regimes: The Case of the Global Environment Facility," *Journal of Environment and Development* 5 (March 1996): 73–86.
51. See Catherine Caufield, *Masters of Illusion: The World Bank and the Poverty of Nations* (New York: Holt, 1996); Doug Bandow and Ian Vàsquez, eds., *Perpetuating Poverty: The World Bank, the IMF, and the Developing World* (Washington, D.C.: CATO Institute, 1994).
52. Horta, "The World Bank and the International Monetary Fund," 138–139. The most influential book on this subject is Bruce Rich, *Mortgaging the Earth: The World Bank, Environmental Impoverishment, and the Crisis of Development* (Boston: Beacon Press, 1994).
53. See Christopher Flavin, "Banking against Global Warming," *World Watch* 10 (November/December 1997): 25–35.

54. Brad Knickerbocker, "World Bank Turns Green, Pleasing Environmentalists," *Christian Science Monitor,* October 13, 1995, 7.
55. See Hilary F. French, "The World Bank: Now Fifty, but How Fit?" *World Watch* 7 (July–August 1994): 10–18.
56. David R. Francis, "IMF and World Bank 50th Birthday Bash: Critics Crash Parties," *Christian Science Monitor,* October 3, 1994, 4.
57. Lily Dizon, "Why the World Bank Gave Its Nod to a Giant Dam," *Christian Science Monitor,* December 3, 1997, 6.
58. See Flavin, "Banking against Global Warming."
59. See Hilary F. French, "An Environmental Security Council," *World Watch* 2 (September/October 1989): 6–7.

3

The Role of Environmental NGOs in International Regimes

John McCormick

The environment has been an issue of critical public concern since the 1970s. As the physical and social sciences have revealed more about the damaging effects of human activity on the environment, opinion polls have found growing levels of public support for government action in response to these effects. However, the record of local and national governments in addressing the causes and the consequences of environmental damage has been mixed at best. Considerable lip service has been paid to the importance of environmental management, but practical action has often fallen short of government pronouncements. As the former executive director of the United Nations Environment Programme (UNEP) noted in 1992, "the commitment [by governments] to set up ministries and to enter into international agreements has not always led to an equal commitment to action. Environment ministries exist, but their role in national decision-making is frequently marginal. Agreements have been entered into freely, but the will to enforce them has often been lacking."[1]

The development of effective environmental policies at the national level has been undermined by a lack of political will, debates generated by uncertainties about the science of environmental problems, and a failure (or an unwillingness) to understand and quantify the costs and benefits of preventive or remedial action. At the international level, the handicaps to effective action have been much greater, for several reasons. First, there is no global legal system (other than international treaties relating to specific regions or problems, or the terms of membership of international organizations), and there is no global authority responsible for proposing and enforcing environmental regulations affecting multiple states. Second, national governments and corporations are less motivated to act on transboundary or global issues than on national issues because they face few legal obligations, are not directly answerable to public constituencies outside their own borders, and find it easier to ignore or transfer the costs of inaction to another party. It is simpler and cheaper, for example, to build tall smokestacks that will carry pollution across borders than to control the sources of that pollution. Finally, because many environmental problems are shared by multiple states, or are common to multiple states, individual states lack the motivation to act unless they can be assured that their neighbors will take similar action.

Against this background, private citizens have stepped into the breach by attempting to generate the pressure for political change through the work of nongovernmental organizations (NGOs). These NGOs have undertaken research into environmental problems, lobbied local and national governments, exerted pressure on international organizations and multinational corporations, raised and spent the funds needed to implement practical management measures, monitored the actions of governments and corporations, built political coalitions in support of public policy, and promoted public awareness of environmental problems. The need to address international problems has led in turn to the creation of international NGOs, formed to bring together the collective interests of national lobbies with a view to influencing multiple governments and publics and to drawing attention to the many environmental problems that are international, regional, or global in nature.

This chapter examines the roots, the structure, the work, and the effects of environmental NGOs. It argues that they have collectively played an important role in influencing the nature of various international regimes—such as those dealing with trade and development—and have become important sources of pressure for international action on environmental management. As such, they have contributed to the development of a global civil society within which humans have increasingly come to appreciate that most economic and social problems—and environmental problems in particular—are not limited by national boundaries but are part of the common experience of humanity and must be addressed accordingly.

The Rise of International Regimes

The period since 1945 has seen an unprecedented growth in the activity of international organizations, a phenomenon that has forced us to rethink the way we try to understand global politics. We still see the world in terms of states, we still see ourselves as citizens of one country or another, and the study of international relations has been heavily influenced by realist theory, which argues that the state is the fundamental unit of analysis. Realists believe that global politics is best understood by a study of the nature of relations among states: forming alliances, going to war, imposing sanctions, protecting and promoting individual interests, and pursuing self-interested goals of security, open markets, and autonomy.

By contrast, idealist theory—which focuses on individuals, groups, and communities rather than the state—argues that values predominate over military strength and strategic resources and that humans can place higher causes above self-interest, can pursue ideals in the interests of improving the quality of life, and can thus work to avoid conflict. Idealists support the development of international organizations as a means to bridging differences among states and avoiding destructive competition. Idealism is also based on a belief in the notion of globalism, where institutions and ideals other than the state attract the loyalty of humans.[2]

The idealist view has been promoted in part by increased doubts about the wisdom and efficiency of the modern state system. The most notable failure of the system lay in the inability of the superpowers during the cold war (1945–1990) to guarantee global peace through anything less than mutually assured nuclear destruction. The state system has also failed to respond effectively to demands for self-determination from national groups divided by state lines (such as the Kurds, the Basques, and the Hutus) and has promoted the kind of nationalism that has encouraged conflict and war rather than cooperation and compromise. It has also failed to resolve pressing economic and social issues, so that the rich industrial states have become richer, while one in every three people—according to World Bank calculations—remain poor.

Finally, the state system has failed to develop an effective response to issues that transcend state lines. The modern industrial state may have improved the quality of life of many of its citizens, but it has done so at the expense of encouraging people to think of themselves as competing citizens of individual states rather than as cooperating members of the human race. Among the consequences, charge its critics, has been a worsening of trans-boundary environmental problems, driven by a combination of three main factors. First, there has been a lack of scientific agreement concerning the causes and effects of environmental problems, which has encouraged states—out of concerned self-interest—to err on the side of caution in making their policy calculations. Scientific debate, for example, has encouraged major industrial states to be slow in reaching agreement on global warming, concerned as many have been about the loss of comparative economic advantage arising from the costs of controlling emissions of greenhouse gases such as carbon dioxide.

Second, states have been concerned about economic costs, both internally and relative to other states. The United States, for example, was slow to take action on acid pollution in part because of the potential costs to auto-manufacturing and coal-producing states (Michigan and West Virginia), and the lack of political concern for Canada, which received many of the emissions generated by power stations in upwind U.S. states. Similarly, Britain was largely unmoved during the late 1970s and early 1980s by the appeals of downwind Scandinavian states to reduce its pollution emissions; it took action only when it discovered forest damage within its own borders and was compelled to do so by European Union law.[3]

Third, there has been a lack of legal requirements. National governments have obligations by virtue of their membership in international organizations, but such organizations lack powers of coercion, and membership often commits the governments to adhere to principles rather than to meet specific objectives. A typical example can be found in the 1979 Convention on Long-Range Transboundary Air Pollution, which committed signatories to "endeavour to limit, and as far as possible, gradually reduce and prevent air pollution . . . [using] the best available technology which is economically feasible." Governments may have obligations as signatories of international treaties and conventions, but they are not obliged to sign, will only sign once compromises have been reached with which they can agree, and—during negotiations—may work to ensure that the obligations are as weak as possible.

One of the consequences of weaknesses in the state system since World War II has been the dramatic growth in the number, reach, and activities of nongovernmental organizations. Known also as interest groups or pressure groups, NGOs consist of groups of people (or coalitions of organizations) who come together outside the formal structures of government in an institutionalized and regularized manner with a view to trying to achieve social, economic, or political change. They may try to effect change just among their own members, mobilizing citizens or member organizations to act in their collective interests, but they will often try to influence public opinion, the media, elected officials, and bureaucrats with a view to influencing the actions of government.

Weaknesses in the state system since World War II have also contributed to a dramatic growth in the number, reach, and activities of international organizations (IOs). In their attempts to address and remove the causes of interstate conflict, and to address matters of shared interest collectively, national governments have created and joined IOs dealing with everything from defense, trade, and economic development to humanitarian issues, education, environmental management, and consumer safety. According to the Union of International Associations, there were just over 200 international organizations at the turn of the century; by 1969, the number had grown to about 2,000, by 1981 had risen to 15,000, and by 1997 stood at nearly 38,000.[4]

IOs broadly take the form either of intergovernmental organizations (IGOs), international nongovernmental organizations (INGOs), or multinational corporations (profit-making organizations that function in more than one country). IGOs are made up either of states or of national government bodies, generally lack autonomy in decision making, have few assets, lack the power to impose taxes or enforce their rulings, and are normally used as forums within which states can negotiate or cooperate with one another. The most influential IGOs are those in the network of United Nations specialized agencies, such as the World Bank, the Food and Agriculture Organization (FAO), and the United Nations Development Programme. Equally important IGOs have been created to deal with defense issues (the North Atlantic Treaty Organization, or NATO), global trade (the World Trade Organization, or WTO), and regional economic development (the Organization for Economic Cooperation and Development, or OECD).

A leading international scholar, Harold K. Jacobson, has identified five major categories of IGOs: informational, meaning agencies that gather, analyze, exchange, and disseminate data, such as the UN specialized agencies and the OECD; normative, meaning agencies that define standards and declare international principles and goals; operational, referring to agencies that have the power to oversee the implementation of certain functions, such as administering financial or technical assistance (for example, the World Bank and the International Monetary Fund); rule creating, meaning bodies involved in the enactment of formal treaties that are binding on the states that ratify them, such as agreements made under the auspices of GATT (now WTO) and NATO; and rule supervisory, referring to those organizations that have the authority to monitor compliance with treaties and other rules, again such as GATT/WTO and NATO.[5]

INGOs, for their part, normally have memberships consisting of individuals or private associations rather than states and have only the first three of the functions identified by Jacobson. They are rarely in the position to be able to create or to supervise the implementation of rules, other than those that relate to their own operations or those of their members. The most important rules are made by governments and by agreement among governments, so INGOs function outside the rule-making process, offering expert advice, undertaking research, and monitoring the application of these rules. Some are made up of delegations from participating national and local NGOs (examples include the International Chamber of Commerce and the World Federation of Trade Unions), while others work to rise above national identity and to become truly global in their memberships and interests.

IOs have been critical actors in the emergence of international regimes. If national regimes are defined as the common expectations, principles, norms, laws, objectives, and organizations that bind a national government and its citizens, then international regimes can be defined as the same factors applied to a group of states. The scholar Barry B. Hughes defines an international regime as "the principles, norms, rules, and decision-making procedures that facilitate extensive reciprocity in a given issue area."[6] It might be argued that we live in a single global regime driven by the balance of power and expectations among the more than 190 independent states of the world, but regime theory has also been applied to specific issue areas, such as trade (as influenced by decisions taken within the auspices of the WTO), monetary relations (the International Monetary Fund), and transportation (the International Civil Aviation Organization).

International regimes emerge when states need to reach agreement on common problems in a fashion that goes beyond ad hoc action but does not go so far as to oblige them to give up sovereignty to a more permanent decision-making system. At one end of the scale, the ad hoc multilateral Western responses to problems such as the crises in Bosnia or Iraq could not be defined as regimes, while—at the other end—the surrender of national sovereignty involved in the development of the European Union has taken its member states far beyond the creation of a regime.

Environmental issues have become the subject of several different international regimes, a reflection of the difficulty of compartmentalizing environmental issues and divorcing them from other issues (such as international trade) and of the fact that the international response to environmental problems has often demanded managing what are known as "common-pool resources." These are resources that do not belong to any one state but rather are part of the global domain. Prime examples include the atmosphere and oceans outside territorial waters, but it has also been suggested that the tropical rain forests of the Amazon basin, central Africa, and Southeast Asia—because of their role in global weather patterns—are also part of the global commons.

The Growth of the Environmental Movement

Attempts were made in the nineteenth and early twentieth centuries to build cooperation among national governments, but it has only been since 1945 that internationalism has come into its own. Motivated initially by the desire to avoid conflict, then pushed into the competing ideological camps of the cold war, then driven by the rising demands of newly independent African and Asian states for recognition and aid, and finally driven into cooperation through growing international trade and a revolution in international communication, states have found themselves drawn into greater cooperation on issues of mutual interest.

One of those issues has been the environment, which was approached for much of the nineteenth and early twentieth centuries largely as a local matter. Driven by the findings of the scientific revolution of the nineteenth century, by concerns about the effects on urban life of the spread of industry, and of the effects on nature of agricultural intensification, local and national nongovernmental organizations were created in the United States, Canada, and several European countries. Among the first NGOs with a focus on the environment were the Society for the Protection of Birds (created in Britain in 1889) and the Sierra Club (founded in the United States in 1892).

A variety of pressures subsequently indicated that a broader perspective was needed if environmental problems were to be addressed effectively. First, private citizens and scientists began to realize that many problems were common to two or more countries and began communicating with each other and sharing ideas about how best to respond. Second, these communications led to the realization that many problems could not be addressed by individual countries acting alone. Finally, following World War II, the growth of international trade meant that consumer demand in one country often created, or worsened, problems in another.

The Europeans were the first to begin looking outside their borders, both to their colonies and to their immediate neighbors. For example, the protection of colonial wildlife was the motivation for the creation in Britain in 1903 of the world's first international conservation NGO, the Society for the Preservation of the Wild Fauna of the Empire. Meetings among European nature protectionists led in 1913 to the creation of the Commission for the International Protection of Nature. INGOs such as these took a broader view than their national precursors; they encouraged environmentalists to look beyond their immediate circumstances and concerns and promoted cooperation among environmentalists with shared interests in multiple countries.

The growth in the number and reach of environmental IGOs and of INGOs accelerated following World War II. There were IGOs that predated the war—for example, the International Joint Commission was created in 1909 to encourage cooperation between the United States and Canada on the management of the Great Lakes—but the postwar IGOs were more ambitious in their scope and their objectives. The UN Food and Agriculture Organization, for example, was created in 1945 not only to deal with an immediate food supply crisis but also to look at long-term supply, and its founders quickly realized that a more globalized approach was needed to the management of natural resources.[7]

In 1947 the Commission for the International Protection of Nature was reorganized as the International Union for the Protection of Nature, becoming the first INGO with a global outlook on environmental problems. Renamed the International Union for the Conservation of Nature (IUCN) in 1956, it became the precursor to the later creation of many more environmental INGOs, notably the World Wildlife Fund (WWF; later renamed the Worldwide Fund for Nature outside the United States), created in 1961 to raise funds for IUCN projects.

The 1960s saw a rapid rise in public interest in environmental problems in industrial countries, driven by the publication of books such as Rachel Carson's *Silent Spring* (which drew attention to the use of chemicals in agriculture), concerns about the threat of fallout from nuclear testing, a series of well-publicized environmental disasters (including several major marine oil spills), and advances in scientific knowledge.[8] New NGOs were created in response, and public interest reached a new peak in 1972 with the convening in Stockholm, Sweden, of the United Nations Conference on the Human Environment, attended by representatives from 113 countries and more than 400 intergovernmental and nongovernmental organizations.[9] The Stockholm conference was the first meeting at which a combination of governments and NGOs from around the world sat down to address the global aspects of the emerging environmental crisis.

Among the many consequences of the Stockholm conference, three in particular stand out. First, the presence of so many national and international NGOs at the conference drew new public and political attention to their work and encouraged them to be more persistent in their efforts to work with each other and to influence public policy. Second, the presence of many newly independent African and Asian governments encouraged the industrial countries—for the first time—to acknowledge that poorer emerging countries had a different set of priorities and that underdevelopment was as much a cause of environmental problems as overdevelopment. For the United States and Europe, the major problems were a consequence of industrialization and the accelerated exploitation of resources: air and water pollution in particular. For Africa and Asia, by contrast, the major problems were a consequence of poverty and population growth, contributing, for example, to deforestation and soil erosion. Third, the conference resulted in the creation in 1973 of the United Nations Environment Programme, which went on to redefine the interest of the UN in environmental issues and to offer NGOs and INGOs a new forum in which they could attempt to influence public policy.

Environmental NGOs were also active before, during, and after the convening of the United Nations Conference on Environment and Development (UNCED, or the Earth Summit), held in Rio de Janeiro in 1992. The formal input of NGOs began as early as 1982 with the ten-year review of the Stockholm conference, which led to the creation in 1983 of the World Commission on Environment and Development (or the Brundtland Commission). Charged with reporting on progress in achieving the objectives of sustainable development, the commission finished its work in October 1987 and was replaced by a new body called the Center for Our Common Future (COCF).

NGOs influenced the Brundtland Commission through the testimony they provided, but they played a more active role in the work of COCF. The Center's mission was to publicize the goals of the Brundtland Commission, which it did in part through establishing contacts with partners, including NGOs and INGOs. With the official announcement in 1989 that the Earth Summit was to be held in 1992, NGOs played an active role in preparatory hearings, working through COCF and through the Environment Liaison Centre International, which was a conduit for contacts between NGOs and UNEP. NGOs also directly lobbied negotiators at the preparatory meetings for UNCED and had further influence as members of national delegations involved in those meetings.[10] Since the Rio conference, NGOs have played a central role in publicizing the extent to which the goals and objectives of the conference have found (or failed to find) their way into public policy.

The Global NGO Community

There is no authoritative source on the size of the global environmental NGO community, but the number of groups has grown at least in concert with the growth of NGOs more generally, and probably even faster. There has been a particular growth in recent years in the number of national and international NGO networks and coalitions, driven by rapid advances in communications technology.[11] The *World Directory of Environmental Organizations* described more than 2,600 environmental organizations in its 1996 edition,[12] but these are the bigger NGOs, and many are themselves umbrella bodies for smaller local and grassroots organizations, whose numbers are constantly changing. The European Environmental Bureau, for example, which acts as a conduit for contacts between NGOs and the major bodies of the European Union, has 132 European NGO members, which it claims represent about 14,000 member organizations and 260 associate organizations.[13] The Philippines alone has about 18,000 NGOs, India has 12,000, and Bangladesh has 10,000.[14] Extrapolating from cases such as these, and taking into account national and regional umbrella bodies around the world, the total number of environmental NGOs in the world probably runs well into six figures.

It would be wrong to suggest that there is a homogeneous global community of environmental NGOs that is driven by complementary goals and uses similar methods. While it is true that they share a common vision of encouraging a workable relationship between humans and their environment, NGOs use many different methods, often have different priorities and objectives, and vary substantially in size, goals, durability, stability, credibility, and ideological orientations (see Table 3-1).[15] In many cases they have disagreed on both methods and goals.

The most fundamental division within the NGO community is the philosophical one that exists between groups based in the industrial countries of the North and those based in the emerging states of the South. The former tend to focus on the environmental consequences of industrial development and to argue that there need to be adjustments in the goals of the free market, including greater regulation of industry, changes in the nature of consumerism, and investment in pollution control. Meanwhile, the latter argue that many environmental problems result from poverty, the shift of polluting industries from the North to the South, and the demands of northern consumers. While the former argue the need for curbs to be placed on economic growth, the latter argue that the worst problems are created by industry and overconsumption in the North and by inequalities in the global economic system. The philosophical difference was clear to one of the participants at UNCED: "While the North set the agenda with high profile statements on the need to tackle population growth and deforestation, without committing substantial new funds to do so, the South's insistence on the need for justice, relief of crippling international debt, new financial resources for sustainable development including environmental protection, and technology transfer went unheeded."[16]

In addition to these global philosophical groupings, it is important to distinguish among groups driven by differences in philosophy regarding the methods by which change is best achieved. In his study of the NGO community in the United States, for example, Walter A. Rosenbaum identifies three "enclaves": the ideological mainstream of "pragmatic reformist" organizations, the deep ecologists, and the radicals.[17] The pragmatists consist of the largest, most conservative, most politically active and publicly visible groups, which prefer to work within established political processes to influence public policy. In the United States, these include members of what is informally known as the Group of Ten, the biggest and most visible mainline NGOs, such as the National Wildlife Federation, the Sierra Club, and the National Audubon Society. (They have their counterparts in Europe in the form of the Royal Society for the Protection of Birds in Britain, Bund für Vogelschutz in Germany, and the Worldwide Fund for Nature.)

The deep ecologists include groups that emphasize the place of humans as a part of nature, believe that all forms of life have an equal right to exist, challenge the underlying institutional structures and social values upon

Table 3-1 Philosophies, Structures, and Methods of
Environmental NGOs

Philosophy	Structure	Method
Northern NGOs focusing on the environmental consequences of industrial development and consumerism	Federations of national/international groups. Created to facilitate communication and cooperation among member bodies	Working with elected officials, bureaucrats, and employees of corporations
Southern NGOs focusing on the environmental consequences of poverty and inequalities in the global economic system	Universal membership	Raising and spending money on groups, with widespread, global membership and interests
Conservative, pragmatic groups working to achieve change within established political processes	Intercontinental membership groups. Interests go beyond a particular region, but are not necessarily global	Campaigning and organizing public protests
Green organizations seeking fundamental changes in relationship among humans, and between humans and the environment	Regionally defined membership groups. Interests restricted to one continent or region	Promoting media coverage of environmental issues
		Litigation and monitoring the implementation of environmental law
	Internationally oriented national groups. National NGOs partly or wholly focused on international issues	Information exchange
Radical organizations that use confrontation to draw attention to the problems of the environment and argue that conventional political processes are part of the problem		Undertaking research
		Acquiring/managing property
NGOs representing the views of socioeconomic groups with an interest in the environmental debate, such as women, minorities, and business		Generating grassroots involvement

which governments are based and economies function, and argue the need for fundamental social change as a prerequisite for effective environmental management. While other groups generally accept the existing sociopolitical order and do not question the dominant values of society, ecologists reject those values, criticize existing political structures, consumerism, and materialism, and propose the development of a new environmental paradigm more compatible with the realities of environmental limits.[18] In several countries, these views have combined with grassroots movements to produce green political parties that see themselves as the vanguard of a new society in which humans take a holistic approach to their relationship with each other and their environment. Their members see green politics as a clarion call for good sense in a world driven by consumption and acquisition, where greed threatens to undermine the foundations of life on Earth. Their critics see them as a threat to economic development, jobs, and livelihoods, and as a brake on human progress.

The third of Rosenbaum's enclaves—the radicals—consists of groups that have become disenchanted with the methods and goals of mainstream environmentalism and believe in the use of direct action as a means to bring about urgently needed political and social change. Radicalism is apparently difficult to sustain. Notable among such groups in the 1970s were Friends of the Earth (FoE) and Greenpeace, which had a reputation for headline-grabbing tactics such as interfering with whaling activities and having their members tie themselves to bridges to protest shipments of nuclear waste; since then they have become less confrontational and more willing to work within established political procedures. Greenpeace still believes that "determined individuals can alter the actions and purposes of even the most powerful by 'bearing witness,' that is, by drawing attention to an abuse of the environment through their unwavering presence at the scene, whatever the risk."[19] However, the best known of the radicals now is Earth First!, founded in 1980, which argues that extreme methods are needed to deal with extreme problems and has opted for militant action, variously termed *ecotage* or *monkeywrenching*, such as hammering metal spikes into trees so as to discourage lumber companies from cutting them down.

Finally, the NGO community is also divided among groups that represent the viewpoints of specific socioeconomic groups, such as women, racial minorities, the poor, consumers, or business. For example, the Women's Environment and Development Organization was set up in 1990 to lobby for the inclusion of gender equity concerns in the documents for the Earth Summit and has gone on to become a network of 20,000 individuals and groups in more than 100 countries that believe in the need to encourage environmental activism among women's groups. Similarly, the World Business Council for Sustainable Development acts as a federation representing the interests of business councils and corporations in the debate over environmental issues and sustainable development. Within these philosophical and stylistic groupings, NGOs also vary in their internal structures and the methods and strategies they use.

Internal Structures

A structural typology developed by the Belgian-based Union of International Associations divides INGOs as follows:

Federations of International and National Organizations. These are bodies set up to facilitate communication and cooperation among their member bodies. They can be global networks of national offices of the same NGO, such as Greenpeace, the Worldwide Fund for Nature, or Friends of the Earth. These three have national offices, respectively, in thirty-two, fifty-three, and fifty-five countries, but the national offices are autonomous and have their own funding and strategic priorities. Cooperation is promoted by international secretariats in Amsterdam and, for WWF, Switzerland.

Federations also take the form of umbrella bodies, bringing together different organizations that act either as conduits for contacts between those NGOs and an IGO (for example, the Environment Liaison Centre International, with 840 NGO members in 1996,[20] provides a point of contact between NGOs and the UN Environment Programme), or as a channel for contacts among NGOs, as is the case with the more than 530 NGO members of the African NGOs Environment Network.[21]

Universal Membership Organizations. These are bodies that have a widespread, geographically balanced membership. The only environmental INGO that really fits this category is IUCN, which brings together both nongovernmental and government agencies. IUCN is one of the oldest environmental INGOs, tracing its roots back to the creation in 1947 of the International Union for the Protection of Nature. It has since undergone several name changes and now confusingly calls itself the World Conservation Union while retaining the IUCN acronym of its previous identity, the International Union for Conservation of Nature and Natural Resources.

Headquartered in Switzerland, IUCN is an unusual hybrid of governmental and nongovernmental members. Its membership in 1997 consisted of 74 governments (the United States, for example, is a member), 105 government agencies (including the U.S. Environmental Protection Agency, the Kenyan Ministry of Tourism and Wildlife, and the Chilean Forest Service), and 716 national and international NGOs.[22] This arrangement not only brings together equivalent organizations from different states but also allows national NGOs to take part in the work of an organization that includes their own governments and government agencies. IUCN also has six commissions (covering issues such as protected areas, education, communication, and law) within which networks of more than 8,000 technical, scientific, and policy experts are brought together to provide IUCN with the information it needs for its work.

IUCN provides governments and NGOs with information, acts as a clearinghouse for the exchange of ideas, and carries out its own environmental management projects, notably the creation of national parks and other protected areas and gathering information on the status of threatened species and ecosystems. It has also been active in the drafting of international treaties, such as the Convention on Biological Diversity and the Convention on International Trade in Endangered Species.

It is one of the more conservative INGOs, shying away from controversy and—unlike the FoE or Greenpeace—doing little to draw media attention to itself. This is because it is not a campaigning organization so much as a meeting place for government bodies and NGOs, and it sees its job as less to change policy and public opinion than to facilitate the exchange of ideas and information.

Intercontinental Membership Organizations. These are bodies whose interests go beyond a particular region but not to the point where they become universal membership groups. Among these are environmental INGOs with more focused interests, such as Birdlife International and Wetlands International. Birdlife International is a network of "partner" organizations in 115 countries that work collectively to gather and share information and to build strong national bodies working to protect birds and their natural habitats. It has a global secretariat in Britain and regional offices in Ecuador, Indonesia, and Belgium. Wetlands International is a federation bringing together national delegations in 48 countries, promotes research and information exchange, and has played an active role in the development and application of the 1971 Ramsar Convention on Wetlands of International Importance. It has three regional offices in Canada, the Netherlands, and Malaysia, and thirteen subregional offices.

Regionally Defined Membership Organizations. These are bodies whose interests are restricted to a particular continent or region, such as the African Wildlife Foundation (Kenya) and the Caribbean Conservation Association (Barbados). The European Environmental Bureau facilitates contacts between groups in the member states of the European Union (EU) and the main policymaking bodies of the EU.

Internationally Oriented National Organizations and National NGOs That Are Partly or Wholly Focused on International Issues. The former include the Sierra Club and the Natural Resources Defense Council, and the latter the World Resources Institute and the Worldwatch Institute (all based in the United States). The Sierra Club is mainly active on the domestic political front in the United States but also campaigns on issues such as human rights and the environment, environmentally compatible trade policies, global warming, and population growth control. The World Resources Institute, meanwhile, focuses on policy research, publishing—among other things—the well-respected annual World Resources series.

In addition, it is important to appreciate that NGOs also have different interests and priorities, and different constituencies. At one end of the scale are the single-issue groups, which pursue a specific, focused objective, such as clean water, opposition to toxic waste storage sites, or even the welfare of a single species of wildlife (as is the case with the U.S.-based Mountain Lion Preservation Foundation and the Bat Conservation International). At the other end of the scale are environmental organizations, which take a broader view of the place of humans in their environment, quality of life issues, and the damaging consequences of human activities. Many of these groups grew out of the expansion of environmental consciousness during the 1960s and address issues as broad as nuclear power, acid pollution, toxic waste disposal, chemicals in the environment, oil spills, and global warming.

A phenomenon of relatively recent emergence (mainly since the mid-1970s) has been the creation of groups with an interest in promoting sustainable development. This is a term that replaced *conservation* in the dictionary of environmentalism and means economic development that takes place within the carrying capacity of the natural environment. The sustainable development lobby focuses on managing resources for continued use. For example, it supports promotion of the management of forests and fisheries with a view to preventing clearcutting and overfishing, arguing that sustainable use will allow them to be a constant source of resources. Although the term is usually applied to African, Asian, and Latin American states, it has been a central factor in environmentalism in industrial states for decades.

Methods and Strategies

Environmental NGOs also differ according to the means they use to achieve their objectives. A distinction is commonly made among groups that attempt to persuade, to bargain, and to coerce,[23] but groups have multiple methods available to them.

Working with Elected Officials, Bureaucrats, and Employees of Corporations. Lobbying is the method most commonly used by national groups at the national level, with care being taken not to compromise their nonprofit or charitable status. In the United States, several major NGOs have created political action committees to channel funds to political parties and candidates running for office; they also work to provide support and information for their favored candidates. Elsewhere, umbrella NGOs such as the European Environmental Bureau and Environment Liaison Centre International act as a conduit between their member bodies and IGOs.

Groups can also exert influence by providing advice and expert testimony during legislative hearings and the development of international treaties, or by submitting proposals to government departments and working with government commissions.[24] Several groups are active, for example, on Antarctic issues: the Scientific Committee on Antarctic Research is an independent advisory body that approves all scientific activity in the Antarctic, and the Antarctic and Southern Ocean Coalition represents more than 200 NGOs at meetings of the signatories of the 1959 Antarctic Treaty.[25] Similarly, many groups have maintained a close relationship with the International Whaling Commission, which has allowed the number of NGOs participating in its meetings to rise to more than fifty.[26]

A notable example of how NGOs have developed a constructive relationship with an IGO is found in the World Bank. In 1983, six U.S. NGOs—including the National Wildlife Federation and the Natural Resources Defense Fund—placed pressure on the World Bank to pay more attention to the environmental effects of its projects, using hearings before the U.S. Congress on World Bank appropriations to draw attention to some of those projects.[27] The World Bank subsequently encouraged NGO involvement in an increasing number of its projects, and now meets regularly, mainly with NGOs based in Washington, D.C. Since the creation of the United Nations, and most notably since the 1972 Stockholm conference, NGOs have been increasingly active in attending and observing international conferences and in holding parallel NGO conferences. For example, more than 1,000 NGOs attended negotiations held in Geneva and New York in preparation for the 1992 Earth Summit, and more than 22,000 representatives from more than 9,000 NGOs attended the summit itself.[28]

Raising and Spending Money. The Worldwide Fund for Nature was founded to raise money that could then be channeled to conservation activities. It was originally charged with raising funds for IUCN projects but quickly went off on an independent course of its own. While it still has a close relationship with IUCN, it is very much a separate organization with its own set of methods and priorities.[29]

As its title implies, WWF initially raised money to spend on projects aimed at protecting animal and plant species. It discovered very early, however, that threatened wildlife could not be protected in isolation and that natural habitats had to be protected first. This meant eliciting the support of local communities and using economic arguments in favor of environmental management. It was no good trying to protect birds and animals in a Brazilian rain forest, for example, unless local farmers could be convinced that the rain forest had more economic value to the local community if it was maintained intact rather than being cut down for timber or to clear land for farming. The result was that WWF became increasingly involved in lobbying local and national governments and in promoting international treaties to achieve its interests.

WWF has its international headquarters in Switzerland and a network of offices in more than fifty countries. It raises funds through a combination of grassroots activities and national and international campaigns, which have gone beyond a focus on individual species and have moved into habitat protection (for example, endangered seas and forests campaigns), attempts to encourage tourists not to buy the products of endangered species, and recently even global environmental issues such as climate change.

Campaigning and Organizing Public Protests. These are methods most commonly associated with groups such as Friends of the Earth and Greenpeace, which are among the best-known environmental NGOs in industrial countries because of their focus on generating publicity for their causes. Both were founded at about the same time (the FoE in 1969 and Greenpeace in 1971), and both have since gone on to open national offices all over the world (the FoE in fifty-five countries and Greenpeace in thirty-two). Between them they now have nearly four million individual members, and they use similar methods to draw attention to similar problems.

The FoE was founded in the United States after a fallout between the Sierra Club and its executive director, David Brower. The Sierra Club is one of the oldest U.S. environmental NGOs (dating back to 1892) but had become too conservative for Brower's tastes. He argued that the solution to environmental problems lay not in temporary remedies but in fundamental social change and that vigorous campaigning was needed to achieve maximum publicity.[30] Similar motivations led to the creation of Greenpeace, which was born as the Don't Make a Wave Committee, a group that sailed a ship into northern Pacific waters to protest nuclear weapons tests. It has since used a combination of public protests and political lobbying to draw attention to issues such as deforestation in Russia, Canada, and Brazil; the dangers of nuclear energy and toxic wastes; and the problem of overfishing.

Promoting Media Coverage of Environmental Issues. Almost every NGO uses this channel, mainly through the provision of information and through being available for media interviews. Studies have repeatedly found that environmental groups believe the media to be generally sympathetic to their cause, and most groups actively use the media to get their message across to the public, mobilize potential allies, give legitimacy and support to their work, and influence policymakers.[31]

Litigation and Monitoring the Implementation of Environmental Law. The former is a method used particularly by groups in the United States, such as the Environmental Defense Fund and the Natural Resources Defense Council, which have exploited citizen suit provisions included in several major pieces of federal environmental law since the early 1970s. These allow private citizens to sue private parties for noncompliance with the law and to recover legal fees and even fines, which then help fund their activities.[32]

Among groups that monitor the implementation of laws at the international level are the Wildlife Trade Monitoring Unit, Trade Records Analysis of Flora and Fauna in Commerce (TRAFFIC), and the Environmental Investigation Agency. These groups were at the forefront of efforts to stop international trade in ivory in the 1980s and to monitor compliance with the ivory trade ban imposed under the Convention on International Trade in Endangered Species (CITES) in 1989.[33]

Information Exchange. NGOs can play an important role in information exchange and dissemination, helping to strengthen the operations of other groups. A prime example is the Indonesian Environmental Forum (WALHI), an umbrella body for more than 400 other groups, which organizes education and training programs, provides technical assistance to its members on issues such as fundraising, and coordinates the activities of its members in lobbying government officials and bringing lawsuits.[34]

Undertaking Research. The British-based International Institute for Environment and Development carries out research on behalf of governments, international agencies, and NGOs into issues such as forestry, sustainable agriculture, and human settlements. Similarly, the Austrian-based International Institute for Advanced System Analysis undertakes scientific research into a variety of environmental problems, such as air pollution.

Acquiring and Managing Property. One of the biggest NGOs in Britain is the National Trust, which buys or is given buildings of historical significance and land of natural significance and manages such property in perpetuity. In the United States, the Nature Conservancy and Ducks Unlimited purchase land, which is then set aside as wildlife habitat.

Generating Local Community Involvement in Environmental Protection. Several organizations focus on mobilizing grassroots support for their objectives. Such groups are most common in rural and urban communities in poorer countries and have been active, for example, in mobilizing forest dwellers in Brazil, India, and Malaysia to block the activities of lumber companies. The most famous of these was Chipko Andalan, or the movement in 1973–1974 to "hug trees" in India, by which local villagers (mainly women) were encouraged to band together to physically block the felling of trees by timber companies. In Kenya, the Green Belt Movement encourages people (again, mainly women) to find public areas and plant tree seedlings to form tree belts. Local community mobilization has also been effective in stopping the building of nuclear power stations, new highways, and toxic waste dumps in industrial countries.

Environmental Groups and International Regimes

The last thirty years has seen the evolution of a large and varied community of environmental NGOs that has exerted a powerful influence on national governments, intergovernmental organizations, and negotiations on international environmental agreements. As suggested in this chapter, these NGOs have goals, philosophies, styles, structures, and methods that are often very different. In some respects, this has been their strength, because they have been able to develop a variety of methods to deal with a variety of problems at a variety of levels. It has also been a weakness, however, because the fragmentation of the environmental NGO community has prevented it from presenting a united front to policymakers and has thus impeded its policy impact.[35]

At the national level, NGOs have government institutions and bodies of law that they can monitor, influence, lobby, and attempt to change. They can appeal to elected officials, use their members and funds to exert influence on the electoral process, and work through the media, elected officials, the courts, and the bureaucracy to exert influence over the policy process. They exist within a civil society, an organized society over which a state rules and in which citizens participate. In most cases, NGOs were created because citizens felt that the state was not dealing effectively with a particular problem—such as environmental management—and they organized in order to use their numbers to put pressure on the state, or to respond themselves to the shortcomings of the state.

The same cannot be said for NGOs working at the international level, where they face at least three major handicaps. First, there is no central authority to which NGOs can appeal, other than the United Nations and its specialized agencies, which have only limited powers and certainly lack the kind of elected officials needed to provide a connection between an institution and those who live under its authority. For environmental NGOs, the

United Nations Environment Programme comes closest to being an international authority, but it suffers a number of critical handicaps: it is a junior member of the UN system, it has no executive powers, it has little scope for carrying out its own projects, and it was intended from the outset to be an agent of cross-cutting policy coordination, working through the other UN specialized agencies.[36] UNEP has achieved the most when it has been a facilitator—bringing together governments and institutions with shared interests and encouraging them to negotiate and reach agreement on those interests. It cannot compel governments to act against their will.

Second, international treaties and organizations are the result of agreements among states, and citizens of those states have an influence over such compacts only indirectly through their own national governments. While it is true that NGOs have worked around this handicap and have played an active role in, for example, the development of international treaties and were obvious by their presence at Stockholm and Rio de Janeiro, there is no formal provision for public review and comment on such treaties, nor is there a formal mechanism by which citizens or NGOs can bring suit before the World Court against IGOs or states failing to meet their obligations.[37]

Finally, while there is a body of international law and a series of international courts with various jurisdictions, there are no international bureaucrats with the power to ensure the implementation of that law. Neither is there an identifiable constituency of citizens that NGOs can mobilize to bring pressure to bear to ensure implementation.

NGOs have nevertheless been able to exploit their strengths to overcome the handicaps inherent in exerting influence over the international regime, in several ways:

- They have acted as information brokers, becoming the source of much of the research upon which policy decisions are taken. Reports to the Stockholm conference and the Earth Summit, and the intergovernmental discussion leading up to many of the most important international environmental treaties, have been heavily influenced by research generated by NGOs and by NGO influence over media coverage of these events.
- They have been whistle-blowers, helping IGOs keep track of progress (or lack thereof) in the implementation of international treaties in signatory states. Indeed, it is arguable that without NGO pressure, there would be little obligation upon states to agree to substantial goals, and there would be little transparency in the process of agreeing and implementing international treaties.
- They have promoted democracy (albeit in limited form) in the work of IGOs and the deliberations preceding agreement of international treaties by ensuring that the views of their members have been taken into consideration.
- They have played a valuable role as opponents of national government policy, drawing attention to the failures of domestic policies

and bringing international pressure to bear with a view to changing those policies.

- They have provided models for new government programs, using their resources and their links with other NGOs to develop and offer solutions to environmental problems. In many instances, NGOs have themselves carried out the work of government by undertaking necessary research, raising necessary funds, and carrying out practical environmental management projects.
- They have built international coalitions that have occasionally bypassed states and helped make up for some of the weaknesses of IGOs.

In the absence of an international body of environmental law backed up by a global governmental authority with responsibility for—and powers of—enforcing that law, much of the responsibility for promoting environmental concern at the international level since World War II has fallen to—or been adopted by—an increasingly complex network of nongovernmental organizations. These organizations operate at several different levels, use many different methods, and have multiple objectives and underlying principles. As well as identifying problems, proposing solutions, and monitoring the responses of states and the international community, environmental NGOs have contributed to the promotion of international regimes and a global civil society within which states and their citizens have redefined their relationships to one another and have helped us better understand the nature of global society.

Notes

1. Mostafa K. Tolba et al., *The World Environment 1972–1992: Two Decades of Challenge* (London: Chapman and Hall, 1992).
2. Gordon C. Schloming, *Power and Principles in International Affairs* (San Diego: Harcourt Brace, 1991); see chap. 2 for a discussion of the characteristics of realism and idealism.
3. John McCormick, *Acid Earth: The Politics of Acid Pollution*, 3d ed. (London: Earthscan, 1997).
4. World Wide Web, Union of International Associations Homepage, http://www.uia.org/welcome.htm (1998).
5. Harold K. Jacobson, *Networks of Interdependence: International Organizations and the Global Political System*, 2d ed. (New York: Knopf, 1984), 88–90.
6. Barry B. Hughes, *Continuity and Change in World Politics: The Clash of Perspectives* (Englewood Cliffs, N.J.: Prentice-Hall, 1991), 264.
7. John McCormick, *The Global Environmental Movement*, 2d ed. (New York: London: John Wiley, 1995), 29–36.
8. Ibid., chap. 3.
9. Ibid., 119.
10. For more details on the role of NGOs in UNCED, see Matthias Finger, "Environmental NGOs in the UNCED Process," in *Environmental NGOs in World Politics*, ed. Thomas Princen and Matthias Finger (London: Routledge, 1994).
11. World Resources Institute, *World Resources 1992–93* (New York: Oxford University Press, 1992), 215.

12. Thaddeus C. Trzyna and Roberta Childers, *World Directory of Environmental Organizations,* 5th ed. (London: Earthscan, 1996).
13. European Environmental Bureau, *Activity Report 1995* (Brussels: EEB, 1996), 28.
14. World Resources Institute, *World Resources 1992–93,* 218–220.
15. For further discussion, see Princen and Finger, *Environmental NGOs in World Politics,* 6–9.
16. Andrew Simms, "If Not, Then When? Non-Governmental Organizations and the Earth Summit Process," *Environmental Politics* 21 (spring 1993): 94–100.
17. Walter A. Rosenbaum, *Environmental Poltics and Policy,* 3d ed. (Washington, D.C.: CQ Press, 1995), 24–27.
18. Russell J. Dalton, *The Green Rainbow: Environmental Groups in Western Europe* (New Haven: Yale University Press, 1994); Stephen Cotgrove, *Catastrophe or Cornucopia: The Environment, Politics, and the Future* (New York: Wiley, 1982); Lester Millbrath, *Environmentalists: Vanguard for a New Society* (Albany: State University of New York Press, 1984); Ronald Inglehart, *The Silent Revolution: Changing Values and Political Styles among Western Publics* (Princeton: Princeton University Press, 1977).
19. World Wide Web, Greenpeace Home Page, http://www.greenpeace.org:80/ gpi.html (1998).
20. World Wide Web, IDS Homepage, http://www.ids.ac.uk/ids/ids.html (1998).
21. Donald T. Wells, *Environmental Policy: A Global Perspective for the Twenty-First Century* (Upper Saddle River, N.J.: Prentice Hall, 1996).
22. World Wide Web, IUCN Home Page, http://w3.iprolink.ch/iucnlib/info_and_ news/about_iucn/index.html (1998).
23. Ralph Turner, "Determinants of Social Movement Strategies," in *Collective Behavior,* ed. T. Shibutani (Englewood Cliffs, N.J.: Prentice-Hall, 1970).
24. Dalton, *The Green Rainbow,* 189–195.
25. Margaret L. Clark, "The Antarctic Environmental Protocol: NGOs in the Protection of Antarctica," in Princen and Finger, *Environmental NGOs in World Politics.*
26. Princen and Finger, *Environmental NGOs in World Politics,* 5.
27. Bruce Stokes, "Storming the Bank," *National Journal,* December 31, 1985, 3521–3522, and Ken Conca, "Greening the UN: Environmental Organizations and the UN System," in *NGOs, the UN, and Global Governance,* ed. Thomas G. Weiss and Leon Gordenker (Boulder, Colo.: Rienner, 1996).
28. Princen and Finger, *Environmental NGOs in World Politics,* 4.
29. McCormick, *The Global Environmental Movement,* 46–48.
30. Ibid., 170–172.
31. Dalton, *The Green Rainbow,* 185–186.
32. Michael S. Greve, "Private Enforcement, Private Rewards: How Environmental Suits Become an Entitlement Program," in *Environmental Politics: Public Costs, Private Rewards,* ed. Michael S. Greve and Fred L. Smith (New York: Praeger, 1992), 105–109.
33. Thomas Princen, "The Ivory Trade Ban: NGOs and International Conservation," in Thomas Princen and Matthias Finger, *Environmental NGOs in World Politics* (London: Routledge, 1994).
34. World Resources Institute, *World Resources 1992-93* (New York: Oxford University Press, 1992), 230.
35. Lynton K. Caldwell, *Between Two Worlds: Science, the Environmental Movement, and Policy Choice* (Cambridge: Cambridge University Press, 1990), 89-97.
36. McCormick, *The Global Environmental Movement,* chap. 6, n. 7.
37. Hilary French, "The Role of Non-State Actors," in *Greening International Institutions,* ed. Jacob Werksman (London: Earthscan, 1996).

4

The European Union as an
Environmental Governance System

Regina S. Axelrod and Norman J. Vig

The creation of the European Union (EU) has transformed western Europe. The objective of establishing a common internal economic market has contributed to the openness of national borders and the harmonization of many policies once in the exclusive domain of individual member states. The EU also has established some of the strongest and most innovative environmental protection measures in the world and has increasingly taken the lead on international environmental issues such as global warming. In principle, environmental protection now enjoys equal weight with economic development in EU policy making.

Political will and public support have been the keys to EU success in approaching the environment from an integrated perspective. First, the legal foundations have been firmly established so that the EU has an unchallenged right to protect the environment. Second, all states recognize that without common environmental policies, barriers to free trade develop. Common environmental policies therefore strengthen the prospects for creation of a single economic market. Third, political, economic, and geographic diversity have challenged policy makers to develop innovative strategies for overcoming differences and sharing burdens equitably.

The European Union is therefore an important model to study, both as the most advanced regional organization of states and as a comprehensive environmental policy regime. But the EU also has become an important actor in global environmental diplomacy. In addition to individual member states, the EU is a party to most international conventions in the 1990s.[1] Since the 1992 United Nations Conference on Environment and Development, known as the Earth Summit, in Rio de Janeiro, the EU has played a leading role in pushing the United States and other nations to adopt more stringent environmental agreements on matters such as climate change. Under current plans to enlarge the EU to include Cyprus and five countries in central and eastern Europe and eventually to include more of the former communist bloc states, the EU has the potential to shape environmental policy from the Baltic to the Aegean.

Nevertheless, the EU also faces a number of important problems and opportunities as it becomes a larger and more integrated governance system. This chapter explores the history, institutions, current environmental policies, and future challenges of this unique organization.

The Political Origins of the European Union
and Environmental Policy

The quest for political and economic union in Europe had its origins in the 1920s and 1930s, when it was recognized that some kind of supranational organization was needed to avoid brutal competition, protectionism, and war. But it was the experience of World War II that convinced statesmen to seek a new type of unity. U.S. economic assistance under the postwar Marshall Plan also called for regional cooperation.

The first step toward building a more integrated Europe was the formation of the European Coal and Steel Community (ECSC). The idea of French economic planner Jean Monnet and foreign minister Robert Schumann, the ECSC was created by the Treaty of Paris on April 18, 1951. The original members were Belgium, France, Germany, Italy, Luxembourg, and the Netherlands. Its economic goal was to pool the production of coal and steel for the benefit of all six countries. Its other purpose was to lock Germany politically and economically into a stable partnership with western Europe.

Other cooperative activities were slow to develop, but in June 1955 the six ECSC members decided to move toward closer economic integration. They saw a European free trade area or "common market" as a means to increase industrial and agricultural exports, to redistribute resources to economically depressed areas, and to encourage travel among countries. The result was the 1957 Treaty of Rome, which established the European Economic Community (EEC) and the European Atomic Energy Authority (Euratom). In the 1970s Denmark, Ireland, and the United Kingdom joined the EEC, and Greece, Portugal, and Spain had followed suit by 1986. Austria, Finland, and Sweden became full members in 1995, bringing the current membership to fifteen.[2]

The Treaty of Rome contained no explicit provisions for protection of the environment. EEC policy on the environment dates instead from the 1972 Paris summit of the community's heads of state and government, which was inspired in part by the Stockholm Conference on the Human Environment held earlier that year. Under Article 235, which permits legislation in new areas if consistent with EEC objectives, the summit proposed the creation of an Environmental Action Programme. In effect, the members added an environmental agenda to the Treaty of Rome.

Over the next dozen years, they adopted three environmental action plans (for 1973–1976, 1977–1981, and 1982–1986, respectively), and enacted more than twenty major environmental directives covering air and water pollution, waste management, noise reduction, protection of endangered flora and fauna, environmental impact assessment, and other topics. They took most of these actions under Article 235 and later Article 100a of the Treaty of Rome, which authorizes actions that "directly affect the establishment or functioning of the common market." The motivation for these laws was to avoid trade distortions caused by different environmental standards while dealing with problems that were inherently transboundary in nature.[3]

The Single European Act of 1987 was the next milestone in the development of the treaties. This act accelerated the integration process by calling for establishment of a single internal economic market by the end of 1992. It set out more precise goals for harmonizing economic policies and eliminating border controls and other barriers to the free movement of goods, services, labor, and capital across Europe. Equally important, the act added a new section to the Treaty of Rome (Articles 130r, 130s, 130t) that formally defined the goals and procedures of EC environmental policies and called for "balanced growth" by integrating environmental policy into all other areas of EC decision making. The volume of new environmental legislation reached a peak during the 1987–1992 period.

The Maastricht Treaty (also called the Treaty of European Union), which entered into force in 1993, called for closer political and monetary union, including development of a common European currency, by the end of the decade. It also created two new "pillars"—to promote common foreign and security policies and cooperation in justice and home affairs—that, together with the European Community (EC), now form the European Union. In addition, the treaty further strengthened the legal basis and procedures for environmental policy making. This trend was continued in the most recent revisions of the Treaty of Union adopted at Amsterdam in June 1997. Article 3d states explicitly that "environmental protection requirements must be integrated into the definition and implementation of Community policies and activities . . . in particular with a view to promoting sustainable development."[4]

As a result of these and other developments, the European Union has created the most comprehensive regional environmental protection regime in the world. Although scholars still debate whether the EU is primarily an "intergovernmental" organization dominated by the interests of individual member states or a "functional" regime that represents common transnational interests and actors, the EU is increasingly regarded as a "multi-level governance structure" in environmental policy.[5]

EU Institutions and Policy-Making Processes

Institutions

The European Union's primary institutions are the council, the commission, the parliament, and the European Court of Justice. There are also eleven secondary agencies including the European Environment Agency (EEA).

The EU Council meets in Brussels and consists of representatives from the governments of each of the member states. When the heads of government meet, it is known as the European Council or "summit." Usually, council meetings involve the fifteen ministers responsible for the topic under discussion; for example, environmental decisions are made by a council made up of the fifteen environment ministers. The presidency of the council rotates among the member states every six months, and the country in charge can shape the agenda. For example, the new German Social Democratic-Green government, elected in September 1998, was expected to push for new energy taxes when it assumed the council presidency in January 1999. The council is the most important EU body because it must approve all legislation. Its directives must be adopted by the individual member states and incorporated into national law within a specified period of time, usually two years. The EU can enact regulations that automatically apply to the states, but they are less common. The council also makes decisions on international treaties and agreements. In general, the council's actions reflect the national interests of the states. However, many decisions can now be taken by a qualified majority of the council, that is, by a special voting procedure that gives greater weight to larger states than smaller states and does not require unanimity.[6]

The EU Commission is a body of twenty commissioners (and their staffs) who head twenty-three directorates-general (DGs). DG XI is responsible for the environment, nuclear safety, and civil protection. The commission's task is to initiate EU legislation and to oversee its implementation by member states. Its president, Jacques Santer (1995–1999) is sometimes referred to as the "European president." A multinational bureaucracy of some thirteen thousand serves the commission and its directorates in Brussels.[7]

The 626-member European Parliament (EP), by contrast, is elected directly by voters in each country and tends to reflect the diverse interests of political parties and groupings across Europe. The parliament has a moving seat. It holds plenary sessions in Strasbourg, France, but much of its staff is in Luxembourg, and it holds most of its committee meetings in Brussels. Draft legislation from the commission is submitted to the EP, which can either accept the draft as is or propose amendments. The parliament also must approve the commission budget and EU treaties, and it votes on the appointment of the president and commissioners.[8]

The EP is not regarded as a true legislature because it cannot initiate measures. However, the Maastricht Treaty allows a majority of members to request that the commission develop a proposal if it concerns implementation of the treaty, and EP committees also can informally influence policy formation in other ways. Under the Amsterdam treaty revisions, a "co-decision" procedure was extended to many more areas of environmental legislation. Under this procedure, if the EP does not agree with the council position after a second reading, a conciliation committee is formed to resolve differences. If agreement still cannot be reached, the EP can reject the proposal by majority vote, giving it a de facto veto. The new procedure could increase the EP's role in policy making, make decision making more transparent, and reduce the "democratic deficit" until parliament receives full legislative powers.

The European Court of Justice (ECJ), located in Luxembourg, considers cases brought before it by the commission, the council, or member states concerning the application of EU treaties. ECJ decisions are binding on member states, but the court must depend on national courts to carry them out, making enforcement difficult. Under the Maastricht Treaty, the ECJ can levy fines against member states that fail to comply with its decisions. The court also has made it easier for citizens to enforce their EU rights in national courts.[9]

Some ECJ decisions have helped define the rights of member states to enact environmental legislation that may violate EU treaty provisions prohibiting restraints of trade. For example, in the 1988 Danish bottle case, the court upheld Denmark's law requiring the use of returnable bottles for beer and soft drinks on grounds that its environmental benefits were sufficient to justify a minor restraint on trade.[10] Like courts in the United States, the ECJ is emerging as an important policy maker in balancing economic and environmental interests.

The European Environment Agency was approved in 1990 and established in 1994 in Copenhagen, after a long battle over its location. Although it does not have the regulatory and enforcement powers of the Environmental Protection Agency in the United States, the EEA is becoming an important actor in EU policy making. Its mission is to compile a scientific database on environmental conditions in Europe and develop analytical models for understanding environmental processes and improving decision making. It published the first comprehensive assessment of the state of Europe's environment in 1995 and issued a critical assessment of progress toward implementing the Fifth Environmental Action Programme (see below).[11]

The Policy Process

Policy making within the EU is more "political" than a description of the institutions might suggest.[12] Because the EU is a fluid and developing institution, policy making is complicated by uncertainty over roles, powers, and decision rules. As we have seen, the council, commission, and parliament perform functions different from those of the three branches of the U.S. government.

The commission and parliament can be viewed as supranational bodies, whereas the council remains essentially intergovernmental. Under their terms of appointment, the commissioners and their staffs are international civil servants who are not supposed to serve any national interest; therefore, the commission's proposed legislation tends to favor greater "harmonization" of European policies. Parliament also tends to favor stronger EU policies, especially in fields such as environmental and consumer protection that are popular with the electorate. The council, in contrast, is usually more cautious because of its sensitivity to national political interests and the costs of implementing EU policies (which largely devolve on national governments). The council is more likely to invoke the principle of *subsidiarity*, under which actions are to be taken at the EU level only if they cannot be carried out more efficiently at the national or local level.[13]

Conflicts of interest among the states are evident in the council. In the past, a fluid coalition of Denmark, Germany, and the Netherlands has pushed the hardest for environmental protection. These "green" countries often have higher regulatory standards than the EU and have tried to get the EU to adopt them, a process that has been called "regulatory competition."[14] For example, Germany was influential in proposing tough air pollution controls on large combustion plants, while the Netherlands convinced the council to adopt its high standards for small car and truck emissions. More recently, Austria, Finland, and Sweden have joined Denmark and the Netherlands as the forerunners, with Germany taking a somewhat more cautious position because of economic difficulties at home.[15] At the other end of the spectrum, the poorer countries, such as Greece, Ireland, Portugal, and Spain, have been more reluctant to carry out EU policies, while Belgium, Britain, France, Italy, and Luxembourg tend to fall in between. One of the principal challenges facing the EU has been to find ways of accommodating different levels of environmental commitment and regulatory capacity without weakening ultimate goals.

Lobbying by private interests is also omnipresent in the EU.[16] Industry is very concerned about the impact of new environmental legislation on business and maintains an army of lawyers in Brussels. Both the commission directorates and parliamentary committees regularly consult such interests, which tend to represent the largest companies and trade associations. Environmental, consumer, and other public interest groups also have representation. An umbrella organization in Brussels, the European Environmental Bureau, represents some 120 national groups. It closely monitors DG XI and tries to influence proposed legislation. Other international environmental NGOs (nongovernmental organizations) such as the Worldwide Fund for Nature and Greenpeace also lobby intensely and are regarded as among the most effective pressure groups.[17] A broad range of stakeholders and policy networks thus influence the EU policy process at all levels.

Environmental policy is closely related to other issues such as economic competition, taxation, research and development, energy, and transportation. Effective policy making therefore requires interaction and cooperation among many EU directorates and parliamentary committees. Formal and informal working groups and task forces try to work out mutually compatible strategies. For example, the development of efficiency standards for electrical appliances involved a working group of members from DG XI and the energy directorate (DG XVII). The divergent perspectives of these directorates often lead to different policy preferences, as do those of the agriculture, transportation, trade, and other "economic" directorates. The requirement of Article 3d that environmental protection must be integrated into all fields of EU policy gives weight to the issue. As a relatively new and understaffed directorate, however, DG XI is often in a weak position in negotiating with its counterparts, especially the leading economic directorates for industry (DG III) and trade (DG I). Final policy resolution by the commission and council usually involves extensive political compromise, which sometimes takes the form of "side payments." For example, in an effort to gain approval for an overall EU target for reducing CO_2, a burden-sharing plan was worked out under which some states agreed to exceed EU targets so that other states have lower burdens to meet. Such differentiated obligations, along with "derogations" allowing some countries more time to comply with EU directives, are creating a "multispeed" Europe despite efforts to integrate and harmonize policies.

The Harmonization of Environmental Standards

The general rationale for creating common EU policies and "harmonizing" standards is to level the economic playing field. The danger is that the lowest common denominator will prevail and, in the case of environmental standards, result in EU norms that are considerably weaker than those of the leading states. Specific provisions have been added to the Treaty of Rome to mitigate this problem.

Article 130r of the treaty guarantees that the EU will take action "to improve the quality of the environment." This statement implies that there will be a minimum standard that is not the lowest; rather, it means that all areas should be brought up to a high level of protection. Article 130s allows the council to define which environmental matters can be decided by a "qualified majority." Article 130t further specifies that "measures taken by the EU do not prevent any Member State from maintaining or introducing more stringent protective measures, provided that these are compatible with the treaty."[18]

Environmental legislation can be based on these clauses of Article 130 or on Article 100a, which authorizes actions to establish a single market. A revised provision was added to the treaty at Amsterdam. It allows states to maintain laws or introduce new measures that exceed EU requirements if they can be justified on scientific grounds and do not constitute an obstacle to the functioning of the internal market.[19]

It appears that the lead states will be able to retain higher environmental standards than other countries so long as the commission or the ECJ does not find them in violation of other sections of the treaty. Naturally, they would rather bring the EU norms up to their level so they are not at a competitive economic disadvantage. In some areas, states have moved ahead of the EU. For example, Denmark, Germany, and the Netherlands require high levels of materials recycling, and Denmark, Finland, the Netherlands, and Sweden have enacted CO_2 taxes, even though the EU as a whole has been unable to reach agreement on this issue.

The Maastricht Treaty allowed most environmental legislation to be enacted by a qualified majority in the council, whereas previously unanimity was normally required. In an offsetting provision, the treaty placed greater emphasis on the principle of subsidiarity, under which actions should be taken by the member states unless the objectives can be better achieved through EU actions. Since 1992 some states have used this principle as a rationale for slowing down new legislation (see below). The Amsterdam Treaty did not alter the provisions on majority voting and failed to clarify the meaning of subsidiarity, leaving this conflict unresolved.

The Fifth Environmental Action Programme

As noted, since 1972 the commission has developed an agenda, called environmental action programmes, to guide its activities for a multiyear period. Although these programs are not legally binding, they have had substantial influence on actual policy development at the EU level and among member states. The Fifth Programme, entitled "Towards Sustainability," was adopted in 1992 and runs through 2000.[20] As the title suggests, its guiding principle is sustainable development, and it represents the EU's attempt to implement the Agenda 21 proposals adopted at the 1992 Earth Summit (see Chapter 8). The program, which was also strongly influenced by the Dutch National Environmental Policy Plan (see Chapter 12), called for "integration of environment considerations in the formulation and implementation of economic and sectoral policies, in the decisions of public authorities, in the conduct and development of production processes, and in individual behavior and choice."[21] All EU policies are said to be dependent on achieving sustainable practices. New strategies are suggested for dealing with problems, such as cross-media pollution and pollution prevention at the source, and for the use of new policy instruments such as environmental taxes. The sectors targeted are industry, energy, transportation, agriculture, and tourism. However, the program goes beyond environmental cleanup and pollution mitigation by also calling for "shared responsibility" for the environment by all sectors of society and, where necessary, long-term changes in human behavior. (For a list of basic problems cited in the program, see box, next page.)

The success of the Fifth Action Programme has been a source of considerable controversy. In January 1996 the European Commission issued a progress report on implementation of the program, which showed mixed results, but was generally optimistic in tone.[22] A technical evaluation published by the European Environment Agency in fact detailed many shortcomings in meeting environmental quality goals set in 1992.[23] The environment commissioner, Ritt Bjerregaard, received harsh criticism—not all of which was justified—from environmental groups and from the environment committee of the European Parliament for the commission's failure to enact specific targets and deadlines for pollution reduction and for failing to implement priorities such as energy conservation and renewable energy development.[24] After more than a year of heated debate, parliament and the commission finally reached an agreement that reaffirmed the goals of the program, identified five priorities, and called for accelerated action to implement them. A new Sixth Action Programme scheduled to go into effect in 2000 is likely to focus on problems of implementation.

Major Environmental Threats in the European Union

Air. "Air quality . . . continues to give cause for concern in most towns and cities due to the increasing emissions of the principal pollutants into the air from motor vehicles. . . . Simulations for the year 2000 suggest there will be some improvement, but at the same time further deterioration in urban and industrial growth areas."

Water. "Despite the investments made over the last 20 years or so, on the whole there has been no improvement in the state of the Community's water resources. There have been more cases of deterioration in quality than of improvement. With demand rising as it is at present, the impending depletion of freshwater resources in certain regions may create major problems in the future, particularly in the Mediterranean countries."

Soil. "Physical degradation of the soil is widespread throughout the Community. The soil was long thought to have unlimited absorptive capacity, but now it is becoming increasingly difficult for it to perform its many vital functions, as a source of biomass in the form of crops and timber, as a habitat and as an ecosystem stabilizer. An increase in the pollution content has been observed at many sites. Pollution . . . by heavy metals and organic products is increasing not only . . . around industrial centres . . . but also in some rural areas, as a result of the combination of air pollution and farming."

Waste. "The volume of waste generated is increasing at a far greater rate than treatment and disposal capacity. A major effort to set up . . . household refuse collection networks has ensured that virtually all the urban waste in the Community is actually collected. Nevertheless, landfill remains the commonest disposal method. Processes such as composting or recycling are gaining ground but remain too limited to alleviate the growing landfill problem."

The quality of life. "Urban population growth will continue at a rapid rate in the cities of southern Europe, particularly along the coast, putting further pressure on the population's quality of life. Without rigorous measures to protect the rural environment in places where desertification is becoming acute, the countryside will continue to deteriorate."

High-risk activities. "As man learned to protect himself from natural risks, he also began to apply more and more high-risk techniques. Not only the workers employed in these activities are at risk but also the local population as well. The nuclear power industry, the chemical industry, the transport of hazardous substances and, more recently, the genetic engineering industry all pose new risks."

Source: *Fifth Programme on the Environment of the European Commission,* 1992.

Legislative Action

The EU has more than two hundred pieces of environmental legislation in force.[25] Most of this legislation was enacted during the 1970s and 1980s to address the major sources of pollution noted in the box. Since 1992 there has been a marked slowdown in the passage of legislation for several reasons. First, the principle of subsidiarity was elevated to a prominent place in the Maastricht Treaty to gain the support of several states that were reluctant to move toward further economic integration. According to Article 3b, the EU can take action only "if and in so far as the objectives of the proposed action cannot be sufficiently achieved by the Member States and can therefore, by reason of the scale or effects of the proposed action, be better achieved by the Community." Although the exact meaning of this wording is unclear, one consequence is that the commission has been more cautious in proposing new regulations and directives since 1992. Second, the commission has had to devote increasing attention to other issues under the Maastricht and Amsterdam treaties, notably completion of the monetary union and preparations for the inclusion of countries in central and eastern Europe. Third, there has been substantially increased pressure from industry and from some governments for deregulation or at least greater flexibility in the design and implementation of policies. Sluggish economic growth and high unemployment have made pivotal states such as Germany and France more reluctant to impose new costs on industry. As a result of these and other factors, the council has adopted little new legislation since 1992. Rather, there has been a shift in emphasis toward consolidation of existing policies and improving implementation and enforcement before extending regulation in new areas.

Nevertheless, there has been some progress in the post-Rio period. The EU has enacted or is considering several directives that consolidate existing policies and promote more integrated decision making across media and sectors; it has taken a relatively aggressive stance on certain global issues such as climate change. The commission also has issued a series of white papers and other communications suggesting options for new policy measures and approaches that may be adopted in the future. One of the most important of these was the "Communication on Environment and Employment" issued in November 1997, which for the first time spelled out how environmental protection and job creation can be mutually reinforcing.[26]

The following sections discuss some of the recent legislation in greater detail.

Framework Directives

Legislation in the European Union can take the form of either regulations or directives. Regulations are directly binding on member states and require no further legislation at the national level; they are used when technical standardization is necessary. Directives are more commonly used for environmental regulation. Under Article 189 of the treaty, directives "shall be binding, as to the result to be achieved, upon each Member State . . . but shall leave to the national authorities the choice of form and methods." What this means is that directives must be "transposed" into national law— each country must pass or amend legislation to achieve the stated objectives.

The purpose is to allow states to adapt EU policies to their particular legal and administrative traditions, but "choice of form and methods" gives states considerable discretion in deciding how to achieve EU policy goals. For example, a government might try to achieve a certain level of water quality either by controlling industrial discharges or by regulating land use to reduce urban and agricultural runoff. The result has been wide variations among countries in the implementation of EU environmental laws and severe difficulties in monitoring and assessing progress toward common goals.

Framework directives attempt to deal with this problem by establishing comprehensive long-term environmental quality goals and standards that can be used to measure progress across a wide range of specific policy instruments and actions. They provide a mechanism for consolidating, integrating, and simplifying related pieces of legislation (for example, separate directives on drinking water, bathing water, and protection of shellfish) to encourage more comprehensive and efficient management of resources. While allowing countries greater flexibility in pursuing these goals, they can also serve as a catalyst to force states to adopt a more integrated approach to environmental protection. Finally, an explicit purpose of the new directives is to increase "transparency" in environmental regulation by ensuring public access to information in a timely fashion.

Despite these laudable objectives, many environmental groups and members of parliament fear that the trend toward more general framework directives will result in a weakening of existing environmental controls. They are concerned that minimum standards may be set too low and that EU enforcement will become even more difficult than it already is. The European Parliament, therefore, has taken a tough stance on the new legislation, requiring extensive modifications in some cases.

The three environmental framework directives enacted or near to completion at this writing are discussed briefly below.

Integrated Pollution Prevention and Control. The first two framework directives were enacted by the council in September 1996. The Integrated Pollution Prevention and Control Directive (96/61/EC) is intended to provide much of the operational foundation for the others because it imposes common requirements for issuing permits to large industrial sources of pollution throughout the EU. Under the directive, member states will have to require all new and existing facilities to obtain operating permits that ensure that all appropriate measures are taken to prevent or minimize pollution of the air, water, and land. The directive calls for use of both environmental quality and emission standards (the "combined approach"), which accommodates different national systems; for example, the British rely on ambient quality standards, but the Germans insist on strict emission limits. Emission standards are to be based on the "best available techniques," but state authorities are given discretion to determine the specific control technologies to be used and to consider "the technical characteristics of the installation, its geographical location and local environmental conditions." This provision gives states considerable discretion, although the directive reserves the right for the council to set communitywide emission limit values for certain categories of installations and pollutants if necessary.

The larger significance of the directive is that states are encouraged to take a comprehensive, integrated approach to pollution reduction at the source, including waste minimization, efficient use of energy, and protection of soil and groundwater as well as surface waters and air. This approach is in line with the Fourth and Fifth Action Programmes, which called for a shift from end-of-the-pipe controls to pollution prevention; more integrated, long-term environmental management; and greater flexibility in the use of policy instruments. The subsequent air and water directives are designed to consolidate existing legislation and provide a legal framework for integrating policy across these media.

Ambient Air Quality and Auto Emissions Standards. EU legislation to protect air quality goes back to 1970, when the first directive to regulate emissions from automobiles was passed (70/220/EEC). Since then the council of ministers has enacted more than thirty directives on air pollution covering, among other things, diesel engine emissions, the lead and sulfur content of fuels, and emissions from large industrial facilities, power plants, and waste incinerators. Ambient air quality standards also have been set for sulfur dioxide, nitrogen dioxide, particulates, and lead; and regulations to limit chlorofluorocarbons (CFCs) and other ozone-depleting gases have been implemented under the Vienna Convention and subsequent international agreements. Europe generally followed the lead of the United States in setting these standards but lagged somewhat behind, for example, in not requiring the installation of catalytic converters on cars until 1991, and air pollution has become a severe problem in many European cities. Moreover, methods for measuring, assessing, and reporting air quality data varied greatly from country to country, making it difficult to apply common standards.

The commission proposed a new air quality framework directive in July 1994, which, after debate and amendment by parliament, was adopted by the council in September 1996. The primary goals of the directive are to "define and establish objectives for ambient air quality in the Community designed to avoid, prevent or reduce harmful effects on human health and the environment as a whole" and to "assess the ambient air quality in member states on the basis of common methods and criteria." [27] Although the directive does not set specific air quality limits, it requires the commission to propose new limit values and alert thresholds for a total of thirteen pollutants by the end of the decade. The commission proposed the first "daughter directives" spelling out tighter standards for sulfur dioxide (SO_2), nitrogen dioxide (NO_2), lead, and particulates in October 1997, with others following in 1998 and 1999. The SO_2 standards are to go into effect across the EU in 2005, the others in 2010. [28]

At the same time, the commission is developing separate legislation to further reduce acid precipitation (primarily from SO_2 and NO_2) and to cut pollution from automobiles in a series of steps beginning in 2000. The goal is to reduce pollution from road traffic by 60–70 percent by 2010.

The latter effort, known as the Auto-Oil Programme, involved the commission in detailed negotiations with the auto manufacturing and petroleum industries between 1992 and 1996. The proposed plan would regulate the content of fuels and set far more stringent emission limits on new cars. When the details were announced in May 1996, the proposal received strong protests both from the manufacturers (for being too expensive) and environmentalists (for not being strict enough).[29] One of the major issues was whether the higher standards set for 2005 would be "indicative" (voluntary), as the commission proposed, or mandatory. Germany, the Netherlands, and the Nordic countries supported tighter exhaust standards, while countries such as France, Italy, and Spain opposed mandatory controls.[30] The European Parliament largely sided with the former states, passing more than two hundred amendments in early 1997 that would further tighten and make mandatory the emission controls for 2005, while offering additional time to the poorer southern states to meet the fuel standards.[31] The EU council of ministers adopted a common position on the proposals that was somewhat tougher than the commission's position, but parliament passed further amendments on its second reading of the legislation in February 1998. In June a compromise agreement was reached that mandates a 70 percent reduction in tailpipe emissions by 2005.[32]

Meanwhile, talks on a second stage of the program (Auto-Oil II) are already under way. These proposals would further tighten auto and truck emission standards after 2005 and set new limits for large stationary sources of pollution such as power stations, chemical plants, and factories. A variety of nontechnical measures (such as tax incentives) to change consumer behavior and lifestyle patterns are also being considered.

Water Resources Management. The EU has adopted about ten major directives to protect fresh water quality since 1975. These directives cover drinking water, bathing water, fish and shellfish, groundwater, urban waste water, and protection against nitrates from fertilizers and various dangerous chemicals. Other policies cover pollution of European seas and rivers under various international maritime conventions and agreements.

In February 1996 the commission called for a water framework directive that, like the air framework, would establish broad guidelines for the protection and management of all fresh water resources into the next century. The proposed guidelines were strongly criticized in a parliamentary opinion of October 1996, but a revised framework directive was formally proposed by the commission in February 1997.[33] It would replace eight existing or proposed directives and integrate all aspects of surface and ground water management in accordance with principles of sustainable development. Its goal is to "reach and/or maintain 'good' status in all surface waters and groundwaters . . . by the year 2010."[34] The principal means for achieving this goal would be comprehensive river basin management plans to be formulated by the states; these plans would have to be drawn up within ten years after the directive comes into force and fully implemented within six years after that.[35] As in the Integrated Pollution Prevention and Control

Framework, a "combined" approach to pollution control (both water quality and discharge standards) would be allowed. Another guiding principle is that the full costs of water protection and delivery are to be charged to polluters and consumers. The directive also would intensify the monitoring of water quality and the collection and exchange of data to improve implementation and compliance.

The environmental committee of the European Parliament was highly critical of the proposed directive on grounds that it failed to spell out criteria for "good" water quality; in essence, the committee feared that the framework would eliminate the controls embodied in previous directorates without putting any specifics in their place.[36] The result could be to "renationalize" water policy and actually reduce the level of protection. Parliament also resents the fact that under Article 130s of the treaty, "management of water resources" is not subject to qualified majority voting or to the co-decision procedure; hence the council of ministers can act (unanimously) without the consent of parliament in this area. The council reached agreement on the directive in June 1998 but deferred final approval until parliament could express its opinion.

Other Legislation

The EU has enacted legislation on many other aspects of environmental protection, including environmental impact assessment; control of chemicals and other dangerous substances; hazardous waste transfer and management; noise reduction; packaging and recycling; product eco-labeling; eco-auditing and management; development of renewable energy; and protection of forests, wildlife, and biodiversity. Space does not permit analysis of all of these policies, many of which continue to undergo amendment and revision. The following section briefly examines two areas in which the EU has tried to take the lead but has so far enjoyed only limited success: packaging reduction and eco-labeling. In both cases individual states had begun to adopt national legislation that threatened to create barriers to trade, which could trigger action by the European Commission. But each case also illustrates both the technical difficulties of implementing well-intended policies and the political problem of reconciling differences among member states with different levels of environmental commitment.

Packaging and Recycling. Beginning in the 1970s, a number of European countries began to enact laws to reduce the volume of solid waste by requiring the use of returnable beverage containers, encouraging recycling of materials, and limiting waste in packaging. Denmark led the way by banning the use of aluminum cans and requiring that beer and soft drinks be sold in reusable bottles. Denmark's action eventually led to the seminal ruling by the ECJ in 1988 that such restrictions on trade may be justified on environmental grounds provided that they do not unfairly discriminate in favor of domestic producers. Other countries have since passed legislation mandating the reduction or recycling of certain materials, including packaging. In 1991

Germany gained international attention for its novel packaging ordinance (*Verpackungsverordnung*), which required retail stores to take back all used packaging materials from consumers and process them. The ordinance allowed business and industry to set up a private collection system (known as the green dot system) on condition that it could meet ambitious recycling targets for various materials; otherwise a mandatory deposit would be levied on the sale of relevant products. The Netherlands also established an ambitious recycling program that requires industry to reduce its volume of packaging by 2000.[37]

The EC had adopted a directive on beverage containers in 1985, but, in the wake of the German and Dutch laws and the Danish bottle decision, it was moved to draft a packaging directive that would accommodate recycling of other materials while preventing the development of potential trade restrictions. The initial draft of the directive was influenced by the German and Dutch approaches, mandating high minimum recycling targets: within five years, 90 percent of packaging waste was to be collected; 60 percent of each material had to be recycled; and another 30 percent incinerated with energy recovery. However, a coalition of states led by Britain objected to such rigid quotas, and ultimately the mandatory targets were lowered to 50 percent recovery, 25 percent overall recycling, and 15 percent minimum recycling for each material. While states were allowed to exceed these targets, Germany's experience suggested that too high recovery rates could lead to excessive accumulation and export of waste materials because of inadequate processing capacity. Therefore, the final EU packaging and packaging waste directive (94/62/EC) passed in 1994 also set "maximum recovery" rates of 65 percent and recycling rates of 45 percent, over the objections of Denmark, Germany, and the Netherlands.

According to some analysts, this compromise illustrates that the establishment of an integrated market still takes precedence over environmental protection.[38] Implementation of the directive is also considerably behind schedule: in 1997, a year after all states were to have transposed it into national law, only six of the fifteen had done so. Ironically, the commission threatened to take Germany and Denmark to court on grounds that their recycling laws exceed the maximum norms permitted by the directive. It does not seem likely that the packaging directive will survive in its present form.[39]

Eco-Labeling. Another approach to limiting waste and environmental damage generally is to encourage consumers to purchase more ecologically benign products by providing better information. As in the case of packaging, Germany had introduced its own eco-labeling system, and several other countries were planning to do so when the council in 1990 asked the commission to prepare a regulation establishing criteria for an EC labeling scheme. The criteria for granting a "green" label should take into account the environmental impact of the product throughout its entire life cycle, including the materials used, manufacturing technologies, health and safety of workers, and ultimate disposal costs. Under the council regulation (92/880/EEC) of March 23, 1992, member states were authorized to appoint a competent body to receive applications for and award the EC eco-label to manufacturers or importers whose products met the criteria. Participation by industry was voluntary, but it was hoped that consumer demand for "green" products would drive producers to compete for the label (symbolized by a flower) by designing better products.

Like the packaging directive, the eco-labeling regulation has been difficult to implement. Procedures for establishing the technical criteria for labels in each product group (such as washing machines, paper products, and detergents) proved to be extremely cumbersome, essentially requiring agreement among all of the national bodies as well as formal approval by the commission. As of July 1997, the eco-label had been awarded to only 166 products manufactured by twenty companies. To try to speed things up, the commission has proposed that the system be turned over to a semi-private European eco-label organization, which would be responsible for reviewing criteria for labeling, coordinating national authorities, and verifying compliance with criteria (97/C 114 09, COM (96) 603 Final). The commission also has proposed that "graded" labeling be introduced, under which one, two, or three flowers could be awarded depending on how "clean" the product is. Parliament has been critical of this idea on grounds that it would confuse consumers and further weaken the system. It does not appear, however, that the public pays much attention to the current labels. Without stronger consumer support the whole system may be abandoned.

Major Challenges Facing the European Union

Implementation of Environmental Laws

As the examples suggest, the success of the EU commitment to environmental protection depends on the extent to which member states actually take the actions required by EU legislation. States must enact (transpose) EU law into national law, but this action is not sufficient in itself. They must also apply and enforce the law in practice.[40] Although there are no thorough analyses of EU treaty compliance and enforcement to date, it appears from scattered studies that the record is uneven and that in some areas implementation may be deteriorating.[41]

The European Commission monitors policy implementation and seeks to detect violations of EU law, but it has no authority to investigate or inspect specific facilities. In its latest report (for 1997), it recorded 315 suspected violations of environmental law, up from 207 in 1996 and a reversal of a four-year downward trend. Environmental violations account for more than 20 percent of *all* EU cases, more than in any other field of law. However, the rate of alleged violations varies greatly among states: in 1997 Spain had the highest rate with sixty-three, while Finland, Luxembourg, the Netherlands, and Sweden had fewer than ten each. Moreover, except for Belgium, all of the fifteen countries had succeeded in transposing at least 95 percent of EU environmental laws.[42]

The EU has some legal enforcement mechanisms at its disposal. Article 169 of the treaty allows citizens, local authorities, businesses, or interest groups to lodge complaints on the inadequate application or transposition of EU law directly before the commission. Once a complaint is brought, efforts are made to mediate the dispute or to informally persuade the national government to take appropriate action. If a party is found to be in violation of EU law, the commission can issue a formal notice to the state. If all else fails, an infringement case can be brought before the European Court of Justice to force compliance. However, resolution of cases can take many years, and, even if a government is found guilty, compliance is not automatic. Article 171 of the Maastricht Treaty allows the ECJ to levy financial penalties against states that fail to carry out its decisions, but so far the court has only recently begun to use this power.[43]

Some of the variation in compliance among states is related to differences in levels of citizen and interest group awareness. Some states may have proportionately more complaints lodged because their citizens are more alert, informed, and able to bring matters to the attention of the EU. But differential enforcement is also the result of variations in the budgets and other resources of governments to carry out EU mandates. Because states choose their own means of compliance, differences are inevitable in the instruments used and in the severity of penalties levied against violators. For example, the Court of Justice found Italy guilty of noncompliance with an EU directive on protection of wild birds (79/409/EEC). Because Italy had not limited bird hunting or incorporated an amendment (86/411/EEC) to the original directive into Italian law, it was ordered to pay legal costs. In another example, the court censured France for failing to comply with EU directives on air pollution. As a consequence, France incorporated the directives directly into its laws.[44]

A growing volume of such cases has led to calls in the European Parliament and elsewhere for an EU inspectorate, possibly under auspices of the European Environment Agency. However, states have resisted any such extension of supranational powers, and it does not appear likely that a specialized enforcement body will be established any time soon. The commission instead works with an informal network of national environmental officials, known as Impel, to improve compliance.[45] In October 1996 the commission also issued a communication on implementation; it proposed guidelines for states to follow in carrying out inspections, handling public complaints about legal enforcement, and guaranteeing access by NGOs to national courts.[46] The commission also indicated that it might include provisions in future legislative proposals requiring national governments to enforce effective penalties and sanctions for noncompliance of environmental laws. Whether these proddings from the commission improve environmental performance at the national level remains to be seen, but it is likely that new policy strategies will also be required in the future.

New Instruments and Approaches

In part because of the ineffectiveness of some existing legislation but also because new problems loom on the horizon that require different regulatory approaches, the Fifth Environmental Action Programme called for broadening the range of instruments for attaining sustainable development. In addition to traditional regulatory measures, it was argued that the EU should adopt market-based instruments (including taxes and economic incentives, environmental auditing, and voluntary agreements), horizontal supporting instruments (research, information, and education), and new financial support mechanisms.[47] Such new approaches are now widely advocated to improve the economic efficiency of regulation and to involve all sectors of society in "shared responsibility" for the environment. As the costs of environmental regulation rise, they are also supported (at least in theory) by business and industry as an alternative to traditional "command and control" regulation.

Several countries in northern Europe have enacted extensive "green" taxes to promote waste reduction and energy saving.[48] Although the EU does not have the legal competence to impose new taxes directly, it can encourage states to do so on a coordinated or harmonized basis; for example, the European Commission issued a communication in early 1997 setting out guidelines for such taxes.[49] A study prepared for the commission showed that environmental taxes currently make up only 1.7 percent of the total tax revenues in EU states, suggesting substantial potential for increases.[50]

Despite efforts by the commission to promote new policy approaches, relatively little progress has been made by the EU to date. The failure to achieve a communitywide CO_2 tax to combat global warming illustrates the problem, but other measures also have been stalled either in the council or parliament. We comment briefly on two proposed instruments: energy taxes and voluntary industry agreements.

Energy Taxes. Concern over global climate change due to the accumulation of CO_2 and other greenhouse gases in the atmosphere has been particularly strong in Europe. It is widely perceived that continued burning of fossil fuels could produce major disruptions in weather patterns and cause rising sea levels that could imperil countries such as the Netherlands. Recognizing that industrial nations are largely responsible for the problem, a June 1990 meeting of the European Council in Dublin called for an EC strategy to reduce greenhouse emissions. The Dublin summit was followed by a council meeting of environment and energy ministers in October, at which it was agreed that CO_2 emissions should be stabilized at 1990 levels by the year 2000 in the EC as a whole. The council asked the commission to develop a strategy to meet this target, including fiscal and economic instruments to promote energy efficiency.

The commission responded by proposing a substantial communitywide "carbon tax" on oil and other fuels to reduce CO_2 emissions; the tax would rise from $3 a barrel of oil in 1993 to $10 a barrel in 2000.[51] Carlo Ripa di

Meana, the environment commissioner at the time, supported this concept and hoped to make the carbon tax the centerpiece of the EC position on climate change in Rio de Janeiro in June 1992. However, disagreements among EC member states on the tax proposal produced a deadlock before the Rio meeting, and Ripa di Meana angrily refused to attend the conference.

Despite this embarrassment, the European delegation continued to push for binding CO_2 targets in the Framework Convention on Climate Change adopted at Rio and in subsequent negotiations (see Chapter 10). Moreover, the commission has continued to search for an acceptable form of energy tax. In 1994 it proposed a directive under which individual member states could adopt national CO_2 taxes over a flexible time period, with the goal of eventual harmonization. This idea met with strong opposition from several states—some wanted a mandatory tax, while others opposed any extension of tax competency at all—as well as from the environment committee of parliament, which thought the idea was much too weak. A third tax proposal was launched in 1997. Originated in DG XI and supported by tax commissioner Mario Monti, this plan would extend the existing harmonized excise tax duties on mineral oils to coal, natural gas, and electricity, while allowing national governments to offer rebates for environmentally friendly forms of energy production. An agreement on a weaker version of this proposal appeared possible in mid-1998.[52]

The need for energy taxes has become increasingly important as a means for limiting greenhouse gases. In March 1997 the EU council adopted a position calling for a reduction of greenhouse gas emissions to 15 percent below 1990 levels by 2010, a far more ambitious target than the United States and Japan were willing to accept. The agreement reached in Kyoto requires the EU to cut its emissions of six greenhouse gases a total of 8 percent below 1990 levels by 2008–2012. Under the European burden-sharing concept, some countries (Denmark and Germany) have agreed to cut their emissions by up to 21 percent, while poorer nations (Greece and Portugal) will be allowed to *increase* their emissions as much as 25–27 percent.[53]

Environment commissioner Bjerregaard has repeatedly warned that Europe will not be able to meet the Kyoto goals without new energy taxes. At the same time she has argued for a limit on the use of "emissions trading," a strategy preferred by the United States under which countries could buy pollution credits from other countries to meet their obligations.[54] In the absence of some agreement between the United States and the European Union, it is unlikely that the EU will enact strong policy measures.

Voluntary Agreements. Another innovative strategy calls for voluntary agreements between government and industrial sectors or individual companies to pursue pollution prevention and sustainable development. Such agreements or "covenants" have been a central feature of Dutch planning (see Chapter 12) and were endorsed in the Fifth Action Programme. The idea is that voluntary cooperation can supplement (but not replace) legal obligations in many sectors in setting and achieving goals.[55] Examples are industry agreements in Denmark on the phaseout of organic solvents used in paints and varnishes; in Belgium on elimination of CFCs; and on waste management and improving energy efficiency in several states. While such agreements can improve communication and cooperation between regulated industries and governments, environmental groups are generally skeptical of them on grounds that they may not be transparent and may amount to a form of backdoor "deregulation" that allows companies to circumvent existing laws. Members of the European Parliament also have expressed these concerns, and an assessment by the European Environment Agency raises questions about their effectiveness.[56]

The commission consequently issued a communication on voluntary agreements in late 1996 that attempted to clarify the legal and other considerations that should guide such agreements. Under these guidelines, agreements must take contractual form; must be published and open to the public; must have quantified objectives and deadlines; must be monitored, with performance reported to competent authorities; and when appropriate, may include sanctions for nonfulfillment. When they are used to implement EU policy, the European Commission must be notified of all information regarding such agreements. The commission would scrutinize them for conformity with community law and certify their transparency and credibility.[57] In some cases the commission also makes voluntary agreements directly with industry. For example, in 1997 and 1998 the commission conducted negotiations with the European auto manufacturing association on reduction of carbon dioxide emissions on future models, leading to a voluntary agreement to cut emissions of new cars by about one quarter by 2008. This agreement was accepted by the Council of Ministers in October 1998, eliminating the need for new legislation in this area.

Enlargement

Perhaps the greatest challenge to EU environmental policy of the future will be to prepare new member states from central and eastern Europe to meet existing pollution standards. Under the Agenda 2000 plan issued by the commission in July 1997, ten countries in central and eastern Europe plus Cyprus will be considered for admission to the EU in the coming years. Six countries (Cyprus, Czech Republic, Estonia, Hungary, Poland, and Slovenia) were accepted as candidates for accession in the first wave, while five other states (Bulgaria, Latvia, Lithuania, Romania, and Slovakia) were placed in a second category requiring a longer period of preparation. Detailed accession negotiations with the nations in the first group began in March 1998 and are expected to take several years.[58]

Under the treaty, all new members of the EU must comply with the full *acquis communautaire* (body of European Community law), including all environmental directives and regulations. This requirement poses a massive problem for the countries of central and eastern Europe, which have far higher levels of pollution than western countries because of the lax environmental standards under their former communist governments. In addition to outdated coal-burning power plants and factories, several of these countries rely heavily on Soviet-designed nuclear plants that pose substantial safety risks (see Chapter 13). Although some of the worst facilities have been closed down, the EU commission has estimated that the cost of bringing the applicant states into compliance with EU environmental standards could be 120 billion ECU, or some 3 percent to 5 percent of their GDP over the next twenty years.[59]

Where this huge amount of capital is to come from is unknown. The commission has announced that the overall EU budget will not be increased beyond its present level (1.27 percent of member states' GDP) during the 2000–2006 period, meaning that financial aid to accession countries must come from other EU programs.[60] The most obvious candidates are the Common Agricultural Policy and the Structural Funds, which have been used to subsidize economic development in the poorer regions of the EU. Countries that stand to lose this funding and their representatives in the European Parliament have been quite critical of the enlargement process, and it is by no means certain that all states will agree to accession (parliament as well as the council must vote to approve new members). Aside from increasingly bitter divisions over financing, it is unclear how the countries of central and eastern Europe will, under any circumstances, be able to meet current environmental standards within the pre-accession period (perhaps five years). According to a 1997 report to parliament's environment committee, it could take several decades to bring the applicants fully up to western standards.[61] Even with substantial derogations, the new members could hypothetically enter the EU with compliance levels well below even the worst current offenders.

The danger is that enlargement will weaken existing environmental standards and enforcement in some present EU countries while only gradually improving conditions in eastern Europe. What is already a "multispeed" Europe could lose all sense of direction as the potentials for harmonization fade. Finally, the Amsterdam treaty revisions failed to resolve the fundamental institutional question of how voting rights are to be allocated in an enlarged EU council, raising the specter of further divisive negotiations and the possibility that the "green" states may find it more difficult to assert leadership in the future.

Conclusion

The European Union is at a critical stage in its evolution. While proceeding toward further "deepening" of integration through the new monetary union, it is also preparing for the largest "widening" in its history by incorporating the central and east European states.[62] Without question, the EU has made great strides toward environmental protection over the past quarter-century, but it has also entered a transition phase in this area of policy. After two decades of imposing increasingly detailed environmental directives and regulations from Brussels, the EU has begun to revise its approach since adoption of the Maastricht Treaty in 1992 and its emphasis on the principle of subsidiarity. Member states have pressed for greater freedom in implementing EU legislation, while supporting the general principles of sustainable development set out in the Fifth Environmental Action Programme. The European Commission has responded by turning toward the use of broader framework directives that set long-term environmental goals while allowing more flexibility in the choice of means to achieve them; it also has encouraged the introduction of new policy instruments at both the national and EU levels to improve environmental performance and cost-effectiveness. At the same time it has led the world toward the first binding agreement on climate change at Kyoto.

Despite these accomplishments, the EU faces daunting challenges both in extending its policies eastward and in maintaining its standards in the member states. Economic stagnation and high levels of unemployment throughout much of the 1990s appear to have dampened public and government enthusiasm for increased environmental protection. Implementation of EU environmental laws at the national level leaves much to be desired, and the gap between the northern "green" states (including the three new members that joined in 1995) and the less wealthy southern countries seems to be growing. The addition of five to ten transitional states of central and eastern Europe ranking even further behind the leaders threatens to shift the balance of power toward the laggards. On the other hand, from a global perspective, enlargement of the EU to include these countries could improve conditions in the region as a whole if the new members can be forced to significantly raise their standards.

Within the EU generally, sustainable development will require much greater integration of environmental perspectives into other policy areas such as energy, transportation, agriculture, and tourism. The new Article 6 (formerly 3d) of the treaty will legally obligate all EU bodies and member states to pursue such integrated sustainable development strategies. In a communication prepared for the Cardiff Summit of the European Council in June 1998, the commission formulated new guidelines for policy integration and called for urgent efforts to realize this goal in two areas that may define the environmental success of the European Union in the future: Agenda 2000 (enlargement) and the Kyoto Protocol (climate change).[63] The real test of the EU governance system therefore still lies ahead.

Notes

The authors wish to thank Nicolas Colaninno of the EU Delegation to the United Nations and Rita Edwards, librarian at Adelphi University, for assistance in securing documentary resources. Regina Axelrod is also indebted to the EU Commission, Directorate-General XI, Economic Analysis Unit, for the opportunity to work with them in November 1997. Norman Vig would like to thank the Institute for Transnational Legal Research of Maastricht University for use of its facilities in summer 1997.

1. The European Union negotiates on behalf of the member states insofar as they are in agreement and is a signatory to most recent conventions, but it does not have exclu-

sive jurisdiction. Individual member states can sign separately, as a member of the EU, or both. See Angela Liberatore, "The European Union: Bridging Domestic and International Environmental Policy-Making," in *The Internationalization of Environmental Protection*, ed. Mirana A. Schreurs and Elizabeth C. Economy (Cambridge: Cambridge University Press, 1997), 204–206.

2. On the general history and development of the EC/EU, see Clifford Hackett, *Cautious Revolution: The European Community Arrives*, rev. ed. (New York: Praeger, 1996); Desmond Dinan, *Ever Closer Union? An Introduction to the European Community* (Boulder: Lynne Rienner, 1994); and David M. Wood and Birol A. Yesilada, *The Emerging European Union* (White Plains, N.Y.: Longman, 1996).

3. For a summary of the programs and a general description of EC environmental legislation, see Stanley P. Johnson and Guy Corcelle, *The Environmental Policy of the European Communities*, 2d ed. (London: Kluwer Law International, 1995); and David Judge, ed., *A Green Dimension for the European Community* (London: Frank Cass, 1993). See also Robert Barrass and Shobhana Madhavan, *European Economic Integration and Sustainable Development* (London: McGraw-Hill, 1996).

4. Article 3d will become Article 6 when the consolidated Amsterdam Treaty is ratified in 1999. For the Maastricht revisions of the treaty, see Clive H. Church and David Phinnemore, *European Union and European Community* (New York: Harvester Wheatsheaf, 1994); and David O'Keefe and Patrick W. Twomey, *Legal Issues of the Maastricht Treaty* (London: Wiley Chancery Law, 1994).

5. See, for example, Gary Marks et al., *Governance in the European Union* (London: Sage Publications, 1996); and Alan W. Cafruny and Carl Lankowski, eds., *Europe's Ambiguous Unity: Conflict and Consensus in the Post-Maastricht Era* (Boulder: Lynne Rienner, 1997).

6. See Fiona Hayes-Renshaw and Helen Wallace, *The Council of Ministers* (New York: St. Martin's Press, 1997); and Martin Westlake, *The Council of the European Union* (London: Catermill, 1995).

7. Michelle Cini, *The European Commission* (Manchester: Manchester University Press, 1996); Geoffrey Edwards and David Spence, eds., *The European Commission*, 2d ed. (London: Catermill, 1997).

8. Richard Corbett, Francis Jacobs, and Michael Shackleton, *The European Parliament*, 3d ed. (London: Catermill, 1995); and Martin Westlake, *A Modern Guide to the European Parliament* (London: Pinter, 1994). On the role of political parties, see Simon Hix and Christopher Lord, *Political Parties in the European Union* (New York: St. Martin's Press, 1997).

9. L. Neville Brown and Tom Kennedy, *The Court of Justice of the European Communities*, 4th ed. (London: Sweet and Maxwell, 1994); Han Somsen, ed., *Protecting the European Environment: Enforcing EC Environmental Law* (London: Blackstone Press, 1996).

10. "Commission of the European Communities v. Kingdom of Denmark—Case 302/86," *Report of Cases Before the Court*, vol. 8 (Luxembourg: Office for Official Publications of the European Communities, 1988).

11. European Environment Agency, *Europe's Environment: The Dobris Assessment* (Luxembourg: Office of Publications of the European Communities, 1995).

12. See, for example, Jeremy J. Richardson, ed., *European Union: Power and Policy-Making* (London: Routledge, 1996); Helen Wallace and William Wallace, *Policy-Making in the European Union* (Oxford: Oxford University Press, 1996); Stephen George, *Politics and Policy in the European Community* (Oxford: Oxford University Press, 1991); and Carolyn Rhodes and Sonia Mazey, eds., *The State of the European Union, Vol. 3, Building a European Polity?* (Boulder: Lynne Rienner, 1995).

13. See Regina S. Axelrod, "Subsidiarity and Environmental Policy in the European Community," *International Environmental Affairs* 6 (spring 1994): 115–132.

14. Adrienne Héritier et al., *Ringing the Changes in Europe: Regulatory Competition and Transformation of the State: Britain, France, Germany* (Berlin and New York: Walter de Gruyter, 1996).

15. Mikael Skou Andersen and Duncan Liefferink, eds., *European Environmental Policy: the Pioneers* (Manchester: Manchester University Press, 1997); and D. Liefferink and M. S. Andersen, "Strategies of the 'Green' Member States in EU Environmental Policy-Making," *Journal of European Public Policy-Making* 5 (June 1998): 254–270.

16. Sonia Mazey and Jeremy Richardson, eds., *Lobbying in the European Community* (Oxford: Oxford University Press, 1993); Sonia Mazey and Jeremy Richardson, "The Logic of Organisation: Interest Groups," in *European Union*.

17. "Pressure Groups Become a Political Force," *European Voice*, June 11–17, 1998.

18. For explanation of these clauses, see Ludwig Krämer, *EC Treaty and Environmental Law* (London: Sweet and Maxwell, 1995), chap. 4; and Martin Hession and Richard Macrory, "Maastricht and the Environmental Policy of the Community: Legal Issues of a New Environmental Policy," in *Legal Issues*, 151–167.

19. These were sections 100(a)4–5, which are to become part of a new Article 95 in the consolidated treaty upon ratification. The Scandinavian states, especially, fought hard for this "environmental guarantee" in the Amsterdam Treaty negotiations. The commission will approve such measures on a case-by-case basis, but the criteria remain highly uncertain. For example, such measures must deal with problems specific to that particular state and must be based on "new scientific evidence." Many observers believe this weakens the previous safeguard clause.

20. Commission of the European Communities, *Toward Sustainability: A European Community Programme of Policy and Action in Relation to the Environment and Sustainable Development*, COM(92)23 Final (Brussels, March 27, 1992).

21. Ibid., 3.

22. Commission of the European Communities, *Proposal for a European Parliament and Council Decision on the Review of the European Community Programme of Policy and Action in Relation to the Environment and Sustainable Development "Towards Sustainability,"* COM(95)647 Final (Brussels, January 24, 1996).

23. European Environment Agency, *Environment in the European Union 1995: Report for the Review of the Fifth Environmental Action Programme*, summarized in *ENDS Report* 253 (February 1996): 24–27.

24. "Widespread Condemnation of Action Programme Review," *European Voice*, May 30–June 5, 1996; "Vth Environmental Programme: Ritt Bjerregaard Comes Under MEP's Fire Again," *Europe Environment*, No. 488, November 19, 1996.

25. Johnson and Corcelle cite as many as four hundred acts in *Environmental Policy of the European Communities*; see also Sevine Ercmann, *Pollution Control in the European Community: Guide to the EC Texts and Their Implementation by the Member States* (London: Kluwer Law International, 1996).

26. Commission of the European Communities, *Communication on Environment and Employment* COM(97)592 Final (Brussels, November 18, 1997).

27. *Council Directive 96/62/EC of 27 September 1996 on Ambient Air Quality and Assessment*, Article 1.

28. "Air Quality Proposals under the Microscope," *European Voice*, May 15–21, 1997; "New EU Air Quality Standards Proposed," *ENDS Environment Daily*, October 10, 1997.

29. "Outcry Over Plan for Car Emissions," *European Voice*, May 30–June 6, 1996.

30. "Battle Lines Drawn for Confrontation Over Car Emissions," *European Voice*, January 30–February 5, 1997.

31. "MEPs Take Hard Line on Car Emissions," *European Voice*, May 29–June 4, 1997; "Delays Hinder Progress of 'Auto-Oil' Deal," *European Voice*, July 3–9, 1997.

32. Press release, "Auto-Oil Programme Is on the Road" (Parliament-Council Conciliation Committee), General Secretariat of the Council of the European Union, 9924–98 (PRESS 230) (Brussels, June 29, 1998).

33. Commission of the European Communities, *Directive Establishing a Framework for Community Action in the Field of Water Policy*, COM(97)49 Final. (Brussels, February 26, 1997).

34. Ibid., 14.
35. "Environment Ministers Likely to Strike Deal to Protect Union's Lakes and Rivers," *European Voice*, June 11–17, 1998.
36. "Water Quality Proposals Under Attack," *European Voice*, June 5–11, 1997.
37. Markus Haverland, "Convergence of National Governance under European Integration? The Case of Packaging Waste" (paper presented at the Fifth Biennial Conference of the European Community Studies Association, Seattle, May 29–June 1, 1997).
38. Thomas Gehring, "Governing in Nested Institutions: Environmental Policy in the European Union and the Case of Packaging Waste," *Journal of European Public Policy* 4 (September 1997): 337–354.
39. "Packaging Directive Coming Undone," *European Voice*, September 18–24, 1997.
40. For the distinction, see chapter 7, and Peter M. Haas, "Compliance with EU Directives: Insights from International Relations and Comparative Politics," *Journal of European Public Policy* 5 (March 1998): 17–37.
41. Alberta Sbragia, "Environmental Policy in the European Community: The Problem of Implementation in Comparative Perspective," in *Towards a Transatlantic Environmental Policy* (Washington, D.C.: European Institute, 1991); Jeremy Richardson, "Eroding EU Policies: Implementation Gaps, Cheating and Re-Steering," in *European Union*.
42. Commission of the European Communities, *Fifteenth Annual Report on Monitoring the Application of Community Law* (1997), COM (1998) 317 Final (Brussels, May 19, 1998).
43. For example, in December 1997 the commission began or continued infringement suits against twelve of the fifteen member states under Article 169. It announced its first legal proceedings under Article 171 against Italy and Germany in January 1997. "First Request for Penalties for Ignoring EU Court Rulings," *Europe Environment*, No. 493, February 11, 1997; *ENDS Environment Daily*, December 19, 1997.
44. *Europe Energy*, No. 367, November 15, 1991, 1, 7.
45. "Inspectors Agree to Expanded Enforcement Role," *ENDS Environment Daily*, May 20, 1997.
46. Commission of the European Communities, *Implementing Community Environmental Law*, COM(96)500 (Brussels, October 22, 1996).
47. Commission of the European Communities, *Toward Sustainability*, chap. 7.
48. Mikael Skou Andersen, *Governance by Green Taxes: Making Pollution Prevention Pay* (Manchester: Manchester University Press, 1994); Timothy O'Riordan, ed., *Ecotaxation* (London: Earthscan, 1997).
49. Commission of the European Communities, *Environmental Taxes and Charges in the Single Market*, COM(97)9 (Brussels, January 29, 1997).
50. *ENDS Environment Daily*, February 12, 1997.
51. Commission of the European Communities, *Proposal for a Council Directive Introducing a Tax on Carbon Dioxide Emissions and Energy*, COM(92)226 (Brussels, June 30, 1992). See Anthony R. Zito, "Integrating the Environment into the European Union: The History of the Controversial Carbon Tax," in *The State of the European Union, Vol. 3*, 431-448.
52. "End to Six-Year Deadlock over Energy Taxes in Sight," *European Voice*, July 2–8, 1998.
53. *European Voice*, June 18–24, 1998.
54. The use of emissions trading and other instruments is allowed under the Kyoto Protocol, but details remain to be worked out (see chapter 10). The Clinton administration has projected that up to three-fourths of the U.S. reductions could come from such credits; "White House Is Optimistic on Pollution-Reduction Costs," Minneapolis *Star Tribune*, August 1, 1998.
55. In fact, "voluntary" agreements are seldom entirely voluntary and may be a tool for enforcing existing regulations. See Duncan Liefferink and Arthur P. J. Mol, "Volun-

tary Agreements as a Form of Deregulation?" in *Deregulation in the European Union: Environmental Perspectives*, ed. Ute Collier (London: Routledge, 1998).

56. "MEPs Report Doubts Voluntary Agreements," *ENDS Environment Daily*, May 22, 1998; "EEA Cautious About Voluntary Agreements," *ENDS Environment Daily*, May 26, 1997.

57. Commission of the European Communities, *Communication from the Commission to the Council and the European Parliament on Environmental Agreements*, COM(96)561 Final (Brussels, November 27, 1996).

58. Commission of the European Communities, *Communication from the Commission to the Council, European Parliament, the Economic and Social Committee, and the Committee of Regions and the Candidate Countries in Central and Eastern Europe on Accession Strategies for the Environment; Meeting the Challenge of Enlargement with the Candidate Countries in Central and Eastern Europe*, COM(98)294 Final (Brussels, May 20, 1998). The document states, "Environment has been identified as a key priority in the Accession Partnerships and will be given special attention." (Page 19).

59. *ENDS Environment Daily*, September 9, 1997. By contrast, OECD countries spend 1 percent to 1.5 percent of GDP on environmental protection, and the United States about 2 percent. One ECU (European currency unit) equals about $1.10.

60. "Union Enlargement at No Extra Cost," *European Voice*, March 19–25, 1998.

61. *ENDS Environment Daily*, June 10, 1997.

62. See Pierre-Henri Laurent and Marc Maresceau, eds., *The State of the European Union, Vol. 4, Deepening and Widening* (Boulder: Lynne Rienner, 1998).

63. Commission of the European Communities, *Partnership for Integration: A Strategy for Integrating Environment in EU Policies*, COM (1998)333 Final (Brussels, May 27, 1998).

ENVIRONMENTAL LAW

5

The Emerging Structure of International Environmental Law

Edith Brown Weiss

The Peace of Westphalia that ended the Thirty Years' War 350 years ago established a new international order based on sovereign, independent, territorially defined states, each striving to maintain political independence and territorial integrity. Since a state could rely only on self-help if attacked, new rules were needed to constrain state behavior.

The resulting international legal system was European and centered on relations with states with defined territories. It was hierarchic, since states were in control of everything under them and it was based on equality among the sovereign states. It reflected a laissez-faire philosophy, in which all states were equally free to pursue their own interests, whatever their underlying economic or political differences. As the system of sovereign states spread across the globe, so did the system of international law that was based on it.

The classical definition of international law was given by J. L. Brierly: "the body of rules and principles of action which are binding upon civilized States in their relations with one another."[1] The Permanent Court of International Justice articulated this classical view in the 1927 *S.S. Lotus* case: "International law governs relations between independent States. The rules of law binding upon States therefore emanate from their own free will as expressed in conventions or by usages generally accepted as expressing principles of law and established in order to regulate the relations between these co-existing independent communities or with a view to the achievement of common aims."[2]

In this view, international law is instrumentalist. It affects behavior and the interests of states by altering incentives. It does not admit easily that states' interests may change over time in response to events today. It implicitly adopts the realist school view that states are monolithic bodies and does not assign importance to entities within states, transnational entities, or individuals.

This classical framework of international law centers exclusively on states, relies on binding legal instruments to provide solutions to clearly

Adapted from Edith Brown Weiss, "The Changing Structure of International Law," presented at Georgetown University Law Center, May 23, 1996.

defined problems, and assumes that states comply with the obligations they have assumed. The line between international and domestic law is sharply drawn, as is that between public and private international law. Public international law governs intergovernmental relations, while private international law regulates the activities of individuals, corporations, and private entities engaged in transborder transactions (choice of law rules, rules relating to international transactions, such as shipping terms and letters of credit).

The international system is rapidly changing and with it the structure of international law. Two changes have profound implications for the structure of international law: the simultaneous push toward integration and fragmentation; and the rise of thousands of organizations and millions of individuals as relevant actors.

As we approach the third millennium, our world is becoming both more integrated and more fragmented. Evidence of global integration abounds: regional trading units, global communication networks such as the World Wide Web, international regimes covering issues ranging from banking and trade, to human rights, environmental protection, and arms control. The information revolution, the spread of financial markets, the penetration of industries across borders, the rapid technological advances, the global environmental problems, and other economic interdependencies compel greater integration. Future problems will require global cooperation to address them effectively.

At the same time nationalism, ethnicity, and the need for personal affiliations and satisfaction push toward fragmentation and decentralization. Less than 10 percent of the more than 185 states are homogeneous ethnically. Only about 50 percent of the states have one ethnic group that accounts for three-quarters of the population.[3] Scholars write of the rise of "tribalism" and the revealed need for community bonds. States are relinquishing elements of sovereignty to transnational networks of nonstate actors; the sense of community (with intense loyalty and identification) that served to bind together the citizens of the state is not being extended to the networks.

A new divide is fragmenting the international system: a divide between states and their nonstate transnational elites, on the one hand, and the ethnic, nationalistic, orthodox religious, dispossessed, and alienated communities on the other. For example, governments and governing authorities in the Middle East, whatever their expressed differences with each other, find that they have much in common as they try to counter common threats within their country from radical religious, ethnic, and political movements.

The emerging international system is structurally nonhierarchic. It consists of networks of states, nonstate actors, and individuals. Twenty years ago, Harold Jacobson wrote that while the global political system still consists of many sovereign centers of decision making, "effective power is increasingly being organized in a non-hierarchical manner."[4] While the sovereign state certainly continues as the principal actor, its freedom to make decisions unilaterally is restricted more and more, and nonstate entities are performing increasingly complex tasks. States remain as the only actors that can tax, conscript, and raise armies, but the importance of these functions has declined relative to these newly important issues.

Within the community of sovereign states (and within countries), by contrast, elements of hierarchy have emerged. We have moved from an international system of a limited number of states to one with many. At the beginning of this century, there were only 34 generally recognized states, and 51 when the United Nations was formed in 1945. In 1998 there were 185 member states of the United Nations and at least three additional recognized states. While all states are sovereign, they are in fact not equal in their relations with each other, even though the doctrine of sovereign and equal states still prevails in international law. The voting structure of the UN Security Council, weighted voting provisions in international organizations, differential legal obligations depending upon economic ability and principles such as "common but differentiated responsibility"—all reflect a more hierarchical community. Thus, within the nonhierarchic international system, there is new hierarchy among sovereign states.

The emerging system has many new international actors other than states. The 1997–1998 edition of the *Yearbook of International Organizations* records 6,115 intergovernmental organizations and 40,306 nongovernmental organizations (NGOs), for a total of 46,421 international organizations.[5] There are also other relevant actors: multinational corporations, ethnic minorities, subunits of national governments, local NGOs, illicit actors such as transnational drug cartels or terrorist networks, and ad hoc transnational associations of individuals.[6] These new transnational elites are interested in particular outcomes and may have extensive resources at their disposal. They are bound together in complex ways that change frequently. Most are part of the integrative pulse that is sweeping the globe.

New information technologies empower groups other than states to participate in developing and implementing international law. They empower publics to participate in the process of governance. Since 1994, communiques of rebels in Chiapas, Mexico, have been transmitted across the world through Internet bulletin boards to seek support for the rebels' cause. Political factions and separatists in other areas of the world also circulate their messages through the Internet. Pressure groups now form almost instantaneously on the Internet to oppose actions in a given country, as almost every college student knows. Letter-writing campaigns have gone electronic.

In this setting, international law provides the normative framework and the procedures for coordinating behavior, controlling conflict, facilitating cooperation, and achieving values. Rosalyn Higgins has distinguished between the process view of international law and the positivist (in which international law consists of neutral rules).[7] In the emerging system, international law arguably has elements of both. Many of the systemic changes relate to process. Certainly the legitimacy of the development of the norms of international law is as important to their effectiveness as the incentives that a particular rule may provide. But part of the change to a nonhierarchic system invokes a positivist, normative element in the sense that legal rules and principles extend through time as well as spatially, address new issues of equity, and articulate values held in common among the actors in the emerging system.

In the changing structure of international law, states exist in a global civil society that shapes the development of and compliance with international norms. Many nonstate actors contribute to the development, interpretation, and implementation of international law across all fields, including human rights, labor, oceans, environment, economic development and trade, and the use of force. Individuals are also increasingly important nonstate actors in international law, as evidenced in human rights law, in which individual rights can be enforced before human rights commissions and tribunals and in national courts. Individuals can also be held accountable for the commission of war crimes and crimes against humanity.

In the environmental area, NGOs have become prominent players in the negotiation and implementation of international environmental agreements. For example, they have attended all of the negotiations for the 1992 Framework Convention on Climate Change and the 1997 Kyoto Protocol to the Convention, where they distributed information, prepared agreed positions on issues, and developed draft text to advocate to governments. Members of an NGO formally represented the Alliance of Small Island States at the negotiations for a Framework Convention on Climate Change.[8] After a treaty has been concluded, NGOs are often active participants in the subsequent meetings of the parties. Indeed at the biennial Conference of the Parties to the Convention on International Trade in Endangered Species (CITES), NGOs have outnumbered governments.

Nongovernmental organizations can also be assigned important roles in implementing international agreements. The 1972 World Heritage Convention, under which countries list significant natural and cultural sites on a World Heritage List, expressly provides in the text for three organizations, nongovernmental and intergovernmental, to assist in implementing the convention. The International Union for the Conservation of Nature (IUCN), for example, evaluates sites proposed for the World Heritage List and assists in monitoring the listed sites. In CITES, the World Conservation Monitoring Unit for many years computerized the national reports of countries on the trade in endangered species and prepared reports for tracking the trade, as part of implementing the convention's control of international trade in endangered species.

In addition to the above, there are other important changes occurring in the international legal system. The sharp lines between public and private international law are blurring, the divide between international and domestic law is fading, and the difference between the effectiveness of legally binding and nonbinding instruments in international law in changing behavior is under deserved scrutiny. Moreover, with the revolution in information technology, international law will likely extend to widespread international monitoring and tracking of various kinds of transactions and legal obligations.

But the most important role for international law in a global society that is both integrated and fragmented may be as the expression of fundamental norms (or values) among peoples, including care for the interests of future generations. These will be detailed below.

The Emerging Characteristics of International Law

The emerging international legal system has three characteristics that reflect important changes in the international system: the blurring of public and private international law, which reflects the growing role of the private sector; the increasing use of nonbinding legal instruments, which reflects the growth in issues subject to international negotiations and the participation of nonstate actors; and the integration of international and domestic law, which reflects the interconnectedness and globalization of the world.

The Blurring of Public and Private International Law

Public international law has become increasingly concerned with areas that used to be viewed as entirely within the purview of private international law, just as private international law is more often addressing issues that used to be viewed as the primary province of governments.

In the commercial field, formal treaties have codified many rules and norms governing commercial behavior. These include, for example, the United Nations Convention on Contracts for the International Sale of Goods (International Sales Convention) and other agreements such as those governing intellectual property rights and those relating to international litigation and to the enforcement of arbitral awards. There are also numerous examples of nontreaty rules that are widely used: the rules of arbitration governing investment conflicts (for example, those used by the International Centre for the Settlement of Investment Disputes, the American Arbitration Association, and the International Chamber of Commerce) or the commercial terms to be followed in an international transaction (ICC's Incoterms).

In international environmental law, the most important development for the next century may be the emerging interaction of intergovernmental environmental law with transnational environmental law developed primarily by the private sector and by institutions such as the International Standards Organization (ISO). The private sector's development of transnational environmental standards and management practices in part assumes functions traditionally done by governments. Since industry often has the best information and can act far more quickly than governments, this is not only inevitable but desirable. Enforcement of the standards and practices may also be done in the private sector through procurement requirements and other practices, which if done by governments could violate international trade agreements.

Increased Use of Legally Nonbinding Instruments

A significant part of international law now consists of legally non-binding or incompletely binding norms, or what has been called "soft law." Paul Szasz notes that states generally observe these norms even though they are not strictly required to do so, "which gives them a predictive value similar to those norms expressed in hard law"—which, he points out, are also not always observed.[9] These instruments are proliferating in many fields of international law: environment, human rights, trade, and arms control, for example.

In the international environmental field, soft law instruments abound. The 1972 Stockholm Declaration on the Human Environment and the 1992 Rio de Janeiro Declaration on Environment and Development are both non-binding instruments, as are the Forest Principles adopted at Rio. The many guidelines, principles, and recommended practices adopted by the Organization for Economic Cooperation and Development (OECD), the United Nations Environment Programme (UNEP), or the United Nations Food and Agriculture Organization (FAO), while nonbinding, are sometimes influential legal instruments. For example, the 1989 UNEP London Guidelines for the Exchange of Information on Chemicals in International Trade or the 1985 FAO International Code of Conduct on the Distribution and Use of Pesticides, and the 1990 FAO Guidelines on the Operation of Prior Informed Consent (for pesticide trade) have been widely respected, although they are nonbinding.

Nonbinding legal instruments have also been important in other fields of international law. In human rights, many instruments that extend specific human rights to groups or set forth new human rights began as nonbinding instruments. The Helsinki Final Act of the Conference on Security and Cooperation in Europe, which was the end product of the effort by the Soviet Union and its allies to secure recognition by European states and the United States and Canada of the post–World War II division of Europe, was a nonbinding document. The human rights component of the document played a crucial role during the cold war in empowering groups and individuals in central and eastern Europe to challenge the human rights practices of their governments. Even in the trade field, in which most instruments are binding, the OECD Guidelines for Multinational Enterprises are explicitly voluntary, but they have had considerable effect.

One of the most important sources of international soft law is the myriad of guidelines, resolutions, and decisions that are taken by parties to an international agreement in the course of implementing it. The old vision of an international agreement that once negotiated is an unchanging normative document binding upon the parties is obsolete. International agreements need to be viewed as living agreements, into which parties continuously breathe life and to which they give new directions by acting as informal legislatures. The Guidelines for the World Heritage Convention or the many adjustments and decisions, in addition to formal amendments, to the 1987 Montreal Protocol on Substances That Deplete the Ozone Layer have enabled those agreements to evolve over time to meet changing needs.

The negotiation of legally nonbinding instruments is likely to increase more rapidly than the negotiation of formal international conventions in at least certain areas of international law. Agreement is usually easier to achieve, the transaction costs for governments and even NGOs are lower, the opportunity to set forth detailed strategies is greater, and the ability to respond to rapid changes in scientific understanding or economic or social conditions is better.

There is another body of legally nonbinding norms developed largely in the private sector, as referenced earlier: codes of conduct by industrial associations such as chemical manufacturers, agricultural associations, business groups, professional bodies, or ad hoc coalitions for particular issues. Private codes of environmental management have emerged as a major force in industry.

The most prominent private sector efforts to set environmental management norms include the ISO 14,000 series, the Chemical Manufacturers Association's Responsible Care Program, the Coalition for Environmentally Responsible Economies, and the International Chamber of Commerce's Business Charter for Sustainable Development. The European Union has developed a parallel effort in the private sector in its Environmental Management Auditing System. Although these codes differ, they require industry to follow certain environmental management practices and provide for audits. They seek to use market, peer, and public pressure to motivate firms to undertake major changes in their management procedures and rely on procurement practices of other companies and governments and on individual consumers to enforce them.

Robert Cooter, in analyzing voluntary norms in the domestic context, has characterized them as "the new law merchant."[10] The associations are increasingly transnational, and the resulting norms are also transnational. Compliance with the norms depends largely on the private sector.

The Integration of International and National Law

We have become accustomed to sharply differentiating international law from national law. International law applies between states; national law governs relations within states. But there is no longer such a sharp line.

International law has always been linked with national law, for it is implemented through national, provincial, and local laws. In other cases, national laws, independent of any treaty, provide protection to other countries or their citizens for harm that occurs within the country but injures those outside, as in Canadian and U.S. national legislation on air pollution, which long before the Canada–United States acid rain agreement provided for reciprocal access to administrative decision making.

In still other cases, states may apply their own national laws extraterritorially, as for example, U.S. antitrust or civil rights legislation. There have been proposals to extend the U.S. National Environmental Policy Act's requirement of a formal environmental impact statement to all projects abroad. Since there is no international agreement setting forth criteria for extraterritorial application, the practice of doing so creates considerable conflict.

Increasingly, the sharp line between international and national law is disappearing because subnational units of governments are concluding legal instruments on transborder issues independently with subnational units of governments in other countries. This is particularly occurring in the environmental field, as evidenced, for example, by the 1982 New York–Quebec Agreement on Acid Precipitation.[11] While the legal instruments may not rise to the level of an international agreement, they nonetheless shape transborder relations and, more generally, affect the structure of international law.

But there is another sense in which the line is becoming blurred: namely, the increasing acceptance of issues formerly regarded as within "domestic jurisdiction" as issues that raise international concern. For example, the growing transnational human rights consciousness has contributed to pressure on the United Nations Security Council to authorize interventions for humanitarian purposes in cases that earlier might have been viewed as falling within "domestic jurisdiction." As Lori Fisler Damrosch notes in her introduction to a multiauthored study on the issue, the case studies establish that large segments of the international community have been willing to endorse strong collective action in such situations as "genocide, ethnic cleansing . . . interference with the delivery of humanitarian relief to endangered civilian populations . . . collapse of civil order . . . and irregular interruption of democratic governance."[12]

The same trend is apparent in environmental law. Agreements address the management of natural resources within national jurisdiction such as wetlands, forests, and other biologically diverse areas; fresh water; soils; and energy resources. The Framework Convention on Climate Change and the accompanying Kyoto Protocol address countries' energy policies and land use practices, matters traditionally within domestic jurisdiction.

Substantive Directions for International Law

International law will bear an unusually heavy challenge in the decades ahead: to provide the norms that connect the many parts of our global society. Political theory tells us that viable communities need shared values, either globally or locally. They need to feel that they are linked to each other. The new transnational elites need to share common values with each other and with the fragmented communities who are not directly part of the elites.

One might argue that international law will be viewed as irrelevant to the needs of the numerous decentralized communities that are forming on the grounds that it is a product of elite structures in which they have been denied effective participation. But it is equally plausible that international law will be seen as providing the normative content and a voice to the needs of all groups who feel dispossessed, discriminated against, and deprived of basic human rights. Developments in human rights law illustrate this.

The field of human rights has exploded since World War II. Television and advances in information technology have brought violations of the norms into living rooms everywhere. The Helsinki process for implementing the human rights commitments in the 1975 Helsinki Final Act armed those that were fighting oppression. In central and eastern Europe in the late 1980s and early 1990s, environmental rights provided a rallying cry for those seeking democratic rule. In 1995, women's rights provided important norms that women are seeking to implement across the globe. Calls for environmental justice in the United States, calls that will likely be heard in various forms across the world, demonstrate the importance of the norms in uniting and mobilizing people. The emerging information age makes possible global communications that link disparate groups to express common values and common ends.

Intergenerational Norms

One fundamental norm is that concerning our relationship with present, past, and future generations. Until recently international law has addressed intertemporal issues primarily by relating the present to the past. The intertemporal doctrine in international law applies to territorial claims, to certain rules of customary international law, and to several aspects of treaties. In private international law, intertemporal questions relate to choice of time, such as the rules governing conflict of laws.

Increasingly, intertemporal issues relate the present to the future, as in economic development, environmental and natural resource protection, and cultural heritage issues. The mandate for sustainable development is inherently intergenerational. Elsewhere I have articulated a theory of intergenerational equity that argues that we are part of the natural system and that we hold the global environment in common with past, present, and future generations of the human species. We have both rights to use it for our own benefit and obligations to care for it for our generation and for future generations.[13] This in turn gives rise to principles of intergenerational equity, which must be articulated and can provide the normative link between the living generation and future generations.

Three principles frame intergenerational equity. First, each generation should be required to conserve the diversity of the natural and cultural resource base so that it does not unduly restrict the options available to future generations in addressing their problems and meeting their values, and each generation should be entitled to diversity, or options, comparable to that enjoyed by previous generations. Second, each generation should maintain the planet's quality so that it is bequeathed on balance in no worse condition than received. The principle of quality assumes that development will take place and that trade-offs will be made, but it requires that, on balance, quality be maintained. It calls for the development of predictive indexes of environmental quality, baseline measurements, integrated monitoring networks, and most important, scientific and technical research to use resources efficiently, develop substitutes, and monitor and prevent environmental degradation. The third principle, access, provides that the members of every generation should have comparable rights of access to the legacy of past generations and should conserve this access for future generations. People living today have a nondiscriminatory right to use the natural and cultural resources and a right not to suffer a disproportionate share of environmental burdens. This has important implications for the distribution of environmental burdens and benefits within countries.

While intergenerational equity as a principle seemed remote from the daily practice of international law when first articulated in the late 1980s, there has now been considerable scholarly, policy, and judicial attention, both in national and international courts, to fairness to future generations. In particular, Judge Christopher Weeramantry, the Vice President of the International Court of Justice since the mid-1990s, has recognized in his separate and dissenting court opinions the principle of intergenerational equity as an established part of international law.[14] In the Philippines, the Supreme Court recognized intergenerational equity by granting constitutional standing to a group of children to represent the interests of future generations in their effort to stop the leasing of very biologically diverse forested lands.[15]

Principles of intergenerational equity can provide unifying norms to counter alienation associated with fragmentation. To be effective, they must be articulated and implemented at all levels—international, national, and local.

New International Monitoring and Tracking Regimes

Political scientists are pointing to unprecedented global threats in the coming decades to our security, economic welfare, and well-being. While commonly held international norms may be one response, another will surely be unprecedented tracking of international transactions and monitoring of compliance with international obligations.

Materials increasingly cross national borders, and transactions do so electronically. It can be argued that we will need increased international regulatory tracking of dangerous security-related transactions such as weapons sales, nuclear material movements, chemicals trade, and so forth.[16] As the world becomes more fragmented this is seen by many as essential to containing the growing threats to the security of the planet. Technology advances, particularly in communications and monitoring technology, will greatly help, for they will provide the means for near-real-time tracking of transactions and movements of material. Highly sophisticated technologies are also available to track national compliance with certain international treaties and to assess their effectiveness. This applies not only to arms control but to environmental and other agreements. Agreements such as CITES, the Montreal Protocol on Substances That Deplete the Ozone Layer, and the 1989 Basel Convention on the Control of Transboundary Movements of Hazardous Wastes and Their Disposal, to cite but a few examples, require increasingly sophisticated technology to track exports and imports of controlled items.

Many problems will arise, however, with the surge in monitoring and tracking of products and transactions. Countries will have to absorb further inroads on national sovereignty. Individuals, corporations, and business will face potential invasions of individual and corporate privacy. And the international community will have to address the potential vulnerability of systems to renegade actors.

Compliance with International Law

Traditionally there has been little attention to the nuances of compliance with international legal instruments. In this view, states assume that other states will have the capacity to comply with their treaty obligations and do not consider that a treaty's primary purpose may be to build the capacity of member states to comply or to encourage nongovernmental participation in discharging international obligations. In this approach, compliance can be measured in a snapshot. Compliance is regarded hierarchically: governments join treaties and adopt national implementing legislation or regulations, with which domestic units comply.

But in fact, agreements evolve over time and, very important, compliance by countries changes over time. States do not necessarily comply fully with their obligations, either because they do not have the capacity or because they lack political will, or both. The situation is somewhat analogous to that of compliance with countries' domestic laws, which are not always fully complied with either.

Compliance involves a dynamic process between governments, secretariats, international organizations (including international financial institutions), NGOs, subnational units, the private sector, and all actors whose behavior is targeted by the agreements. The many actors interact in complex ways in patterns that vary among agreements and within countries.

A large international study of national compliance with international environmental agreements found, based on empirical research, that in general, national compliance increased over time. But it also declined for periods in certain countries for particular agreements in response to factors such as economic chaos, political instability, and sudden decentralization.[17]

Strategies to ensure compliance must be aimed at engaging countries, which means that a different mix of strategies will be needed for different countries and different agreements. International legal strategies to encourage compliance may be grouped into three categories: negative incentives in the form of penalties, sanctions, and withdrawal of membership privileges; sunshine methods such as monitoring, reporting, on-site visits, transparency of governmental actions to comply, nongovernmental participation, industry tracking, and secretariat persuasion; and incentives such as special funds for financial or technical assistance, access to technology, or training programs. In addition, there are institutional measures, such as noncompliance procedures, that can be built into the implementing structure of the agreement. The precise mix of strategies that will be needed for any particular country will vary among countries and agreements and, importantly, over time.[18] In general, in international environmental law, countries have relied primarily upon the sunshine and incentive strategies to secure compliance. Sanctions have rarely been used, although in certain instances the mere possibility of using them may offer indirect persuasion to comply.

Understanding the Emerging Framework in Operation

Classical international law looked only to the actions of states to understand the development, implementation, and enforcement of international law. Political scientists and some legal scholars have penetrated this form and suggested that it is essential to look both inside the states and externally to international organizations to understand development of and compliance with international law.

Since space does not permit a critique of various approaches, I want to focus only on one: the concept that two-level games, international and domestic, are being played in all international negotiations and in the implementing and compliance theater that ensues after agreements go into effect. Robert Putnam offered in 1988 a theory of two-level games in which a state is engaged in separate games at the international and the national level, each influencing the other. "At the national level," he said, "domestic groups pursue their interests by pressuring the government to adopt favorable policies, and politicians seek power by constructing coalitions among those groups. At the international level, national governments seek to maximize their own ability to satisfy domestic pressures, while minimizing the adverse consequences of foreign developments. Neither of the two games can be ignored by central decision-makers, so long as their countries remain interdependent, yet sovereign."[19]

Those who have been involved in international negotiations, whether over trade, environment, military security, or energy, have experienced this first hand. For the United States, the negotiations for the Kyoto Protocol to the climate change convention involved competing interests among the executive branch, Congress, and the many different domestic constituencies and at the same time international pressures from other countries and their domestic constituencies, all of which were dynamically joined.

There are other more subtle ways in which the two-level game is played and which affect international law. International organizations, such as the international financial institutions, require, at the request or with the tacit approval of national leaders, legal or policy measures that are politically unpopular domestically with significant groups but are viewed as necessary for sustainable economic development. Domestic leaders can use international events to shift power balances within the country for given issues. In international trade law, particular disputes before the General Agreement on Tariffs and Trade, now the World Trade Organization, can arguably be understood only in terms of a two-level game, with national leaders implicitly using international resolution of the dispute to constrain or reinforce the influence of particular domestic pressure groups or constituencies. For example, the international trade dispute between Venezuela and Brazil on one side and the United States on the other over the treatment of reformulated gasoline, in which the United States formally lost the decision, reflected a two-level game in which the World Trade Organization's dispute settlement procedures strengthened the environmental interests within the United States government against protectionist interests that were capturing Congress.[20]

The two-level game now needs to be extended to understanding nonstate actors who are negotiating and concluding transnational law, particularly transnational law that addresses issues that governments could also address in the exercise of their sovereignty. The theory could be extended more generally to understanding development and implementation of the emerging transnational "law merchant." Negotiators for industry or for any of the other actors must similarly play in two arenas: their own domestic arena and the international arena. Industry associations, and the corporation itself, are not monolithic structures but can be unpacked to reveal groups or individuals who are pressing for different policies. Leaders similarly must consider the effects of these negotiations upon the alignments, although the structure is likely to be much more authoritarian than in democracies.

The New Issues

The emerging structure of international law raises two additional important issues: manageability and accountability.

Management Issues

Since World War II we have witnessed a legalization of the relationship among states. There are now more than 33,000 international agreements registered with the United Nations, as compared with 61 multilateral treaties recorded between 1918 and 1941. In addition, thousands of other international legal instruments are not registered with the United Nations, and new rules of customary international law have emerged. Thousands of legally nonbinding instruments or voluntary norms have emerged among states and among nonstate actors. All of these developments lead to the question of whether the international legal system is manageable and whether there are steps that need to be taken to increase efficiency and promote equity.

While the subject is far too complex to explore in detail here, three aspects need highlighting: systemic congestion, an advance in bringing states and other actors under a "rule of law" and in peacefully settling disputes, and a revolution in information technology, which may help maintain a coherent and commonly held body of international law.

Treaty congestion can perhaps most easily be seen in the international environmental field, where there are more than 900 international legal instruments with one or more important provisions concerned with the environment. Transaction costs in negotiating international agreements can be high. Four or five intergovernmental negotiating sessions of one to two weeks each during less than two years, as in the negotiations for the Framework Convention on Climate Change, put large demands on countries with limited resources to staff and fund participants and also on interested NGOs and industry coalitions. Moreover, with such a large number of international legal instruments, there is great potential for duplication, inconsistencies, and unnoticed but significant gaps.

The multiplicity of international agreements and other legal instruments also potentially challenges the development of a consistent, commonly held body of law. This is particularly so since there are multiple forums available for settling particular disputes. For example, ocean issues may go to the International Court of Justice, the new Law of the Sea Tribunal, or other organs. Different bodies may give differing interpretations on similar issues, such as the validity of jurisdictional reservations to judicial settlement (as in the Turkish case before the European Court of Human Rights and decisions of the International Court of Justice). This in turn may encourage forum shopping. In contrast to national legal systems, there is no international body that serves as the ultimate body of appeal.

But the proliferation of sources and associated institutions also has a very positive implication: that more actors, state and nonstate, are acting under the rule of law and resolving disputes peaceably according to "the rule of law." International law is becoming central to community concerns across the world, in part because there are more international legal instruments defining its content in more subject areas for more actors, and more forums are available to resolve disputes. From this perspective, a hierarchy for authoritative determinations of law might stifle the attractiveness of peacefully settling disputes by imposing costly and time-consuming procedures, or by discouraging creative resolutions.

Louis Sohn has noted the need to develop a systematic collection of international law.[21] The information revolution can be helpful in providing the technology with which to compile and monitor the commonly held body of international law. We need to explore building a computerized database that would include judicial and arbitral decisions from forums in specialized fields as well as important national court decisions bearing on international law. Information technology may also facilitate the chronicling of the practices of states in order to determine the development of rules of customary international law and otherwise help to maintain a consistent, commonly held body of international law and to monitor changes in it.

Accountability

Traditionally, states have been accountable to each other as sovereign independent states for assuring compliance with international law. This is still true. But the communications revolution has made governance more transparent and hence public involvement greater. The negotiations in June 1995 between the prime minister of Russia and the Chechen rebel leader for a truce in the Chechen republic and the release of hostages from a hospital in Budyonnovsk took place on television for the public to observe. Meetings of the parties to the convention controlling trade in endangered species and to the World Heritage Convention are promptly available on the Internet. Televised images of civilians suffering in internal conflicts have generated pressure on governments by NGOs and domestic public opinion to take collective action in response. However, accountability for the many nonstate actors has yet to emerge. Many are constructive in their influence; others not. Their sheer number poses congestion problems.

In a very important sense, participation by nonstate actors in the international legal system greatly enhances accountability, because it can give a voice to citizens who would otherwise be unrepresented, ensure that actions taken meet local needs, counter effects of high-level government corruption, and therefore produce outcomes that maximize human welfare efficiently. Information technology can assist because it makes information readily accessible to groups and individuals across the world and empowers them. It makes governments and international organizations more transparent. International nongovernmental organizations have been particularly effective in helping to develop, implement, and promote compliance with international environmental agreements, although to be sure not all organizations share interests congruent with those in the treaties.

The problem is that nonstate actors in the new international legal order are not necessarily held accountable for their actions. As noted before, states have always had powers to tax, conscript, and form armies. These are traditional needs in international affairs, for which states are accountable to their citizens in democratic governments. But actions of nonstate actors are not subject to such direct public accountability.

Two problems arise: how to structure constructively NGO and private sector participation in international governmental and international organization deliberations and how to ensure that the transnational norms developed largely outside of governments are responsive to public needs and concerns.

Particularly in international environmental law, nonstate actors are now prominent participants, either formally or informally, in international negotiations, conferences of parties, and other meetings. Some are membership-based and accountable to their members, while others are loosely accountable to their funders, who may be dispersed. While the United Nations Economic and Social Council still determines accreditation to intergovernmental meetings, the sheer number of NGOs suggests that the system needs to be reconsidered to ensure effective representation. Moreover, it is time to consider additional processes that legitimate NGO participation in the international legal system.

However, NGOs also need to be held accountable for their actions. Spurious information, unrelenting pressures for special interest pleading outside the intergovernmental forum, unlimited demands for transparency, and similar concerns mean that pressures are building for at least an informal code of conduct. Leading NGOs, which have contributed so much to developing and implementing international law in fields such as human rights and the environment, may find it in their best self-interest to take the lead in initiating this.

A second major issue of accountability stems from the emerging transnational standards and management practices being developed, largely in the private sector. In the West, at least, industries and corporations are accountable through the market system. Thus, nonstate actors should eventually find that consumer preferences both drive and limit what they can do. But accountability through the marketplace is tenuous and works imperfectly.

One of the main functions of international law is to provide a process for legitimating norms. It is essential to build processes for legitimating the norms developed by transnational industrial actors. Otherwise they will not be acceptable in the long run. This means giving a voice to governments and to the public in developing the norms, whether they be environmental management practices, eco-labels (or green labels on products), or banking practices. The industrial sector may resist because the situation is moving too fast for meaningful consultation or because other actors are believed to be not sufficiently well informed and hence could corrode and delay the process. While information technology should assist in providing informed and rapid consultation, the process would still be messier and longer. But unless the process for developing the norms is viewed as legitimate, the norms will ultimately not be accepted by the broader community to which they are addressed.

International law in the next century must become more central and relevant if we are to address both global and local problems effectively. While we will continue to draw on the classical structure of international law, and states will continue to be central, the emerging structure that reflects the rise of a global civil society is better suited to the international problems that we face. It engages new actors and enlists important new resources, although it also raises new dangers. Thomas Jefferson said, as inscribed on the walls of the Jefferson Memorial, "I am not an advocate for frequent changes in laws and constitutions, but laws and institutions must go hand in hand with the progress of the human mind. As that becomes more developed, more enlightened, as new discoveries are made, new truths discovered and manners and opinions change, with the change of circumstances, institutions must advance also to keep pace with the times." While the international legal system is more complicated and far less crisp than before, this is inevitable and desirable for the complex integrated and fragmented world of the twenty-first century.

Notes

1. J. L Brierly, *Law of Nations*, 6th ed. (Oxford: Clarendon Press, 1963).
2. "The Case of the S.S. Lotus (*France v. Turkey*)," Permanent Court of International Justice, Series A, no. 10, Manly O. Hudson, *World Court Report*, vol. 2, p. 20.
3. Joseph S. Nye Jr., "What New World Order?" *Foreign Affairs* 71 (1992): 83, 91.
4. Harold K. Jacobson, *Networks of Interdependence: International Organizations and the Global Political System*, 2d ed. (New York: Knopf, 1984), 386.
5. *Yearbook of International Organizations, 1997–1998*, 34th ed. (Brussels: Union of International Associations, 1997), 1762.
6. See James Rosenau and Ernst-Otto Czempiel, eds., *Governance without Government: Order and Change in World Politics* (New York: Cambridge University Press, 1992); Jessica Mathews, "Power Shift," *Foreign Affairs* 76 (1997): 50.
7. Rosalyn Higgins, *Problems and Process: International Law and How We Use It* (Oxford: Clarendon Press, 1994), 8.
8. The Alliance includes forty-two low-lying, small, coastal and island states from all regions of the world. The United Nations defines small island states as islands with less than 10,000 square kilometers in land mass and less than 500,000 inhabitants.
9. Paul C. Szasz, "International Norm-making," in *Environmental Change and International Law,"* ed. Edith Brown Weiss (Tokyo: United Nations University Press, 1992), 70; see also Alexandre Kiss, "The Implications of Global Change for the International Legal System," in ibid., 315, 319–325.
10. Robert Cooter, "Structural Adjudication and the New Law Merchant: A Model of Decentralized Law," *International Review of Law and Economics* 14 (1994): 143, 144. See also Anne-Marie Slaughter, "International Law in a World of Liberal States," *European Journal of International Law* 6 (1995): 503.
11. "New York–Quebec Agreement on Acid Precipitation," July 26, 1982, *International Legal Materials* 21 (1982): 721.
12. Lori Fisler Damrosch, ed., *Enforcing Restraint: Collective Intervention in Internal Conflicts* (New York: Council on Foreign Relations Press, 1993), 12–13.
13. Edith Brown Weiss, *In Fairness to Future Generations: International Law, Common Patrimony, and Intergenerational Equity* (Dobbs Ferry, N.Y.: Transnational Publishers, 1989).
14. Judge Weeramantry noted that "the rights of future generations have passed the stage when they were merely an embryonic right struggling for recognition. They have woven themselves into international law through major treaties, through juristic opinion and through general principles of law recognized by civilized nations." International Court of Justice, Advisory Opinion on the Legality of the Threat or Use of Nuclear Weapons, 1996, reprinted in *International Legal Materials* 35 (1996): 809. Opinion of Judge Weeramantry, 17.
15. Judgment of June 30, 1993 *(Juan Antonio Oposa et al. v. the Honourable Fulgencio Factoran, Secretary of the Department of the Environment and Natural Resources, et al.)*, Supreme Court of the Philippines, G.R. no. 10183; see also Ted Allen, "The Philippine Children's Case: Recognizing Standing for Future Generations," *Georgetown International Environmental Law Review* 6 (1994): 713.
16. Presentation on international relations by John Steinbrunner of the Brookings Institution to faculty at Georgetown University Law Center, March 1996.
17. Edith Brown Weiss and Harold K. Jacobson, eds., *Engaging Countries: Strengthening National Compliance with International Environmental Accords* (Cambridge: MIT Press, 1998).

18. Harold K. Jacobson and Edith Brown Weiss, "Assessing the Record and Designing Strategies to Engage Countries," in Brown Weiss and Jacobson, *Engaging Countries.*

19. Robert D. Putnam, "Diplomacy and Domestic Politics: The Logic of Two-Level Games," *International Organization* 42 (1988): 427, 434.

20. "United States Standards for Reformulated and Conventional Gasoline *(Brazil, Venezuela v. United States),*" World Trade Organization, Appellate Body, AB-1996-1, April 22, 1996.

21. Louis B. Sohn, "Making International Law More User-Friendly," Address to the United Nations Congress on Public International Law, New York City, March 17, 1995.

6

Environmental Protection in the Twenty-first Century: Sustainable Development and International Law

Philippe Sands

This chapter identifies the emerging principle of international law for the protection of the environment. A decade or so ago a discussion of this topic would probably have begun with a question as to whether the subject of international environmental law even existed: there were no treatises or journals specifically on the subject, only a very small number of law school seminars were being taught, and most treatises on public international law were able to avoid dealing with the environment at all with little risk of being criticized for incompleteness.

Today the situation is entirely different. The International Court of Justice has confirmed the "obligations of States to respect and protect the natural environment" and that their "general obligation . . . to ensure that activities within their jurisdiction or control respect the environment of other States or of areas beyond national control is now part of the corpus of international law relating to the environment."[1] This latter obligation, it is now clear, is applicable at all times and to all activities, even the use of different forms of weaponry, including nuclear weapons.[2]

These general obligations will be further developed in the context of the international community's commitment, at the United Nations Conference on Environment and Development (UNCED) held at Rio de Janeiro in 1992, to integrate environment and development and to cooperate "in the further development of international law in the field of sustainable development."[3] The basic challenge for the next century continues to be that pithily described by Philip Allott: the inherent and fundamental interdependence of the world environment with land, sea, and air spaces of planet Earth that are part of the sovereign areas of independent states.[4] This challenge raises issues about the nature of international society and the structure of the international legal order, the content and reach of international environmental law, and the relationship between international environmental law and other areas of international law, particularly in the economic and social domains. It is not surprising that the World Commission on Environment and Development indicated in its report (known as the Brundtland Report) that "international law is being rapidly outdistanced by the accelerating pace and expanding scale of impacts on the ecological basis of development."[5]

There is no novelty in environmental issues, even if they have become more complex. International legal efforts to protect the environment go back at least to the 1880s, when a dispute was submitted to international arbitration as a consequence of United States efforts to prevent British vessels from exploiting fur seals in international waters of the Bering Sea. Although the Pacific Fur Seal Arbitration Tribunal did not find in favor of the unilateral U.S. approach to conservation (early shades of current issues in the context of the General Agreement on Tariffs and Trade, or the GATT, which became the World Trade Organization in 1995), it did adopt regulations for the "proper protection and preservation" of fur seals. These regulations have served as an important precedent for the subsequent development of international environmental law, reflecting a recognition that environmental problems transcend national boundaries and can be addressed only by international law.[6]

The first part of this chapter briefly describes the historic development of this emerging area of international law, including the institutional arrangements, and the traditional legal order within which environmental challenges failed to be addressed. The general principles are then described. The last part sets out basic rules of international environmental law, as well as the principal legal techniques that exist for implementing them.

International Environmental Law: Context, Sources, and History

This part of the chapter describes the international legal order, including the fundamental concepts of sovereignty and territory, identifies the main international actors, and describes the principal sources of international environmental law. It then summarizes the four stages in the development of the field.

The International Legal Order

International law and international organizations provide the basis for international cooperation and collaboration between the various members of the international community in their efforts to protect the local, regional, and global environment. At each level the task becomes progressively more complex as new actors and interests are drawn into the legal process: whereas just two states, representing the interest of local fishing communities, negotiated the early fisheries conventions in the middle of the nineteenth century, more than 150 states were involved in negotiations sponsored by the UN General Assembly that led to the 1992 UN Framework Convention on Climate Change, and its 1997 Kyoto Protocol (see Chapter 10).

In both cases, however, the principles and rules of public international law, together with the international organizations that have been established thereunder, are intended to serve similar functions. The overall objective of the international legal order is to provide a framework within which the various members of the international community may cooperate, establish norms of behavior, and resolve their differences. As with national law, the functions of international law are legislative, administrative, and adjudicative. The legal principles and rules that impose binding obligations requiring states and other members of the international community to conform to certain norms of behavior are accomplished through the legislative function of international law. In relation to the environment these obligations place limits upon the activities that may be conducted or permitted because of their actual or potential impact upon the environment. Such impact may be entirely within national borders, across territorial boundaries, or in areas beyond national jurisdictions (global commons).

The administrative function of international law allocates tasks to the various actors to ensure that the standards imposed by the principles and rules of international environmental law are carried out. The adjudicative function of international law aims, in a limited way, to provide mechanisms or forums for the pacific settlement of differences or disputes that arise between members of the international community involving the use of natural resources or the conduct of activities that will affect the environment.

Sovereignty and Territory

The international legal order thus seeks to regulate the activities of an international community that comprises states, international organizations, and a growing number of nongovernmental actors. States continue to play the primary and dominant role in the international legal order, both as the principal creators of the rules of international law and the principal holders of rights and obligations under those rules. As the dominant actors in the international legal order, states are sovereign and equal, imbued with equal rights and duties as members of the international community, notwithstanding differences of an economic, social, or political nature. The sovereignty and equality of states means that each has prima facie exclusive jurisdiction over its territory and the natural resources found there; each also has a duty not to intervene in the area of exclusive jurisdiction of other states. The sovereignty and exclusive jurisdiction of the 190 or so states over their territory means, in principle, that they alone have the competence to develop policies and laws in regard to the natural resources and the environment of their territory. That territory comprises

- land within its boundaries, including the subsoil;
- internal waters, such as lakes, rivers, canals;
- territorial sea, which is adjacent to the coast, including its seabed, subsoil, and the resources thereof; and
- airspace above its land, internal waters, and territorial sea, up to the point at which the legal regime of outer space begins.

States may also have more limited sovereign rights and jurisdiction over other areas, including: a contiguous zone adjacent to their territorial seas; the continental shelf, its seabed and subsoil; certain fishing zones; and "exclusive economic zones."

As a result of these arrangements certain areas are left to fall outside the territory and exclusive jurisdiction of any state. These areas, which are sometimes referred to as the "global commons," include the high seas and its seabed and subsoil, atmosphere, outer space, and, according to a majority of states, the Antarctic.

This apparently straightforward international legal order was a satisfactory organizing structure until technological developments permeated national boundaries. The structure does not coexist comfortably with an environmental order that consists of a biosphere of interdependent ecosystems that do not respect artificial territorial boundaries between states.[7] As an ecological matter, if not a legal one, many natural resources and their environmental components are shared, and the use by any one state of the natural resources within its territory will invariably have consequences for the use of natural resources and their environmental components in other states.

Ecological interdependence therefore poses a fundamental problem for international law, and it explains why international cooperation and the development of shared norms of behavior in the environmental field are indispensable. The challenge for international law in the world of sovereign states is to reconcile the fundamental independence of each state with the inherent and fundamental interdependence of the environment. A question arises as to how to protect areas beyond the national jurisdiction of any state as a result of existing territorial arrangements that leave certain areas outside any state's territory.

International Actors

Although states remain far and away the most important actors, the history of international environmental law reflects the central role played by international organizations and nongovernmental actors in the legal order and its associated processes. As with the human rights field, environmental law provides clear evidence of an evolution away from the view that international society comprises only a community of states, to one that extends its scope to encompass individuals, groups, and corporate and other entities within and among those states. This new reality is now reflected in many international legal instruments, especially the Rio Declaration on Environment and Development and Agenda 21 adopted at UNCED (see Chapter 8), which recognize and call for the further development of the role of international organizations and nongovernmental actors in virtually all aspects of the international legal process that relate to environment and development.

These various actors have different roles and functions, both as subjects and objects of international environmental law. These functions and roles include, principally, participating in the law-making process; monitoring implementation, including reporting; and ensuring enforcement of obligations. The extent to which each actor contributes to that process turns upon the extent of its international legal personality and the rights and obligations granted to it by general international law as well as the rules established by particular treaties and other rules. The Rio Declaration and Agenda 21, as well as an increasing number of international environmental agreements, envisage an expanded role for international organizations and nongovernmental actors in virtually all aspects of the international legal process.

States. States remain the primary and principal subjects of international law. It is still states that create, adopt, and implement international legal principles and rules, create international organizations, and permit the participation of other actors in the international legal process. In 1998 there were 185 member states of the United Nations, and several others that were not members. The members include both developed and developing countries. Developed countries include the 24 member states of the Organization for Economic Cooperation and Development (OECD) and the 11 states that previously formed part of the Soviet bloc. The latter are currently referred to as "economies in transition." Some 155 member states are the developing states that form an association referred to as the Group of 77. The Group of 77 often works as a single negotiating bloc within the United Nations. Within the UN system states are also arranged into regional groupings, usually for the purpose of elections to UN bodies. The five groupings are: Latin America and the Caribbean; Africa; Asia; western Europe and others; and central and eastern Europe.

Frequently in environmental negotiations these rather simple distinctions tend to break down as states pursue what they perceive to be vital national interests, including their strategic alliances. The UNCED negotiations illustrated the extent of the differences that exist between and among developed states and developing states on the particularly contentious issues: atmospheric emissions, conservation of marine mammals, protection of forests, institutional arrangements, and financial resources.

International Organizations. The international organizations involved in environmental matters make up a complex and unwieldy network at the global, regional, subregional, and bilateral levels. It is unlikely that any international organization today will not have some responsibility for environmental matters. The lack of coordination between international organizations in the environmental field makes it difficult to assess their role by reference to any functional, sectoral, or geographic criteria. To help understand their activities and interests they can, however, be divided into three general categories: global organizations under the auspices of, or related to, the United Nations and its specialized agencies; regional organizations outside the UN system; and organizations established by environmental and other international agreements.

International organizations perform a range of different functions and roles in the development and management of international legal responses to environmental issues and problems. International organizations fulfill judicial, legislative, and administrative roles. The actual functions of each institution will depend to a great extent upon the powers granted to it as subsequently interpreted and applied by the parties to it and by the practice of the organization. Apart from very specific functions required of particular organizations, five separate but interrelated legal functions and roles are performed by most international organizations.

First, they provide a forum for general cooperation and coordination between states on matters of international environmental management. Second, they play an informational role, receiving and disseminating information, facilitating information exchange, and providing for formal and informal consultation between states and between states and the organization. The third function is the contribution of international organizations to the development of international legal obligations, including "soft law," or nonbinding commitments. International organizations develop policy initiatives and standards and may adopt rules that establish binding obligations or that reflect rules of customary law in relation to the development of procedural standards and the establishment of new institutional arrangements.

Once environmental and other standards and obligations have been established, a fourth function for institutions is in ensuring the implementation of and compliance with those standards and obligations. A fifth function is to provide an independent forum, or mechanism, for the settlement of disputes, usually between states.

Nongovernmental Organizations (NGOs). Nongovernmental organizations have historically played an important role in developing international environmental law and continue to do so in a variety of different ways. They identify issues that require international legal action, frequently participate as observers in international organizations and in treaty negotiations, and make efforts to ensure the national and international implementation of, and compliance with, standards and obligations that have been adopted at the regional and global level. In the past two decades at least six different types of NGO have emerged as actors in the development of international environmental law: the scientific community; nonprofit environmental groups and associations; private companies and business concerns; legal organizations; the academic community; and individuals. The Rio Declaration and Agenda 21 affirm the important partnership role of NGOs and call for their "expanded role."[8]

Transnational corporations are also increasingly the subject of international environmental regulation even though they are not yet traditional subjects of international law. This is a result of the fact that they conduct their activities across national boundaries in an increasingly interdependent world that recognizes the limits of national control and the need for minimum international standards of behavior. Transnational corporations have themselves begun to consider the need for the further development of international environmental law.

Sources of International Environmental Law

International law consists of rules that are legally binding on states and other members of the international community in their relations with each other. The sources from which the binding rights and obligations of states and other members of the international community arise include

- bilateral or multilateral treaties;
- binding acts of international organizations;
- rules of customary international law; and
- judgments of an international court or tribunal.

Additionally, rules of soft law play an important role by pointing to the likely future direction of formally binding obligations, by informally establishing acceptable norms of behavior, and by "codifying" or reflecting rules of customary law.

In practice, the most important binding international agreements are treaties (also referred to by such names as conventions, protocols, agreements) that can be adopted bilaterally (between two states), regionally (between states in a particular region geographically or politically defined), or globally (participation open to all states). With more than 185 states now in existence, the number of bilateral environmental agreements runs into the thousands, supplemented by dozens of regional agreements and a smaller, but increasing, number of global treaties. European (in particular the European Union) and other industrial countries have adopted a large body of regional environmental rules that frequently provide a basis for similar regional and global measures adopted in other parts of the world. Regional treaties are less well developed in Africa, the Caribbean, and Oceania and are even more limited in Asia and parts of the Americas. All industrial activity is, however, prohibited by treaty in the Antarctic.

The second principal source of international obligation is acts of international organizations. Almost all international environmental agreements establish institutional organs with the power to adopt certain acts, make decisions, or take other measures. Such acts of international organizations, sometimes referred to as secondary legislation, can provide an important source of international law; they may be legally binding in themselves, or if they are not legally binding per se they may amend existing obligations or authoritatively interpret treaty obligations. Nonbinding acts can contribute to the development of customary law. Binding acts of international organizations derive their legal authority from the treaty on which their adoption was based and can therefore be considered part of treaty law; some of the more far-reaching international measures affecting the use of natural resources have been adopted in the form of acts of international organizations rather than by treaty. Many environmental treaties allow the institutions they create a choice of adopting acts with or without binding legal effects. Those acts that do not have binding legal consequences could, however, subsequently be relied upon as reflecting a rule of customary international law.

The primary role of international environmental obligations adopted by treaty and acts of international organizations should not obscure the important, albeit secondary, role that is played by customary international law. Customary law fulfills a number of functions by creating binding obligations and by contributing to the codification of obligations in the form of treaty rules and other binding acts. The significance of customary law lies in the fact that, as a general matter, it establishes obligations for all states (or all states within a particular region) except those that have persistently objected to a practice and its legal consequences. Establishing the existence of a rule of customary international law requires evidence of consistent state practice. Such practice will rarely provide clear guidance as to the precise content of any particular rule. Article 38(1)(b) of the statute establishing the International Court of Justice identifies the two elements of customary international law: state practice and *opinio juris* (the belief that practice is required as a matter of law).

These sources of binding obligation are supplemented by nonbinding sources of soft law, reflected in guidelines, recommendations, and other non-binding acts adopted by states and international institutions. These can provide evidence of state practice that might support the existence of a rule of customary international law, and they often reflect trends that lead to the development of binding rules. The most important sources of soft law are the Declaration of Principles, produced at the United Nations Conference on the Human Environment, held in Stockholm in 1972, the World Charter for Nature, adopted by the UN General Assembly in 1982, and the 1992 Rio Declaration.

The case law of international courts and tribunals, and arguments presented to such bodies, identify some general principles and rules of international environmental law. The importance of arbitral awards, in particular, in the development of international environmental law should not be understated. Mention has already been made of the Pacific Fur Seal Arbitration, and before states had adopted many "international statutes," important principles had been elaborated by arbitral tribunals in the Trail Smelter case (concerning transboundary air pollution), between the United States and Canada, and the Lac Lanoux arbitration (concerning the use of a shared river), between France and Spain. Judgments of the International Court of Justice have also contributed to the development of international environmental law, particularly in the Icelandic fisheries cases (on fisheries conservation), the nuclear tests cases of 1974 and 1995 (on the legality of atmospheric nuclear tests), and the opinions on the legality of the use of nuclear weapons.

History

The "greening" of international law has occurred over four periods, responding to particular factors that influenced legal developments.[9] Until recently it was evident that international environmental law had arisen without a coordinated legal and institutional framework. The 1972 Stockholm conference and then UNCED attempted to create such a framework.

To 1945. The first distinct period in the greening process began with nineteenth-century bilateral fisheries treaties and the Pacific Fur Seal Arbitration and concluded with the creation of the new UN family of international institutions in 1945. This period might be characterized as one in which states first acted internationally upon their understanding that the process of industrialization and the rapid expansion of economic activities relying on natural resources required limits to be placed on the exploitation of certain natural resources (flora and fauna) and the adoption of appropriate legal instruments.

Until the United Nations was created in 1945 there was no international forum in which to raise environmental concerns, and most of the agreements adopted in this initial period did not create arrangements to ensure that legal obligations were complied with or enforced. Many initiatives grew from private activities by private citizens, an early harbinger of the more intensive activism of nongovernmental organizations that marks international negotiations today.[10]

The Creation of the United Nations: 1945–1972. The establishment of the UN introduced a second period in the development of international environmental law, which culminated with the 1972 UN Conference on the Human Environment. During this period many international organizations with competence in environmental matters were created, and legal instruments were adopted to address particular sources of pollution and the conservation of general and particular environmental resources. These included oil pollution, nuclear testing, wetlands, the marine environment and its living resources, freshwaters, and the dumping of waste at sea.

The UN provided a forum for the discussion of the consequences of technical progress and introduced a period characterized by international organizations, involvement with environmental issues, and the addressing of the causes of pollution and environmental degradation. The relationship between economic development and environmental protection began to be understood. However, the UN Charter did not, and still does not, explicitly address environmental protection or the conservation of natural resources.

In 1949 the UN convened its first environmental conference, entitled the Conservation and Utilization of Resources, which presaged the 1972 Stockholm Conference and the 1992 UNCED.[11] The conference was significant also because it recognized the UN's competence in regard to environmental and natural resource issues. In 1954 the UN General Assembly convened its first major conference, the Conference on the Conservation of the Living Resources of the Sea, which led to the conservation rules adopted in the 1958 Geneva Conventions.[12] The following year the General Assembly adopted the first of many resolutions on atomic energy and the effects of radiation, which led to the 1963 Nuclear Test Ban Treaty and, ultimately, the political context for Australia and New Zealand to bring to the International Court of Justice a case calling on France to stop all atmospheric nuclear tests.[13]

Stockholm and Beyond. The third period began with the 1972 Stockholm conference and concluded with UNCED in 1992. In this twenty-year span the UN attempted to put in place a system to address a growing range of environmental issues in a more coordinated and coherent way. A raft of regional and global conventions addressed new issues, and new techniques of regulation were employed.

The 1972 conference, convened by the General Assembly, adopted three nonbinding instruments: a resolution on institutional and financial arrangements; the Declaration of Twenty-six Guiding Principles; and an Action Plan setting forth 109 recommendations for more specific international action.[14] These represented the international community's first effort at constructing a coherent strategy for the development of international policy, law, and institutions to protect the environment.

For international law the significant developments proved to be the creation of the United Nations Environment Programme (UNEP); the establishment of coordinating mechanisms among existing institutions; the definition of a framework for future actions to be taken by the international community; and the adoption of a set of general principles to guide such action, including Principle 21. UNEP has subsequently been responsible for the establishment and implementation of its Regional Seas Programme, including some thirty regional treaties, as well as important global treaties addressing ozone depletion, trade in hazardous waste, and biodiversity.

Stockholm catalyzed other global treaties adopted under the UN's auspices. The most important agreement, over time, may be the 1982 United Nations Convention on the Law of the Sea (UNCLOS).[15] This established a unique, comprehensive framework for the establishment of global rules for the protection of the marine environment and marine living resources, including detailed institutional arrangements and provisions on environmental impact assessment, technology transfer, and liability. Its provisions have provided an influential basis for the language and approach of many other environmental agreements. Stockholm was followed by other new regional agreements.[16] Also in this period economic and financial institutions began for the first time to address environmental issues.[17]

By 1990, when preparations for UNCED formally began, there existed a solid body of rules of international environmental law. States were increasingly subject to limits on the right to allow or carry out activities that harmed the environment. New standards were in place and a range of techniques were sought to implement those standards. Environmental issues, moreover, had begun to intersect with economic matters, especially trade and development lending. But in spite of these relatively impressive achievements, environmental matters remained on the periphery of the international community's agenda and the activities of most institutions.

UNCED and Beyond. UNCED launched a fourth period for international environmental law, which might be characterized as the period of integration, requiring environmental concerns to be integrated into all international activities. In this period international environmental law was merged into international law in the field of sustainable development.

In December 1987 the UN General Assembly endorsed the Brundtland Report, and the following year it called for a global conference on environment and development.[18] UNCED was formally proposed in December 1989 by General Assembly Resolution 44/228, and after four preparatory negotiating sessions 176 states, several dozen international organizations, and several thousand NGOs converged on Rio de Janeiro for two weeks in June 1992. The purpose of the conference was to elaborate strategies and measures to halt and reverse the effects of environmental degradation in the context of strengthened national and international efforts to promote sustainable and environmentally sound development in all countries. UNCED adopted three nonbinding instruments: the Rio Declaration on Environment and Development (the Rio Declaration); a Non-legally Binding Authoritative Statement of Principles for a Global Consensus on the Management, Conservation, and Sustainable Development of All Types of Forest (the Forest Principles); and Agenda 21.[19] Two treaties were also opened for signature at UNCED: the Convention on Biological Diversity and the United Nations Framework Convention on Climate Change.[20]

It is still too early to fully assess UNCED's contribution to the progressive development of international law.[21] Nevertheless, it is clear from the recent case law of the International Court of Justice that the environment is now recognized as falling within the mainstream of international law.

International Environmental Law: General Principles

The relationship between environmental protection and international law has been transformed in recent years. International environmental issues are now a central concern of the UN and other international institutions and of all governments. Scientific and political concern about global and regional environmental issues is indicated by an increase in the number of international agreements and acts relating to the protection of the environment. Though at any time negotiations are in progress for many different instruments in different forums, it is virtually impossible for all but the most highly resourced states to maintain effective, and consistent, negotiating positions.

Despite impressive achievements, there is reason to doubt the impact of this body of law on actual governmental and human behavior. Limited implementation and enforcement suggests that international environmental law remains in its formative stages. Lawmaking is decentralized, with legislative initiatives being developed in literally dozens of different intergovernmental organizations at the global, regional, and subregional levels. Coordination between the initiatives is inadequate, leading to measures that are often duplicative and sometimes inconsistent. Moreover, the lawmaking process tends to be reactive and somewhat ad hoc in nature, often vulnerable to the vagaries of political, economic, and scientific events and findings. These themes are further developed in the next part of this chapter.

This part describes international environmental law as it currently stands—the general principles, the basic rules, and the emerging legal techniques for their implementation and enforcement. Although no single international legal instrument establishes binding rules or principles of global application, the pattern of state behavior has given rise to an emerging set of guiding principles and minimum standards of acceptable behavior in relation to particular environmental resources. These principles and standards are considered in the following sections.

Principles of General Application

Several general principles and rules of international law have emerged, or are emerging, specifically in relation to environmental matters, as reflected in treaties, binding acts of international organizations, state practice, and soft law commitments. They are general in the sense that they are potentially applicable to all members of the international community across the range of activities that they carry out or permit to be carried out and that they address the protection of all aspects of the environment.[22]

Sovereignty and Responsibility for the Environment. The rules of international environmental law have developed in pursuit of two principles that pull in opposing directions: that states have sovereign rights over their natural resources and that states must not cause damage to the environment. These objectives are now reflected in Principle 21 of the Stockholm Declaration and Principle 2 of the Rio Declaration and provide the foundation of international environmental law.

The first element (sovereignty) reflects the preeminent position of states as primary members of the international legal community. It is tempered by the second element (environmental protection), however, which places limits on the exercise of sovereign rights. In an environmentally interdependent world, activities in one state almost inevitably produce effects in other states or in areas beyond national jurisdiction (such as the high seas).

In the form presented by Principle 21 and Principle 2, the responsibility not to cause damage to the environment of other states or of areas beyond national jurisdiction has been accepted as an obligation by all states.[23] As indicated in the introduction, the International Court of Justice has now confirmed that the second element reflects customary international law.[24]

The emergence of the responsibility of states not to cause environmental damage in areas outside their jurisdiction has historical roots that predate the Stockholm conference. These relate to the obligation of all states "to protect within the territory the rights of other states, in particular their right to integrity and inviolability in peace and war" and the principle endorsed by the arbitral tribunal in the much-cited *Trail Smelter* case, which stated that "no state has the right to use or permit the use of territory in such a manner as to cause injury by fumes in or to the territory of another of the properties or persons therein, when the case is of serious consequence and the injury is established by clear and convincing evidence."[25]

Good Neighborliness and International Cooperation. The principle of "good neighborliness," as enunciated in Article 74 of the UN Charter, concerning social, economic, and commercial matters, has been extended to environmental matters by rules promoting international environmental cooperation. It applies particularly where activities carried out in one state might have adverse effects on the environment of another state or in areas beyond national jurisdiction. The commitment to environmental cooperation is reflected in many international agreements and is supported by state practice. In general, the obligation includes commitments to implement treaty objectives or to improve relations outside a treaty or in relation to certain tasks. Specifically, the obligation can require information sharing, notification, consultation or participation rights in certain decisions, the conduct of environmental impact assessments, and cooperative emergency procedures, particularly where activities might be ultrahazardous. The construction of nuclear power plants on borders is an example where cooperative obligations are reasonably well developed, at least in some regions.

The extent to which this obligation has been complied with was one of the central issues in the dispute between Hungary and Slovakia over the construction of the Gabcikovo Dam and the proposed diversion of the Danube River, which was referred to the International Court of Justice in 1993.[26] Hungary claimed that Czechoslovakia (now just Slovakia) violated its obligation to cooperate in good faith in the implementation of principles affecting transboundary resources, including the obligation to negotiate in good faith and in a spirit of cooperation, to prevent disputes, to provide timely notification of plans to carry out or permit activities that may entail a transboundary interference or a significant risk thereof, and to engage in good faith consultations to arrive at an equitable resolution of the situation. On September 25, 1997, the International Court gave judgment, finding that Hungary had not been entitled to terminate work on the construction of the barrages or to terminate the treaty, and that Slovakia was operating an alternative barrage illegally. The parties subsequently undertook negotiations to implement the judgment, which implied that Hungary was not required to build a second barrage. However, in the absence of agreement, in September 1998 Slovakia returned to the International Court, with a further request that the Court should lay down guidelines on the conduct of the negotiations.

Sustainable Development. Another emerging principle requires states to ensure that they develop and use their natural resources in a manner that is sustainable. Although the ideas underlying the concept of "sustainable development" have a long history in international law, the term has only recently begun to be used in international agreements. It has also been confirmed as having a role in international law by the International Court of Justice in the Gabcikovo-Nagymaros Case.[27] The ideas underlining "sustainability" date at least to the Pacific Fur Seal Arbitration in 1893, when the United States asserted a right to ensure the legitimate and proper use of seals and to protect them, for the benefit of humankind, from wanton destruction.

What "sustainable development" means in international law today is, however, a more complicated matter. Where it has been used it appears to refer to at least four separate but related objectives that, taken together, might comprise the legal elements of the concept of "sustainable development" as used in the Brundtland Report.[28] First, as invoked in some agreements, it refers to the commitment to preserve natural resources for the benefit of present and future generations. Second, in other agreements sustainable development refers to appropriate standards for the exploitation of natural resources based upon harvests or use; examples include use that is "sustainable," "prudent," "rational," "wise," or "appropriate." Third, yet other agreements require an "equitable" use of natural resources, suggesting that the use by any state must take account of the needs of other states and people. And a fourth category of agreements require that environmental considerations be integrated into economic and other development plans, programs, and projects, and that development needs are taken into account in applying environmental objectives.

The instruments adopted at UNCED reflect each of these four objectives, and translate them in Agenda 21 and the Rio Declaration into more specific proposals and principles to govern human activity.

Common but Differentiated Responsibility. This principle has emerged from the application of the broader principle of equity in general international law, and from the recognition that the special needs of developing countries must be taken into account in the development, application, and interpretation of rules of international environmental law if they are to be encouraged to participate in global environmental agreements. The principle is reflected in a handful of international environmental agreements and is applicable in the Climate Change convention to require parties to protect the climate system "on the basis of equity and in accordance with their common but differentiated responsibilities and respective capabilities."[29]

The principle of common but differentiated responsibility includes two important elements. The first expresses the common responsibility of states to protect certain environmental resources. The second element relates to the need to take account of differing circumstances, particularly in relation to each state's contribution to the creation of a particular environmental problem and its ability to respond to, prevent, reduce, and control the threat. In practical terms the application of the principle of common but differentiated responsibility has certain important consequences. It entitles, or possibly requires, all concerned states to participate in international response measures aimed at addressing environmental problems. And it leads to the adoption and implementation of environmental standards that impose different commitments for states.

Precautionary Principle. The precautionary principle emerged in international legal instruments only in the mid-1980s, though it had previously been relied upon in some domestic legal systems. It aims to provide guidance to states and the international community in the development of international environmental law and policy in the face of scientific uncertainty and is, potentially, the most radical of environmental principles, generating considerable controversy. Some of its supporters invoke it to justify preemptive international legal measures to address potentially catastrophic environmental threats such as ozone depletion or climate change. Opponents, however, have decried the principle for allowing overregulation of a range of human activities. The core of this emerging legal principle, which has now been endorsed in a number of agreements, is reflected in Principle 15 of the Rio Declaration, one part of which provides that "[w]here there are threats of serious or irreversible damage, lack of full scientific certainty shall not be used as a reason for postponing cost-effective measures to prevent environmental degradation." [30]

Polluter-Pays Principle. The polluter-pays principle refers to the requirement that the costs of pollution be borne by the person or persons responsible for causing the pollution and the consequential costs. The precise meaning, international legal status, and effect of the principle remains open to question, since international practice based upon the principle is limited. It is doubtful whether it has achieved the status of a generally applicable rule of customary international law, except perhaps in relation to states in the European Union (EU), the UN Economic Commission for Europe (UNECE), and the OECD. It has nevertheless attracted broad support and relates closely to the development of rules on civil and state liability for environmental damage, on the permissibility of state subsidies, and the growing acknowledgment by developed countries of the "responsibility that they bear in the international pursuit of sustainable development in view of the pressures their societies place on the global environment," as well as the financial and other consequences that flow from this acknowledgment.[31] Supporting instruments include Principle 14 of the Rio Declaration, OECD Council Recommendations, the EC Treaty of Rome (as amended) and related instruments, and the 1992 agreement establishing the European Economic Area.

Basic Rules and Emerging Legal Standards

As international environmental law has developed, standards have been adopted to address a widening range of environmental resources. These standards tend to address particular resources, of which the most important have been flora and fauna, water quality, air quality, hazardous substances, and waste. Agenda 21 identifies the priority environmental issues and divides them into two categories. The first category addressed the priority needs for the protection and conservation of particular environmental media. These needs are

- the protection of the atmosphere, in particular by combating climate change, depletion of the ozone layer, and ground level and transboundary air pollution;
- protection of land resources, including farmlands, by, for example, combating desertification and drought and protecting mountain ecosystems;
- halting deforestation;

- the conservation of biological diversity;
- the protection of freshwater resources; and
- the protection of oceans and seas (including coastal areas) and marine living resources.

The second category of major issues identified the products of human technological and industrial innovation that are considered to be particularly harmful to the environment and that require international regulation. These are

- the management of biotechnology;
- the management of toxic chemicals, including their international trade;
- agricultural practice;
- the management of hazardous wastes, including their international trade;
- the management of solid wastes and sewage-related issues; and
- the management of radioactive wastes.

The difficulty with an approach that regulates sector by sector is that it tends to transfer harm from one environmental medium to another, or to substitute one form of harm for another. Thus, the prohibition on the dumping of radioactive wastes at sea may result in harm to land-based resources resulting from long-term storage. Efforts to address this problem have led to the emergence of the concept of integrated pollution control, which requires states and other persons to consider and minimize the impact of activities on all environmental resources at each stage of the processes that contribute to that activity.

Protection of Flora and Fauna

The protection of flora and fauna was the subject of the earliest international environmental regulation and there are now widely accepted standards that prohibit interference with endangered species in particular. Important global instruments regulate wetlands, trade in endangered species, and, most recently, the conservation of biodiversity generally (also regulating the sustainable use of the components of biodiversity and the sharing of benefits arising out of the use of genetic resources).[32] However, efforts to adopt a convention on forests at UNCED proved to be fruitless in the face of sustained opposition from many developing countries. Apart from early fisheries conservation agreements, including the regulations adopted by the tribunal in the Pacific Fur Seal Arbitration, regional conservation agreements were adopted as early as 1900 in Africa and 1940 in the Americas.[33] Subsequent arrangements have been put in place in East Africa; Southeast Asia; Europe, including the European Union; the South Pacific; and the Caribbean.[34] Acts adopted by international organizations have contributed significantly to the development of this area of international law. Notable examples include the 1982 decision by the International Whaling Commission to adopt a moratorium on commercial whaling and the 1985 decision of the parties to the 1972 London Dumping Convention to adopt a moratorium on the dumping of radioactive waste at sea.

Protection of the Marine Environment

International law to prevent pollution of oceans and seas is now relatively well developed at the global and regional levels. At the global level the 1982 UN Convention on the Law of the Sea, which entered into force in November 1994, establishes a comprehensive framework to address marine pollution from various sources, including dumping at sea, land-based sources, vessels, and off-shore installations, such as oil rigs.[35] Detailed obligations for these sources of marine pollution have been adopted both prior to and after UNCLOS. At the global level, there are agreements on the dumping of waste at sea, protection of the environment during salvage operations, and oil pollution preparedness and response.[36] However, no global agreement regulates pollution from land-based sources, which is particularly consequential because pollution from this source accounts for more than 70 percent of the total.

At the regional level early agreements addressed dumping from ships and pollution from land-based sources.[37] These have since been supplemented by an extensive network of conventions adopted under the UNEP Regional Seas Programme, which was initiated in 1975 and now includes programs covering ten regional seas: the Caribbean, East Asian, East African, Kuwait, Mediterranean, Red Sea and Gulf of Aden, South Asian, South Pacific, Southeast Pacific, and West and central African. More than 120 coastal states now participate in this UNEP program, and framework conventions and supplementary protocols are in force for the Caribbean, Kuwait, the Mediterranean, the Red Sea and Gulf of Aden, the Southeast Pacific, the South Pacific, and West and central Africa.[38] Additional commitments have been adopted for the EU and Antarctic regions.

Protection of Freshwater Resources

Freshwater resources include rivers, lakes, and groundwaters. Many individual rivers and river systems are now subject to special rules governing their use and the maintenance of the quality of their waters. Noteworthy examples include the Rhine in Europe, the Zambezi in Africa, and the Plate in South America, each of which has been subject to treaty protection for many years. More recently, efforts have been made to develop rules that apply to all rivers in a particular region or to all rivers globally.[39] Lakes have also been subject to protective regimes, especially in North America and other areas where acid rain and other deposits have threatened to cause long-term damage.[40] Protection of groundwaters remains less well developed in international law.

Air Quality

International law for the protection of the atmosphere addresses transboundary air pollution, ozone depletion, and climate change. Measures now place limits for many states on permissible atmospheric emissions of certain substances. This has important implications for production patterns and, particularly, energy use.

In this new area of international regulation, the first instrument was the regional 1979 UNECE Convention on Long-Range Transboundary Air Pollution, which has since been supplemented with protocols on sulphur dioxide, nitrogen oxides, and volatile organic compounds.[41] The transboundary air pollution model has since been relied upon in global efforts to protect the ozone layer with the 1985 Framework Convention for the Protection of the Ozone Layer, as supplemented by a 1987 protocol subsequently amended in 1990 and 1992.[42] The 1992 Framework Convention on Climate Change and its 1997 Kyoto Protocol are also of global application. The 1992 convention entered into force in March 1994, aiming to limit emissions by industrial countries of carbon dioxide and other greenhouse gases, and creating a framework for cooperation and commitments to ensure that greenhouse gas concentrations in the atmosphere do not lead to dangerous anthropogenic interference with the climate system.[43]

Waste

Binding international regulation of waste management is currently limited to regulating or prohibiting trade in certain wastes, as well as the provisions prohibiting the disposal at sea of certain hazardous wastes. These measures encourage waste prevention and minimization by increasing costs and are likely precursors to measures that might limit industrial wastes produced, including packaging.

Three recent agreements establish regulations and prohibitions on trade in hazardous waste. The only global agreement is the 1989 Basel convention, which aims to control traffic and trade in hazardous wastes by requiring importing countries to be notified of, and grant consent for, shipments before they occur (prior informed consent).[44] The 1990 Fourth Lomé Convention, an agreement between the EU and African, Caribbean, and Pacific (ACP) countries, goes beyond the Basel agreement by prohibiting exports and imports between the EU and certain ACP countries.[45] And the 1991 Bamako Convention on the Ban of the Import into Africa and the Control of Transboundary Movement and Management of Hazardous Wastes within Africa, which also prohibits imports, redefines "hazardous waste" to include all substances the use of which is banned in the exporting country.[46] Global regulation of radioactive waste movements is governed by a nonbinding 1990 International Atomic Energy Agency Code of Practice, which establishes regulatory guidelines and is far less stringent than any of the three treaty agreements.[47]

Hazardous Substances

The management of hazardous substances other than waste, including chemicals and pesticides, is not yet subject to any binding global legal instruments. Within the past few years, however, a large body of detailed, non-binding regulations and other instruments dealing with the management of hazardous substances, including in particular international trade and chemical safety at work, have been adopted.[48] The OECD has developed a broad range of recommended practices that address product registration, dealer licensing, classification, packaging, labeling, advertising, international trade, and transport.

Conclusion

As the century draws to a close there is now in place a significant body of principles and rules of international law for the protection of the environment and the conservation of natural resources. The principles, in particular, provide guidance to states and other international actors, but they fall short of giving the clear and practical direction necessary to assist in enhancing environmental conservation. In the next phase of lawmaking in this area the essential issue will be enforcement. And this means not merely the mechanical application of techniques to give effect to principles and norms. Rather, what will be needed is a shift out of the legislative domain and into the judicial and quasi-judicial domain, with international courts and other such bodies filling the gaps left by the legislators. This applies equally to economic instruments and approaches, which inevitably rely on a traditional regulatory structure to establish the framework within which they can be given effect. Judging by recent decisions of the International Court of Justice there is still some way to go before the more established judicial bodies will feel comfortable dealing with environmental issues and providing leadership in this next phase. By contrast, the European Court of Justice and the European Court of Human Rights are beginning to address environmental issues across the range of their competencies. And it may well be that in application of the principle of sustainable development the World Trade Organization dispute settlement bodies may, too, contribute to the further implementation of the essential principles and techniques described in this chapter.

Notes

1. "Request for an Examination of the Situation in Accordance with Paragraph 63 of the Court's Judgment of 20 December 1974 in the Nuclear Tests (*New Zealand v. France*) Case," Order of September 22, 1995, *International Court of Justice Reports* (hereafter *ICJ Reports*) 1995:306, para. 64; *Legality of the Threat or Use of Nuclear Weapons,* Advisory Opinion, July 8, 1996, para. 29.
2. *Legality of the Threat or Use of Nuclear Weapons,* para. 33.
3. See the Rio "Declaration on Environment and Development," Principle 27; *Report of the UN Conference on Environment and Development,* A/CONF.151/26/Rev.1, 2:3 (1993), reprinted in *International Legal Materials* (hereafter *ILM*) 31 (1992): 874. As

an international legal concept, "sustainable development" remains in an early stage of development. Thus, although references to "sustainable development" and international law abound in Agenda 21, none of the formulations apparently follow that of Principle 27 ("international law in the field of sustainable development"), and there remain occasional references to "international environmental law." Whether the variable terminology arises by accident or design is unclear. Anecdotal evidence suggests that the head of the Brazilian delegation persuaded Working Group III of UNCED's Preparatory Committee to replace every reference to "international environmental law" in Agenda 21 to "international law in the field of sustainable development" (the diplomat Pedro Motta Pinto Coelho apparently remarked that this change would "keep you lawyers busy well into the 21st century": see Philippe Sands, *Principles of International Environmental Law* (Manchester, England: Manchester University Press, 1995), 17.

4. Philip Allott, *Eunomia: New Order for a New World* (New York: Oxford University Press, 1990), para. 17.52.

5. World Commission on Environment and Development, *Our Common Future* (New York: Oxford University Press, 1987), 4.

6. See "Great Britain v. United States," *Moore's Report of International Arbitration Awards* 1 (1893): 755.

7. See generally Philippe Sands, "The Environment, Community, and International Law," *Harvard International Law Journal* 30 (1989): 393.

8. "Agenda 21," chap. 38, paras. 38.42 to 38.44.

9. For a general history of international environmental law, see Sands, *Principles of International Environmental Law.*

10. For the agreements that were adopted nevertheless, see ibid., 26.

11. *United Nations Yearbook, 1948–1949* (New York: United Nations, 1950), 481–482.

12. UN General Assembly Resolution 800 (IX), December 14, 1954; the conference report is in *International Protection of the Environment* 8:3969. "Convention on the High Seas," Geneva, April 29, 1958, United Nations Treaty Series, *Treaties and International Agreements Registered or Filed or Reported with the Secretariat of the United Nations* (hereafter cited as UNTS), 450:82; "Convention on Fishing and Conservation of the Living Resources of the High Seas," Geneva, April 29, 1958, UNTS, 559:285; "Convention on the Continental Shelf," Geneva, April 29, 1958, UNTS, 499:311.

13. UN General Assembly Resolution 912 (X), December 3, 1955. "Treaty Banning Nuclear Weapon Tests in the Atmosphere, in Outer Space, and Under Water," Moscow, August 5, 1963, UNTS, 480:43. Nuclear test cases: Australia v. France, *ICJ Reports* 1974:253; New Zealand v. France, *ICJ Reports* 1974:457. These years also saw the adoption of the first global conventions on oil pollution prevention, high seas intervention for clean-up, liability and compensation, high seas fishing and conservation, and the protection of wetlands; see "International Conventions for the Prevention of Pollution of the Sea by Oil," London, May 12, 1954, UNTS, 327:3; "International Convention Relating to Intervention on the High Seas in Cases of Oil Pollution Damage," Brussels, November 29, 1969, reprinted in *ILM* 9 (1970): 25; "International Convention on Civil Liability for Oil Pollution Damage," Brussels, November 29, 1969, UNTS, 973:3; "International Convention on the Establishment of an International Fund for Compensation for Oil Pollution Damage," Brussels, December 18, 1971, reprinted in *ILM* 11 (1972): 284.

14. *Report of the U.N. Conference on the Human Environment,* UN Doc. A/CONF/48/14 at 2-65, and Corr. 1 (1972), reprinted in *ILM* 11 (1972): 1416. For an excellent account of the conference and the Declaration, see Louis B. Sohn, "The Stockholm Declaration on the Human Environment," *Harvard International Law Journal* 423 (1973).

15. "United Nations Convention on the Law of the Sea," Montego Bay, December 10, 1982, reprinted in *ILM* 21 (1982): 1261.

16. "Convention on the Conservation of Migratory Species of Wild Animals," Bonn, June 23, 1979, reprinted in *ILM* 19 (1980): 15; "Convention on the Conservation of European Wildlife and Natural Habitats," Berne, September 19, 1979, United Kingdom Treaty Series, 56 (1982) Cmnd, 8738; "Convention on Long-Range Transboundary Air Pollution," Geneva, November 13, 1979, reprinted in *ILM* 18 (1979): 1442.

17. For more details see Sands, *Principles of International Environmental Law*, 39.

18. UN General Assembly Resolution 42/187, December 11, 1987, endorsement of World Commission on Environment and Development, *Our Common Future*; UN General Assembly Resolution 43/196, December 20, 1988.

19. *ILM* 31 (1992): 881; *Report of the United Nations Conference on Environment and Development*, vol. 1.

20. *ILM* 31 (1992): 822, 849.

21. For more details see Sands, *Principles of International Environmental Law*, 48–61, esp. 58.

22. For the general distinction between rules and principles see Ronald Dworkin, *Taking Rights Seriously* (Cambridge: Harvard University Press, 1977), 24, 26.

23. "Request for an Examination of the Situation in accordance with paragraph 63 of the Court's Judgement of 20 December 1984 in the Nuclear Tests (New Zealand v. France) Case," *ICJ Reports* 1995:306.

24. *Legality of the Threat or Use of Nuclear Weapons*, para. 29. See also "Case Concerning the Gabcikovo-Nagymaros Project" (Hungary/Slovakia), *ICJ Reports* 1997, paras. 53 and 112.

25. Permanent Court of Arbitration, Palmas Case (1928), *HCR* 2:93. "United States v. Canada," *Reports of International Arbitral Awards* 3 (1941): 1907; citing Clyde Eagleton, *Responsibility of States* (New York: New York University Press, 1928), 80.

26. See original Hungarian Application, October 22, 1992, paras. 27, 29, and 30, in *Documents in International Environmental Law*, ed. Philippe Sands, Richard Tarasofsky, and Mary Weiss, vol. 2A (Manchester, England: Manchester University Press, 1995), 691, doc. 28.

27. "Case Concerning the Gabcikovo-Nagymaros Project," para. 140.

28. World Commission on Environment and Development, *Our Common Future*.

29. Art. 3(1), *ILM* 31 (1992): 881.

30. See in addition suggestions of Judge Weeramantry in his Dissenting Opinion in "Nuclear Test II," *ICJ Reports* 1995:342.

31. "Declaration on Environment and Development," Principle 7.

32. "Convention on Wetlands of International Importance," Ramsar, Iran, February 2, 1971, UNTS, 996:245; *Report of the U.N. Conference on the Human Environment*, reprinted in *ILM* 31 (1992).

33. Allott, *Eunomia*; the regional African agreements have now been superseded by the African "Convention on the Conservation of Nature and Natural Resources," Algiers, September 15, 1968, UNTS, 1001:4; Sands, "The Environment, Community, and International Law," *Harvard International Law Journal* 1989:393–420.

34. See the "Nairobi Protocol Concerning Protected Areas and Wild Fauna and Flora in the Eastern African Region," June 21, 1985, *International Environmental Law Multinational Treaties* 985:47; "ASEAN Agreement on the Conservation of Nature and Natural Resources," Kuala Lumpur, July 9, 1985, *Environmental Policy and Law* 15 (1985): 64; Council Directive 79/409/EEC of April 2, 1979, on the conservation of wild birds, *Official Journal*, L series, 1031 (April 25, 1979): 1; Council Directive 92/43/EEC of May 21, 1992, on the conservation of natural habitats and of wild flora and fauna, *Official Journal*, L series, 206 (July 22, 1992): 7; "Convention for the Protection of the Natural Resources and Environment of the South Pacific Region," Nouméa, New Caledonia, November 24, 1986, reprinted in *ILM* 26 (1987): 38; "Protocol Concerning Specially Protected Areas and Wildlife in the Wider Caribbean

Region," Kingston, Jamaica, January 18, 1990, *Yearbook of International Environmental Law* 1 (1990): 441.

35. "Convention on the Prevention of Marine Pollution by Dumping of Wastes and Other Matter," December 29, 1982, UNTS, 1046:120.

36. "International Convention Relating to Intervention on the High Seas in Cases of Oil Pollution Damage," Brussels, November 29, 1969, reprinted in *ILM* 9 (1970): 25; "International Convention on Salvage," London, April 28, 1989, *International Journal of Estuarine and Coastal Law* 1989:300; "International Convention on Oil Pollution Preparedness, Response, and Co-operation," London, November 30, 1990, *ILM* 30 (1991): 733.

37. "Convention for the Prevention of Marine Pollution by Dumping from Ships and Aircraft," Oslo, February 15, 1972, UNTS, 932:3; "Convention for the Prevention of Marine Pollution from Land-Based Sources," Paris, June 4, 1974, reprinted in *ILM* 13 (1974): 352.

38. See generally, UNEP, "Status of Regional Agreements Negotiated in the Framework of the Regional Seas Programme," Nairobi, August 1990.

39. "Convention on Long-Range Transboundary Air Pollution," reprinted in *ILM* 18 (1979): 1442; "ILC Draft Articles on the Law of Non-Navigational Uses of International Watercourses," reprinted in *ILM* 30 (1991): 1575.

40. "Agreement between the United States and Canada Concerning the Water Quality of the Great Lakes," Ottawa, April 15, 1972, reprinted in *ILM* 11 (1972): 694.

41. "Convention for the Protection of World Cultural and Natural Heritage," Paris, November 16, 1972, reprinted in *ILM* 11 (1972): 1358; "Protocol on the Reduction of Sulphur Emissions or Their Transboundary Fluxes by at Least Thirty Percent," Helsinki, July 8, 1985, reprinted in *ILM* 27 (1987): 707; "Protocol Concerning the Control of Emissions of Nitrogen Oxides or Their Transboundary Fluxes," Sofia, October 31, 1988, reprinted in *ILM* 28 (1988): 214; "Protocol on the Control of Emissions of Volatile Organic Compounds and Their Transboundary Fluxes," Geneva, November 18, 1991, reprinted in *ILM* 31 (1992): 568.

42. "Framework Convention for the Protection of the Ozone Layer," Vienna, March 22, 1985, reprinted in *ILM* 26 (1987): 1529; "Protocol on Substances That Deplete the Ozone Layer," Montreal, September 16, 1987, reprinted in *ILM* 26 (1987): 1550.

43. *ILM* 31 (1992): 881.

44. "Convention on the Control of Transboundary Movements of Hazardous Wastes and Their Disposal," Basel, March 22, 1989, reprinted in *ILM* 28 (1989): 649.

45. Lomé, December 15, 1989, *ILM* 29 (1990): 783, Articles 39 and 40.

46. "Convention on the Ban of the Import into Africa and the Control of Transboundary Movement and Management of Hazardous Wastes within Africa," Bamako, January 30, 1991, reprinted in *ILM* 30 (1991): 775.

47. International Atomic Energy Agency, Doc. GC(XXXIV)/920, June 27, 1990, *Yearbook of International Environmental Law* 1 (1990): 537.

48. 1985 UN Food and Agriculture Organization Code of Conduct on the Distribution and Use of Pesticides; 1987 UNEP London Guidelines for the Exchange of Information on Chemicals in International Trade, as amended in 1989. "Convention Concerning Safety in the Use of Chemicals at Work," Geneva, June 24, 1990, *Yearbook of International Environmental Law* 1 (1990): 295.

7

Compliance with International Environmental Agreements

Michael Faure and Jürgen Lefevere

The United Nations Conference on the Human Environment, held in Stockholm in 1972, set off an unprecedented development of new international environmental treaties. Before 1972 only a dozen international treaties with relevance to the environment were in force; twenty-five years later more than a thousand such instruments could be counted.

With the intensified use of international treaties as a means to combat environmental degradation, concerns have arisen regarding the compliance of states with the commitments to which they agreed. Even within relatively strong regional organizations such as the European Union, compliance problems are more and more overshadowing successes in the adoption of new instruments. In a hearing some years ago by the British House of Lords on the subject, a member of the European Parliament even warned that "we have now reached the point in the EC where, if we do not tackle implementation and enforcement properly, there seems very little point in producing new environmental law."[1]

In recent decades new approaches to the drafting, adoption, implementation, operation, and enforcement of international environmental treaties have been attempted in an effort to improve the compliance of states with international environmental treaties. This chapter will give a brief overview of the problems experienced with treaty compliance and the solutions sought, both in theory and in practice. The findings of this chapter will be related to three international treaty regimes, the Montreal Protocol on Substances That Deplete the Ozone Layer, the United Nations Framework Convention on Climate Change (FCCC), and the EU environmental regime. In addition, other examples of environmental treaties will be given as well.

First, we will discuss the theory of compliance as it has been developed in recent literature and in practice.[2] Second, we will give an overview of the sources of compliance and noncompliance. Then we will examine the methods developed to improve compliance with international environmental treaties. We will end with some concluding remarks.

Theory of Compliance

The term *compliance* is often not used in a consistent way, but confused with related terminology such as *implementation, effectiveness,* or even *enforcement.* To avoid unnecessary confusion, however, one should be careful in using these terms. *Implementation, compliance, enforcement,* and *effectiveness* refer to different aspects of the process of achieving international political and legal cooperation.

Implementation refers to the specific actions (including legislative, organizational, and practical actions) that states take to make international treaties operative in their national legal system. Implementation therefore establishes the link between the national legal system and the international obligations. The aim of establishing this link should be compliance. *Compliance* is generally defined as the extent to which the behavior of a state, party to international treaty, actually conforms to the conditions set out in this treaty. Some authors make a distinction between compliance with the treaty's explicit rules and compliance with the treaty's objective.[3] It is, however, difficult to assess compliance with the "spirit" of an agreement, since this evaluation can be quite subjective. The third term, *enforcement,* indicates the methods that are available to force states to implement but also to comply with treaty obligations. Where compliance and implementation concern the actions of the states themselves, *effectiveness* is more concerned with, as the term indicates, the effect of the treaty as a whole. *Effectiveness* addresses the question whether treaties that are correctly complied with actually achieve the objectives stated in the treaty, or whether the treaty actually helped to reach the environmental goal for which it was designed.

The terms *compliance* and *effectiveness* are often used interchangeably, but in fact have very distinct meanings. Compliance is in most cases a condition for effectiveness, if by *effectiveness* we understand the reaching of the treaty's goals. If a treaty is complied with, however, it does not automatically mean that it is effective in reaching the environmental goal for which it was originally designed. Effectiveness also depends on the actual treaty design, the instruments and goals contained in the treaty, as well as other external factors, such as a changing political situation or even changing environmental conditions. An example of this could be the Montreal Protocol: compliance with that document can be perfect, but the protocol itself can be ineffective in reducing harm to the ozone layer. Hence, compliance is only a proxy for effectiveness: greater compliance will usually lead to environmental improvement, but whether this is actually the case will to a large extent depend upon the contents of the treaty concerned. One could even imagine a treaty that is so badly drafted that noncompliance would even contribute to its effectiveness. This ironic result is reached in treaties that on paper protect the environment (or potential victims) but that in fact protect industrial operators, for example, by introducing financial caps on their liability. One could argue that potential victims would be better off in cases of noncompliance, but this is obviously true only in those cases where special interests (and not primarily environmental concerns) dictated the contents of the treaty.

We will concentrate here on the issue of compliance as a requirement for an effective treaty. The issue of compliance is receiving increasing attention in recent practice and scholarly writing. This increasing attention has led to the development of a new approach to the compliance issue. The traditional view of compliance was very much connected to the principle of sovereignty of states. According to this principle states are sovereign actors in the international arena, meaning that they are free to act as they find necessary, unrestricted by any external authority or rules. Starting from this principle of sovereignty one tended to believe that governments therefore accepted only those international treaties that were in their own interest. A breach of these treaties was thus not seen as likely. If a state was in breach of its treaty obligations, it was usually considered to be intentional. Enforcement measures were thus often limited and considered to be severe actions. Examples of these enforcement measures are the state complaints procedures, where states can file an official complaint against the violating state, or trade sanctions. Because of the gravity of these sanctions, however, they are hardly ever applied in practice. Even in the European context direct complaints of one state against another are still highly exceptional.[4]

In recent scholarly writings this traditional view of compliance problems is now being abandoned. This change of view goes hand in hand with the new approach to sovereignty. States are no longer seen as completely sovereign entities but have to accept limitations on their originally sovereign rights, for the benefit of the environment, future generations, or the international community as a whole.[5] The international community is increasingly organized in *regimes*.[6] These regimes consist of a framework of a relatively well developed set of rules and unwritten norms concerning a specific subject matter. The development of regimes can be placed between the traditional concept of sovereignty, leaving the states unbound, and a comprehensive world order, placing the states within a new world governance. Examples of important regimes are the climate change regime, constructed around the FCCC, and the world trade regime, based on the General Agreement on Tariffs and Trade (GATT; now the World Trade Organization, or WTO) rules. With the development of these regimes "sovereignty no longer consists in the freedom of states to act independently, in their perceived self-interest, but in membership in reasonably good standing in the regimes that make up the substance of international life."[7] States' interests are increasingly determined by their membership in, but also good reputation under, these regimes.

The new approach to compliance tries to place compliance problems in this increasingly complicated international context, with a multitude of regimes, interdependent actors, and different interests and obligations. Within this new context many factors can lead countries to conclude treaties. These factors also affect the states' willingness and, more important, their ability, to comply with the obligations. In this more complex perception of compliance, the actors at the international level can no longer be seen as utilitarian decision makers weighing the benefits and costs of compliance. The compliance record of states is influenced by a large number of factors, in which the willful desire to violate rules plays only a minor role. Often it is rather practical obstacles, outside this will or control of states, that make compliance difficult.

This new concept of compliance also necessitates new solutions to compliance problems. The traditional sanction mechanisms, based on the notion that states intentionally do not comply, have proven largely ineffective. Moreover, some of these are now often unlawful under other international arrangements. Military action is strictly regulated under international law and now only allowed in a limited number of situations.[8] Economic sanctions become increasingly difficult to apply with the development of an increasingly comprehensive international trade regime. Approaches to compliance problems now need to take into account the actual abilities of states to comply, and sanctions for noncompliance need to be developed that fit within the new international regimes. Solutions for compliance problems need to be based more on what is referred to as a "managerial approach" rather than on a more traditional "enforcement approach."[9]

Sources of Compliance and Noncompliance

Having discussed the theory of compliance in general, we will now address a few factors that may affect compliance with environmental agreements and possible sources of noncompliance.

Country Characteristics

The chances of compliance with international environmental accords will first of all depend to a large extent upon the characteristics of the parties involved in negotiating and adopting international environmental treaties, that is, the states concerned. These country characteristics—but also the relationship between the various states involved in the treaty-negotiating process—will have an impact on the chances of treaty adoption; in addition, they will have a considerable influence on the chances of compliance.

There may be many reasons why states sign treaties but nevertheless do not comply. States may sign an agreement because of international pressure or to serve domestic interests. Domestic interests, however, may also oppose compliance. Hence, it may well be in the states' interest to sign the agreement but not to comply. Moreover, compliance with international environmental agreements seldom is a black or white situation: states may view most provisions of a treaty in their interest, thus complying with those provisions and violating a few others.

Other factors that may play a role are, for example, the cultural traditions, the political system, and the administrative capacities of the country concerned, as well as economic factors. Also the strength of nongovernmental organizations (NGOs), an issue that we will discuss below, may influence compliance.

An important question is whether a country has a democratic form of government. Many features of democratic governments contribute to improved implementation and compliance. There may be more transparency and hence easier monitoring by citizens who can bring pressure to improve the implementation record. Also NGOs generally have more freedom to operate in democratic countries. Hence, it could be argued that democracies do have a number of features that may facilitate compliance.

A considerable role can also be played by individuals, such as the heads of state. In many cases the personal enthusiasm of a particular head of state has facilitated compliance, usually during the treaty negotiating process.[10]

As was indicated above, compliance may also fail because of incapacity. This could be due to the country's lack of administrative capacity to implement the treaty, which in turn may have to do, for example, with the level of education and training of the bureaucrats. The level of administrative capacity is also dependent upon another factor, economic resources. In addition, sometimes compliance with treaties requires investment in technologies that countries with less resources simply lack.

Role of NGOs

We already indicated that the political system of a country can have a bearing on the compliance record because democracies may have a stronger tendency to allow activities of NGOs.[11] NGO activity can beneficially influence the compliance record of a country in various ways. In the first place international environmental NGOs may influence international public opinion, shaping the agenda that determines the issues to be dealt with in a treaty. For instance, activities of NGOs contributed, through an increasing pressure on the international community, to the agreement on the Framework Convention on Climate Change, leading to the adoption of the Kyoto Protocol in December 1997. Once a treaty has come into being, NGOs can play a crucial role in ensuring compliance. As watchdogs they can pressure their governments to uphold the key provisions of specific regimes. This so-called bottom-up approach to compliance is increasingly stressed in the literature.[12] The role of NGOs here also illustrates that their actions can lead to what is referred to as "compliance as self-interest," or at least nontreaty induced. Through pressure by environmental groups public opinion may be influenced in such a manner that the country views the costs of a potential violation of treaty provisions as prohibitively high.[13]

Finally, NGOs can also provide information about activities that are addressed in international environmental treaties. Greenpeace, for instance, is an important source of information about ocean dumping.[14] Hence, NGO activity may foster transparency both at the negotiating and at the implementation and compliance stages.

These factors generally merit the conclusion that the stronger and more active NGOs are with respect to the issue area of the treaty, the larger the probability of compliance.

Number of States and the "International Environment"

The third aspect relates to the number of states involved in the treaty and the pressure that other signatory states can exercise toward compliance of all. The greater the number of countries that have ratified an accord, and the greater the extent of their implementation and compliance, the greater also the probability will be of compliance by any individual country. Non-compliance would then run counter to international public opinion.[15] There is also a relationship between the area to be regulated in the environmental treaty and the number of countries that can be expected to comply. For instance, the international whaling commission faces a trade-off between, on the one hand, maintaining a moratorium on commercial whaling in a treaty to which fewer countries are willing to be parties, or on the other hand, allowing some commercial whaling to keep a larger number of countries under the scope of the treaty and thus achieving a higher compliance record.[16] Thus, having a large number of countries accept the contents of a treaty comes at a price, and it may lead to a lowering of the standard to be achieved.

The general "international environment" will have an influence on the willingness of a country to engage in the treaty obligations and on the subsequent compliance record as well. This can be analyzed in terms of the "free riding" and "prisoners' dilemma" problems.[17] *Free riding* relates to the fact that individual states may hope that others will take the necessary measures to reduce the sources of a transboundary pollution problem, thus "free riding" on their efforts. The game-theoretical prisoners' dilemma in this context refers to the fact that although mutual compliance may be in the interest of all states in order, for example, to reduce transboundary industrial pollution, the absence of enforcement may lead all parties to believe that they can violate. Because of these problems enforcement was traditionally advocated to guarantee compliance.

Compliance also depends on the distribution of power among nations, which can influence individual states' compliance strategies. A dominant state, perceiving sufficient benefits from complying, may force compliance by other, weaker states.[18] In those cases compliance does not even require explicit enforcement: the power of the dominant states can lead the weaker ones to comply. Obviously, the division of power between states may change. These changes in the asymmetries of power will also produce changes in the incentives to comply.[19]

Moreover, states sign numerous international treaties. Usually, negotiations concerning treaties and compliance concern situations in which similar states will encounter each other repeatedly in the context of various treaties (often referred to as repeat player games); such multiple encounters may have a beneficial influence on compliance. Thus the fear of free riding can be overcome if the record of compliance is related to potential benefits for states in existing and future international agreements.[20] In other words, states may comply because future agreements with the same partner states will be possible if they have an acceptable compliance record.

This "international environment" perspective underscores the point made in the "Theory of Compliance" section above that states increasingly belong to various "regimes," which engage them in a repeat player game. Hence, the incentives to comply may emerge from these regimes, reducing the need for formal enforcement of one particular treaty.

Primary Rule System

The most important factor determining the likelihood of compliance is probably the primary rule system. The primary rule system is the actual contents of the treaty that is agreed upon by the parties. This primary rule system defines the behavior that is required by the specific treaty, or in other words, the duties imposed upon the participatory states under the specific treaty. The primary rules are directly related to the activity that the environmental accord is supposed to regulate. Even during the negotiations, when the primary rules are defined, the degree of treaty compliance can be determined to a large extent.

A first important aspect of the design of the primary rule system relates to whether it requires any behavioral change, what the costs of this change will be, and by whom this behavioral change is required. It is easier to achieve compliance if the degree of behavioral change and the costs of this change are low. It is therefore argued that, for instance, compliance with the FCCC might be harder to achieve than compliance with the Montreal Protocol, since more people and industries must make bigger behavioral changes. The Montreal Protocol mainly requires behavioral changes by the producers of a limited number of regulated substances. The goals of the FCCC, however, require large-scale behavioral changes, not only by industry, but also by individuals.

There are a number of cases where treaty rules require no change in behavior of the industry in a specific country. This is often the case when industry is already meeting a specific pollution (for example, emissions) standard. Those industries may even lobby in favor of treaties that will impose on their foreign competitors the standards the industries already have to comply with at the national level.[21] In those cases the industries already meeting the specific standard will obviously easily comply, since the treaty in that particular case merely erects a barrier to entry for the foreign competitors.

In some cases the treaties are clearly in the interest of industry for other reasons. One example is the treaties relating to liability for nuclear accidents and oil pollution. On paper these treaties serve the interests of victims, but in fact the contents are often such that the liability of operators is limited (for example, through financial caps). The nuclear liability conventions that originated at the end of the 1950s came into being as a reaction against the growing nuclear industry's fear of unlimited liability. Hence, compliance with the conventions, which included limited liability of nuclear operators, was relatively high.[22]

The amount of detail or specificity of a treaty may affect future compliance. States can facilitate their own compliance by negotiating vague and ambiguous rules, for example, if they agree to provisions that seem to be in the environmental interest on paper but are sufficiently vague to allow business as usual. However, primary rules can also often increase compliance through greater specificity. Specific obligations make compliance easier by reducing the uncertainty about what states need to do to comply. Specific treaty language will, moreover, remove the possibility of the excuse of inadvertence and misinterpretation in case of noncompliance. Moreover, the advantage of conventions with relatively precise obligations (such as the Montreal Protocol) is that it is easier to judge whether states do in fact comply. If the obligations are vaguer, assessing implementation and compliance becomes more difficult.

One obvious remedy to inadvertence as a source of noncompliance is, therefore, to draft specific, detailed obligations. These, together with an information campaign, can at least prevent the situation of states justifying noncompliance by the lack of information or clarity with respect to their obligations. A general formulation of the obligations may, however, be unavoidable in some cases simply because political consensus may not support more precision. Article 4(2)(a) of the FCCC is an example of diplomatically formulated "obligations." The article leaves unclear whether there is any specific obligation at all.[23]

When discussing the country characteristics, we indicated that one source of noncompliance may be the incapacity of states to fulfill the treaty obligations due to a lack of resources or a lack of technological abilities. Hence, when these problems are recognized during the drafting stage, noncompliance may be prevented by designing the primary rules in such a manner that differing capacities are taken into account. This can either take the form of a differentiation of the treaty obligations, related to the various capacities or of a transfer of resources or technologies. This is, again, an example of a managerial approach, where instead of blunt sanctions instruments are developed that take into account the varying capacities and thus prevent noncompliance in the treaty design stage.

The idea of differentiated standards according to a state's capacities is predominant in the FCCC. This convention divides its signatory states in different categories, imposing different obligations for each group. Although all signatory states commit themselves to the general commitments, such as developing national greenhouse gas inventories, only the developed states and states in transition that are listed in Annex I of the FCCC are required to stabilize their emissions. Annex II lists the developed countries that additionally need to provide for financial resources to facilitate compliance by developing countries.[24] The transfer of funds from developed to developing states can also be observed in other treaties. The Montreal Protocol, for instance, provides for a framework within which financial support as well as transfer of technology is possible. The EU uses the instrument of structural funds to promote economic and social development of disadvantaged regions within the EU.

One concept used in the area of climate change, which also takes into account differing abilities of states, is joint implementation. When a treaty contains specific obligations (for example, concerning emissions reduction), joint implementation implies that one state can fulfill its emission reduction goals by investing in pollution reduction in a second state, in which the marginal costs of emission reduction are lower.[25] Joint implementation is somewhat similar to the economic concept of "tradeable emission rights" to the extent that it causes a flow of "emission rights" to industrial states in exchange for financial aid and technologies to developing countries. Hence, this can also remedy the incapacity problem. Instruments such as financial or technology transfer mechanisms all should facilitate compliance.

The only problem with these inducements is that they are vulnerable to "moral hazard." Moral hazard refers to the fact that the incentives for the prevention of emissions may be diluted if states are subsidized through financial or technological transfers. States may indeed misrepresent their abilities in order to have others pay for their compliance costs. The approach of using differentiated standards and financial and technological transfers lies at the basis of the more comprehensive noncompliance response systems that we will discuss below (see box on the Montreal Protocol as an example of the managerial approach).

Reporting and Information

The likelihood of compliance will also depend upon informational issues. Information plays a role at several stages. First, accurate information on the environmental risks concerned seems important both for the chances of adoption of a treaty on the specific subject and to the likelihood of compliance. Second, information plays a role in increasing the transparency of implementation and compliance records of states through monitoring or reporting systems.

With respect to the first aspect, it is broadly assumed that the more information there is about an environmental issue, the more effective implementation and compliance will be.[26] This understanding is rather straightforward: the clearer the activities and risks that are the subject of the treaty are presented, the easier it will be to build political pressure (through, among others, NGOs) via public opinion to induce compliance. One of the reasons that the swift adoption of the Montreal Protocol came as a surprise to the international community was the fact that it was adopted in a time of still important scientific uncertainties surrounding the causes and effects of the changing ozone layer.[27] Scientific uncertainties about the causes, existence, and effects of climate change are still influencing to an important extent the negotiations concerning climate change. The scientific reports of the Intergovernmental Panel on Climate Change play an important role in forming international consensus about the problem. Still, some states and industries persistently deny the existence of a problem altogether.[28]

With regard to the second aspect, information increases the transparency of implementation and compliance records of states. If it is known that states do not comply, international and domestic groups can take actions aimed at improving a state's compliance. Whether there is transparency with respect to the compliance record will to a large extent depend upon the complexity of the issue covered by the treaty and upon the democratic character of the complying state. Transparency can lead to public pressure to increase compliance. In this respect one can think of the actions of NGOs to identify noncompliance. These actions toward transparency can increase compliance even without formal sanctions. Transparency is considered to be an almost universal element of compliance management strategy. Indeed, NGOs can provide valuable information (thus increasing transparency) on violations, thereby giving incentives for compliance without a need for formal sanctioning. Also, domestic environmental groups can point at noncompliance by states or multinational corporations, thus increasing the costs of noncompliance.[29]

Transparency can be achieved through an effective compliance information system that is laid down in the treaty. To a large extent treaties rely on self-reporting by states. As we have already seen above, in a regime system with often delicate political links and pressures, the "status" of a state is often very important. States are generally careful about "losing face" toward other states and toward their own population. This fear of losing face has traditionally been used in many treaties, including those outside the field of the environment, by imposing a requirement for the state to report on its compliance with the treaty. This report would then allow other states and citizens to hold it accountable for its compliance record. Although reporting procedures can be found in most environmental treaties, they are often vaguely formulated and the reports are badly drafted. Hence the reporting procedure is often criticized for its "weak" character and the absence of sanctions in case of noncompliance with the reporting requirements.

Self-reporting is also criticized, however, because it may lead to self-incrimination. If states take their duties with respect to self-reporting seriously, they should report their own noncompliance. The hesitancy of states to incriminate themselves may be one of the reasons why the reporting requirements of environmental treaties are often violated. Moreover, governments, particularly of smaller states, are sometimes overburdened with administrative tasks, and filing reports is seen as yet another burden. Reporting by states is, therefore, a first step, but obviously no guarantee of compliance.[30]

Compliance can be improved through monitoring by an independent third party. The likelihood of compliance will indeed to a large extent be influenced by the possibilities provided for in the treaty to monitor compliance effectively. This in turn also depends on the contents of the primary

The Montreal Protocol . . .

The approach to international environmental treaty design has changed in the past decades, mainly because of the new, more realistic "managerial" approach. Prime examples of this new approach are the Vienna Convention for the Protection of the Ozone Layer and, more important, its subsequent Montreal Protocol on Substances That Deplete the Ozone Layer, adopted under this convention, are used.

The Vienna Convention was adopted in 1985. This convention did not contain any substantive commitments for the states but provided for a general framework, including the possibility of adopting protocols in the Conference of the Parties, the main institution set up under the convention. Only two years after the adoption of the convention the 1987 Montreal Protocol on Substances That Deplete the Ozone Layer was adopted under the Vienna Convention. The Vienna Convention and more particularly its Montreal Protocol surprised the international community by their swift adoption, their specific goals, their effectiveness, and the large and still increasing number of states party to it (163 as of January 1997). One of the main reasons given for this effectiveness is the design of the treaty system. This system has several "modern" characteristics that make it very suitable for dealing with environmental problems in the modern international context. In many of the more recent international environmental treaties the Vienna/Montreal system is used as a model. One of the main reasons is the flexibility of its primary rule system.

The Vienna Convention establishes the Conference of the Parties (Article 6), which is to meet "at regular intervals," in practice every three to four years. The Montreal Protocol adds to this Conference of the Parties a Meeting of the Parties. These meetings now are held annually to discuss the implementation of the commitments and possible improvements to or adoption of new commitments. They are organized by the Ozone Secretariat, set up under Article 7 of the Vienna Convention and Article 12 of the Montreal Protocol. The regular convening of the Conference of the Parties has proven very useful in keeping the treaty objectives on the political agenda and has ensured a continuous updating of the treaty goals and standards. The continuous updating of the treaty goals and standards was made possible by the framework structure chosen by the Vienna Convention. Although this framework structure was not new (it was also used in the 1979 UN-ECE Convention on Long-Range

rules. The Montreal Protocol, for instance, regulated the production of chlorofluorocarbons (CFCs) because it was easier to monitor a few producers than thousands of consumers.

Some treaties, such as those on nuclear weapons, allow on-site monitoring. This obviously is one of the most effective instruments to control whether states not only formally adopt legislation implementing a treaty, but also in fact comply with the contents. On-site monitoring is, however, still heavily debated, since it constitutes an important infringement on state sovereignty. Even in the EU, on-site monitoring by a European authority of member state violations of environmental directives is still not allowed. The compliance record will inevitably depend upon the ability to monitor violations. This brought Gro Harlem Brundtland, the Norwegian prime minister

... A "Managerial" Primary Rule System

Transboundary Air Pollution), it proved particularly effective. Whereas the Vienna Convention only lays down the framework for further negotiations, the real commitments are laid down in the Montreal Protocol, the first and, to date, only adopted protocol under this convention. At the meetings of the parties to the conference unexpected agreement could be reached on a regular updating of the protocol. The Montreal Protocol has in its short existence already seen three adjustments and amendments, in 1990 at the London meeting, in 1992 at the Copenhagen meeting (at which the timetable for a total phase-out of ozone depleting substances was accelerated), and most recently in September 1997 at the Montreal meeting. This shows how the likelihood of compliance can be influenced in the treaty design stage, by adopting primary rules that allow for flexibility.

The Montreal Protocol also provides an example of how the individual capacities of states may determine this willingness to accept treaty obligations in the first place. India and China would not become parties to the Montreal Protocol until the agreement about compensatory financing had been adopted at the London meeting in 1990. This agreement provided for financial support to developing states in return for and in order to allow these states to become party to the protocol and actually be financially capable of complying with its obligations.

Under the Montreal Protocol various instruments have been developed to remedy the incapacity problem: a Multilateral Fund was set up (Article 10) in order to provide this financial assistance. The implementing agencies of this fund—the International Bank for Reconstruction and Development (World Bank), the United Nations Environment Programme, and the United Nations Development Programme—draw up "country programmes" and "country studies" consisting of a combination of financial support, assistance, and training. Furthermore, the Montreal Protocol provides for the transfer of technology under its Article 10A. On the basis of this article all states party to the protocol "shall take every practicable step" to ensure that "the best available, environmentally safe substitutes and related technologies are expeditiously transferred" to developing countries (as defined in Article 5[1] of the protocol) and that those transfers "occur under fair and most favourable conditions."

and chair of the World Commission on Environment and Development, to recommend the establishment of "an international authority with the power to verify actual emission and to react with legal measures if there are violations of the rules" in order to ensure compliance with carbon dioxide emission targets.[31]

The problems with reporting procedures have led to the development of *compliance information systems*.[32] Such compliance information systems contain elaborate procedures for the provision of information by member states, the possible review of this information by independent experts, and the availability of this information to the general public. By developing a more elaborate and transparent system for the provision of information on the compliance of member states with a treaty, the accountability of member states automatically increases.

For example, the FCCC contains in Articles 4 and 12 elaborate provisions concerning member states' communication of their implementation of the convention. Although the word *reporting* is avoided in the context of the convention and replaced by the word *communicate*, these communications have the character of national reports. The first FCCC Conference of the Parties (COP 1) in 1995 promulgated guidelines for the preparation of national communications, and more important, procedures were adopted for the in-depth review of individual reports from Annex I countries. At COP 2, which took place in July 1996 in Geneva, more extensive guidelines were drawn up for the country reports. By May 15, 1997, thirty-two in-depth reviews of national communications from Annex I countries were drawn up by experts. Although written in "non-confrontational language" (Decision 2/COP1) the in-depth review procedure does provide an important impetus for member states to increase the efforts of complying. All national communications and the in-depth reviews are collected by the FCCC Secretariat in Bonn (Germany). Under Article 12(10) of the FCCC the Secretariat makes these communications publicly available. The Secretariat has improved the availability to the public by publishing these reports on the Internet at the Secretariat's site (http://www.unfccc.de).

This increased attention to compliance information systems and to reporting procedures is part of the transformation from an enforcement to a managerial approach to compliance. Traditionally, the incentives for states to report their own noncompliance were low, since such an admission could only lead to "bad news," such as the imposition of sanctions. The situation totally changes, however, when noncompliance is not necessarily considered as the intentional act of a sovereign state, but may be due, for example, to incapacity. In that case, reporting this capacity problem may lead the other partners in the regime to look for remedies to overcome the capacity problems of the state concerned, for example, through a transfer of finance or technology. In this managerial approach to compliance, reporting noncompliance should not be threatening but may well be in the state's interest. The desired result of this new approach is that in the end a higher compliance record is achieved than with traditional enforcement methods. Thus, the reporting of noncompliance under the Montreal Protocol leads the Implementation Committee to investigate the possibilities of financial and technical assistance instead of threatening with traditional sanctions.

Responses to Noncompliance

Finally, the likelihood of compliance with an environmental treaty will depend upon the possibilities of coercive or other measures being imposed in reaction to violations.

As we have discussed, traditional treaty mechanisms for noncompliance were restricted to adversarial dispute settlement procedures (DSPs). Traditional dispute settlement procedures, used generally under international environmental law, mostly involve a sequence of diplomatic and legal means of dispute settlement. Diplomatic settlement procedures usually involve negotiation and consultation in a first instance. If this negotiation and consultation does not lead to a solution, often some form of mediation or conciliation is prescribed. This mediation or conciliation involves third parties or international institutions. In case of deeper conflicts parties often can have recourse to legal means of dispute settlement, either arbitration or the International Court of Justice. In July 1993 the International Court of Justice even set up a special chamber for environmental matters.

This standard sequence of dispute resolution—negotiation, mediation, and finally arbitration or submission to the International Court of Justice—can still also be found in more recent treaties, such as the Vienna Convention for the Protection of the Ozone Layer, 1985, and the FCCC. Article 11 of the Vienna Convention prescribes negotiation as the first means of dispute resolution (para. 1). If this fails, parties must seek mediation by a third party (para. 2). As an ultimate remedy, arbitration or submission to the International Court of Justice, or in absence of agreement over this remedy a conciliation committee, is prescribed (paras. 3 to 5). Article 14 of the FCCC contains similar wording.

Although the number of cases brought under dispute settlement proceedings has increased in the last few years, they are still very rare, especially considering the compliance problems with most environmental treaties. The International Court of Justice has so far never dealt with a purely environmental conflict.[33] Conflicts under dispute settlement proceedings mostly involve either trade relationships or territorial disputes. One of the reasons for the small use of dispute settlement instruments is the fact that these procedures are characterized by an adversarial relationship between the parties, and are only used as a last resort. States are rarely willing to risk their relationship with other "sovereign" international actors by openly challenging them. As we have already stated above, even in a close community of states such as the EU the state complaints procedure under Article 170 of the treaty establishing the European Community (EC Treaty) has rarely been used. Not only are traditional dispute settlement procedures not often used, they are also considered less effective and appropriate in environmental treaties. The result of noncompliance with environmental treaties is often damage to the global commons in general, affecting all states, rather than several well-identifiable parties.

The ineffectiveness of dispute settlement proceedings in international environmental agreements has led to the development of a new system of responding to noncompliance, called noncompliance procedures (NCPs). Such procedures, rather than "punishing" noncompliance, are aimed at finding ways to facilitate compliance by the state that is in breach of its obligations. They provide a political framework for "amicable" responses to noncompliance that cannot be considered "wrongful." This tendency toward NCPs reflects the new managerial approach, which no longer assumes that noncompliance is the result of a willful desire to violate.

One of the consequences of shifting from an adversarial approach to a more managerial approach is that sanctions play only a minor role in the noncompliance response system. Three categories of sanctions can be distinguished: the treaty-based sanctions, membership sanctions, and unilateral sanctions.[34] The latter category of unilateral sanctions is now severely restricted under international law. As we have discussed above, resort to the use of military force is exceptional. Trade sanctions are increasingly difficult to invoke under the rapidly developing international trade regimes. Treaty-based sanctions have also not proven very effective. The European Union treaty, for instance, has had since November 1993 a provision for the imposition of a financial penalty upon a member state that is in breach of its obligations (Article 171 of the EC Treaty). Although this provision was introduced in 1993, the EU Commission (which supervises the application of the EC Treaty) started the first procedures in 1997, which indicates the political difficulties involved in the use of such a system. Sanctions against states party to an international treaty, including expulsion or suspension of rights and privileges, are also not considered an effective response in the case of noncompliance with an environmental treaty, since one of the aims of environmental treaties is to achieve global membership (see box on the non-compliance procedures of the Montreal Protocol).

Toward Comprehensive Noncompliance Response Systems

In this chapter we have tried to give an overview of recent developments concerning compliance with international environmental treaties. We have observed a clear shift from the "old" approach, including dispute settlement proceedings and sanctions in treaties, to the "managerial" approach, which tries to use a more comprehensive system of different methods for solving compliance problems. Increasingly, more recent treaties have included a comprehensive combination of different instruments for responding to noncompliance. These systems, also referred to as comprehensive noncompliance response systems, contain not only methods to sanction violations but, more important, methods to facilitate compliance, improve transparency, improve reporting procedures, and prevent violations.[35]

As we have already discussed, the various capacities of states can also be taken into account in the design of the primary rule system by allowing financial or technology transfer mechanisms. These differing capacities can also be taken into account in the noncompliance response system. The fact that self-reporting of noncompliance should not immediately lead to "negative" sanctions but can lead to actual support to remedy incapacity can in turn also increase the reporting record. Although the managerial approach is proving very successful in treaties such as the Vienna Convention and the Montreal Protocol, one should not forget that we are only at the beginning of new efforts to find solutions to compliance problems. The instrument of joint implementation under the FCCC, for instance, is still to be tested. In

Noncompliance Procedures: Montreal Protocol

In the more recent environmental treaties one can observe new noncompliance procedures, often side by side with the traditional dispute settlement procedures. A prime example of a well-functioning noncompliance procedure is the procedure set up under Article 8 of the Montreal Protocol. This article states that the parties to the protocol "shall consider and approve procedures and institutional mechanisms for determining noncompliance with the provisions of this Protocol and for treatment of Parties found to be in noncompliance."

At the Copenhagen meeting in November 1992 the Meeting of the Parties adopted the procedure under this article. Under this noncompliance procedure an Implementation Committee is set up. The committee consists of ten representatives elected by the Meeting of the Parties based on equitable geographical distribution. Although under the noncompliance procedure parties can also submit reservations regarding another party's implementation of its obligations under the protocol, this adversarial action has in practice not become the main function of the procedure. The focus has instead been put on the nonadversarial functions. The procedure allows states, when they believe they are unable to comply with their obligations, to report this inability to the Secretariat and the Implementation Committee. The Implementation Committee also discusses the general quality and the reliability of the data contained in the member states' reports. The Implementation Committee, meeting three to four times a year, has in fact assumed a very active role in improving the quality and reliability of the data reported by the member states and by seeking in a cooperative sphere solutions for parties with administrative structural and financial difficulties.

The noncompliance procedure under the Montreal Protocol operates independently from the dispute settlement procedure laid down in Article 11 of the Vienna Convention. Although it is tempting to see the noncompliance procedures as a prelude to the heavier dispute settlement procedure,[a] the international community has so far been very hesitant to take this approach. This hesitancy again appears in the current discussions on the adoption of a noncompliance procedure under Article 13 of the FCCC.[b] The resistance against linking the two procedures can be explained by the fear of states that linking them will reduce the use of the noncompliance procedure, and thus that it might be followed by an "uncomfortable" dispute settlement proceeding.

[a] See Jacob Werksman, "Designing a Compliance System for the UN Framework Convention on Climate Change," in *Improving Compliance with International Environmental Law*, ed. James Cameron, Jacob Werksman, and Peter Roderick (London: Earthscan, 1996), 103.

[b] See Article 4 of the set of functions and procedures that could serve as a basis for further discussion on a multilateral consultative process, Annex II to *Report of the Ad hoc Group on Article 13 on the Work of Its Fifth Session*, Bonn, July 28–30, 1997, FCCC/AG13/1997/4, August 29, 1997.

many other areas it remains difficult to reach any international consensus at all on the protection of our global environment.

International environmental law is still in a phase in which the adoption of standards is more of a concern than the actual compliance with these standards. One should not forget, however, that it is especially in the phase of adoption that a well-designed noncompliance response system can prove decisive in getting states to agree to new commitments.

Notes

1. United Kingdom, House of Lords, Select Committee on the European Communities, "Implementation and Enforcement of Environmental Legislation," Session 1991–1992, 9th report, HL paper 53-I, March 10, 1992, sec. 39.
2. Harold K. Jacobson and Edith Brown Weiss, "Strengthening Compliance with International Environmental Accords: Preliminary Observations, from a Collaborative Project," *Global Governance* 1 (1995): 119–148. The authors rightly point to the fact that there are very few studies of the compliance with international environmental treaties and even fewer studies that focus on factors at the national level that affect compliance. Their crosstreaty and crosscountry evaluation of compliance is an important exception. See also Ronald B. Mitchell, "Compliance Theory: An Overview," in *Improving Compliance with International Environmental Law*, ed. James Cameron, Jacob Werksman, and Peter Roderick (London: Earthscan, 1996), 3–28; and most recently David G. Victor, Kal Raustiala, and Eugene B. Skolnikoff, eds., *The Implementation and Effectiveness of International Environmental Commitments: Theory and Practice* (Cambridge: MIT Press, 1998).
3. Jacobson and Brown Weiss, "Strengthening Compliance," 124.
4. Article 170 of the treaty establishing the European Community, one of the treaties forming the basis of the EU, contains the possibility for one or more member states to bring another member state before the European Court of Justice. In practice this procedure is used very rarely. One example is the Court's judgment in the fisheries conflict between France and the United Kingdom (Case 141/78). In this case the UK was held to have breached EC law when searching a French trawler and convicting its master.
5. This new idea is probably best formulated by Abraham Chayes and Antonia Handler-Chayes, *The New Sovereignty: Compliance with International Regulatory Agreements* (Cambridge: Harvard University Press, 1995); see especially chap. 1.
6. For a review of the literature on regimes, see Marc A. Levy, Oran R. Young, and Michael Zürn, "The Study of International Regimes," *European Journal of International Relations* (1995): 267–330.
7. Chayes and Handler-Chayes, *The New Sovereignty*, 27.
8. Articles 2 (3) and 2 (4), in combination with Articles 42 and 51 of the UN treaty.
9. Chayes and Handler-Chayes, *The New Sovereignty*, 22–28.
10. Jacobson and Brown Weiss, "Strengthening Compliance," cite the important role of the Brazilian president Fernando Collor in the UNCED conference (142).
11. For a general discussion of the role of NGOs in international environmental law, see Patricia Birnie and Alan Boyle, *International Law and the Environment* (Oxford: Clarendon Press, 1992), 76–78.
12. See, for example, James Cameron, "Compliance Citizens and NGO's," in Cameron, Werksman, and Roderick, *Improving Compliance with International Environmental Law*, 29–42, and see more particularly the book review by Oran R. Young in *International Environmental Affairs* 9 (winter 1997): 84. The role of NGOs is also discussed in Chayes and Handler-Chayes, *The New Sovereignty*, 250–270.
13. Mitchell, "Compliance Theory," 9.
14. For further details see Jacobson and Brown Weiss, "Strengthening Compliance," 129 and 140–142.
15. Ibid., 129.
16. Mitchell, "Compliance Theory," 24.
17. Jacobson and Brown Weiss, "Strengthening Compliance," 143; and Oran Young, *International Governance, Protecting the Environment in a Stateless Society* (Ithaca: Cornell University Press, 1994), 110–115.

18. Young, *International Governance*, 37–39.

19. Mitchell, "Compliance Theory," 15.

20. Ibid., 11.

21. Examples of this can be found in European environmental law. See Michael Faure and Jürgen Lefevere, "The Draft Directive on Integrated Pollution Prevention and Control: An Economic Perspective," *European Environmental Law Review* 5 (April 1996): 112–122.

22. See, with respect to nuclear accidents, Organization for Economic Cooperation and Development, *Liability and Compensation for Nuclear Damage: An International Overview* (Paris: OECD, 1994); Michael Faure and Göran Skogh, "Compensation for Damages Caused by Nuclear Accidents: A Convention as Insurance," *The Geneva Papers on Risk and Insurance* 17 (October 1992): 499–513; J. Deprimoz, "Régime juridique des assurances contre les risques nucléaires," *Juris. Classeur* 555 (1995): 1; with respect to civil liability for marine oil pollution, see Michael Faure and Günter Heine, "The Insurance of Fines: The Case of Oil Pollution," *The Geneva Papers on Risk and Insurance* 17 (January 1991), 39–58; and for recent developments, see E. H. P. Brans, "Liability for Ecological Damage under the 1992 Protocols to the Civil Liability Convention and the Fund Convention and the Oil Pollution Act of 1990," *Tijdschrift voor Milieuaansprakelijkheid* 94, nos. 3, 4 (1994): 61–67 and 85–91.

23.   2. The developed country Parties and other Parties included in Annex I commit themselves specifically as provided for in the following: (a) Each of these Parties shall adopt national policies and take corresponding measures on the mitigation of climate change, by limiting its anthropogenic emissions of greenhouse gases and protecting and enhancing its greenhouse gas sinks and reservoirs. These policies and measures will demonstrate that developed countries are taking the lead in modifying longer-term trends in anthropogenic emissions consistent with the objective of the Convention, recognizing that the return by the end of the present decade to earlier levels of anthropogenic emissions of carbon dioxide and other greenhouse gases not controlled by the Montreal Protocol would contribute to such modification, and taking into account the differences in these Parties' starting points and approaches, economic structures and resource bases, the need to maintain strong and sustainable economic growth, available technologies and other individual circumstances, as well as the need for equitable and appropriate contributions by each of these Parties to the global effort regarding that objective. These Parties may implement such policies and measures jointly with other Parties and may assist other Parties in contributing to the achievement of the objective of the Convention. . . .

24. For details see Jacob Werksman, "Designing a Compliance System for the UN Framework Convention on Climate Change," in Cameron, Werksman, and Roderick, *Improving Compliance with International Environmental Law*, 85–112; and see Philippe Sands, *Principles of International Environmental Law*, vol. 1, *Frameworks, Standards and Implementation* (Manchester: Manchester University Press, 1995), 217–280.

25. For further details on this concept of joint implementation, see Farhana Yamin, "The Use of Joint Implementation to Increase Compliance with the Climate Change Convention," in Cameron, Werksman, and Roderick, *Improving Compliance with International Environmental Law*, 229–242.

26. Jacobson and Brown Weiss, "Strengthening Compliance," 126.

27. Richard Benedick, *Ozone Diplomacy, New Directions in Safeguarding the Planet* (Cambridge: Harvard University Press, 1991); Benedick describes this process of decision making under scientific uncertainty.

28. British Petrol surprised the international community with the speech of its group chief executive John Browne at Stanford on May 19, 1997, in which BP officially acknowledged the existence of a climate change problem and stressed the need for international action, the first major oil company to do so.

29. Mitchell, "Compliance Theory," 8–9 and 21.

30. Several varieties of reporting and data collection are discussed by Chayes and Handler-Chayes, *The New Sovereignty,* 154–173.
31. Gro Harlem Brundtland, "The Road from Rio," *Technology Review* 96 (1993): 63.
32. Mitchell, "Compliance Theory," 14; and Lynne M. Jurgielewicz, *Global Environmental Change and International Law* (Lanham, Md.: University Press of America, 1996), 113.
33. A recent example of a case that does not explicitly deal with environmental issues, but in which the environment plays an important role, is the one concerning the Gabcikovo-Nagymaros Dam on the Danube River in which the International Court of Justice pronounced judgment on September 25, 1997.
34. Chayes and Handler-Chayes, *The New Sovereignty,* 30.
35. Mitchell, "Compliance Theory," 14; Chayes and Handler-Chayes, *The New Sovereignty,* 25; Werksman, "Designing a Compliance System," 115–116.

PART III. INTERNATIONAL ENVIRONMENTAL POLICIES AND IMPLEMENTATION

8

Agenda 21: Myth or Reality?

Gary C. Bryner

The 1992 United Nations Conference on the Environment and Development (UNCED), held in Rio de Janeiro and also known as the Rio Earth Summit, was an extraordinarily ambitious undertaking. Its aim was to integrate efforts to protect the planet's ecosystems with the economic development of the poor nations of the world. Its roots were in the 1972 United Nations Conference on the Human Environment, held in Stockholm, where delegates from 113 countries met in the Stockholm Opera House to examine the ecological health of the planet. The conference produced a Declaration of Principles to guide a new era in global environmental cooperation, and an action plan for forming a new generation of global, national, and nongovernmental institutions dedicated to improving environmental quality. A 1987 report issued by the World Commission on Environment and Development, entitled *Our Common Future,* renewed the promise of the Stockholm meeting, arguing that economic growth and the production and consumption of goods could be accomplished in ways that were consistent with limited global resources. "Sustainable development" promised to improve the quality of life of current residents without compromising the resource base on which future generations will depend.[1] In 1989 the United Nations General Assembly called on leaders from the nations of the earth to meet in three years to explore what was required to shift the planet toward sustainable development.

The Earth Summit was the first global meeting to link expressly the plight of the planet's ecosystems with the poverty that plagues so many of its inhabitants. More than thirty thousand government officials, environmental activists, corporate officials, religious leaders, and others gathered in Rio for twelve days of speeches, demonstrations, and negotiations. Delegates from 178 countries gathered, the largest collection of national political leaders ever assembled, to debate and ratify a number of agreements. The earnestness of the negotiations over the conference's documents and treaties was matched by the energy and exuberance of the Global Forum, a festival dedicated to the earth and its citizens. Members of 7,892 nongovernmental organizations (NGOs) from 167 countries congregated at the festival to make their own case for protecting the earth's ecosystems. More than a thousand women held an all-night vigil on the beach near the park in which the Global Forum was held to focus attention on lack of representation of women in the official delegations. Each day speeches, dances, and concerts took place under a large bronze statue, the Tree of Life, for which some one million paper leaves had been sent from throughout the world as an expression of hope and solidarity.[2]

The Rio Declaration on Environment and Development, or Earth Charter, adopted by consensus by the delegates to the conference, is a brief statement calling the world to action and outlining the broad responsibilities of the rich and poor nations. It recognizes a "right to development" for the poorer nations and calls on all nations to commit to assisting with the "developmental and environmental needs of present and future generations."[3] While the Rio Declaration itself is nonbinding, it was a symbolic effort by the leaders of most of the nations of the earth to make at least some commitment to sustainable development and environmental preservation.[4] The declaration reaffirmed that states have "the sovereign right to exploit their own resources pursuant to their own environmental and development policies," although they also have the "responsibility to ensure that activities within their jurisdiction or control do not cause damage to the environment of other States or of areas beyond the limits of national jurisdiction."[5] The Earth Summit culminated in two important global agreements: a climate convention aimed at encouraging nations to reduce emissions of greenhouse gases, and a convention aimed at protecting the world's biodiversity by having the wealthy nations fund efforts to protect endangered species and ecosystems and by regulating biotechnology.[6]

UNCED also produced and adopted by consensus Agenda 21, an outline of what nations and international organizations agreed to do to protect the environment and promote sustainable development in the developing world.[7] The various chapters in the document required participating states to commit to achieve sustainable levels of consumption in the industrial nations, address population growth, consider market-oriented reform of their economies, encourage prices to be set that incorporate and internalize the environmental costs of production and disposal, ensure increased participation by women in development and environmental policies and programs, facilitate the transfer of technologies from the developed to the developing world, take actions to maintain or increase biodiversity, eliminate subsidies for unsustainable harvesting of natural resources, expand their institutional capacity to encourage sustainable development, increase access to natural resources by indigenous peoples, control the export of hazardous wastes, and a host of other tasks.[8] (See box, p. 162.) UNCED also resulted in the creation of a new agency, the UN Commission on Sustainable Development, to collect data on environmental and development activities and monitor implementation of the provisions of Agenda 21 by participating states through national action plans.

The Earth Summit and Agenda 21 in particular reflected the view that achieving the global agenda of environmental sustainability requires the participation of the developing countries, the South, as well as the industrial nations, the North, and that the North must play a major role in funding investments in sustainable development. That view is based on at least three major arguments that are central to understanding and assessing Agenda 21 and the Earth Summit itself. First, the countries of the South play a key role in accomplishing the goals of these and other global environmental accords, such as the Montreal Protocol to the 1985 Vienna Convention for the Protection of the Ozone Layer. The Montreal Protocol, and subsequent agreements negotiated in London and Copenhagen, placed limits on the production and consumption of several ozone-depleting substances such as chlorofluorocarbons (CFCs). The southern countries are a growing source of greenhouse gas and ozone-depleting emissions, and their forests play an important role in absorbing carbon dioxide from the atmosphere.[9] Their lands are also home to much of the world's biodiversity.[10] Second, the North has a moral obligation to provide financial and technical assistance to the South: the North is the primary source of greenhouse and ozone-threatening gases but also has the resources to mitigate many of the effects of changes to the atmosphere; the South is less responsible for the problem but much more likely to suffer the adverse consequences because its residents lack the resources to mitigate the effects.[11] Industrial nations control the technology that can solve the problem, but cooperation from the developing countries is essential. Third, the interests of the North largely dominate the global environmental protection and economic development agendas; the conference at Rio de Janeiro and subsequent meetings have recognized that more of the interests of the South might be pursued if they are linked to the interests of the North.[12]

Agenda 21 created an expectation of North-South partnership that is critical to the achievement of protecting the global environment and minimizing the environmental impact of economic growth. A key question for both the North and South is whether that partnership has been firmly established. In order to answer that question, two other questions must first be addressed: what are the goals of Agenda 21 and how well were they achieved in the first five years? Five years is, of course, not sufficient to provide clear answers to these questions, since solutions to these environmental problems will likely require decades of compliance efforts, depending on what happens to environmental conditions, technological innovation, and other factors. But five years is sufficient for an initial assessment of whether policies seem to be headed in the right direction and whether the base has been formed on which subsequent agreements and efforts can be built.

The Goals of Agenda 21

The Preamble to Agenda 21 lays out the main impetus for its creation:

Humanity stands at a defining moment in history. We are confronted with a perpetuation of disparities between and within nations, a worsening of poverty, hunger, ill health and illiteracy, and the continuing deterioration of the ecosystems on which we depend for our well-being. However, integration of environment and development concerns and greater attention to them will lead to the fulfillment of basic needs, improved living standards

for all, better protected and managed ecosystems and a safer, more pros-
perous future.[13]

Agenda 21 emphasizes that all nations and all people have a responsibility to pursue the idea of sustainable development but gives particular
responsibility to the United Nations system. Agenda 21 was conceived as a
plan of action to be pursued at all levels of government to give concrete
expression to the idea of sustainable development. The eventual agreement
suggested steps that individuals and families, communities, local and
national governments, and global organizations should take to ensure the
compatibility of economic activity with ecological limits and to expand the
knowledge of how to preserve the environment so it would support future
generations. The agenda promised to produce a new global partnership
between the more and less developed world that would secure the interests
and meet the basic needs of all people. It includes 40 separate sections and
120 action programs that seek to lay out the problems and challenges in
some detail while also emphasizing their interconnectedness.

One way of summarizing Agenda 21 is to divide its provisions into two
categories. The first set of issues includes specific environmental and development problems and challenges and actions to be taken. This set can be further divided into two areas: improving the quality of life of the poor and
fostering sustainable economic growth, and conserving natural resources and
reducing pollution and the release of toxic chemicals. The agenda for
improving the quality of life includes expanding the provision of primary
health care, reducing risks from communicable and environmental-related
diseases, providing shelter, developing environmental and transportation
infrastructures to serve the poor, stabilizing population growth, and developing sustainable patterns of production and consumption in the wealthy
world and reducing poverty in the poorer nations. Sustainable economic
growth requires the creation of new incentives and penalties that promote
sustainable activity; revising national economic indicators to reflect environmental considerations; reforms that ensure that market prices include more of
the true costs of production; and addressing the problem of falling commodity prices that encourages developing countries to export natural
resources at unsustainable rates. Conserving natural resources includes developing new data systems, coordinating local and international land-use planning, increasing the productivity of land and decreasing the pressure to farm
marginal lands. It also means conserving genetic resources, giving developing
countries access to scientific knowledge concerning biotechnology, conserving
forests, assisting drought-prone areas, protecting the marine environment and
aquatic ecosystems, ensuring sustainable fishing yields, preserving drinking
water, and giving developing countries technical assistance for sustaining natural resources. Reducing pollution and toxic chemicals includes steps to preserve the ozone layer, reduce transboundary pollution, improve the disposal of
toxic chemicals, prevent the illegal transportation of hazardous substances,
minimize the production of solid wastes and encourage reuse and recycling,

reduce fossil fuel consumption, and give developing countries the technical infrastructure to regulate pollution sources. Agenda 21 also includes provisions aimed at implementing the International Convention on Biological Diversity and the Framework Convention on Climate Change (both also signed at the Rio conference in 1992).

The second category of Agenda 21's provisions focuses on increasing the capacity of governments, at all levels, to pursue sustainable development goals. The agreement calls for increasing participation by women in all decision-making forums at all levels; improving health and education for children, particularly girls; empowering indigenous peoples to participate in decisions affecting them; increasing the interaction between NGOs, governments, and international organizations; strengthening the role of public participation in development decisions; giving increased voice to workers and unions; and supporting new venture capital commitments for small businesses.

The most expensive undertaking by far is to make urban life more sustainable by helping the poor gain access to housing, land, and credit; increasing clean water, waste collection, and sanitation services; developing mass transit, improving energy efficiency, and taking other steps to reduce air pollution; reducing poverty through development of the informal economic sector; and improving rural conditions as a way to reduce urban migration. Other efforts that will require the greatest level of funding include social and economic needs, such as improving public health, reducing poverty, and increasing employment opportunities, and natural resource priorities, such as protecting and developing freshwater sources, conserving forests and planting trees, expanding agricultural output, providing solid waste and sewer services, reducing air pollution and protecting the atmosphere, reducing ocean pollution, and developing and disseminating the benefits of biotechnology for food production and human health. The range in projected spending is remarkable, from less than $2 million for children and youth (although they would benefit from health, education, and many other efforts), to $218 billion to combat urban ills.[14] Some efforts, such as reducing consumption of resources in the developed world, are not funded at all.

Agenda 21 was the result of years of preparatory work, and a broad consensus had been achieved on the agenda before the 1992 summit, except in the area of financing. Part of the task in Rio de Janeiro was to specify the resources required. While Agenda 21 did not establish priorities or provide funds, it estimated that implementation would require an annual contribution from the developed world of $125 billion a year, or about 0.7 percent of their gross national product (GNP). An additional $400 billion a year was to be spent by governments and businesses in the developing world in order to achieve Agenda 21's goals. Chapter 33, the section that deals with how the changes are to be paid for, was not even included in the document until the final negotiations were concluded in Rio de Janeiro. It was recognized in the chapter that most of the funding for sustainable development would come from public and private sources within each developing country, and devel-

The Chapters of Agenda 21

1. Preamble

Section One: Social and Economic Development
2. International Cooperation to Accelerate Sustainable Development in Developing Countries
3. Poverty
4. Changing Consumption Patterns
5. Demographic Dynamics and Sustainability (Population)
6. Protecting and Promoting Human Health
7. Promoting Sustainable Human Settlements
8. Policy-Making for Sustainable Development

Section Two: Conservation and Management of Resources for Development
9. Protecting the Atmosphere—Making the Energy Transition
10. An Integrated Approach to Land-Resource Use
11. Combating Deforestation
12. Managing Fragile Ecosystems: Combating Desertification and Drought
13. Protecting Mountain Ecosystems
14. Meeting Agricultural Needs and Rural Development
15. Sustaining Biological Diversity
16. Environmentally Sound Management of Biotechnology
17. Safeguarding the Oceans' Resources
18. Protecting and Managing Freshwater Resources
19. Safe Use of Toxic Chemicals
20. Managing Hazardous Wastes
21. Seeking Solutions to Solid Waste and Sewage Problems
22. Management of Radioactive Wastes

Section Three: Strengthening the Role of Major Groups
23. Preamble to the Contribution of Social Groups
24. Action for Women: Sustainable and Equitable Development
25. Youth
26. Indigenous Peoples
27. Non-Governmental Organizations
28. Implementing Agenda 21 at a Community Level
29. Workers and Trade Unions
30. Strengthening the Role of Business and Industry
31. Science and Technology
32. Strengthening the Role of Farmers

Section Four: Means of Implementation
33. Financial Resources and Mechanisms
34. Transfer of Environmentally Sound Technology, Cooperation, and Capacity-Building
35. Science for Sustainable Development
36. Promoting Environmental Awareness
37. Capacity-Building in Developing Countries
38. International Institutional Arrangements
39. International Legal Instruments and Mechanisms
40. Bridging the Data Gap

Note: For the full text of Agenda 21 see United Nations, *Agenda 21: Programme of Action for Sustainable Development,* 1992, E.92-38352, A/CONF. 151/26, vols. 1–3.

oped countries' commitment to increase Official Development Assistance (the term used by nations and international organizations for aid to developing countries) in order to meet the costs of implementing Agenda 21 was reaffirmed. Table 8-1 summarizes the estimated costs for implementing Agenda 21.

Achieving the Goals

It is too early to determine whether or not the goals of Agenda 21 are being achieved, since the problems at which it is aimed and the nature of the goals themselves—improving the quality of life, encouraging sustainable economic growth, conserving natural resources, reducing pollution, and improving governmental capacity—require long-term efforts. However, several indicators can shed light on the questions of whether some progress has been made, whether progress is likely in the future, and whether the foundation for more ecologically sustainable economic activity is in place.

Improving Quality of Life and Encouraging
Sustainable Economic Growth

The developing countries have made great progress since the 1950s in reducing poverty: child mortality and malnutrition have significantly declined; life expectancy, access to clean water and sanitation, opportunities for education, and health care have expanded.[15] But the progress of the 1960s and 1970s did not continue in the 1980s and 1990s. About a hundred countries, for example, have suffered from economic stagnation during this period. Conflict in thirty countries has made economic and social progress almost impossible. The rise in health threats from communicable diseases like HIV/AIDs has been greater than expected and poses a major threat to well-being in many developing nations, particularly those in Sub-Saharan Africa.[16] Only modest progress has been made in recent years in reducing poverty and malnourishment and in increasing access to clean air, clean water, sanitation, and health care. Incomes in Africa are 1.4 percent lower than in 1992.[17] In the Commonwealth of Independent States (C.I.S.), life expectancy has dropped five years or more since the breakup of the Soviet empire.[18] The economic growth that has occurred has often bypassed the poor and has failed to increase their earnings and employment opportunities.

The 1996 *Human Development Report*, published by the United Nations Development Programme (UNDP), emphasized another indicator of the lack of progress in achieving Agenda 21's goals—the increasing gap between the world's rich and poor. In 1960, for example, the difference between the per capita income of the developed and the developing countries was $5,700; in 1993 the difference had almost tripled to $15,400. In 1960 the bottom 20 percent of the world's population received 2.3 percent of the total global income; in 1991, they received 1.4 percent; in 1994 they received only 1.1 percent of global income. In 1991 the ratio of the income of the richest 20

Table 8-1 Estimated Costs of Implementing Agenda 21

Agenda 21 program	Total cost of Agenda 21 program (in millions of dollars)	Developed countries' share (in millions of dollars)
Human settlements	$218,000	$29,500
Fresh water	54,800	17,000
Human health	51,000	6,400
Agriculture	31,800	5,100
Deforestation	31,200	5,700
Poverty	30,000	15,000
Solid waste/Sewage	23,300	6,900
Atmosphere	21,000	21,000
Biotechnology	20,000	200
Education/Training	14,600	6,000
Oceans	13,100	900
International cooperation	8,900	8,900
Population	7,100	3,600
Hazardous wastes	4,200	1,300
Biological diversity	3,500	1,800
Science	2,900	2,000
Information	2,100	2,100
Toxic chemicals	650	200
Creating capacity	650	650
Technology transfer	500	500
Workers/Trade unions	300	300
Making decisions	63	63
Land	50	50
Women	40	40
Scientists/Technologists	20	20
Radioactive wastes	8	8
Indigenous peoples	3	3
Children/Youth	2	2
Local authorities	1	1
NGOs	a	a
Farmers	a	a
Organizations for sustainable development	a	a
International law	a	a
Consumption patterns	a	a
Total	$561,500	$141,900

Source: Adapted from Michael Keating, *The Earth Summit's Agenda for Change* (Geneva: Centre for Our Common Future, 1993): 53.

Note: Numbers do not add to total because of rounding;   [a] No estimate.

percent of global income. In 1991 the ratio of the income of the richest 20 percent of the world's population to the poorest 20 percent was 61:1; in 1994 it had grown to 78:1. Seventy-seven percent of the people of the world earn only 15 percent of its income. The average income in the North is 18 times greater than that in the South.[19] The globalization of markets and economic activity has benefited some interests in the developing world but has not reached the poorest of the poor, especially those in rural areas, where three-fourths of the developing world's poor reside.[20]

The United Nations Development Programme measures poverty in two ways. First, *income poverty* is a function of daily income: poverty is defined as less than $1.00 per day in the poorest regions of the world, less than $2.00 per day in Latin America and the Caribbean, less than $4.00 per day in the C.I.S., and less than $14.40 per day in the developed world. Some 1.3 billion people live below the income poverty line.[21] Second, *human poverty* is more broadly measured in terms of the percentage of people who die before age forty, are illiterate, and lack access to safe drinking water and basic health care, and the percentage of children who are underweight. In 1997 the UNDP concluded that, in the developing world, 507 million people were not expected to reach the age of forty, 1.2 billion lacked access to safe water, 842 million adults were illiterate, and 158 million children under the age of five were malnourished.[22]

Women and children bear much of the brunt of poverty in the world: they suffer from maternal-related deaths, respiratory diseases (from inhaling the smoke of cooking fires), and other maladies that result from poverty. Much of the work done by women is underpaid and undervalued. Wide disparities exist between men and women, and female literacy is only about two-thirds that of males. Women are often prevented from owning property. Primary school enrollment for girls is only a little over half that of boys. Women's wages remain at two-thirds those of males.[23] Discrimination, which is manifest in land ownership laws, employment practices, education, and development programs, contributes to the global feminization of poverty. Because of the low status of women in most societies, development projects often ignore their role in local economies, despite the fact that women make up 50 percent of the agricultural labor force and more than 70 percent of some industries, such as clothing manufacturing.[24] Development projects often ignore the plight of women because their efforts are largely outside of the formal economy.[25]

Other indicators paint a sobering picture of Agenda 21's task. Although the number of deaths from communicable diseases has fallen and is expected to continue to do so during the next twenty-five years, maternal mortality rates have changed little: about 585,000 women die each year from complications arising during pregnancy and childbirth, and more than 99 percent of these deaths are in the developing world. For every death, an additional 30 women suffer from debilitating health problems resulting from problem pregnancies and childbirth. Most of these deaths and disabilities could be prevented with adequate prenatal and postnatal care.[26] Linguists estimate that only 6,000 of the 10,000–15,000 languages that were once spoken simultaneously in the world are still spoken, and that number is expected to continue to decline, one measure of the loss of indigenous culture and global diversity.[27]

Trends in food production are also worrisome. According to a World Watch Institute analysis, the world grain harvest, measured in kilograms of grain for each person on earth, fell from a peak of 342 in 1984 to 299 in 1995 and has fluctuated between 299 and 328 during the past five years.[28] There seems to be complacency over levels of food production, but grain yields have been increasing at less than 1 percent a year in the 1990s, compared with a 2.1 percent increase throughout the 1980s.[29] Per capita soybean production peaked in 1994 and then fell slightly; one troublesome sign is that China has recently become a net importer of soybean and grain, and its transformation from exporter to importer puts increased pressure on global food supplies.[30] The global fish catch per capita has also declined, from a high in 1988 of 17.2 kilos to 15.9 in 1996; thirteen of the fifteen major global fisheries are in decline. "If current trends of overexploitation and habitat destruction continue," the Worldwatch report warned, "fish will no longer be 'the protein of the poor.'" [31]

Population growth may undermine most of what Agenda 21 seeks to accomplish. The rate of global population increase has slowed slightly: in 1996, it grew by 80 million, an increase of 1.4 percent. The rate of population growth has gradually declined since its peak of 2.2 percent in 1963. Some 98 percent of the growth occurs in the developing countries. The slowed growth rate is due to a number of factors, including declining fertility rates, a decrease in the life expectancy in the C.I.S., and diseases such as AIDs that have slowed growth rates in Sub-Saharan Africa.[32] The number of people considered by the UN to be eligible for assistance as refugees declined slightly between 1995 and 1996, to 26.1 million, but has otherwise grown steadily since the 1970s. This number does not include refugees who are displaced within their own country, most of whom do not receive international assistance, nor does it include the estimated 100 million to 250 million people a year who are displaced because of natural disasters such as floods and earthquakes and who compete with other types of refugees for scarce relief assistance.[33]

Conserving Natural Resources and Reducing Pollution

Some critical indicators of natural resource use and pollution production show the daunting challenges in achieving Agenda 21's goals. Consumption of fossil fuel, which provides 85 percent of the world's commercial energy, continues to grow, and the use of coal, oil, and natural gas all set new records in 1996: coal use grew by 1.8 percent, oil by 2.3 percent, and natural gas by 4.5 percent. Worldwide carbon emissions from the burning of fossil fuels increased by 4 percent between 1992 and 1996 and by 2.8 percent between 1995 and 1996, the highest increase since 1988. These emissions have increased by 400 percent since 1950.[34] The use of CFCs and halons peaked in 1988 but fell by 76 percent by 1995. CFC use has largely ended in the developed world, which must now try to reduce methyl bromide and hydrofluorocarbons (HCFCs). In contrast, in some areas of the developing world, CFC use has risen rapidly. Between 1986 and 1994, for example, CFC use rose by 95 percent in China, 109 percent in the Philippines, and 193 percent in India.[35] Between 1991 and 1995 there has been a net loss of tropical forests of about 12.6 million hectares a year, a continuation of the annual loss throughout the 1980s of 12.8 million hectares. Tropical forest cover, wetlands, and other sensitive areas have declined by 3.5 percent since 1992.[36] These figures likely understate the problem, since some logging leaves a residual cover and is not counted as deforestation but nevertheless disrupts ecosystems, nor does it differentiate between plantation forests, planted and harvested in cycles, and old-growth forests, which are much richer in biodiversity.[37]

A 1996 World Resources Institute study concluded that while significant progress has been made in reducing urban environmental problems, cities "remain significant contributors to regional and global environmental burdens," are themselves areas of serious environmental problems such as air pollution and inadequate water and sanitation, and are "expanding into fragile ecosystems" in ways that threaten surrounding ecosystems and resources.[38] Other global trends are also alarming. While some developing countries "are moving rapidly toward population stability . . . other countries are experiencing rapid population growth, usually accompanied by high levels of poverty, limited progress for women, and high levels of internal and international migration." The continued growth of global population "places enormous pressure on natural resources, urban infrastructure and services, and governments at all levels, especially in the poorest countries where growth is most rapid."[39] Demand for water is rapidly increasing and "many current patterns of water withdrawals are currently unsustainable." Some 1 billion people have no access to clean water, and about 1.7 billion have inadequate sanitation. Between 13 and 20 percent of the world's population will live in water-scarce countries by the year 2050, according to one estimate. Water scarcity contributes to agricultural problems and combines with soil erosion and degradation to threaten our ability to increase global food production. Even if food production is expanded, "the inability of poor nations to pay for food imports, along with an inadequate distribution infrastructure and the inability of poor families to buy food, means that many people will continue to go hungry."[40] Projections of energy use suggest that increased consumption is inevitable, particularly in the developing world, and that will translate into increased levels of local and regional air pollution and global greenhouse gases. Other major environmental threats that will likely increase are degradation of coastal habitats and destruction of old-growth forests.[41]

Improving Governmental Capacity

Agenda 21 and UNCED spawned a number of institutional changes. Perhaps the most important was the Commission on Sustainable Development, established in 1993 by the UN General Assembly to monitor implementation of the Rio agreements, and Agenda 21, in particular. The commission is a body within the UN Economic and Social Council, and its primary responsibility is to monitor progress in implementing the policies suggested in Agenda 21 and to encourage international and national governments, businesses, and NGOs to integrate environment and economic development objectives. The commission has fifty-three seats distributed among countries in each region of the world. It has no legal authority and must make recommendations to the UN General Assembly.[42] The commission seeks to facilitate international efforts to exchange information, study problems, and develop collaborative solutions. It has provided a forum for negotiating global environment and development agreements, and it helped organize a number of subsequent meetings to deal with human rights, sustainable development of small island developing states, population and economic development, social development, women, trade and development, human habitats, and global food production and consumption.[43]

Other important institutions have been created to work with the UN Environment Programme (UNEP), UN Development Programme, and other organizations involved in issues related to Agenda 21. The Global Environment Facility was established to provide new funding sources. New NGOs include the World Business Council for Sustainable Development, the Earth Council, and the International Council for Local Environmental Initiatives. These new institutions were superimposed on the existing structure of international agencies, with little effort to deal with problems of overlaps, duplication, and coordination. The Economic and Social Council was created under the UN Charter as the principal body to coordinate economic and social activities, and it oversees a bewildering array of agencies and organizations, including the International Atomic Energy Agency, the International Research and Training Institute for the Advancement of Women, the United Nations Centre for Human Settlements (Habitat), the United Nations Conference on Trade and Development, the United Nations Development Programme, the United Nations Environment Programme, the United Nations Population Fund, the Office of the United Nations High Commissioner for Refugees, the United Nations Children's Fund, and the World Food Council.[44]

A 1997 UNEP report argued that "significant progress" has been made during the past decade "in the realm of institutional developments, international cooperation, public participation, and the emergence of private-sector action." The report highlighted the spread of new environmental laws, environmental impact assessments, economic incentives, and other policy efforts, and the development of cleaner, less polluting production processes and technologies. These innovations, it argued, resulted in several countries reporting "marked progress in curbing environmental pollution and slowing the rate of resource degradation as well as reducing the intensity of resource use."[45] However, the report concluded, "from a global perspective, the environment has continued to degrade during the past decade, and significant environmental problems remain deeply embedded in the socio-economic fabric of nations in all regions. Progress towards a global sustainable future is just too slow." The report argued that while technologies are available to remedy environmental problems, a "sense of urgency is lacking" as are the financial resources and the "political will" to reduce environmental degradation and protect natural resources. There is a "general lack of sustained interest in global and long-term environmental issues," global "governance structures and environmental solidarity remain too weak to make progress a world-wide reality," and, consequently, the "gap between what has been done thus far and what is realistically needed is widening." There has been insufficient development of effective national environmental legislation and "fiscal and economic instruments," and the environmental innovations made by transnational corporations "are not reflected widely in the practices of small- and medium-sized companies." [46]

One of the major challenges in building governing capacity in the developing countries is the drop in support for Overseas Development Assistance (ODA) in the developed countries. Only a few countries have met the 0.7 percent of GNP target for foreign aid. By 1995, total ODA had dropped to $59 billion, representing about 0.3 percent of the GNP of the developed countries. New financial resources and technology sharing are needed to help developing countries implement Agenda 21, but foreign debt remains in many developing countries an imposing barrier. [47] The indebtedness of developing countries grew rapidly in the 1960s and 1970s and resulted in the debt crisis in the 1980s, when countries had to submit to new rounds of borrowing to maintain debt payments. The developing countries require massive amounts of capital to upgrade their industrial infrastructure, but their indebtedness is a major barrier. They owe some $1.8 trillion to banks and international lending institutions. The debt-GNP ratio—the dollar value of outstanding medium- and long-term debt as a percentage of GNP—is nearly 40 percent in the developing world, and as high as 80 percent in the poorest African nations. [48] Despite some restructuring of the debt in the early and mid-1990s, debt service still comprises from 15 to 19 percent of debtor countries' export revenues. Debt levels are particularly high in Sub-Saharan Africa: debt service payments are $10 billion a year, four times the annual amount these countries spend on health and education. The debt burden of the poorest nations continues to rise: the 41 most indebted nations owed $183 billion in 1990; by 1997, their debt was $215 billion. [49] The share of debt of the lowest-income countries to multilateral institutions grew from 15 percent of total debt in 1980 to 24 percent in 1992. [50]

In 1995 the Group of Seven major industrial nations asked the World Bank and the International Monetary Fund (IMF) to devise a program of debt relief for poor nations. The request was in response to studies such as one issued by Oxfam International, which found countries like Uganda spending $3 per person a year on health care and $17 per person a year on servicing international debt. In 1996 the Bank and the IMF proposed a plan to reduce the debt of twenty of the world's poorest and most indebted nations, including Bolivia, Madagascar, Nicaragua, Tanzania, Uganda, Zaire, and Zambia. These countries would first undergo a three-year economic reform program outlined by the Bank and the IMF and would then be eligible for forgiveness of up to two-thirds of the debt they owed. [51] After another three years, up to 90 percent of their debt could be forgiven; the

Bank would pay off some of the debts owed to multilateral lending institutions, and the IMF would lend money at a low interest rate (one-half of 1 percent) to the countries to pay off some of their debt. Their debt would eventually be no greater than 350 percent of their annual export earnings. The proposal was approved in September 1996, the first time that debts to international lending agencies had been forgiven and the largest reduction in indebtedness ever agreed to. But critics argued that the six-year plan would take too long to reduce the crushing burden of debt and did not reach enough needy countries.[52]

Assessing the Impact of Agenda 21

One of the most important assessments of Agenda 21 was undertaken by the United Nations itself. In 1992 the UN General Assembly endorsed Agenda 21 and promised to convene a special session after five years to review progress. In June 1997 the UN General Assembly Special Session to Review Implementation of Agenda 21 (UNGASS) heard assessments of the progress made toward Agenda 21 by 197 heads of states, ministers, and UN representatives. The General Assembly adopted a Programme for the Further Implementation of Agenda 21, which began with an assessment of progress made since the Earth Summit in Rio de Janeiro and painted a pessimistic picture of the lack of progress in achieving the Agenda's goals. Globalization has accelerated and foreign direct investment and world trade have increased in a limited number of developing countries, but the impact has been uneven, and many areas continue to be plagued by foreign debt and receive little assistance. Poverty has prevented them from participating in and benefiting from the global economy, and they require assistance to meet basic needs. The total number of poor people in the world has increased since the Rio meeting and the gap between the wealthy and poor countries "has grown rapidly in recent years."[53] While some countries have reduced emissions of pollutants and resource use, and population growth rates have declined in most areas, overall, global environmental conditions have worsened and "significant environmental problems remain deeply embedded in the socio-economic fabric of countries in all regions." Persistent poverty continues to contribute to ecological decline and threats to fragile ecosystems. "Overall trends remain unsustainable." Foreign debt remains in many developing countries "a major constraint on achieving sustainable development."[54]

UNGASS outlined a number of issues requiring urgent attention in order to implement Agenda 21 and urged the reactivation and intensification of international cooperation and the "invigoration of a genuine new global partnership, taking into account the special needs and priorities of developing countries."[55] It outlined three sets of strategies. First, integrate economic, social, and environmental objectives in national policies; foster a dynamic economy "favourable to all countries"; eradicate poverty and improve access to social services; change unsustainable consumption and production patterns; make trade and the environment "mutually supportive";

further promote the decline in population growth rates; enable all people to "achieve a higher level of health and well-being"; and improve living conditions throughout the world.[56] Second, it made recommendations to improve conditions in key sectors: freshwater, oceans and seas, forests, energy, transportation, the atmosphere, climate change, toxic chemicals, hazardous and radioactive wastes, land and agriculture, desertification and drought, biodiversity, sustainable tourism, small island developing states, and responses to natural disasters.[57] Third, it reaffirmed the goal of the ODA, encouraged increased private investment and foreign debt reduction in developing countries, called for more transparency of subsidies, called for increased transfer of environmentally sound technologies to developing countries, and urged other efforts to build developing countries' capacity for effective policy-making.[58] A final set of recommendations focused on policy coordination of efforts to implement Agenda 21 within the United Nations, such as enhancing the roles of the United Nations Development Programme and the Commission on Sustainable Development.[59] UNGASS agreed to review progress in the implementation of Agenda 21 in the year 2002.[60]

One indicator of the success or shortcomings of Agenda 21 in reshaping our discourse on economic growth and environmental preservation is a comparison of the 1997 UNGASS with the 1992 meeting. The problems confronting the delegates to the 1992 Rio conference largely resurfaced in the 1997 meeting. There was in 1997 little discussion of regulating private capital flows, corporate behavior, and the impact of trade on environmental quality. On the positive side, there is increasing discussion and monitoring of concrete indicators of reproductive health care and consumption and production patterns. The meeting was a frank assessment of the lack of progress rather than an attempt to "paper over the cracks in the celebrated 'global partnership' for sustainable development and pretend that things are better than they are." However, the question of funding for the implementation of Agenda 21 in the developing countries seemed as vexing in 1997 as it was five years earlier. The UN meeting reminded global leaders of the idea of sustainable development but seemed to lack any ability to identify strategic plans or generate commitments to specific actions. UN documents dutifully catalog the myriad global environmental challenges but fail to take on the dominant force in economic activity and development—international trade and private investment decisions—and are unable to focus attention on a limited set of actions that deserve priority, or even impose some direction to and coordination of the activities that are undertaken under the auspices of the United Nations. A major area of progress in 1997 was the decision to establish an intergovernmental forum for negotiations on the sustainable management of forests. Despite that one positive development, UNGASS provided little evidence that Agenda 21 has become an effective guide for economic activity. The "question dominating debate at UNGASS," according to one observer, was "where to go from here?"[61]

Multilateral institutions, bilateral assistance, and the efforts of national governments, NGOs, and industries have contributed to debt relief and institutional capacity building in the South. The idea of sustainable development has become a part of economic planning in a few nations, and the principles of Agenda 21 are being pursued through local sustainable development programs. Some businesses have become greener. New institutions have been created and public-private collaboration has increased.[62] Progress has been made in implementing the two treaties signed in Rio de Janeiro, particularly the climate change agreement, which was strengthened considerably in December 1997 when the industrial countries agreed to reduce their emissions of six greenhouse gases by an average of 5 percent below 1990 levels during the years 2008–2012.[63]

However, the progress that has been made is dwarfed by the remaining tasks. The goodwill and cooperation that was generated during the 1992 Earth Summit has already dissipated and may deteriorate further without a renewed commitment on the part of the North to work with the South in providing an alternative to traditional economic development. There has been relatively little debate about the idea of sustainable development itself, for example, and whether it is even possible. Skeptics argue that sustainable development is a thinly veiled attempt to justify business as usual, that businesses promise to make minor accommodations to the idea of environmental sustainability while continuing to pursue economic growth. From this view, economic growth is simply not possible because humans have already exceeded the carrying capacity of the planet, and future generations are already destined to have a lower quality of life than the current one. Even if this pessimistic view of sustainable development is discarded, it still requires a major shift in effort to reduce the consumption and waste of the developed world and increase economic growth without increasing pollution or resource degradation in the developing countries, and there has been little movement toward that goal during the past five years. It is difficult to envision how the political will for such a shift in priorities could be fostered. There has been little discussion of sustainable development or more precise efforts such as limits on consumption and production, investment in conservation and efficiency, or the integration of the poor into the global economy.

Assessments of the success of Agenda 21 ultimately depend on how it is understood. From one perspective, it is a catalog of policies that countries can embrace as they seek to become more sustainable. Agenda 21 has clearly triggered some policy innovations in some nations and has served as a vehicle for sharing information and ideas. It can be judged more or less successful depending on the extent to which more and more nations, over time, choose to implement more and more of the policy prescriptions it offers and the extent to which economic, political, and social goals underlying the policies are achieved. A great deal of activity in these areas has occurred, although it is difficult to know what can and cannot be attributed to Agenda 21. Within the first two years of UNCED, 103 of the 178 nations attending the meeting in Rio de Janeiro had established national sustainable development commissions. Many countries reported progress in reducing lead exposures and cleaning up freshwater resources.[64] Agenda 21 will likely become increasingly important in the future as a source of ideas for sustainable development.

From another view, Agenda 21 represents a national commitment to a new set of policies that domestic political groups can use to pressure their governments. The governments that signed Agenda 21 but have failed to implement it can be aggressively criticized by environmental and other groups for failing to keep their pledges. Governments can be nudged and urged from within to make sustainable development a national policy, and Agenda 21 can be a useful vehicle for drawing attention to commitments and suggesting concrete steps.

Perhaps most important, Agenda 21 can be viewed as an attempt to change the discourse surrounding economic growth. The key here is whether Agenda 21 has altered the global economic and environmental protection agenda, whether it has reshaped the way we think about economic growth, international trade, and international relations. From this perspective, Agenda 21 has not produced a major commitment to rethinking our approaches to development and to the globalization of the world's economy. It has not become a central idea in international trade agreements and the operation of the World Trade Organization. It has not been a major factor in shaping negotiations over the proposed Multilateral Investment Agreement that would facilitate the flow of capital worldwide.

In the United States the idea of sustainable development has had some influence in the development of national policies and programs, but that influence has largely been limited to the executive branch. The Clinton administration has pursued a number of initiatives it has described as part of its commitment to sustainable development, while Congress has largely failed to even address the idea. The President's Council on Sustainable Development, for example, was created by the Clinton administration in 1993. Its purpose was to bring together representatives from environmental groups, industry, and government to advise the president "on matters involving sustainable development," defined as "economic growth that will benefit present and future generations without detrimentally affecting the resources or biological systems of the planet."[65] The council's "vision statement" argues that a "sustainable United States will have a growing economy that provides equitable opportunities for satisfying livelihoods and a safe, healthy, high quality of life for current and future generations."[66] The structure of the council reflects one of its primary themes: "Our most important finding is the potential power of and growing desire for decision processes that promote direct and meaningful interaction involving people in decisions that affect them."[67] The role of government is to "convene and facilitate, shifting gradually from prescribing behavior to supporting responsibility by setting goals, creating incentives, monitoring performance, and providing information."[68] The council may be laying a framework for future commitments to sustainability, but its recommendations are not currently being translated into law.

The United States has not embraced sustainable development as a
guiding principle for public policymaking, for several reasons. First, political
leaders, and Congress and the White House in particular, continue to debate
the question of whether there should be more or less environmental regulation. Rather than asking more fundamental questions about how to balance
and integrate economic growth and ecological sustainability and the other
issues raised in Agenda 21, policymakers are mired in efforts to defend or
attack the regulatory system that has been in place since the 1970s. There is
little question that the system of environmental regulation could be
improved. But congressional regulatory reformers have given more attention
to devising new rules to require risk assessment and cost-benefit analysis and
make them subject to legal challenges, than dealing with more fundamental
changes in economic activity. While most every proponent of regulatory
reform calls for improved analysis underlying regulation, Congress's attempts
to simply add an exhaustive set of requirements and then subject each of
them to judicial review are not likely to achieve that goal.[69]

Second, political leaders have been unwilling to take on the broader
questions of American values of economic growth, consumption, technology,
land use, transportation, and individual freedom. Most Americans seem
determined to view economic growth as limitless, constrained only by unwise
policy or business choices. They resist strongly the idea that limits should be
placed on material consumption and exhibit tremendous faith in technological solutions to whatever problems confront them. Their strong commitment
to private property rights places major limits on political decisions to limit
private property use for environmental purposes. Their insistence on single-
occupant vehicles and dislike for mass transit is intertwined with their fundamental commitment to individual freedom, which includes their ability to
travel wherever and whenever they please. Jimmy Carter was the last major
political leader to talk about limits and constraints, and he was widely derided
for violating the American creed of unbridled growth and opportunity.

A third barrier to the more expansive and aggressive policies suggested
by a real commitment to sustainable development may be the movement
toward policy devolution, toward a weakened federal government and more
responsibility for environmental regulation to be assumed by states, and
toward more choice and variety across communities in how they choose to
balance environmental preservation and economic growth. Reducing
national regulatory power has been embraced across the political spectrum.
A 1995 report commissioned by Congress and completed by the National
Academy of Public Administration, for example, concluded that Congress
needs to give the Environmental Protection Agency (EPA) more flexibility
and discretion in order to accomplish the nation's environmental goals; in
turn, the EPA must give more decision-making authority to the states and
local governments and to regulated industries.[70]

A fourth difficulty has been the priorities of the EPA and the statutes
the agency is responsible for implementing, which have primarily focused on
public health rather than broader environmental quality. In 1987 the EPA

completed a study that compared the risks of thirty-one major categories of environmental and health problems, ranging from global warming to oil spills, and also examined risks from four perspectives that represent the major responsibilities of the EPA: cancer risks, noncancer health risks, ecological risks, and effects on the general welfare. There were significant differences between the study's estimation of the seriousness of risks and EPA's operating priorities: "EPA has been more concerned about pollution that affects public health, as opposed to protection of natural habitats and ecosystems, in all programs except surface water."[71] In some areas of high risk, such as for indoor air pollution, carbon dioxide and global warming, and nonpoint sources of water pollution (for example, runoff from fields and lawns), neither the EPA nor any other federal agency has any significant statutory authority. Other studies have built upon the EPA assessments and criticized Congress and the EPA for failing to compare and rank risks so that the most serious are given priority.[72] Congress has not yet responded to the challenge of overhauling environmental laws in ways that ensure that the most serious problems are addressed and regulations are more efficient and effective.

A final challenge has been the unwillingness of Congress and the inability of the EPA to create more effective incentives to push industries and consumers toward pollution prevention. In 1989 the EPA commissioned a review of its comparative risk assessment by the agency's Science Advisory Board. The board's report in 1990 concluded that the agency had largely been a "reactive" agency, insufficiently oriented toward "opportunities for the greatest risk reduction." Not all risks can be reduced, but not all problems are equally serious, and the agency had failed to set priorities for reducing the most important problems. The agency had usually imposed "end-of-pipe controls that often cause environmental problems of their own" rather than "[p]reventing pollution at the source—through the redesign of production processes, the substitution of less toxic production materials," and so on. Pollution prevention approaches avoid transferring "pollutants from one environmental medium to another" (from air to water, for example) and "often bring substantial economic benefit to the sources that use them."[73]

One policy area, energy production and use, illustrates the failure of the United States to move in directions suggested by sustainable development and Agenda 21. Early in his presidency, Bill Clinton proposed a broad tax on all forms of energy in order to raise federal revenue to reduce the budget deficit. The proposed tax, called a Btu tax because it was based on the heating ability of different fuels, as measured by British thermal units, would have raised the prices of gasoline, electricity, and other energy sources. Environmentalists supported the measure as a way to promote conservation and to begin to move away from fossil fuel consumption. The tax would have cost the American people only about $22 billion a year, a tiny fraction of the $6 trillion U.S. economy, but opposition from Democratic and Republican senators representing energy-producing states killed the idea.[74] The administration was successful in raising gasoline taxes by 4.3 cents a gallon in 1993 as part of the president's deficit reduction plan. Even this very modest step toward less energy use did not enjoy strong political support. During the 1996 campaign, when gas prices jumped 17 percent during the summer, Republican candidate Bob Dole called for a repeal of the gas tax, and President Clinton called for an investigation of the oil companies and ordered the release of 12 million barrels of oil from the nation's Strategic Oil Reserve in order to soften the price increase.[75] Increasing energy taxes sufficiently for significant conservation or revenue purposes requires more political skill than recent presidents and their congressional allies have been able to muster. Congress has refused to pass recent bills to increase the Corporate Average Fuel Economy standards required of new automobiles sold in the United States or other proposals to increase energy conservation. The failure of this policy debate is particularly significant. After adjusting for inflation, the price of crude oil in 1996, not including taxes, is less than one-half what it was in 1981. The average fuel efficiency of cars climbed from 15.9 miles per gallon in 1981 to 21.4 miles per gallon in 1994; as a result, the average fuel cost per mile driven dropped during those years from 12.11 cents per mile to 3.38 cents per mile.[76] Thus rather than an increase in the cost of gas, which might contribute to conservation, the country has seen a decline in cost in inflation-adjusted terms, which has led to higher use.

However, while many national policymakers refuse even to discuss Agenda 21 and the idea of sustainability, some local governments in the United States have actually taken action. Communities in the Pacific Northwest are leaders in sustainable development. The region has undergone dramatic economic growth in the years since the 1960s and its economic base has been transformed. Metropolitan areas have aggressively developed policies to control urban sprawl and develop mass transit. Timber and ranching businesses in the region have emphasized stewardship and responsibility for sustainable use of resources. State officials in Oregon have devised indicators of sustainable development to help guide policymakers.[77] Other communities have also aggressively pursued sustainable development initiatives. The East-West/Gateway Coordinating Council in St. Louis, Missouri, for example, has developed a twenty-year transportation plan that integrates transportation decisions with economic, environmental, and community goals, such as supporting mobility for low-income residents and ensuring that development along rail lines is based on sustainability principles. Some communities have formed sustainable development forums to bring community members together to discuss issues and formulate plans. Nonprofit organizations throughout the nation formed the Sustainable Communities Network to share information on demonstration projects and conduct outreach programs.[78]

Many U.S. cities have joined the International Council for Local Environmental Initiatives (ICLEI), which has established a global program to assist local governments in implementing Agenda 21 programs. The first effort, Model Communities, focused on community planning. A second program established Local Agenda 21 networks to report on the implementing, monitoring, and reporting of Agenda 21 programs.[79] While it is too early to be able to assess the impact of these initiatives on local and global environments, they represent important efforts to gain binding commitments for participation in the kinds of efforts envisioned in Agenda 21.[80]

ICLEI's Cities for Climate Protection program is another example of local communities implementing plans to address global issues. Many cities have embraced the goal of a 20 percent reduction in carbon dioxide emissions, and several major cities have reduced emissions by as much as 15 percent since 1995. Most of the progress is being made in retrofitting municipal buildings, community energy efficiency programs, and waste management initiatives.[81]

A number of U.S. communities have also developed their own greenhouse gas reduction programs. Twenty-three states, according to one count, have developed action plans for reducing greenhouse gases.[82] In 1993, Minnesota's Public Utilities Commission began requiring power companies to assign a dollar value to the environmental impact of each ton of carbon dioxide their plants emit and to add that amount to their estimate of the total cost of operating their plants for the purpose of setting electric rates. This effort to deal with power plant externalities was a planning tool rather than a regulatory requirement. Minnesota industries that burn coal sued the commission, challenging the science behind fears of climate change and warning of economic collapse. The judge ruled in favor of the commission but ordered it to value the carbon dioxide at from $0.30 to $3.00 a ton; advocates of the charge had pushed for a tax range some ten times greater. The Minnesota state legislature considered a bill in 1997 that would have cut income and payroll taxes and imposed a new tax on carbon dioxide emissions, but opponents successfully blocked the action, claiming that it was a tax increase rather than a tax shift. In some states, climate change efforts are a tool used by industries to protect themselves against greenhouse gas agreements.

In Oregon a new electric power deregulation law, enacted in 1997, requires utilities to offset 17 percent of the carbon dioxide they emit, based on emissions when operating at full capacity; if they operate below capacity, they must still offset 17 percent of the maximum carbon dioxide they could generate with reductions of that amount from other sources. The Oregon law stipulates that new plants must emit 17 percent less carbon dioxide than the cleanest facility in the nation, creating a continual incentive to develop cleaner technologies. As facilities elsewhere emit less pollution, new plants in Oregon must become even cleaner. Utilities can offset the carbon dioxide themselves or give money to the Oregon Climate Trust, a nonprofit organization responsible for seeing that offset projects actually reduce carbon dioxide levels. Vermont officials have proposed a carbon tax, to be offset by income and sales tax cuts. Wisconsin is exploring options for a major shift to energy efficiency and shifting from coal to natural gas to produce electricity. While Agenda 21 and the idea of sustainability have not reshaped national policy debates, some of their provisions and underlying values are being taken seriously in a few U.S. communities.

Major Issues in Implementing Agenda 21

Agenda 21 and the sustainability goals underlying it are dynamic, moving targets. No country will ever implement all of Agenda 21's provisions, but the Agenda may play a greater role in the future than it has during its first five or six years in reshaping the dominant discourse of economic growth, social equity, and environmental protection. If it is to be successful in reshaping that discourse, it will need to help us rethink our understanding of a number of issues. Two issues are critical: our understanding of economic development in the developing world, and economic policy and globalization.

Rethinking Development

Much of the spending for development since the beginning of the cold war in the late 1940s was driven by national security concerns rather than the needs of the recipient nations. Development programs devised by the North have often emphasized large-scale, politically visible projects that impose Western technologies and ways of thinking on cultures and societies that are organized and structured much differently. Relief or short-term assistance is often not integrated with long-term, sustainable interventions that promote self-sufficiency.

An alternative view of development begins with the interests and desires of local residents, who identify their problems, propose solutions, and work alongside those who can provide external technological and financial support. Crops are produced primarily for domestic consumption rather than export. Sustainability and development are emphasized along with environmental concerns. Women are empowered and gain resources to improve the quality of life for their families through access to capital from microcredit banks. These efforts are sensitive to how change affects traditional cultures and to the need to reinvent community and individual identity in response to change. They provide opportunities for native peoples to examine their cultures and to reconcile traditional beliefs and practices with the imperatives of change. They respect the energy of culture, which can "energize a people to renew themselves and their society," "mobilize individuals, groups, and communities to a heightened sense of purpose," and help "people to reach within themselves to find a previously hidden reservoir of strength and resolve." Cultural energy grows with use in awakening the "latent power" of individuals and groups.[83]

Technology plays a central role in this model of development. The emergent model of integrating culture and development promises to ensure that the technologies employed are compatible with and serve to strengthen local cultures and practices. Such alternative technologies are appropriate, small-scale, compatible with local knowledge and culture, and can be built and maintained by the people who will use them. Most modern technologies used in development projects are dependent on fossil fuels and other limited resources, are poorly integrated with natural processes, are large-scale, and are justified by relying on a relatively narrow concept of efficiency and rationality. Alternative, or soft, technologies generally are adapted to natural cycles, minimize pollution, use renewable matter and energy, are labor intensive, minimize per capita use, take long-term costs into account, are smaller and simpler and less dependent on a specialized technical elite than hard technologies, and adapt to societal needs and ecological constraints. They rely on materials that are often a combination of old and new technologies. And, especially, they reject the idea that society must adapt to technological developments; here, technologies are shaped by societal concerns and are controlled by collective decision making.[84]

Such development efforts are also comprehensive and incorporate a wide range of solutions. They address health care, education, literacy, food production, environmental quality, and other considerations. Development includes efforts to reduce population growth, since unchecked growth will simply overwhelm other efforts to produce food and preserve ecological systems. Perhaps most important, development takes place through people, not to them or for them, as it reinforces local cultures and traditions.

Rethinking Economic Policy and Globalization

The theory of environmentally sustainable development is compelling, but much more needs to be done to harmonize the goals of economic development and environmental preservation. The most promising source of funds for achieving global environmental goals, for example, is broad-based economic policy. Many countries in the North and South "continue to mismanage their economies—tolerating inefficiency for political ends, squandering precious resources on wars, [and investing] too little in education."[85] The countries of both the North and the South need to improve economic policy. Ending environmentally damaging subsidies, increasing taxes on pollution and cutting taxes on payroll, and redefining economic indicators and measures are critical steps countries can take to pursue economic, environmental, and social goals.

Some studies argue that from $500 billion to $1 trillion in resources could be made available for environmentally sustainable economic activity by ending subsidies on fossil fuels, pesticides and fertilizers, agriculture, irrigation, logging, resource development, and other actions that contribute to environmental harm.[86] Subsidies that protect workers from job loss are similarly important to end because of their environmental and economic impact. Subsidies require higher taxes and diversion of resources that could be used to fund environmentally sustainable economic activities. Many such subsidies seek to protect jobs and profits that will inevitably decline as natural resources are exhausted. Price controls and other subsidies that seek to keep prices of food, energy, water, and other products artificially low also encourage excess use, fail to encourage more environmentally safe alternatives, and divert resources from other productive activities; they also represent significant opportunity costs. Among the biggest subsidies are for agriculture and irrigation, fossil fuel and power, highways, logging, fishing, and mineral production. Subsidies for road building help mask the true cost of driving vehicles. Many subsidies aim to block economic progress and change by protecting domestic industries that are unable to compete effectively.[87]

Ending subsidies is a tremendously powerful way to protect resources and generate funds for environmentally sustainable growth.[88] However, there are tremendous challenges in ending subsidies. It is difficult to ensure that such changes will achieve their goals: a cutback in subsidies for kerosene use in Ghana, for example, led to more cutting of trees from mangrove forests, which are critical habitats for marine life and stabilize coastlines. Some subsidies encourage energy conservation and the development of renewable energy sources, but distinguishing between good and bad subsidies, and anticipating the consequences of ending them, are extremely difficult policy tasks. One approach is simply to try to eliminate all subsidies: even though environmentally beneficial subsidies might be lost, efforts to distinguish between them and the damaging ones will be so difficult that a straightforward opposition to all subsidies is more feasible. It is clear, however, that some subsidies are environmentally valuable, such as those that help overcome the barriers facing new technologies. Subsidies can be narrowly tailored and applied and involve the least cost possible. All the costs, particularly the environmental ones, of giving subsidies can be included in the assessments of costs and benefits. Much work needs to be done in developing complete cost-benefit analysis of existing and proposed subsidies in order to be able to determine which subsidies should be provided and which should be dropped.[89] More daunting is the political challenge. Beneficiaries of subsidies are concentrated and have great incentives to ensure their perpetuation, while the consumers who pay the taxes to fund subsidies and are adversely affected by the environmental damage are widely dispersed and have only weak economic incentives to act. Those subsidies are politically quite entrenched and it would take enormous political energy to end them.

As difficult as subsidies are to eliminate, even more difficult is the creation of tax-based policies that could reduce environmental problems and generate resources for investments in environmentally sustainable economic activity. Tax policies create incentives and disincentives for a host of activities that have environmental and economic consequences. Taxes on sales, income, payrolls, and profits create a disincentive for productive economic activities, but it makes little economic sense to tax activities that are socially beneficial. Governments "tend to undertax destructive activities, such as pollution and resource depletions and environmental quality."[90] The failure to tax air and water pollution ensures that polluters will avoid the full costs of production.

Tax policy provides a clear means of integrating and improving economic and environmental policy. Shifting taxes away from desirable actions such as earning profits and paying salaries, and directing them toward the undesirable actions of producing pollution and harvesting scarce resources can strengthen economies and make them more ecologically sustainable at the same time. Taxing pollution has several advantages: it ensures that producers of pollution take some responsibility for the harms they create; it guarantees that those who benefit economically from industrial production also pay the costs and do not impose them on others who do not enjoy the benefits; it creates clear incentives for people to reduce harmful activities without the heavy hand of government regulators and the inherent loss of flexibility and freedom that comes from command and control regulation; and it encourages pollution reduction to be efficient. Taxes can permit us to include in current price calculations the interests of future generations, who, if present, would also demand clean air and water and old growth forests, and force up the prices for them. It is difficult to calculate the appropriate level of these taxes, since pollution levels differ significantly across similar sources (motor vehicles vary tremendously in their emissions, for instance, as a result of kinds of fuel, weather and climate, driving patterns, and other factors). Placing economic values on environmental quality or scarce resources is similarly difficult. Taxes must be integrated with other laws and policies. The benefits of increased gasoline taxes, for example, are countered by land-use decisions that encourage urban sprawl and more driving. Increasing taxes may not solve the problems of how pollution sources are distributed and their tendency to be concentrated in low-income communities.[91]

Making markets work through true cost pricing is critical but may not be enough. Markets do not account for real scarcity, for example. Markets "tend to break down when confronted with absolute scarcity." In cases such as famines, the market for food may simply collapse or "degenerate into uncontrolled inflation, because the increased price is incapable of calling forth an equivalent increase in supply."[92] Consumers may not respond to rising prices in ways predicted by economic theory. Some consumer decisions are rather independent of price increases; increasing the price of gasoline is likely to have little impact, in the long run, on driving, unless the price increases are so dramatic that they discourage people from driving their own vehicles. Other consumer decisions, such as the kind of energy used to heat a home, are essentially locked in because of the high capital costs involved in converting to another energy system. High prices may not be enough to deter ecologically unsustainable activities. Nevertheless, emissions taxes and other pollution fees can make important contributions to environmental quality by raising money and encouraging conservation.[93]

The third element of the economic policy reform agenda is to change the way we assess national economies. Current economic analysis, Robert Repetto argues, ignores the loss of environmental and natural resources in its assessing of economic progress in developing countries; economists today concentrate on only two kinds of assets: human resources and invested capital, treating natural sources as some sort of "freebie." If a country's balance sheet shows the income gains made from the timber industry, then it should also account for the loss in the forest's natural resources to show the real net gain from production. However, although developing nations are usually the most dependent on their natural resources, they "use a national accounting system that almost completely ignores their principal assets." "A country can cut down its forests, erode its soils, pollute its aquifers and hunt its wildlife and fisheries to extinction," Repetto warns, "but its measured income is not affected as these assets disappear. Impoverishment is taken for progress."[94] This type of approach eventually results in a substantial depletion in natural resources, which will ultimately bankrupt these developing countries.[95] Much of the reason for this approach is that these countries are forced to take whatever prices are offered by the large transnational corporations that dominate international trade and are not in a position to raise prices to encourage conservation or account for the true costs of exploiting limited resources.[96]

One preliminary but promising such effort is the World Bank's proposal to measure a country's wealth by estimating not only how much it produces but also its investments in natural and human resources. The new system breaks down national wealth into three major attributes: "natural capital," or the economic value of timber, mineral deposits, land, water, and other environmental assets; "produced capital," or the value of a nation's machinery, factories, roads; and "human resources," such as the educational level of a population. National wealth is ultimately viewed as the value of produced goods minus consumption, depreciation of produced assets, and use of natural resources. These indicators, not yet widely used, provide a more realistic assessment of national wealth and take into account environmental depletion and degradation in measuring wealth.[97] There are several advantages that arise from this kind of broad balancing of national economic books. First, it focuses attention on the value of investments that increase human capital. Education, health, and other social services are critical in the development of human resources. Second, as data are developed over time, relative changes in a country's development can be identified and adjustments made. Third, the development of information on natural resource wealth can help identify the long-term consequences of selling off natural resources in the short term; while rapid harvesting of resources might appear as gains in immediate economic figures such as gross national product, they will be reflected in reductions in indicators of natural resource wealth.[98]

The Importance of a Development Regime
for the Global Environment

One of the primary challenges that continue to plague efforts to implement Agenda 21 is the lack of coordination among international agencies, which persist in pursuing their own agendas and resist efforts to reshape their work. The issues raised in Agenda 21 and by the concept of sustainable development require a complicated balancing of economic, environmental, and social goals; making difficult tradeoffs; and coordinating disparate efforts. As one study concluded, this requires a "structure which is capable of making complex assessments and reaching carefully calibrated judgments in a manner which is open and accountable. No UN agency meets these criteria."[99] Agenda 21 emphasized the interrelationship between reducing poverty and protecting environmental quality. Reducing poverty is central to the idea of sustainable development. But the implementation of Agenda 21 has focused more on environmental issues than on poverty reduction. The UN Commission on Sustainable Development, the agency responsible for monitoring progress in implementing Agenda 21, for example, has "not made poverty a theme of its discussions."[100] The Global Environmental Facility has been the primary mechanism for providing additional funding for Agenda 21 but has not emphasized the connection between environment and poverty. The UN Commission on Social Development, created to monitor implementation of the agreement signed in the 1995 World Summit for Social Development, has not focused on environmental quality. As one UNDP report put it, "In the five years since UNCED the need to contribute to poverty reduction while attempting to apply Agenda 21 has been ignored."[101] The same UN department that provided administrative support services for the Commission on Sustainable Development, for example, also provided such services for the 1995 World Summit for Social Development, but the summit made virtually no effort to pursue the agenda of sustainable development. Building institutional capacity is an essential element in pursuing the provisions of Agenda 21, but that task seems to overwhelm UNEP and other UN and global institutions.[102]

The most troubling conclusion to be drawn from a brief review of the first five years after the signing of Agenda 21 is the failure to establish a new regime of international development, that is, "persistent and connected sets of rules and practices that prescribe behavioral roles, constrain activity, and shape expectations" and bureaucratic institutions created to formulate and implement policies.[103] Relatively little changed during the five years in the structure of the global community and its capacity to organize for sustainable development. There are a great number of programs but little coordination, and there does not appear to be the capacity to bring about more fundamental change in economic activity. Trade and economic growth continue to dominate the global agenda. When attention is briefly directed to environmental issues like climate change, little effort is made to explore the interaction of free trade and investment agreements with the imperatives of sustainable development. Nevertheless, some reason exists for optimism. International organizations, for example, can play key roles in expanding the capacity of national governments, and their motivation and commitment, to help preserve environmental quality and natural resources. As international agreements are made through the sponsorship of international organizations, domestic environmental and other groups can help hold national governments accountable for their global commitments and pressure them to make changes in national policies.

International environmental organizations have been able to increase the level of concern about environmental threats, facilitate the negotiating of global accords, and help build national governmental capacity while still respecting the integrity of nation-states. These regional and international institutions such as UNEP and commissions and secretariats responsible for implementing regional environmental agreements for acid rain and protection of oceans create networks that transfer technical and managerial expertise, information, and funds. The influence of international environmental institutions has not been in their direct exercise of authority but in their role as catalysts: they link environmental issues with other concerns, create and disseminate scientific information, and facilitate the application of domestic political pressure on governments. They provide forums for negotiations that reduce transaction costs and facilitate decision making, and they monitor compliance and related environmental quality.[104]

One study of the effectiveness of international organizations whose goal is to transfer resources to the developing countries to facilitate their cooperation with and participation in global environmental agreements concluded that these transfers have not been and will not likely be in the future sufficient to remedy major environmental problems. Additional resources will be needed. But the "strategic use of environmental aid can make a difference in environmental quality in some situations by alleviating political obstacles to environmental reforms [and] altering the incentives and capabilities of key players." Environmental assistance can create windows of opportunity that permit political leaders to give more attention to environmental problems, build political coalitions, make environmental projects more appealing to constituents normally not so disposed, redistribute political resources and clout, increase levels of concern about problems, contribute to institutional capacity, and create incentives for other donors to contribute funds.[105] Problems include the dominant role played by donors in setting the assistance agenda, the ways in which donations are actually aimed at solving political problems rather than environmental ones, the defection from commitments once funding is reduced or ends, and difficulties in linking aid with specific environmental reforms. The most "significant sources of aggregate ineffectiveness in environmental aid are coordination failures. . . . Many aid projects and programs are duplicative while others work at cross-purposes."[106] Aid seems most promising when it is aimed at building the capacity of recipient states and of national and local environmental NGOs who can provide internal pressure for environmental protection policy actions.[107]

Agenda 21 and other agreements represent important statements concerning emerging global expectations. Part of their strength comes from the fact that they represent cooperative efforts on the part of participating countries and that it is in everyone's interest to protect the global environment and promote environmentally sustainable economic growth. But the agreements in place are built on the expectation that the wealthy world will provide major new sources of funding to accomplish these goals, and that expectation has not been realized. Nevertheless, these agreements have overcome significant obstacles. The tension between the developing and developed nations, rooted in the history of colonialism, economic exploitation, military adventurism, nationalism, and other factors, is considerable. The tension has become more pronounced as the debate over addressing global environmental problems has evolved during the past two decades. Those in the South fear that their aspirations of economic growth, reduced poverty and starvation, and improved health and education are now to be sacrificed in the name of environmental preservation. They worry that global efforts fashioned by wealthy nations will prevent them from harvesting their natural resources and expanding their industrial base. They believe that their dreams of an improved life will give way to a global effort to reverse the excesses of the wealthy nations that have precipitated environmental threats. The agreements in place are not enough to secure our environmental future, and new agreements will need to be negotiated for decades into the future. If commitments already made are not kept, future agreements will be all the more difficult to produce, and the goals of the agreements in place will not be realized. The future of all the planet's residents, rich and poor, is inextricably intertwined.

Notes

1. World Commission on Environment and Development, *Our Common Future* (New York: Oxford University Press, 1987).
2. For a review of the UNCED meeting, see Michael Keating, *Agenda for Change: A Plain Language Version of Agenda 21 and the Other Rio Agreements* (Geneva: Center for Our Common Future, 1994); Michael Grubb et al., *The Earth Summit Agreements: A Guide and Assessment* (London: Earthscan, 1993); Adam Rogers, *The Earth Summit: A Planetary Reckoning* (Los Angeles: Global View Press, 1993); Daniel Sitarz, *Agenda 21: The Earth Summit Strategy to Save Our Planet* (Boulder, Colo.: Earthpress, 1993).
3. For a review of the UNCED meeting see ibid. and United Nations, *Agenda 21: Programme of Action for Sustainable Development; Rio Declaration on Environment and Development; Statement of Forest Principles*, 1992.
4. "PrepCom 4 Adopts Draft Declaration of Principles for Rio Summit," *Earth Summit Update*, April 1992, 2.
5. "Declaration on Environment and Development," Principle 2.
6. "United Nations Framework Convention on Climate Change" (http://www.unep.ch/iucc/begincon.html); "Convention on Biological Diversity" (http://www.unep.ch/biodiv.html).
7. United Nations, *Agenda 21: Statement of Forest Principles*. "Pressure for Specific Funding Level Expected in Rio," *Earth Summit Update*, May 1992, 2.
8. "PrepCom 4 Forwards Agenda 21 to Rio; Many Ambitious Proposals Are Blocked," *Earth Summit Update*, April 1992, 1, 5; "Agenda 21 Chapter-by-Chapter Summary," *Earth Summit Update*, May 1992, 4–5.
9. See Lester R. Brown, Michael Renner, and Christopher Flavin, *Vital Signs, 1997* (New York: Norton, 1997), 57–61.
10. See E. O.Wilson, ed., *Biodiversity* (Washington, D.C.: National Academy Press, 1988), 3–18.
11. Brown, Renner, and Flavin, *Vital Signs*.
12. Paula DiPerna, "Five Years after the Rio Talkfest: Where Is the Money?" *Earth Times*, January 25, 1997 (http//www.earthtimes.org).
13. Preamble to Agenda 21, reprinted in Sitarz, *Agenda 21*, 28. For the entire document, see United Nations, *Agenda 21*, UN doc. E.92-38352; A/CONF.151/26 (vols. 1–3).
14. All costs are expressed in U.S. dollars unless otherwise noted.

15. United Nations Development Programme (UNDP), *Human Development Report 1997* (New York: Oxford University Press, 1997), 2.
16. Ibid., 3. See also Robert Pear, "New Estimate Doubles Rate of H.I.V. Spread," *New York Times,* November 26, 1997, A8.
17. World Bank, *Advancing Sustainable Development: The World Bank and Agenda 21* (Washington, D.C.: World Bank, 1997), 3.
18. UNDP, *Human Development Report 1997,* 5.
19. UNDP, *Human Development Report 1996* (New York: Oxford University Press, 1996), 9.
20. Ibid., 9–10.
21. Ibid., 27.
22. UNDP, *Human Development Report 1997,* 13–14, 27.
23. World Resources Institute, *World Resources 1990–91* (Washington, D.C.: World Resources Institute, 1990), 256–264.
24. Jodi L. Jacobson, "The Forgotten Resource," *World Watch,* May–June 1988, 35, 36–38.
25. Ann Misch, "Lost in the Shadow Economy," *World Watch,* April 1992, 18–19.
26. Ibid., 128.
27. Ibid., 130.
28. Lester R. Brown, Michael Renner, and Christopher Flavin, *Vital Signs 1997* (New York: Norton, 1997), 27.
29. World Bank, *Advancing Sustainable Development,* 35.
30. Brown, Renner, and Flavin, *Vital Signs 1997,* 29.
31. Ibid., 32–33.
32. Ibid., 80.
33. Ibid., 82.
34. Ibid., 46, 58.
35. Ibid., 102.
36. World Bank, *Advancing Sustainable Development,* vii, 3.
37. The UN Food and Agriculture Organization defines deforestation as depletion of crown cover to less than 10 percent; even if 10 percent or more of crown cover remains, however, significant damage to forest ecosystems may occur. Brown, Renner, and Flavin, *Vital Signs 1997,* 96.
38. World Resources Institute, *World Resources: A Guide to the Global Environment* (New York: Oxford University Press, 1996), x.
39. Ibid., xi.
40. Ibid., xi–xii.
41. Ibid., xiii–xiv.
42. World Resources Institute, *World Resources 1994–95* (Washington, D.C.: World Resources Institute, 1994), 224.
43. Ibid., 224–225.
44. The source of the listings of UN organizations is Lee Kimball, *Forging Environmental Agreements* (Washington, D.C.: World Resources Institute, 1992), 70.
45. United Nations Environment Programme, *Global Environmental Outlook* (New York: Oxford University Press, 1997), 2.
46. Ibid., 3.
47. DiPerna, "Five Years after the Rio Talkfest."
48. World Bank, *World Development Report 1988* (New York: Oxford University Press, 1988).
49. Ibid., 11.
50. Gary Gardner, "Third World Debt Is Still Growing," *World Watch,* January–February 1995, 37–38.
51. Jyoti Shankar Singh, "How to Reduce the Debt Burden," *Earthtimes,* October 1–15, 1996, 12.

52. This debt is actually owed to the Paris Club, a body of official creditors that represents the major industrial nations in decisions affecting the debt owed by developing countries; Club members hold 42 percent of the debt owed by developing countries; the World Bank, IMF, and other multilateral institutions hold 21 percent; other bilateral creditors, such as Arab countries and the former Soviet Union nations, also hold 21 percent of the debt; and 16 percent of the debt is owed to private creditors. Paul Lewis, "Debt-Relief Cost for the Poorest Nations," *New York Times,* June 10, 1996, C2; Paul Lewis, "I.M.F. and World Bank Clear Debt Relief," *New York Times,* September 30, 1996, C2; "The Third-World Debt Crisis," *New York Times,* June 26, 1996, A14 (editorial).

53. United Nations General Assembly, Nineteenth Special Session, Agenda Item 8, "Overall Review and Appraisal of the Implementation of Agenda 21" (June 27, 1997), sec. 2. See also *Assessment of Progress Made Since the United Nations Conference on Environment and Development,* paras. 7–8 (gopher://gopher.un.org:70/00/ga/docs/S-19/plenary/AS19-29.TXT).

54. Ibid., paras. 9–10, 17.

55. UNGASS, "Implementation in Areas Requiring Urgent Action," sec. 3, para. 22.

56. Ibid., paras. 23–32.

57. Ibid., paras. 33–75.

58. Ibid., paras. 76–115.

59. Ibid., paras. 116–136.

60. Ibid., para. 137.

61. *Earth Negotiations Bulletin* 5 (June 30, 1997), http://www.iisd.ca/linkages/csd/enb0588e.html#1.

62. Ibid., paras. 11–12.

63. Ibid., para. 13.

64. Natural Resources Defense Council and Cape 2000, *Four in '94 Assessing National Actions to Implement Agenda 21: A Country-by-Country Progress Report* (New York: Natural Resources Defense Council, 1994).

65. Executive Order 12852, June 29, 1993, amended on July 19, 1993, *U.S. Code,* vol. 42, sec. 4321.

66. President's Council on Sustainable Development, *Sustainable Development: A New Consensus* (Washington, D.C.: U.S. Government Printing Office, 1996), iv.

67. Ibid., 7.

68. Ibid.

69. Sheila Jasanoff, *The Fifth Branch: Science Advisers as Policymakers* (Cambridge: Harvard University Press, 1990); Paul Portney, "Cartoon Caricatures of Regulatory Reform," *Resources,* fall 1995, 21–24; Terry Davies, "Congress Discovers Risk Analysis," *Resources,* winter 1995, 5–8.

70. National Academy of Public Administration, *Setting Priorities, Getting Results* (Washington, D.C.: NAPA, 1995).

71. U.S. Environmental Protection Agency, *Unfinished Business: A Comparative Assessment of Environmental Problems* (Washington, D.C.: U.S. EPA, 1987), 96.

72. Terry Davies, ed., *Comparing Environmental Risks: Tools for Setting Government Priorities* (Washington, D.C.: Resources for the Future, 1996).

73. U.S. Environmental Protection Agency, Science Advisory Board, *Reducing Risk: Setting Priorities and Strategies for Environmental Protection* (Washington, D.C.: U.S. EPA, 1990), 22.

74. Susan Dentzer, "R.I.P. for the Btu Tax," *U.S. News and World Report,* June 21, 1993, 95.

75. Howard Gleckman, "Gas Pump Politics," *Business Week,* May 13, 1996, 40–41.

76. "Resource Facts," *Resources,* summer 1996, 4; U.S. Department of Commerce, *Statistical Abstract of the United States, 1997* (Washington, D.C.: U.S. Bureau of the Census, 1997), 638.

77. President's Council on Sustainable Development, *Building on Consensus: A Progress Report on Sustainable America* (Washington, D.C.: PCSD, 1997), 10–11.
78. Ibid., 13.
79. Ibid., 9.
80. "Local Agenda 21," *Initiatives* (International Council for Local Environmental Initiatives), July 1997, 9.
81. "Cities to Report Success to COP3," *Initiatives* (International Council for Local Environmental Initiatives), November 1997, 1, 3.
82. The discussion in this and the following paragraph on state innovations is based on Josh Wilson, "Power Plays," *MotherJones* Interactive: http://bsd.mojones.com/news_wire/wilson.html.
83. Charles Kleymeyer, "Cultural Energy and Grassroots Development," in *Cultural Expression and Grassroots Development*, ed. Charles Kleymeyer (Boulder, Colo.: Rienner, 1994), 28.
84. William Ophuls and A. Stephen Boyan Jr., *Ecology and the Politics of Scarcity Revisited* (New York: Freeman, 1992), 176–177.
85. Sylvia Nasar, "Third World Embracing Reforms to Encourage Economic Growth," *New York Times*, July 8, 1991.
86. DiPerna, "Five Years after the Rio Talkfest."
87. Ibid., 104–105.
88. David Malin Roodman, *Paying the Piper: Subsidies, Politics, and the Environment*, WorldWatch Paper 133 (Washington, D.C.: WorldWatch Institute, 1996).
89. DiPerna, "Five Years after the Rio Talkfest."
90. David Malin Roodman, "Public Money and Human Purpose: The Future of Taxes," *World Watch* 8 (September–October 1995): 13.
91. Taxes can be used to help workers. Pollution taxes are often regressive, since they raise the price of energy, transportation, manufactured goods, and other essentials, and take a larger bite out of the total income of poor households than of more wealthy ones. They must be combined with wage and income tax cuts aimed at low-income families, rebates for energy taxes, and other adjustments. See Roodman, "Public Money and Human Purpose."
92. Ophuls and Boyan, *Ecology and the Politics of Scarcity*, 219.
93. Ibid., 220.
94. Robert Repetto, "Accounting for Environmental Assets," *Scientific American*, June 1994, 94.
95. Ibid., 96.
96. Commission on Developing Countries and Global Change, *For Earth's Sake* (Ottawa: International Development Research Centre, 1992), 22–23.
97. See World Bank, *Expanding the Measure of Wealth: Indicators of Environmentally Sustainable Development* (Washington, D.C.: World Bank, 1997).
98. See World Bank, *Monitoring Environmental Progress: A Report on Work in Progress* (Washington, D.C.: World Bank, 1995); Ismail Serageldin, "Third Annual World Bank Conference on Environmentally Sustainable Development," paper presented at the Third Annual World Bank Conference on Environmentally Sustainable Development, Washington, D.C., October 1995.
99. Konrad Moltke, "Why UNEP Matters," in *Green Globe Yearbook 1996*, ed. Helge Ole Bergesen and Georg Parmann (New York: Oxford University Press, 1996), 61.
100. Ibid., 114.
101. Ibid.
102. Ibid., 61–63.
103. Robert O. Keohane, Peter M. Haas, and Marc A. Levy, "The Effectiveness of International Environmental Institutions," in *Institutions for the Earth*, ed. Robert O. Keohane, Peter M. Haas, and Marc A. Levy (Cambridge: MIT Press, 1993), 5.

104. Robert O. Keohane, Peter M. Haas, and Marc A. Levy, "Improving the Effectiveness of International Environmental Institutions," in Keohane, Haas, and Levy, *Institutions for the Earth*, 397–426.
105. Barbara Connolly, "Increments for the Earth: The Politics of Environmental Aid," in *Institutions for Environmental Aid*, ed. Robert O. Keohane and Marc A. Levy (Cambridge: MIT Press, 1996), 327–328.
106. David Fairman and Michael Ross, "Old Fads, New Lessons: Learning from Economic Development Assistance," in Keohane and Levy, *Institutions for Environmental Aid*, 45.
107. Connolly, "Increments for the Earth," 327–366.

9

Economic Integration and the Environment
Daniel C. Esty

No mention was made of the word *environment* in the original General Agreement on Tariffs and Trade (GATT)—the central pillar of the international trading system—negotiated just after World War II. At that time, no one saw much connection between trade liberalization and environmental protection. For the next forty years, trade and environmental policymakers pursued their respective agendas on parallel tracks that rarely, if ever, intersected. In recent years, however, trade and environmental policymaking have increasingly appeared to be linked, and the two realms have often seemed to collide. Environmental advocates have come to fear that freer trade means increased pollution and resource depletion. And free traders worry that protectionism in the guise of environmental policy will obstruct efforts to open markets and integrate economies around the world.

This chapter explores the trade-environment relationship. It argues that freer trade and economic integration more broadly offer the promise of improved social welfare—as do programs aimed at pollution abatement and improved natural resource management. While theoretically not inconsistent, in practice these goals are often not in perfect alignment. Only through concerted policy attention and efforts to overcome conflicts and tensions can both aims be addressed simultaneously and progress be made toward sustainable development.

Origins of the Trade and Environment "Conflict"

The trade and environmental policy agendas have been driven together by a number of factors. First, environmental issues have taken on increased salience in the last several decades. Trying to accommodate new issues on the public agenda often creates strain.[1] Interest in environmental protection as a component of "quality of life" emerges in almost all societies as wealth rises. The precise focus of the public's environmental interest will vary from nation to nation, and particularly from industrialized to developing countries. But, in almost every corner of the world, there has been a marked increase in the attention paid to environmental problems over the last several decades. This trend reached a crescendo in 1992 with the Earth Summit in Rio de Janeiro. Formally known as the United Nations Conference on Environment and Development (UNCED), this global convocation drew 120 presidents and prime ministers to Brazil and helped to focus global attention on pollution control and resource management issues. It highlighted the link between environmental problems and economic development and consolidated the environment as a first-tier international agenda item.[2]

The end of the cold war also augmented interest in environmental issues. Reduced East-West tensions allowed public officials (and citizens more generally) to shift their foreign policy gaze from traditional politico-military concerns to a more extensive array of international issues.[3] As a result of this wider international affairs perspective, a broader definition of "national security" has begun to emerge that encompasses environmental matters.[4]

Recognition of a set of inherently global pollution and resource problems has further propelled environmental issues up the international policy agenda. Notably, scientific advances have transformed the environmental policy landscape. From the threat of global climate change arising from a build-up of greenhouse gases in the atmosphere to ozone layer destruction from emissions of chlorofluorocarbons (CFCs) and other related chemicals to the depletion of fisheries in most of the world's oceans, over-exploitation of the "global commons" has added to the sense of priority given to the environment on the international scene.[5]

Economic integration has also helped to transform environmental protection from a clearly domestic, highly localized issue into one of inherently international scope. In a world of liberalized trade, where the competition for market share is global, the stringency of environmental regulations in each nation and subjurisdiction becomes an important determinant of the competitiveness of the enterprises located within that territory. Thus, for example, while hazardous waste management requirements have long been viewed as simply a function of local pollution control priorities and risk tolerances, today these policy choices are understood to have important consequences for the production costs of the enterprises that must meet the standards.[6] Concerns about competitiveness transform even the most local of environmental issues into a matter of some international significance.

Triggering Events

Government commitments to freer trade and liberalized investment regimes have helped to sharpen the focus on the intersection of trade and environmental policies. Indeed, it was the 1989 announcement by President George Bush that he intended to negotiate a free trade agreement with Mexico that first brought "trade and environment" issues to the fore. The prospect of a free flow of goods across the U.S.-Mexico border struck fear in the hearts of environmentalists. With visions of the highly polluted "maquiladora" (duty-free) zone along the border expanding and a nervousness that a trade agreement with Mexico might mean explicit lowering ("harmonizing") of U.S. environmental standards to match lax Mexican regulatory requirements or, worse, trigger a downward spiral in environmental standards on both sides of the border as industry claims of competitive disadvantage induced governments to relax their environmental rules, the U.S.

environmentalists demanded that attention be paid to the environmental consequences of freer North American trade. The Bush administration's commitment to discuss environmental issues with Mexico and Canada in parallel with the trade negotiations that led to the North American Free Trade Agreement (NAFTA) marked a watershed in international economic policy—establishing clearly that trade and environmental goals must be pursued in tandem.[7]

While NAFTA set the environmental pot on the trade fire, the decision of a GATT dispute resolution panel in the 1991 "tuna-dolphin" case caused a simmering issue to boil over. The GATT declared the U.S. law requiring an embargo on Mexican tuna that were caught in nets that killed dolphins to be illegal under the rules of international trade.[8] U.S. environmentalists saw the decision as an affront to American environmental "sovereignty."[9] How could some obscure set of trade experts sitting in Geneva judge a U.S. law (the Marine Mammal Protection Act) to be unacceptable? The environmental community saw in the tuna-dolphin decision proof that in a conflict between trade and environmental goals, the trade liberalization principles would trump the environmental values. Outraged environmentalists decried "GATTzilla" and began a campaign to "green" trade law and policymaking.[10]

This "trade and environment" initiative now has widened and evolved. In fact, the call for further regional free trade agreements, including a Free Trade Agreement of the Americas (FTAA) and the push by the eighteen members (including the United States) of the Asia-Pacific Economic Cooperation (APEC) forum to advance free trade throughout the Pacific Basin, as well as new commitments to multilateral trade liberalization through the World Trade Organization (WTO), have continued to keep trade and environment issues on the international agenda.[11]

There have been some successes in making trade and environmental policymaking more mutually supportive. NAFTA, as noted above, represents such a case. In other circumstances, trade policy has been pushed forward without regard to any environmental consequences. But policymakers are learning that they ignore the trade-environment link at some peril. For example, negotiations within the Organization for Economic Cooperation and Development (OECD) to establish a Multilateral Agreement on Investment (MAI) faltered in the face of environmentalists' outcry over the lack of attention to pollution control and resource management issues in the draft treaty.

The 1992 Rio Earth Summit established broad support for the notion that economic growth must be pursued on a sustainable basis.[12] While the concept of "sustainable development" remains somewhat murky and contested, a general consensus has emerged that this concept means that economic goals cannot be pursued in a manner that disregards the environmental consequences of growth.[13] Similarly, sustainable development also means that environmental aims must be understood in the context of a need for economic growth and improved material conditions, especially in the developing world.

Efforts to make trade and environmental policies more compatible have faced significant obstacles. The trade and environmental communities have distinct goals, traditions, operating procedures, and even language. The ultimate good for environmentalists—"protection"—is the consummate bad for free traders. Both in terminology and substance, bringing these two worlds together continues to be a significant challenge.

Core Environmental Concerns about Free Trade

Environmentalists worry that economic integration and more globalized markets will make environmental protection harder to achieve. Their concerns can be boiled down to a few key propositions:[14]

Expanded trade will cause environmental harm by promoting economic growth that, without environmental safeguards, will result in increased pollution and the unsustainable consumption of natural resources. Environmentalists who adhere to a traditional "limits to growth" perspective would reject the possibility that environmental safeguards might make trade liberalization environmentally acceptable. They see free trade resulting in environmentally damaging economic growth. Of course, many environmentalists today adhere to the "sustainable development" paradigm, which would accept the possibility that environmental improvements might arise from economic growth so long as pollution control and resource consumption issues are expressly addressed.[15] They also recognize that poverty leads to short-term decision making that is often environmentally harmful. Thus, to the extent that trade promotes growth and alleviates poverty, it can yield environmental benefits.

Trade liberalization and trade agreements often entail "market access" commitments that can be used to override environmental regulations unless appropriate sensitivity to pollution and resource issues is built into the structure of the trading system. Many environmentalists fear that the "disciplines" to which countries bind themselves as part of a trade agreement will result in a loss of regulatory sovereignty. Specifically, they worry that the market access obligations and other trade principles designed to permit the free flow of imports and exports will override environmental policies and goals, resulting in the harmonization of environmental standards at baseline levels or worse.[16] This outcome might arise, they believe, through negotiated commitments to common regulatory rules. Alternatively, they fear that a free trade zone might make it hard for high-standard countries to keep their strict environmental requirements in the face of industry claims of competitive disadvantage from producers in low-standard jurisdictions whose environmental compliance costs are lower.

Even where pollution does not spill across national borders, countries with lax environmental standards will have a competitive advantage in a global marketplace, putting pressures on countries with high environmental standards to reduce the rigor of their environmental requirements. The fear of competitive disadvantage in an integrated North American marketplace was the central trade and environment issue in the course of the NAFTA debate. Ross Perot's memorable suggestion that low labor costs and lax environmental standards in Mexico would result in a "giant sucking sound" of U.S. factories and jobs going down the drain to Mexico resonated broadly.[17] Although in academic circles there is an ongoing debate over the seriousness of fears about a "race toward the bottom" in environmental standard setting,[18] business leaders, environmentalists, and politicians seem convinced that the fear of competitive disadvantage arising out of divergent environmental standards deserves attention.

Variations in the stringency of regulations are not always a problem. Differences in environmental standards can be seen as an important component of comparative advantage. Indeed, the fact that countries have different levels of commitment to environmental protection—and thus different pollution control costs—makes gains from economic exchange and trade more generally possible. Competitiveness pressures may also induce "regulatory competition" among jurisdictions as governments work to make their location attractive to industry. In some circumstances, these pressures will induce governments to provide services and regulate efficiently. Competition of this sort enhances social welfare.[19] But in other circumstances, competition among horizontally arrayed jurisdictions (national governments versus national governments) may precipitate a welfare-reducing cycle of weakening environmental commitments as political leaders seek to relax their environmental standards to attract investment and jobs.[20] In fact, governments rarely lower their environmental standards overtly to improve their competitive position. They do, however, relax the enforcement of their standards or fail to raise standards to optimal levels for fear of exposing their industries to higher costs than their competitors.[21] Competitiveness pressures thus create a "political drag" on environmental policymaking.[22]

The debate over the seriousness of concerns about environmental-regulation-based competitiveness turns on the question of why standards diverge. If the stringency of the rules varies because of differences in climate, weather, population density, risk preferences, level of development, or other "natural" factors, the variations in standards should be considered legitimate and appropriate. Any competitive pressure created is simply the playing out of socially beneficial market forces. Divergent standards may also arise, however, from regulatory authorities failing to monitor fully the harms that spill across their borders onto other jurisdictions, resulting in part of the costs of pollution control being "externalized"; regulatory "incapacity" leading to suboptimal environmental standards or lax enforcement of environmental requirements; or special interest manipulation of the regulatory process or other distortions in environmental policymaking, which lead regulators to deviate from what would be the optimal environmental policies (what academics call "public choice" problems), causing the authorities in other jurisdictions to respond strategically.

Under-regulation that permits pollution to spill over onto neighboring jurisdictions or into a global commons represents an unfair (and economically inefficient) basis on which to establish a competitive advantage. Likewise, suboptimal standards that arise from "regulatory failures"—including results driven by weak government performance and inadequate environmental decision making or outcomes manipulated by special interests through lobbying, campaign contributions, or outright corruption of public officials—break the promise of improved social welfare through interjurisdictional competition.[23] And where one's competitors have selected, for whatever reason, suboptimal environmental policies, governments must generally respond strategically and set their standards with an eye on those adopted by their trade competitors.[24] In each of these circumstances, international cooperation in response to environmental challenges promises to improve policy outcomes. Insofar as trade negotiations generate the competitive pressures that trigger a race toward the bottom, they also provide an occasion to advance the "collective action" required to avoid a downward regulatory spiral.

The likelihood of a "race" dynamic increases as economic integration deepens. As long as Jurisdiction A is a comparatively unimportant destination of Jurisdiction B's exports or if Jurisdiction A is an insignificant international competitor, then differential environmental standards matter very little. B will be relatively unaffected by environmental policy choices in A. But if the level of interaction grows, so too does B's exposure to "economic externalities" arising from suboptimal environmental policies in A. For example, in 1985, U.S. exports to China totaled $7 billion and imports from China stood at $3 billion. In 1995, Chinese exports to the United States topped $24 billion and U.S. exports to China amounted to $16 billion.[25] This extraordinary growth in U.S.-China trade makes U.S. industries much more sensitive to cost disadvantages that they suffer in relation to Chinese competitors—and will focus increasing attention on whether any such disadvantages that arise from environmental conditions are appropriate and legitimate.

Trade restrictions need to be available as a tool for enforcing international environmental agreements, and the market opening commitments made in the course of trade agreements may reduce the availability of trade measures as an enforcement tool. Environmentalists fear that commitments to trade liberalization will forbid the use of trade measures as a way of obtaining leverage over countries that are refusing to sign or are not living up to their obligations under international environmental agreements. The need to discipline "free riders"—those who are benefiting from but not paying for pollution control or resource management—is well understood. Trade officials, however, would argue that it is not appropriate to use trade policy tools as a way of achieving environmental goals. They reason that it is hard enough to keep markets open without trying to carry environmental burdens at the same time. Environmentalists respond that there are very few ways of exerting pressure in the international domain (for example, bombing environmental treaty violators would probably not be considered reasonable) and therefore that trade measures must be available as an enforcement tool.

The Free Trade Response

Free traders worry that the environmentalists' critique of trade is misplaced and could result in the disruption of efforts to promote trade liberalization and to obtain the benefits promised by more open markets around the world. Trade advocates note, in particular, that trade and environmental policy goals can be made compatible. As the members of the just-created World Trade Organization (WTO) declared at their meeting in Marrakesh in 1994: "There should not be, nor need be, any policy contradiction between upholding and safeguarding an open, nondiscriminatory and equitable multilateral trading system on the one hand, and acting for the protection of the environment and promotion of sustainable development on the other."[26]

Free traders note that both freer trade and environmental protection efforts are aimed at promoting efficiency and reducing waste. They posit that, to the extent that environmental policies seem to be in tension with freer trade, the conflict generally arises from poorly constructed environmental policies rather than any inherently antienvironmental bias embedded in the trading system. Trade experts further observe that environmental policies that seek to internalize externalities through the application of the Polluter Pays Principle represent virtually no conflict with freer trade.[27]

Trade supporters also maintain that, as an empirical matter, as the wealth of the society increases, its spending on environmental protection almost always goes up. Thus, they contend that environmentalists should support freer trade as a way of achieving economic growth and greater wealth, some part of which can be devoted to expanded pollution control and resource conservation programs. More dramatically, trade advocates observe that poverty is the source of a great many environmental harms. And indeed, poor people often make bad environmental choices because of the short-term time frame forced upon them. For example, those who lack modern conveniences must cut down nearby trees to cook their evening meal. They are unable to focus on the longer-term consequences of deforestation such as soil erosion and pollution of nearby water bodies.

Professors Gene M. Grossman and Alan B. Krueger have demonstrated that some environmental problems seem to worsen during the early stages of development, peak at a per capita gross domestic product of about $8,000, and improve as countries become wealthier beyond that point.[28] Two other scholars, Dua and Esty, have suggested that the relationship between environmental harms and income is somewhat more complicated.[29] They argue that some problems are so localized and pressing that even the poorest countries will be under pressure to address them as economic growth begins and incomes start to rise. Governments, for example, seek to provide drinking water to their people at even the lowest levels of development. Other problems appear to follow the inverted-U "Kuznets" curve that Grossman and Krueger hypothesize, rising in the initial stages of industrialization, but falling as wealth increases. Local air pollution problems seem to fall into this category. Dua and Esty note, however, that some indicators of environmental

quality continue to deteriorate even as incomes rise. For instance, greenhouse gas emissions may go up at a less rapid rate, but they do not fall even when high income levels are achieved.

This more nuanced understanding of the relationship between economic growth and environmental protection leads to the conclusion that trade for trade's sake does not make sense as an economic strategy. Trade can be a mechanism for advancing economic growth and social welfare. These gains *can* permit resources to be made available for investments in environmental protection. But there are no guarantees that this positive result will always emerge. In fact, welfare losses from trade-exacerbated environmental harms could outweigh the benefits of freer trade. It is therefore important that environmental policy tracks and evolves in parallel with commitments to trade liberalization.

NAFTA First Steps

Environmental Protection Agency (EPA) administrator William Reilly described the North American Free Trade Agreement in testimony before the U.S. Congress as "the greenest trade agreement ever."[30] Reilly's conclusion was based on a number of procedural and substantive advances in integrating trade and environmental policy goals that were achieved in the course of the NAFTA negotiations.

On the procedural front, the need to address environmental issues in the context of a commitment to trade liberalization was recognized and taken seriously for the first time ever in the agreement. The Bush administration launched environmental negotiations with the Mexicans and Canadians on a "parallel track" set up alongside the trade negotiations. These environmental talks generated a joint U.S.-Mexico commitment to address pollution issues along their shared border. The "integrated border environmental plan" that emerged cataloged comprehensively for the first time the spectrum of environmental concerns arising along the 2,000 mile border between the two countries. The initiative also offered a game plan for addressing the issues identified and a set of priorities to be undertaken jointly by Mexican and U.S. environmental officials.

In addition to the border plan, the parallel track negotiations led to an Environmental Side Agreement to NAFTA. The Side Agreement, concluded by the administration of Bill Clinton and Al Gore, set up a "development bank" to promote environmental infrastructure investments along the U.S.-Mexico border, and established a Commission for Environmental Cooperation (CEC) to oversee the environmental issues associated with closer trade links across North America.[31] The CEC provides a mechanism for facilitating cooperation among the NAFTA countries on the full range of environmental issues and resource challenges that they face, serves as a forum for regular high-level meetings, provides an independent secretariat to report on significant environmental issues confronting the NAFTA parties, and ensures that environmental enforcement remains a priority in all three countries and that opportunities exist for public participation in the development and implementation of environmental laws and programs in Mexico, the United States, and Canada.

In addition to the parallel track environmental negotiations, environmental officials were included, for the first time, in the trade negotiations themselves. EPA negotiators participated in several of the issue-specific working groups. A senior EPA official served on the high-level negotiating team of the U.S. Trade Representative (USTR). Likewise, environmental groups were considered an important constituency in the course of the NAFTA debate—a role they had never played before. USTR officials regularly briefed environmental advocates. In addition, trade representative Carla Hills placed four environmental group leaders on her public advisory committees on various aspects of trade policymaking.[32]

Perhaps the most important procedural advance associated with NAFTA was the decision to undertake an environmental review of issues associated with freer trade across North America. This analysis helped to focus the U.S. negotiators on the environmental challenges and opportunities they faced. The NAFTA environmental review, produced in draft in the fall of 1991, was made available for public comment and sparked considerable debate at six hearings around the country.[33] The final review, including a series of recommendations to the negotiating team, was released in February 1992—in time to be incorporated into the U.S. negotiating strategy. The review helped to focus the negotiators on both large and small issues, ranging from the benefits of broadening Mexico's economic development beyond the maquiladora zone along the border to finding ways to reduce the traffic jams (and resulting air pollution) that resulted from backups at customs in Texas, New Mexico, Arizona, and California.

Substantive advances were also made in the course of the NAFTA process. The Preamble to the agreement makes environmental considerations a central focus of the effort to promote freer trade. It calls on the parties to pursue their program of trade liberalization so as to promote "sustainable development" and to "strengthen the development and enforcement of environmental laws and regulations."[34]

The NAFTA parties further agreed that major environmental agreements with trade provisions should be given precedence if there were to develop a conflict between the party's obligations under the environmental agreement and under NAFTA. Similarly, NAFTA makes clear in its chapter on "sanitary and phytosanitary" provisions that each party to the agreement retains an unrestricted right to set and maintain environmental health and safety standards at its own chosen level of protection. By clarifying that the NAFTA parties are free to make their own risk assessments and apply their own risk policies, NAFTA acknowledges that some legitimate environmental policies will have impacts on trade but should still be permitted.

NAFTA's investment chapter also breaks new ground in addressing environmental issues. Specifically, each country is assured of the right to adopt and enforce any pollution control or resource management measure it deems necessary to protect its environment. This language prevents trade commitments from trumping environmental policies and programs as long as they are based on scientific foundations and are not disguised barriers to trade. The treaty also contains a "pollution haven" proviso that declares that a NAFTA party cannot seek to attract investments by relaxing environmental standards or cutting back on enforcement. This provision is backed by a structure of binding arbitration and the possibility of trade penalties being imposed for noncompliance.

NAFTA also establishes more environmentally sensitive dispute resolution procedures. Specifically, where environmental issues are in question in a trade dispute, the agreement provides procedures for convening a board of scientific or technical experts to advise the dispute settlement panel. It also forbids countries from taking disputes out of NAFTA to the WTO in order to obtain less environmentally protective ground rules.

The NAFTA efforts to make trade liberalization and environmental protection mutually compatible have generally worked quite well. Fears of industrial migration to Mexico based on a promise of lax environmental standards have not been realized. In fact, NAFTA's broadly based program of environmental cooperation has greatly increased the focus on pollution control in Mexico. While many problems remain and the attempt to finance new environmental projects on the U.S.-Mexico border has gotten off to a slow start, environmental conditions across large parts of Mexico are beginning to improve.

Some environmentalists remain concerned that environmental issues are still not being taken seriously in the trade context. And in the 1997–1998 debate over "fast track" legislation to extend NAFTA to all of the Western hemisphere, these complaints rang true. The proposals put forward for negotiation of a Free Trade Agreement of the Americas devoid of any environmental provisions represented a significant step back from the progress made by NAFTA in integrating environmental sensitivity into efforts at trade liberalization.

It is also true that the NAFTA Side Agreement's Commission for Environmental Cooperation has proceeded in fits and starts. It has undertaken several studies designed to ensure that environmental considerations are factored into trade policy across North America. But the CEC has also faced pressure not to pursue its environmental goals too aggressively. The lack of clear political support drove the CEC to back away from several controversial "trade and environment" issues, including questions about Mexico's environmental performance and efforts to address clear-cutting in the U.S. Northwest and British Columbia. In addition, the executive director of the CEC, Victor Lichtinger (a Mexican), was forced to resign in early 1998 when U.S. and Mexican officials concluded that his environmental advocacy was disruptive to their national pollution control and resource management programs. Whether the CEC will mature into an effective mechanism for environmental coordination among the United States, Mexico, and Canada remains to be seen.

The Broader Policy Response

While the first steps toward integrating environmental protection and trade liberalization were taken in NAFTA, a broader effort to make trade and environmental policies mutually reinforcing has yet to be launched. The World Trade Organization, the international body set up in 1994 to implement the General Agreement on Tariffs and Trade and to manage international trade relations, has come under considerable criticism for its lack of environmental sensitivity. Although the WTO has a Committee on Trade and the Environment (CTE) that has been meeting for several years, the CTE is dominated by trade experts, has demonstrated little understanding of the trade effects on environmental policy, and has almost nothing in the way of results to show for its first four years of efforts. Moreover, the OECD hosted from 1995 to 1998 an ill-fated negotiation to produce a Multilateral Agreement on Investment designed to promote freer flows of capital across the world. The draft agreement, which contained virtually no recognition of the link between economic integration and environmental protection, has come under harsh criticism and now appears to be dead.

Ironically, an MAI could generate significant environmental gains.[35] The flow of private capital to developing countries, especially through joint ventures with companies in developed countries, offers the promise of more modern plants and equipment (almost always less polluting than those of the existing industrial infrastructure) and access to the latest pollution control technologies and strategies, environmental management systems, and training programs. It is, moreover, clear that the resources necessary for environmental investments in the developing world will have to come from the private sector. The funds of the World Bank and other multilateral development banks are declining, as is foreign aid.[36] Developing countries recognize that they must find ways to attract private sector investors to build drinking water, waste treatment, and other environmental infrastructure projects. They also understand that they must ensure that appropriate pollution controls are enforced in the building of every factory, bridge, and power plant. In China, for example, private foreign investments topped $42 billion in 1997. How this private capital is deployed has a far greater impact on China's growth trajectory and environmental future than the $2.5 billion in World Bank and other official development assistance.

New disputes have added to the trade and environment policy focus. Notably, the European Union (EU) challenged U.S. efforts to block wine imports containing procymidone, an "unregistered" fungicide used on grapes.[37] The EU also challenged the U.S. Corporate Average Fuel Economy (CAFE) car mileage standards, arguing that this policy tool unfairly penalized European automobile manufacturers (for example, BMW, Mercedes, and Volvo) that sell only at the upper (low-gas-mileage) end of the car market. The United States brought a successful WTO claim against the EU

Reformulated Gasoline (1994)

The United States Clean Air Act of 1990 mandated that producers "reformulate" (reducing the levels of olefins and other pollutants) the gasoline sold in regions of the country with air pollution problems. Venezuela and Brazil protested the Environmental Protection Agency's implementation of this law, in particular the regulations that permitted U.S. refiners to calculate the reduction they were required to make from baselines derived from data on the quality of their past gasoline but forcing foreign companies to apply a baseline derived from the average level of U.S. contaminants, on the presumption that their actual data would be unavailable or unreliable.

After a WTO panel ruled that the EPA had discriminated against foreign refiners in violation of U.S. obligations under the GATT, the Clinton administration agreed to allow importers of Venezuelan and Brazilian gasoline to employ the same technique used by U.S. refineries to determine their baselines.

---

for obstructing exports to Europe of U.S. beef found to contain growth homones.[38] Canada forced the EU to back off on plans to forbid fur imports where the animal was caught through the use of a "leghold" trap. Brazil and Venezuela won a case against the United States based on a claim of discrimination against foreign refiners in the EPA's implementation of the "reformulated gasoline" regulations under the 1990 Clean Air Act (see box). And Thailand and several other countries in Southeast Asia got a WTO panel to agree that U.S. trade limitations imposed on shrimp fishermen who refused to use turtle excluder devices (TEDs) to protect endangered sea turtles were illegal under the GATT.[39]

As the pace of economic integration increases, the number of trade-environment conflicts do as well. The pressure for a more systematic commitment to building environmental considerations into the international trading system shows little sign of abating. In fact, the WTO has been criticized for failing to advance trade-environment harmony and specifically for focusing almost exclusively on the trade effects of environmental policy with little attention being paid to the environmental consequences of trade policy. At the OECD, a Committee of Trade and Environmental experts has been meeting periodically since 1990. While more balanced and systematic than the WTO efforts, the OECD initiative has produced only modest recommendations and no concrete guidelines.

Strengthening the Global Environmental Regime

Many observers of the trade and environment debate have concluded that part of the explanation for the ongoing perceived conflict lies in the weakness of the international environmental "regime." The centerpiece of international environmental protection efforts, the United Nations Environment Programme (UNEP), is in serious disarray.[40] Global environmental responsibilities are spread, moreover, across a half dozen other UN agencies (including the United Nations Development Programme, the United Nations Commission on Sustainable Development, and the World Meteorological Organization), the secretariats to various international environmental treaties (including the Climate Change Convention, the Montreal Protocol, the Desertification Treaty, and the Basel Convention), as well as the Bretton Woods institutions (the World Bank, the regional development banks, and the WTO). This fragmented institutional structure results in disjointed responses to global pollution and resource challenges, difficulty in clarifying policy and budget priorities, little coordination across related problems, and lost opportunities for synergistic responses. In sum, effective and efficient action is difficult to achieve.

The presence of a "global environmental organization," able to operate in tandem with the WTO and to provide some counterbalance to the WTO's trade emphasis, would be advantageous.[41] But fears of lost national sovereignty and unhappiness about creating a new UN bureaucracy make the prospect of establishing a comprehensive and coherent international umbrella environmental institution any time soon seem remote. In the absence of a functioning global environmental management system capable of addressing trade and environment issues, much of the responsibility for integrating these two policy realms inevitably falls to the WTO. A serious effort to make the international trading system more environmentally sensitive would require action on many fronts.

First, the activities of the WTO must become more transparent—that is, more open and easily followed by average people. Currently, most of the activities of the international trading system occur behind closed doors. This secrecy generates hostility from those who feel excluded from WTO processes or who are simply put off by the prospect that important decisions are being made without public input or even understanding. What's more, the WTO's legitimacy and authoritativeness would be broadly enhanced by allowing representatives of nongovernmental organizations (NGOs) to participate in or at least observe its proceedings.[42] This logic has been advanced by the United States with a series of proposals to open up the WTO. But to date, the efforts to promote transparency have been blocked by representatives from various developing countries.

This opposition reflects many concerns. Most notably, many free traders fear that the presence of environmentalists and others within the walls of the WTO would result in special interest manipulation of trade policymaking. It seems unlikely, however, that the presence of outside observers would really distort the decision processes of the international trading system. The system is not free of special interest manipulation now, and inviting environmental groups in might produce some countervailing influence to the existing producer and business lobbying and other activities. Allowing NGOs to make submissions where they have a position on issues that are being addressed by dispute settlement panels or more broadly by the WTO Governing Council would improve the knowledge base of the WTO and might assist the organization's decision making, especially in relation to environmental policy outcomes, which are so fraught with uncertainty.[43]

Over the longer term, the WTO must find a more refined way of balancing trade and environmental goals. The current mechanism (found in Article XX of the GATT) requires a country whose environmental policies have been challenged as an obstacle to free trade to demonstrate that they have selected the "least GATT-inconsistent" policy tool available. This standard sets an almost impossibly high hurdle for environmental policies because, in almost every case, there is some environmental strategy or approach that would intrude less on trade. A variety of proposals have been advanced that would amend Article XX and make it easier for legitimate environmental policies to be maintained in the face of trade challenges.[44]

In addition, while the trade system permits restrictions on imports when the product itself fails to meet environmental standards, current GATT rules forbid discrimination against imports based on the environmental conditions associated with their production process or method (PPM).[45] This means that cars without the requisite pollution control devices can be banned. Similarly, imports of strawberries containing chemical residues can be barred. But GATT rules do not permit a country to block imports of cars because the steel that goes into them was made in polluting mills. Nor do they allow the strawberries to be turned back just because the farmers polluted nearby rivers with pesticides and fertilizers. The prohibition against PPM-based environmental requirements is, however, untenable in a world of ecological interdependence.

Today, *how* things are made as well as *what* is traded is an issue. If a semiconductor is produced using chlorofluorocarbons in violation of the ozone-layer-protection provisions of the Montreal Protocol, GATT rules would not permit an importing nation to bar the offending chip.[46] Even if the current blanket prohibition on PPM-based regulation were swept aside, the WTO would face additional questions at the trade-environment interface. Whose regulatory standards should be adopted? Who will determine compliance with agreed-upon standards? And who assesses penalties or takes other enforcement actions when a violation is uncovered?

These questions persist even if the standards in question arise from an international agreement. The WTO remains vulnerable to challenges arising from the imposition of trade measures under multilateral environmental agreements. This is especially true where a WTO member is not a party to the environmental accord. A strong possibility exists that under current interpretations of the GATT a country facing trade penalties for failing to sign or adhere to a multilateral environmental agreement would be able to argue that those imposing the trade sanctions for environmental reasons are in violation of their GATT obligations. As noted above, NAFTA addresses this problem by declaring that trade actions taken consistent with multilateral environmental agreements are not NAFTA violations. A similar provision would be beneficial within the WTO.

Beyond finding ways to balance conflicting trade and environmental goals more effectively, those looking to make trade and environmental policies more mutually reinforcing could identify many places where trade and environmental policy aims dovetail. Notably, the elimination of agriculture and energy subsidies and the more careful regulation of fisheries would yield both substantial trade benefits and environmental improvements.[47] Agricultural price supports, for instance, encourage farmers to plant on marginal lands, which often require heavy doses of chemicals to be productive. Reduced agricultural subsidies would diminish the incentives to farm marginal lands and reduce trade distortions, providing new agricultural export opportunities for many developing countries.

Managing Interdependence

Despite the breadth of activities linking trade and environment policies in recent years and the reasonably favorable results arising on this score from NAFTA, some policymakers continue to disregard the trade-environment relationship. In the debate over giving President Clinton the "fast track" negotiating authority necessary to establish a Free Trade Agreement of the Americas, the leadership of Congress has refused to permit environmental issues to be tied to the trade legislation. The call for separation of economic and environmental interests is, however, not just normatively wrong but practically impossible. The relationship between environmental and trade issues in the context of deepening economic integration is subtle and multilayered. Environmental issues cannot be distinguished from trade policy. The disregard, however, of this inevitable linkage threatens to reduce the gains from trade liberalization and economic integration, and to hasten unnecessarily environmental degradation. Ignoring the environmental implications of trade policymaking poses an acute threat to current and future economic integration efforts, not to mention environmental programs.

The fundamental challenge is to manage interdependence on multiple levels, representing both shared natural resources and a common economic destiny. Governance in this context requires working across divergent priorities—North versus South, economic growth versus environmental protection, and present interests versus future ones. Sustainable development has emerged as the shorthand way of refining the systems-oriented policy approach that would consider all of these conflicting needs simultaneously. Therefore, in many ways, making trade and environmental policies work together stands as a classic example of the on-the-ground challenge of sustainable development.

Notes

1. Kym Anderson and Richard Blackhurst, "Trade, the Environment, and Public Policy," in *The Greening of World Trade Issues*, ed. Kym Anderson and Richard Blackhurst (Ann Arbor: University of Michigan Press, 1992), 3.
2. Richard N. Gardner, *Negotiating Survival: Four Priorities after Rio* (New York: Council on Foreign Relations, 1992); Rio "Declaration on Environment and Development," UNCED, UN Doc. A/Conf. 151/5/Rev. 1, reprinted in *International Legal Materials* 31 (1992): 874, 878; "Agenda 21," UNCED, UN Doc. A/Conf. 151/26/Rev. 1 (1992).
3. Geoffrey D. Dabelko and David D. Dabelko, "Environment Security: Issues of Conflict and Redefinition," in *Environmental Change and Security Project Report*, ed. P. J. Simmons (Washington, D.C.: Woodrow Wilson Center, 1995), 3.
4. See Norman Myers, "Environment and Security," *Foreign Policy* 68 (spring 1989): 23; Jessica T. Mathews, "Redefining Security," *Foreign Affairs* 68 (spring 1989): 162.
5. Daniel C. Esty, *Greening the GATT: Trade, Environment, and the Future* (Washington, D.C.: Institute for International Economics, 1994), 17–20; Andrew Hurrell and Benedict Kingsbury, *The International Politics of the Environment* (Oxford: Clarendon Press, 1992).
6. For a discussion of the far-reaching repercussions of the improper management of hazardous waste, see André Dua and Daniel C. Esty, *Sustaining the Asia Pacific Miracle* (Washington, D.C.: Institute for International Economics, 1997), 41–42.
7. John J. Audley, *Green Politics and Global Trade: NAFTA and the Future of Environmental Politics* (Washington, D.C.: Georgetown University Press, 1997); "Binational Statement on Environmental Safeguards That Should Be Included in the North American Free Trade Agreement," issued by Canadian Nature Federation, Canadian Environmental Law Association, Sierra Club-Canada, Rawson Survival-Canada, Pollution Probe-Canada, National Audubon Society, National Wildlife Federation, Community Nutrition Institute, and Environmental Defense Fund, May 28, 1992.
8. Robert Housman and Durwood Zaelke, "The Collision of the Environment and Trade: The GATT Tuna/Dolphin Decision," *Environmental Law Reporter* 22 (April 1992): 10268.
9. Steve Charnovitz, "Environmentalism Confronts GATT Rules," *Journal of World Trade* 28 (January 1993): 37.
10. For an entertaining depiction of how GATTzilla might devour cities and leave destruction in its wake, see Esty, *Greening the GATT,* 34.
11. Dua and Esty, *Sustaining the Asia Pacific Miracle;* Yoichi Funabashi, *Asia-Pacific Fusion: Japan's Role in APEC* (Washington, D.C.: Institute for International Economics, 1995).

12. For a thoughtful secondary commentary, see Andrew Hurrell and Benedict Kingsbury, *The International Politics of the Environment* (Oxford: Clarendon Press, 1992).

13. For interesting analyses of sustainable development issues, see Edith Brown Weiss, "Environment and Trade as Partners in Sustainable Development," *American Journal of International Law*, October 1992, 700–735; Robert Goodland, Herman Daly, Sarah El Serafy, and Bernd Von Droste, *Environmentally Sustainable Development: Building on Brundtland* (Paris: United Nations Educational, Scientific, and Cultural Organization, 1992).

14. Esty, *Greening the GATT,* 42–55.

15. It is interesting to see how "trade and environment" issues have split the environmental community, separating those who accept the promise of sustainable development from those who believe that economic growth is inherently environmentally harmful. See Audley, *Green Politics and Global Trade: NAFTA and the Future of Environmental Politics.*

16. For instance, in the debate over NAFTA, some environmentalists expressed concerns regarding the likelihood of a deterioration in meat inspection standards along the U.S.-Mexico border. See Lori Wallach, *The Consumer and Environmental Case against Fast Track* (Washington, D.C.: Public Citizen, 1991), 16. But some scholars instead contend that trade can uplift product standards. See Alan O. Sykes, *Product Standards for Internationally Integrated Goods Markets* (Washington, D.C.: Brookings Institution, 1995); David Vogel, *Trading Up: Consumer and Environmental Regulation in a Global Economy* (Cambridge: Harvard University Press, 1995). Further excellent considerations of harmonization issues are provided in *Fair Trade and Harmonization: Prerequisites for Free Trade?* ed. Jagdish Bhagwati and Robert E. Hudec (Cambridge: MIT Press, 1996).

17. Ross Perot, *Save Your Job, Save Our Country: Why NAFTA Must Be Stopped—Now!* (New York: Hyperion, 1993).

18. Judith M. Dean, "Trade and the Environment: A Survey of the Literature," in *International Trade and the Environment,* ed. Patrick Low (Washington, D.C.: World Bank, 1992), 15. Some scholars conclude that no evidence exists that companies migrate to pollution havens. See Adam B. Jaffe, Steven R. Peterson, Paul R. Portney, and Robert N. Stavins, "Environmental Regulation and the Competitiveness of U.S. Manufacturing: What Does the Evidence Tell Us," *Journal of Economic Literature* 33 (March 1995): 132.

19. Charles M. Tiebout, "A Pure Theory of Local Expenditures," *Journal of Political Economy,* October 1956, 416. Wallace E. Oates and Robert M. Schwab, "Economic Competition among Jurisdictions: Efficiency Enhancing or Distortion Inducing," *Journal of Public Economy* 27 (April 1988): 333; Richard L. Revesz, "Rehabilitating Interstate Competition: Rethinking the 'Race to the Bottom' Rationale for Federal Environmental Regulation," *New York University Law Review* 67 (December 1992): 1210.

20. Daniel C. Esty, "Revitalizing Environmental Federalism," *Michigan Law Review* 95 (December 1996): 629–634.

21. William Barron and Jill Cottrell, *Making Environmental Law in Asia More Effective* (Hong Kong: Center for Urban Planning and Environmental Management, 1996).

22. Lyuba Zarsky and Jason Hunter, "Environmental Cooperation at APEC: The First Five Years," *Journal of Environment and Development,* September 1997, 222–252.

23. Regulatory failures resulting from government performance and inadequate decision making could be "technical," that is, arising from weak data or analysis, or "political," that is, emerging from the emphasis of politicians on the here and now (visible economic growth, jobs, and new facilities) rather than long-term policy results, which is where good environmental programs lie.

24. This result is dictated by the Theory of the Second Best, which suggests that when one element of a system is suboptimal, we cannot be sure that optimizing other elements will produce superior results overall.

25. International Monetary Fund, *Direction of Trade Statistics* (Washington, D.C.: International Monetary Fund, 1996).

26. For a discussion of the Marrakesh decision and its implications, see Richard Eglin, "Current Debates at the WTO and Future Directions," in *Trade and Environment: International Issues and Policy Options,* ed. Jong-Soo Lim (Seoul, Korea: Korea Environmental Technology Research Institute, 1996), 9.

27. Steve Charnovitz, "Free Trade, Fair Trade, Green Trade: Defogging the Debate," *Cornell International Law Journal* 27 (1994): 459–525; Sanford Gaines, "The Polluter-Pays Principle: From Economic Equity to Environmental Ethos," *Texas International Law Journal* 26 (summer 1991): 463.

28. Gene M. Grossman and Alan B. Krueger, "Economic Growth and the Environment," *Quarterly Journal of Economics* 110 (May 1995): 353, 369.

29. Dua and Esty, *Sustaining the Asia Pacific Miracle,* 73–77.

30. Senate Committee on Finance, Subcommittee on International Trade, *Environmental Impact of the Proposed North American Free Trade Agreement,* Testimony of William Reilly, Administrator of U.S. Environmental Protection Agency, 102d Cong., 2d sess., September 16, 1992.

31. NAFTA Supplemental Agreements, "North American Agreement on Environmental Cooperation," September 13, 1993, reprinted in *International Legal Materials* 32 (1993): 1480.

32. *Inside U.S. Trade,* August 23, 1991, 7; Trade and Environment Committee of the National Advisory Council for Environmental Policy and Technology, *The Greening of World Trade,* Report to the EPA (Washington, D.C.: EPA, 1993).

33. Office of the U.S. Trade Representative, *Review of U.S.-Mexico Environmental Issues* (Washington, D.C.: Office of the U.S. Trade Representative, 1992).

34. NAFTA Preamble, December 17, 1992, reprinted in *International Legal Materials* 32 (1993): 296 and 605.

35. For a commentary on OECD negotiations over an MAI, see Stephan Schmidheiny and Bradford Gentry, "Privately Financed Sustainable Development," in *Thinking Ecologically: The Next Generation of Environmental Policy,* ed. Marian R. Chartow and Daniel C. Esty (New Haven: Yale University Press, 1997).

36. Given this reality, foreign direct investment offers perhaps the only genuine means of large-scale funding for environmental investment. See Daniel C. Esty and Bradford S. Gentry, "Foreign Investment, Globalization, and the Environment," in *Globalization and the Environment,* ed. Tom Jones (Paris: Organization for Economic Cooperation and Development, 1997).

37. An "unregistered" fungicide is one that has not gone through EPA safety testing to establish a safe residue level under the Federal Insecticide, Fungicide, and Rodenticide Act.

38. Michael B. Froman, "International Trade: The United States–European Community Hormone Treated Beef Conflict," *Harvard International Law Journal* 30 (spring 1989): 549–556.

39. A compilation of many important and interesting trade disputes can be found in Esty, *Greening the GATT,* app. C, 257–274.

40. Even UNEP acknowledges that "global governance structures and global environmental solidarity remain too weak to make progress a world-wide reality. . . .The gap between what has been done thus far and what is realistically needed is widening." See UNEP, *Global Environment Outlook* (New York: Oxford University Press, 1997).

41. For a thorough introduction to the structure and workings of the World Trade Organization, see Bernard Hoekman and Michel Kostecki, *The Political Economy of the World Trading System: From GATT to WTO* (New York: Oxford University Press, 1995).

42. Steve Charnovitz, "Two Centuries of Participation: NGOs and International Governance," *Michigan Journal of International Trade* 18 (winter 1997): 183–286; Daniel C. Esty, "Non-governmental Organizations at the World Trade Organization: Cooperation, Competition, or Exclusion," *Journal of International Economic Law* 1 (1998), 123–147.

43. Daniel C. Esty, *Why the WTO Needs Environmental NGOs* (Geneva: International Centre for Trade and Sustainable Development, 1997); Christophe Bellmann and Richard Gerster, "Accountability in the WTO," *Journal of World Trade* 30 (December 1996): 31–74; James Cameron and Ross Ramsey, "Participation by NGOs in the WTO," Working Paper, Global Environment and Trade Study (GETS), New Haven, 1995.

44. Daniel C. Esty, "Making Trade and Environmental Policies Work Together: Lessons from NAFTA," in *Trade and Environment: The Search for Balance,* ed. Damien Geradin et al. (London: Cameron, May 1994), 382.

45. An astute commentary on the GATT and its interrelationship to U.S. trade policies can be found in John H. Jackson, *The World Trading System: Law and Policy of the World Trading System* (Cambridge: MIT Press, 1989).

46. Duncan Brack, *International Trade and the Montreal Protocol* (London: Royal Institute of International Affairs, 1996).

47. For two interesting analyses of the complex and subtle interaction between trade and the environment within the realm of agriculture, see Richard Eglin, "The GATT's Role in Agriculture, the Environment, and Trade," in *Agriculture, the Environment, and Trade: Conflict or Cooperation,* ed. Caroline T. Williamson (Washington, D.C.: International Policy Council on Agriculture and Trade, 1993); U.S. Congress, Office of Technology Assessment, *Agriculture, Trade, and Environment: Achieving Complementary Policies,* OTA-ENV-617 (Washington, D.C.: U.S. Government Printing Office, May 1995). For a discussion of energy subsidies, see Kym Anderson and Warwick J. McKibbin, "Reducting Coal Subsidies and Trade Barriers: Their Contribution to Greenhouse Gas Abatement," Seminar Paper 97-07 (University of Adelaide: Centre for International Economic Studies, 1997); Dua and Esty, *Sustaining the Asia*

Pacific Miracle. For an examination of some of the recent conflicts regarding fisheries, see C. Ford Runge, *Freer Trade, Protected Environment: Balancing Trade Liberalization and Environmental Interests* (New York: Council on Foreign Relations Press, 1994).

10

The United Nations Climate Change Agreements

Michael R. Molitor

On December 11, 1997, 159 nations adopted the Kyoto Protocol. The protocol and its parent agreement, the 1992 Framework Convention on Climate Change (FCCC), were both adopted under the multilateral treaty-making auspices of the United Nations. Together with some important resolutions of the UN General Assembly and the Governing Council of the United Nations Environment Programme (UNEP), they form the foundation of the United Nations climate change regime (UNCCR).[1]

The principal objective of the FCCC is "to stabilize concentrations of greenhouse gases in the atmosphere at a level that would prevent dangerous anthropogenic interference with the climate system."[2] This statement assumes that the governments participating in the UNCCR will cooperate to control the range of human activities that are capable of altering the climate system as well as manage the predicted future consequences of the resulting changes. To understand and evaluate the FCCC and the 1997 Kyoto Protocol as multilateral policy responses requires knowledge of both these human activities as well as their predictable and measurable consequences.

The negotiating dynamics of the UNCCR have been largely governed by those governments most affected by the regulation of certain economic activities linked to climate change and those parties who believe that they will be most affected by the consequences of climate change. These actors can be characterized along a spectrum of positions that range from the most proactive (for example, the Alliance of Small Island States, or AOSIS) to the very reactive (for example, Saudi Arabia and China).[3] Much of the UNCCR story has been shaped by the actions of key individuals and governments.

Climate change represents an unprecedented policy problem for the international community for a number of important reasons. The FCCC and the Kyoto Protocol are examples of unique responses to a global problem of concern to the entire international community. These multilateral agreements signal a fundamental change in international relations and now characterize a world of increasing global interdependence.

In 1972, at the United Nations Conference on the Human Environment, governments adopted the Stockholm Declaration on the Human Environment.[4] Principle 21 of the declaration, directed at the existing transboundary pollution issues, held that governments enjoy a sovereign right to exploit their natural resources but that, in so doing, they are responsible for any resulting environmental damage that occurs outside their territory. The global impact of human enterprise is now so great that many of the basic industrial and agricultural activities that support national economies produce, for example, greenhouse gas emissions capable of generating consequences on a global scale. The FCCC and the Kyoto Protocol are evidence of an important shift from the regulation of transboundary pollution to global environmental change as the leading environmental issue facing the international community at the end of the twentieth century.

Climate Change as a Unique Policy Problem

There is some debate concerning whether or not environmental issues should be treated as a special set of public policy problems. This suggests to some that there may be something fundamentally unique about environmental problems that requires some important modifications to the national and international public policy processes. Others will argue that environmental issues should be treated like any other public policy issue facing democratic societies, such as public health and crime. Here, it is important to distinguish between different classes of environmental problems. Many environmental problems are local in their causes and effects. Some of these exist as the result of "market failures," where the true costs to society of, for example, different energy options are not signaled by the prices associated with, in this case, using different fuels. The majority of these problems are not unique to the public policymaking process and, therefore, do not require any special categorization or response.

The temporal (decades to centuries) and spatial (global) dimensions of climate change together, however, are sufficient to place this policy problem in a unique category.[5] Consider some other important characteristics of climate change that support a special designation. First, greenhouse gas emissions resulting from human activities are produced by every country in the world. Second, there is no uniform correlation between the level of a nation's emissions and its future vulnerability to the predicted consequences of a climate system modified by human activity. Third, most of the current atmospheric concentrations of the human-produced greenhouse gases were emitted by industrialized countries (the Organization for Economic Cooperation and Development, or OECD). Fourth, at some point early in the next century, emissions from developing countries will surpass OECD emissions.[6] Fifth, most emissions are produced by the burning of fossil fuels (coal, oil, and natural gas), which provide the basic energy that drives the entire world economy. Sixth, and last, scientists' understanding of the climate system, the human impacts on the system, and the consequences of those impacts, is far from complete.

The decision to respond to the predicted future consequences of climate change is in some ways similar to a decision to purchase automobile insurance. Car owners purchase insurance because they believe that there is a reasonable probability that in the future they will be involved in an accident. They also understand that the cost of the accident to them could be extremely high. The cost of hedging against these costs (the insurance premium) is affordable in relation to the possible high costs of an accident.

The Intergovernmental Panel on Climate Change (IPCC) has confirmed that there is a possibility of a climate change "accident" looming out in the future.[7] Unlike the auto insurance analogy, it is very difficult to predict what the costs of such future accidents might be. However, the purchasing of auto insurance does not lower the probability of an accident occurring. Climate change policy responses that lower emissions of greenhouse gases are a type of unique insurance policy that actually lower the probability of a future accident.

The basic questions facing governments in the UNCCR are whether or not to purchase climate change insurance and, if so, how much? This requires comparing two scenarios: the costs that result from doing nothing to lower emissions of greenhouse gases and the costs of complying with any particular target established in the UNCCR. This is the quintessential example of multilateral policymaking under extreme scientific uncertainty.

The Science of Climate Change

The development and evaluation of the range of policy options available to the international community to address the unique characteristics of climate change requires asking and answering the following three questions:

- How does Earth's climate system work?
- In what ways are human activities affecting the climate system?
- What are the possible consequences of these human impacts on the climate system?

In 1988 the United Nations created the Intergovernmental Panel on Climate Change to provide governments with the answers to these questions.[8] The IPCC now includes more than 2,000 climate scientists and other specialists who report regularly on whether there exists any consensus on the answers to these questions. The IPCC has issued two important assessment reports, the first in 1990 and the second in 1995.[9] Much of the following scientific overview was taken from these and other IPCC reports.

The Earth's Climate System

Before it can be established that human activities are causing perturbations in the earth's climate system, it is important to review what is known about the climate system. For this discussion, the single most important aspect of the system is the naturally occurring "greenhouse effect." Energy from the sun reaches the earth in a form (visible light) that allows it to penetrate the atmosphere easily. Some of this energy is absorbed by clouds and the earth's surface. Another part of the incoming energy is re-radiated by clouds and the surface back toward space in the form of longwave (infrared) radiation. Certain naturally occurring gases in the lower atmosphere (water vapor, carbon dioxide, methane, nitrous oxide) trap this outgoing infrared radiation in the form of heat. This heat-trapping mechanism of the lower atmosphere is known as the "greenhouse effect." The balance between the incoming and outgoing solar energy is calculated as the earth's "solar radiation budget."

The changes in the balance between the incoming and outgoing solar energy is a principal feature of the earth's seasons. During fall and winter there is not enough incoming radiation to make up for the outgoing radiation due to, in part, the added reflection provided by snow cover (this is known as albedo). During spring and summer the reverse is true. Greenhouse gases have been present in the atmosphere for much of the 4.5 billion-year history of planet Earth. Without these naturally occurring gases the earth would have average surface temperatures near or below 0 degrees Fahrenheit. As a consequence, this planet would have supported a completely different mix of species that would certainly not have included humans.

The greenhouse effect is one of the basic features of the Earth system that is absolutely critical to human life. The composition and extent of these greenhouse gases in the atmosphere has varied greatly throughout Earth history. Both biological (for example, photosynthesis) and geological (for example, weathering and plate tectonics) processes have a tremendous impact on the amount of different greenhouse gases present in the atmosphere over varying timescales.

The amount of solar energy that is trapped in the atmosphere by greenhouse gases has, on longer timescales, an important effect on the climate and, on shorter timescales, on the weather. Winds and ocean currents are responsible for redistributing the heat produced by the greenhouse effect all over the earth. Evaporation of surface water, and the precipitation that eventually follows, helps to redistribute heat between the earth's surface and the atmosphere and from the equator to higher latitudes. The frequency and intensity of, for example, droughts and floods, is largely a function of the total solar energy available in the atmosphere to drive such events. Hurricanes and cyclones are also driven by the solar energy that is trapped by the earth's climate system. Finally, the greenhouse effect plays a fundamental role in many ocean processes that have important consequences for the climate system. One example is the Gulf Stream, which carries warm surface waters from the equator to the North Atlantic and is responsible for the unusually warm climate of Europe. This can be seen by comparing the winter weather of London and Anchorage, Alaska.

Some natural processes are capable of lowering the heat-trapping service provided by the greenhouse gases in the atmosphere. The most discussed, and misunderstood, may be the role played by volcanic eruptions. The 1991 eruption of Mount Pinatubo in the Philippines, for example, delivered an enormous quantity of sulfate aerosols (very small particles containing sulfur) into the upper atmosphere. Global wind forces initially distributed these particles over a very large portion of the Pacific region and, subsequently, their distribution became global. These particles, acting like little mirrors, reflected a large amount of incoming solar radiation back into space. The effect of these sulfate aerosols was actually to provide a short-term global cooling effect that canceled the increased greenhouse effect of human emissions for approximately one year.

It is important to understand that the greenhouse effect provides the majority of the energy required to support many of the basic features of the Earth system critical to human life. From a policy standpoint, any natural events or human activities that are capable of producing profound impacts on the greenhouse effect must be examined with great care and scrutiny.

Human Impacts on the Climate System

There are, potentially, many ways in which human activities can affect the climate system. The most obvious and important of these concern activities that affect the earth's solar radiation budget on important spatial and temporal scales. That is, certain activities can influence the amount of incoming energy absorbed by the earth's surface (for example, through land-use changes, including deforestation) or the amount of outgoing energy trapped by greenhouse gases (for example, from the burning of fossil fuels). For this discussion, it is more important to focus on the latter.

If human activities add to the total volume of greenhouse gases in the lower atmosphere, then the climate system will trap more outgoing solar radiation, which will consequently increase the surface temperature of the planet. That is, the greenhouse effect will become stronger and add more energy (in the form of heat) to the earth's climate system. Climatologists have concluded, with a high degree of confidence, that the surface temperature of the earth has been rising steadily since scientists began making regular measurements in the late nineteenth century. The important question is whether or not some part of this recent surface temperature increase has been caused by human activity. The popular press uses the term *global warming* to describe this possible human component.

It has only recently become clear that human activities are dramatically altering the composition of greenhouse gases in the atmosphere both by adding to the total volume of naturally occurring gases (for example, carbon dioxide and methane) and by emissions of human-made greenhouse gases (for example, hydrofluorocarbons). This fact was established by the IPCC in its landmark 1995 assessment report. The IPCC stated for the first time that "the balance of evidence suggests a discernible human influence on the climate."[10] "Global warming" had finally arrived.

The burning of fossil fuels (coal, oil, and natural gas) to support the majority of the world's energy requirements is currently responsible for a net transfer of 21 gigatons (21 billion tons) of carbon dioxide to the atmosphere every year (almost 25 percent of these emissions are produced in the United States).[11] The total amount of carbon dioxide in the atmosphere is currently about 370 ppmv (parts per million by volume) and growing at about 2 ppmv per year. The amount of carbon dioxide that was present in the atmosphere before the Industrial Revolution was approximately 280 ppmv. In the last 200 years, human activities have increased the total amount of carbon dioxide in the atmosphere by 30 percent. This is an unprecedented change in the composition of the atmosphere over such a short period of time.

Different greenhouse gases are capable of trapping varying amounts of outgoing solar energy. The actual amount is described by the "global warming potential" (GWP) for each gas. Chlorofluorocarbons (CFCs) are not only capable of depleting the stratospheric ozone layer; in the lower atmosphere they are also extremely potent greenhouse gases. A single molecule of CFC (for example, the refrigerant Freon) has a global warming potential that is several thousand times higher than a single molecule of carbon dioxide. The total increased greenhouse effect is a function of not only the GWP of the different greenhouse gases emitted by human activity but, more important, the relative concentrations of the different gases, the growth rate of their emissions, and their "residence times" (the total time they spend in the atmosphere before being removed by natural processes).

With a global human population rapidly approaching six billion, and the consumption of fossil fuels growing even faster, it is not hard to imagine the reality of a climate system fundamentally altered by human activity. Humans are conducting a global experiment on the earth's climate system by dramatically changing the composition of the atmosphere on a very short timescale. Numerous industrial (for example, cement manufacturing) and agricultural (for example, rice production, cattle and hog farming) activities produce greenhouse gas emissions (carbon dioxide and methane, respectively). It is important to note that every country in the world produces greenhouse gas emissions and that, for the vast majority of countries, such emissions are growing.

Some human activities can actually reduce the effects and extent of growing greenhouse gas emissions. The planting of trees is probably the most well-known example. Through photosynthesis, trees take in carbon dioxide as a source of carbon to assist in their growth and other basic life functions. The more trees, the more carbon dioxide is stored in wood and thereby "sequestered" from the atmosphere. Another interesting example is, paradoxically, the burning of certain fossil fuels that contain sulfur. Much of the coal that is burned in the United States to produce electricity contains sulfur. When the coal is burned to produce the necessary heat energy, sulfate aerosols are emitted into the atmosphere (much like in the volcano example above). The resulting sulfate aerosols act once again like tiny mirrors to reflect incoming solar radiation back out to space and thereby produce a cooling effect. It is important to note that this short-lived cooling effect is eventually overtaken by the longer-term heating effect caused by the carbon dioxide that is also emitted when coal is burned (the sulfate aerosols stay in the atmosphere for weeks; carbon dioxide stays for a century or more).

Predicting and Measuring the Consequences

What if, as predicted, human activities drive the level of carbon dioxide in the atmosphere to 560 ppmv (a doubling of the preindustrial concentration) by the middle of the next century?[12] How might the earth's climate system respond to all the additional energy being trapped by the larger concentration of greenhouse gases? This is obviously an experiment that scientists cannot conduct on the planet to measure the results. It is an experiment that, nevertheless, humanity is unintentionally conducting.

The basic tool that scientists have developed to predict the consequences of human modifications of the climate system are supercomputer programs known as General Circulation Models (GCMs).[13] GCMs attempt to reproduce the physics of the atmosphere and oceans to create a dynamic global model of the climate system. One of the many limitations of GCMs is current computing power. Although the speed and power of supercomputers are growing very fast, GCMs require enormous computational power, which can be provided by only the most sophisticated supercomputers. In fact, there are very high speed communications systems that now link national supercomputing centers together to allow them to work simultaneously on a single GCM program.

Another important limitation on scientists' ability to create supercomputer models that accurately simulate the earth's climate system is insufficient knowledge about all of the components of the system and their complex interactions. The quality of the output of any model is only as good as the quality of the inputs. For example, although scientists now understand that every several years the tradewinds in the Pacific diminish and a large pool of warm surface water moves from the western to the eastern Pacific, causing the well-known "El Niño" events, scientists cannot yet explain what starts the process going. Another vexing problem concerns the role of clouds in climate change. The IPCC predicts that more clouds may exist in a climate system impacted by global warming. However, clouds are capable of both increasing and decreasing the surface temperature of the earth through, respectively, trapping outgoing infrared radiation from the surface or reflecting incoming solar energy back into space (the albedo effect). Therefore, computer modelers are uncertain about how to input the future role of clouds in their GCM programs.[14]

Not all of the data used to measure and predict climate change are produced by computer models. There is an enormous amount of observational data that include everything from satellite measurements, to instruments that measure the amount of carbon dioxide in the atmosphere, to paleoclimate records. The paleoclimate records are essential in helping scientists understand how the climate changed in the past and the consequences of such changes. Excellent records of past climates can be found in lake sediments containing pollen, in ocean sediments containing the shells of small marine organisms (foraminifera), and in air bubbles trapped in ice cores drilled in Greenland and Antarctica. The combination of currently observed data (for example, satellite measurements of sea surface temperature), GCM data, and paleoclimate records provides extensive information about the components of the climate system, how they interact, and what surprises might exist.

The only thing scientists can say with complete confidence about the climate system is that it is dynamic and complex and that as a consequence the weather is highly variable. This all-important variability can be defined by two simple parameters: temperature and precipitation. That is, the weather will get either warmer or colder and wetter or drier. Of course, the four possible combinations of these two parameters can produce the range of variability in the system that can lead from droughts to floods and from hurricanes to snowstorms.

The probability of an extreme weather event (for example, tornadoes and hurricanes) is a function of many factors. However, the total amount of energy in the climate system that is available to produce such events is a critical determining factor. One of the many predictions of a climate system altered by human activity is the greater frequency and intensity of extreme weather events. It is interesting to note that the weather-related claims paid out worldwide by insurance companies has skyrocketed in recent years. For example, the total damages associated with Hurricane Andrew amounted to more than $30 billion following the 1992 event (the insured loss was $16.5 billion).

Of course, the fundamental question that remains is whether or not any particular extreme weather event is the result of human perturbations of the climate system or is strictly the product of natural variability. Although the IPCC reported in 1995 that it had found evidence to support the fact that human activities were modifying the climate system, this influential group has not yet taken the next step to suggest that increased variability in the climate system (extreme weather events) has been driven, in part, by human activity.

In a warmer greenhouse world, the IPCC predicts sea levels to rise and to inundate many important low-lying areas of high human population density. A good example is Bangladesh, where millions of people would be affected by a rise in sea level of one meter. Small, low-lying island nations from the Bahamas to the Seychelles could effectively disappear as rising sea water would completely inundate them.

Maybe the most chilling prediction of a climate system altered by human activity comes from the public health community. Changes in regional temperature and precipitation are already modifying the geographical extent of several important disease vectors.[15] For example, as northern Mexico and the southwestern United States have become increasingly warm and wet, the range of the *aedes aegyptii* mosquito has moved north as well. This mosquito is responsible for transmitting dengue fever to humans. Arizona public health officials have recently documented increased cases of dengue fever near the border with Mexico.

Another climate-disease relationship has been identified with respect to the recent outbreaks of hantavirus in, for example, the Four Corners region of the United States.[16] Unusually high rainfall associated with extreme El

Niño events has led to rapid growth in the grasses that deer mice use for food. This new abundance of food in turn has led to an explosion in the deer mice population. As the competition for living space intensifies, some mice have begun to inhabit the rafters of human dwellings. Feces from mice carrying the hantavirus are deposited in the rafters and eventually are transmitted to humans through the air as dust particles.

Important IPCC predictions include the loss of species that will not be able to adapt to rapid changes in the ecosystems that originally supported them and changes in the availability and distribution of freshwater—a problem that could have serious security implications in the Middle East. All told, the list of predicted changes to the climate system due to human activity is growing longer all the time. Finally, there exists the possibility of unanticipated changes that could take the form of abrupt climate change events fueled by large-scale positive feedbacks to the system. One abrupt climate change scenario focuses on the North Atlantic current, which carries warm water from the equatorial Atlantic Ocean northward and helps maintain Europe's climate.[17] Increased precipitation in northern latitudes may lead to a change in the flow of the current, which would result in, for example, potentially disastrous consequences for European agriculture.

Achieving Scientific Consensus

Although the greenhouse effect was originally theorized in the early nineteenth century by the French mathematician Charles Fourier, the impact of human activity on the climate system became a topic of international scientific concern only following the International Geophysical Year (1957–1958).[18] In 1957, Roger Revelle and Hans Seuss published a paper claiming that the additional greenhouse gases produced by human activity were not, as originally believed, being absorbed through natural processes by the oceans. The scientists made the following important statement: "Human beings are now carrying out a large-scale geophysical experiment of a kind that could not have happened in the past nor be reproduced in the future."[19]

The historic claim made by Revelle and Seuss was supported by the work of their contemporary, Charles Keeling, a geochemist at the Scripps Institution of Oceanography.[20] Keeling had devised a sophisticated device to measure changes in the concentration of carbon dioxide in the atmosphere. His device had recorded a measurement of 315 ppmv in 1955. By the end of the International Geophysical Year in 1958, Keeling's measurements had shown an increase of about 1 ppmv per year. In Revelle's opinion, the increases in atmospheric concentrations of carbon dioxide could only have been explained as a result of human activity.

The intergovernmental community began to consider climate change only in the mid-1970s. The World Meteorological Organization (WMO) created the Ad Hoc Panel of Experts on Climate Change and was the principal sponsor of the First World Climate Conference, held in 1979.[21] The conferences held in Villach, Austria (1985 and 1987), and Bellagio, Italy

(1987), "helped consolidate the scientific consensus regarding global warming and communicate that consensus to policymakers."[22]

When, by 1988, it was clear that there was emerging on the part of governments a range of viewpoints concerning climate change, the WMO and UNEP decided to sponsor jointly the creation of the Intergovernmental Panel on Climate Change.[23] The IPCC's continuing mandate is to review the leading scientific literature on climate change and to report to governments where there is consensus on leading issues. More than 2,000 climatologists, economists, and other specialists now constitute the worldwide IPCC membership.

Originally chaired by the Swedish scientist Bert Bolin, the IPCC began its work attempting to answer a straightforward, yet extremely complex, question: is there evidence to support the possibility of a human influence on the global climate system? The IPCC, upon issuing its first assessment report at the Second World Climate Conference in 1990, stated that although a good deal of evidence pointed in that direction, they were unable to reach consensus on the question of whether human activity affected the variability of the climate system.

As soon as work was completed on the first report, the IPCC process began to direct its efforts toward the Second Assessment Report (SAR).[24] The SAR differed from the first assessment in that, as a result of the Article 3 requirement that all policy responses developed under the FCCC be cost-effective, it also included socioeconomic analyses.[25] Issued in December 1995, the SAR made worldwide headlines with its statement that "the balance of evidence suggests a discernible human influence on the climate." The IPCC had finally answered its most important question but not without substantial controversy.

It is important to remember that the IPCC is a creature of governments and that, consequently, its mandate and reports are subject to their authority and scrutiny. The release of the SAR was preceded by an intergovernmental meeting held in Madrid to approve the language of the report. The landmark phrase above was the subject of intense debate between the proponents of the SAR and some highly reactive governments from the Organization of Petroleum Exporting Countries (OPEC).[26] As a result, all IPCC assessments must be read with the understanding that the resulting consensus language may not be considered completely objective from a purely scientific point of view.

Troubled by the lack of leadership being demonstrated by the White House in addressing climate change and the declining federal funding for climate change research, more than 2,500 American scientists signed the *Scientists' Statement on Global Climatic Disruption* in June 1997.[27] The statement endorsed the findings of the IPCC SAR and went on to claim that "further accumulation of greenhouse gases commits the earth irreversibly to further global climatic change and consequent ecological, economic, and social disruption. The risks associated with such changes justify preventive action through reductions in emissions of greenhouse gases. It is time for the

United States, as the largest emitter of greenhouse gases, to . . . demonstrate leadership in a global effort."[28]

On June 26, 1997, President Bill Clinton, after receiving a copy of the *Scientists' Statement*, made a historic speech to a Special Session of the United Nations General Assembly convened to review the progress in the implementation of the agreements adopted at the Earth Summit held in Rio de Janeiro in June 1992. Here, for the first time, a president of the United States was admitting that, in Clinton's words, "the science [of climate change] is clear and compelling."[29] The president went on to commit the United States "to bring to the Kyoto conference a strong American commitment to realistic and binding limits that will significantly reduce our emissions of greenhouse gases."[30] The nation with the world's largest emissions had finally acknowledged that the science of climate change was sufficiently clear to warrant the negotiation of binding policy responses.

The UNCCR was developed to be flexible and to be capable of responding to advances in the science of climate change. The IPCC is the principal scientific body responsible for making the UNCCR aware of the consensus that emerges on important unresolved questions. The IPCC Third Assessment Report will be completed by 2001 and will focus on regional impacts of climate change.

Many important scientific questions on climate change remain to be answered. For example, there is some debate on the specific point where atmospheric concentrations of greenhouse gases would produce "dangerous anthropogenic interference with the climate system."[31] The IPCC has reviewed numerous computer models that use a doubling of preindustrial concentrations, from 280 to 560 ppmv of atmospheric carbon dioxide, to explore how the climate system might react. More work needs to be done on this question of a definitive greenhouse gas threshold concentration. Finally, the consensus on the science confirms that not only is the total concentration of greenhouse gases in the atmosphere an important factor, but the rate of change appears to be significant as well. This requires some focus on determining the appropriate future emissions path in regard to changes of emissions over time.

Achieving Political Consensus

While the international scientific community was working to identify consensus on climate change, governments were moving much slower in their attempts to achieve political consensus. Some part of the lag between the two processes was the result of a failure to communicate between the two groups. On the one hand, policymakers want definitive answers to questions that address, in this case, scientific questions well beyond their capability to comprehend. Policymakers are generally unaware of the "scientific method" that leads scientists to be cautious and gives policymakers the impression that the science is far from complete. Scientists, on the other hand, are generally not rewarded by their peers for undertaking "policy-relevant" science.

The result is an interesting push-pull process that distorts the science and ultimately leads to dubious policy results.

The political consensus process was catalyzed by a conference convened by the government of Canada in June 1988 to bridge the gap between the science and policy of climate change.[32] Entitled "The Changing Atmosphere: Implications for Global Security," the conference brought together scientists, government officials, members of environmental groups, and industry representatives. The participants adopted the Toronto Conference Statement, which, borrowing from Revelle and Seuss, stated, "Humanity is conducting an unintended, uncontrolled, globally pervasive experiment whose ultimate consequence could be second only to global nuclear war."[33] The statement went on to make some important recommendations:

1. Governments should begin negotiations on "a comprehensive global convention as a framework for protocols on the protection of the atmosphere."
2. Governments should agree to reduce global emissions of carbon dioxide to 20 percent below 1988 levels by the year 2005.
3. A "World Atmosphere Fund" should be created from taxes on fossil fuel consumption in industrial countries.

Later that year, in December 1988, the UN General Assembly adopted Resolution 45/53, "Protection of the Atmosphere for Present and Future Generations of Mankind." The resolution, the first ever to deal with climate change, was introduced by the representative of Malta and had the effect of endorsing the role of the IPCC in its attempts to achieve scientific consensus. The resolution enumerated a list of tasks for the IPCC, which included "comprehensive review and recommendations with respect to: . . . [e]lements for inclusion in a possible future international convention on climate." For the first time, the United Nations had made reference to the need for a multilateral agreement on climate change.

In less than a year, a decision on formal negotiations for a climate change convention was adopted in various high-level government meetings. In March 1989, twenty-two countries called for formal negotiations to begin. This group included Japan, France, Italy, and Canada. The position of the United States was made clear in May 1989, when, at an IPCC Working Group III meeting, it announced its support for a framework convention on climate change. The official mandate to begin negotiations came in the form of resolutions adopted by the UNEP Governing Council and the UN General Assembly. The latter called on governments "to prepare as a matter of urgency a framework convention on climate, and associated protocols containing concrete commitments in the light of priorities that may be authoritatively identified on the basis of sound scientific knowledge, and taking into account the specific development needs of developing countries."[34]

Other important events took place prior to the first negotiating session on the climate change convention.[35] At an October 1990 meeting held in

Luxembourg, the environment ministers of the European Community agreed to a Community-wide goal of stabilizing carbon dioxide emissions at 1990 levels by the year 2000, a target that would have far-reaching implications for the upcoming negotiations. In the following month, governments met in the ministerial portion of the Second World Climate Conference (SWCC) held in Geneva, Switzerland. The SWCC Ministerial Declaration, adopted at the conclusion of the conference, failed to establish any timetables or targets for the stabilization of greenhouse gas emissions.[36]

With both the IPCC and the SWCC calling for negotiations on a climate change convention to begin immediately, the UN General Assembly adopted Resolution 45/212, establishing the Intergovernmental Negotiating Committee as the agency of the General Assembly with authority to launch and manage the negotiations on a climate change convention. The resolution created a deadline for the negotiations to have ready a convention to be signed at the United Nations Conference on Environment and Development (UNCED) to be held in June 1992.[37]

The Intergovernmental Negotiating Committee

The Intergovernmental Negotiating Committee (INC) held five negotiating sessions between February 1991 and May 1992.[38] The negotiations, each lasting approximately two weeks, took place in Chantilly, Virginia; Geneva, Switzerland; Nairobi, Kenya; and New York City. It was agreed early on that the negotiations would follow the format of the UNEP stratospheric ozone depletion agreements. That is, following the approach of the 1985 Vienna Convention for the Protection of the Ozone Layer, the INC would initially work on producing a "framework" agreement on the basic issues of climate change.[39] This would allow for subsequent negotiations on the contentious obligations to control greenhouse gas emissions at a later date when there was more widespread agreement on the science as well as the different response options to climate change. This was the highly acclaimed process that eventually produced the 1987 Montreal Protocol on Substances That Deplete the Ozone Layer.[40]

On May 9, 1992, at the final session of the INC, held at the United Nations in New York, the FCCC was adopted by the parties. The FCCC text would now be sent to Rio de Janeiro for signature. One month later, at UNCED, 154 governments signed the FCCC. The FCCC, by its own terms, entered into force on March 21, 1994, ninety days after the fiftieth instrument of ratification was transmitted to the UN secretary-general. The FCCC makes a basic distinction between two different groups of parties to the convention. The Annex I parties include all of the OECD members plus selected former Soviet and Eastern European governments.[41] Annex I parties have agreed to certain obligations that are not binding on all the other "developing country" parties. As of July 1998, 175 nations had ratified the FCCC.

The Road from Rio to Berlin

In 1993, shortly after taking office, President Clinton announced his support for the FCCC and pledged that the United States would attempt to meet the European target of returning emissions to 1990 levels by the year 2000. After an earlier failed attempt to push through Congress a national energy tax, the president understood that Congress was not prepared to approve new taxes or regulations on energy production and consumption. As a result, he announced that the 1993 White House Climate Change Action Plan would include approximately fifty *voluntary* federal programs promoting, for example, incentives for the use of more energy efficient lighting and building materials.[42] The focus was largely on energy efficiency as a means of lowering U.S. greenhouse gas emissions.

Unfortunately, by the time governments gathered for the First Conference of the Parties (COP 1) in Berlin in the spring of 1995, it was clear that only two of the Annex I governments (Germany and the United Kingdom) were on target to return their emissions to 1990 levels by the year 2000.[43] In the United States, low gasoline prices were partly responsible for an explosion in the sales of gas-guzzling sport utility vehicles. The result was a lower national average gas mileage for automobiles, which eliminated all the gains achieved in energy efficiency under the Climate Change Action Plan. U.S. emissions were now growing faster than ever. The White House announced that the United States was not on schedule to meet its self-imposed roll-back target.

Equally problematic, the IPCC announced the results of a 1994 study that claimed that even if all Annex I governments had met their commitments to return emissions to 1990 levels, it would not be enough to meet the convention's ultimate objective of preventing dangerous human interference with the climate system. As a result, there were two questions before the parties when they met officially for the first time in Berlin in March 1995. The first asked whether Annex I parties should adopt binding emissions reduction obligations to begin in the year 2000, and the second inquired if the emissions reduction obligations should be extended to developing countries.

In Berlin, the United States pushed for an approach that would allow industrialized countries to earn credit for emissions reductions that they financed and implemented in developing countries. This "joint implementation" mechanism would, in the view of the United States, produce a more economically efficient means of lowering emissions by harnessing the large differences in abatement costs between, for example, the United States and China.[44] The parties to the convention agreed in Berlin to initiate "activities implemented jointly" on an interim basis without allowing emissions credits to accrue to the industrial country sponsors. Future changes to the joint implementation program would be negotiated by the parties no later than the Third Conference of the Parties (COP 3), to be held in December 1997.

The most important outcome of COP 1 was the adoption of the Berlin Mandate. The mandate put the FCCC parties on a schedule to negotiate and adopt a protocol or other legal instrument at COP 3, which was held in Kyoto, Japan, December 1–10, 1997. Most important, the parties agreed that any legal instrument emerging from Kyoto would create new emissions reduction obligations for Annex I governments only. There would be no discussion of emissions reduction obligations for developing countries. The parties launched new negotiations for the protocol or new legal instrument under the Ad hoc Group on the Berlin Mandate (AGBM).

The Road from Berlin to Kyoto

At the first AGBM negotiating session (AGBM 1, August 1995), Ambassador Raul A. Estrada-Oyuela of Argentina was elected chairman. The AGBM negotiations took place during eight separate meetings held in Geneva, Switzerland, and Bonn, Germany, between August 1995 and October 1997. The final AGBM negotiating session took place in Kyoto in December 1997 as the central feature of COP 3.

Although most of the attention on the FCCC negotiations centered on the AGBM and COP 3, the parties met in Geneva for the Second Conference of the Parties (and AGBM 4) in July 1996. Here, the FCCC parties adopted a ministerial declaration (the Geneva Declaration) that acknowledged the 1995 IPCC SAR conclusions and, specifically, the need for significant, legally binding emissions reductions. The most important event at COP 2 occurred when the United States reversed its earlier position and agreed that the AGBM process should produce legally binding emissions reductions for Annex I parties.

Five basic issues surfaced during the AGBM negotiations:

1. Which greenhouse gases would be controlled?
2. Would the enhancement of "sinks" be allowed as a means of lowering emissions and fulfilling obligations?[45]
3. Which "quantified emissions limitation and reduction obligation" (QELRO) would be adopted by the Annex I parties?
4. What type of "cooperative measures" would be allowed?
5. Which "policies and measures" to lower emissions would be approved?

The initial phase, and most of the negotiations, focused on the question of which of the many QELRO proposals would form the basis of an agreement adopted in Kyoto. The first QELRO was proposed by AOSIS.[46] It called for Annex I countries to lower their emissions to 20 percent below 1990 levels by the year 2005. This target was subsequently adopted by the leading environmental groups as their unified position. The AOSIS proposal would continue to define the most proactive position throughout the AGBM talks. The other leading QELRO proposals included:

European Union: 15 percent below 1990 levels by 2010
Japan: 5 percent below 1990 levels between 2008–2012

United States: 1990 levels between 2008–2012

G-77/China: 15 percent below 1990 levels by 2010 and 35 percent below 1990 levels by 2020

Australia, claiming that meeting any of the proposed QELRO targets would have a devastating effect on its national economy, opposed the adoption of all QELRO proposals and argued that "differentiation" should form the basis of any emissions reduction obligation. By "differentiation," Australia advanced the idea that Annex I parties should have different QELRO targets based on their differing "national circumstances." This idea would eventually form the basis of the binding QELRO language adopted in Kyoto.

A sixth, and the most contentious, issue was added to the AGBM negotiations late in the game by the U.S. Senate. On June 12, 1997, the Senate adopted a nonbinding resolution with instructions to the president for the U.S. AGBM delegation. In what may be viewed as an attempt to undermine the AGBM negotiations, the Senate made it clear that it would not grant its advice and consent for any agreement emerging from Kyoto that did not include binding obligations for emissions reductions by developing countries. In the words of the Senate resolution:

Resolved, That it is the sense of the Senate that —

(1) the United States should not be a signatory to any protocol to, or other agreement regarding, the United Nations Framework Convention on Climate Change of 1992, at the negotiations in Kyoto in December 1997, or thereafter, which would—

(A) mandate new commitments to limit or reduce greenhouse gas emissions for the Annex I Parties, unless the protocol or other agreement also mandates new specific scheduled commitments to limit or reduce greenhouse gas emissions for Developing Country Parties within the same compliance period, or

(B) would result in serious harm to the economy of the United States.

The other requirement imposed by the resolution, that the protocol should not harm the U.S. economy, touched on the essence of a growing national debate in the United States. A group of American industry associations had paid for television commercials urging the public to reject U.S. participation in any agreement that would emerge from Kyoto.[47] This position was based on their view that the cost of meeting the new binding emissions reductions would be prohibitively high for the United States. Specifically, they warned that fuel costs would soar and that the resulting lower international competitiveness would export U.S. jobs abroad. Furthermore, the industry group argued that the science of climate change was far from complete and that there was, consequently, no immediate need to lower U.S. emissions. These arguments were taken up by Sens. Chuck Hagel

(R-Neb.), Trent Lott (R-Miss.), and Robert C. Byrd (D-W. Va.) and provided the impetus for the resolution.

U.S. negotiators were left with only two opportunities to convince the other parties that they should overlook the terms of the Berlin Mandate and adopt language that would create a mechanism by which developing countries could assume binding emissions reduction obligations. The U.S. delegation put the idea forward at AGBM-7 (Bonn, October 1997), and it was immediately clear that the battle was going to be uphill.

COP 3, Kyoto (December 1–10, 1997)

The final AGBM negotiating session was scheduled to coincide with the Third Conference of the Parties and included only ten days for governments to achieve consensus on the six major issues still largely unresolved. There was no question that the issue of developing country participation was going to remain the largest obstacle. On the fourth day of the negotiations, the representative of New Zealand put forward a proposal that developing countries should be prepared to take on emissions reduction obligations in the period beginning in the year 2014. The proposal was immediately challenged by the Chinese delegation, which reminded all of the parties of their obligations under the Berlin Mandate. Their refusal to allow the New Zealand proposal to be advanced also included an order to the AGBM chairman not to create a special committee to examine this question for further discussion. It was also clear that the Chinese position was shared by many other leading developing countries.

On Monday, December 8, U.S. Vice President Al Gore addressed the conference. He explained that President Clinton had granted the U.S. delegation greater flexibility to help reach agreement on the remaining issues. It was apparent to the conference participants that the United States was now willing to take on reduction obligations beyond the president's earlier proposal of returning emissions to 1990 levels between 2008 and 2012. The deal was subject to the condition that the final Kyoto Protocol would include language that would, at the very least, open the door to reduction obligations for developing countries. The president wanted to create an opportunity for the contentious demands of the U.S. Senate to be met.

On the evening of the final day of COP 3, two major issues still remained unresolved and inextricably intertwined: developing country participation and the individual reduction commitments of Annex I parties. In the early hours of December 11, Chairman Estrada issued the final draft protocol.[48] The document included a provision (draft Article 9) that allowed developing countries to take on emissions reduction obligations on a voluntary basis. Draft Article 9 gave non–Annex I parties the right to select both the base year and the level of emissions reductions. The draft protocol also left the door open for Annex I parties to agree to differentiated emissions reduction obligations for the period 2008–2012.

In the final hours, the United States agreed to reduce emissions to 7 percent below 1990 levels between 2008 and 2012 with the hope that draft Article 9 would also find its way into the final agreement. After a vigorous challenge led by China, and a warning from the chairman that the negotiations were about to completely break down, the chairman finally struck down Article 9 claiming that there was no hope of reaching consensus. The U.S. delegation had achieved its worst case scenario. It had agreed to go well beyond the original U.S. position for reductions and was left without any mechanism for developing country emissions reductions. The almost impossible goal established by the U.S. Senate had clearly not been met.

The FCCC and the Kyoto Protocol: Basic Provisions

There are three general approaches to dealing with climate change: mitigation, adaptation, and geo-engineering. Mitigation (or abatement) approaches are directed at the human activities that affect the climate system. Most mitigation options focus on lowering the emissions of greenhouse gases into the atmosphere that result from human activity. This is the primary focus of the 1992 United Nations Framework Convention on Climate Change and the 1997 Kyoto Protocol.

Adaptation policies are those that recognize that the cost of preventing climate change may be prohibitively high. They allow climate change to occur and subsequently direct their attention exclusively at coping with the consequences. For example, a decision to elevate the dikes protecting much of the Netherlands in anticipation of sea-level rising would be considered an adaptation approach.

The third and most controversial approach concerns the possibility of actually modifying the natural processes that help control the level of greenhouse gases in the atmosphere. For example, scientists discovered that certain mid-ocean regions would bloom with photosynthetic plankton if they supplied the area with a fine dust of iron particles: the critical limiting nutrient.[49] Scientists have distributed iron dust over these areas and watched deep blue ocean water become vibrant and green as dormant plankton used the iron to photosynthesize and capture carbon dioxide in the atmosphere just above the surface of the ocean. The scale of such geo-engineering solutions would have to be so large, however, that, in all probability, they could produce bigger problems than the ones they were designed to solve.

The 1992 Framework Convention on Climate Change

As of July 1998, 175 countries had become parties to the FCCC. The FCCC has as its primary objective the "stabilization of greenhouse gas concentrations in the atmosphere at a level that would prevent dangerous anthropogenic (human) interference with the climate system."[50] Not all governments that are parties to the convention are required to control their emissions of greenhouse gases. The convention recognizes that the industrialized countries and some of the nations of the former Soviet bloc (Annex I parties) are responsible for the majority of the world's emissions and, consequently, they alone should begin the process of meeting the objective set out in Article 2. In this regard, the convention initially created a loosely binding obligation for the Annex I parties to return emissions to their 1990 levels (Article 4). The convention does not specify the time by which this target must be met and thereby renders the obligation meaningless.

Apart from the weak obligations created for Annex I parties, the FCCC is guided by an important set of basic principles (Article 3). The following principles govern the FCCC, the 1997 Kyoto Protocol, and any other future agreements to be concluded under the FCCC:

1. *Equity through "common but differentiated responsibilities"*—the principle that most of the current concentrations of human greenhouse gases were emitted by Annex I countries and that they should take on the largest burden of responding to climate change. Developing countries must also participate but at a level that recognizes their economic development.

2. *Special consideration for disproportionately burdened developing countries*—the principle that certain developing countries (for example, low-lying archipelagic nations: the Bahamas, Kiribati, Maldives, the Seychelles) may face devastating consequences and that they should, consequently, be given special attention.

3. *Scientific uncertainty not an excuse for inaction*— this "precautionary principle" requires FCCC parties to recognize the possible global consequences of climate change and to honor their commitments in the absence of complete scientific certainty.

4. *Cost-effective policy responses*—the principle that any mandated climate change policy response in the FCCC, or any related agreements, is subject to benefit-cost analysis. That is, the cost of the mandated policy prescription must be less than other available options, including the "business-as-usual" scenario.

5. *Responses may be carried out cooperatively*—the principle that parties can work together to share the burden of meeting the ultimate objective of the FCCC. This includes, for example, emissions trading between Annex I parties and "joint implementation" between Annex I and developing country parties.

6. *Promotion of "sustainable development"*—the principle that any mandated climate change policy response in the FCCC, or any related agreements, must not interfere with the developing country parties' sustainable development objectives.

7. *No distortion of international trade*—the principle that any mandated climate change policy response in the FCCC, or any related agreements, must not adversely affect any international trading of goods and services. For example, the FCCC cannot attempt to enforce any of its provisions by using trade sanctions as a means of ensuring compliance.

The Conference of Parties (COP) is the supreme body of the FCCC.[51] All power to make amendments to the FCCC and to negotiate other agreements is held by the COP. Typically, the COP meets once a year to discuss all matters under the FCCC. The Secretariat, based in Bonn, is charged with all of the organizational support functions under the FCCC.[52] The Subsidiary Body for Scientific and Technological Advice provides "timely information and advice on scientific and technological matters relating to the Convention."[53] The Subsidiary Body for Implementation was "established to assist the Conference of the Parties in the assessment and review of the effective implementation of the Convention."[54]

Finally, the FCCC creates a "Financial Mechanism" under Article 11 to assist developing countries in meeting their obligations to report on the climate change information required under Article 12.[55] This requires all parties to produce "[a] national inventory of anthropogenic emissions by sources and removals by sinks of all greenhouse gases not controlled by the Montreal Protocol" and "[a] general description of steps taken or envisaged by the Party to implement the Convention."[56]

The 1997 Kyoto Protocol

The Kyoto Protocol, much like the 1987 Montreal Protocol, is not a free-standing multilateral agreement. That is, only governments that are parties to the FCCC may join the protocol.[57] The primary objective of the protocol, as authorized by the Berlin Mandate, is to create binding emissions reduction obligations for Annex I parties beginning in the year 2000. In this connection, the focus of the protocol establishes differentiated targets for the thirty-nine Annex I parties (Article 3). The percentages listed in Annex B of the Kyoto Protocol (see box, p. 230) correspond to obligations to reduce national emissions from reported 1990 levels between 2008 and 2012.

The protocol includes an agreed-upon list of policies and measures that Annex I parties should consider implementing to meet their emissions reduction targets. The European Union had hoped that the list would be mandatory for all Annex I parties. The United States disagreed and advanced the idea that the list should be interpreted as recommendations only. As is evident from the text of Article 2.1.a, the U.S. position prevailed (see box, p. 231).

The protocol provides five options for Annex I parties to meet their emissions reduction obligations specified in Article 3. The first is to make use of the "policies and measures" outlined in Article 2 and to put regulations in place that actually lower national emissions. For many countries, especially the United States, this is the most politically difficult option. An easier approach is to make use of the sinks enhancement opportunities under Article 3.3: "The net changes in greenhouse gas emissions from sources and removals by sinks resulting from direct human-induced land use change and forestry activities, limited to afforestation, reforestation, and deforestation since 1990, measured as verifiable changes in stocks in each commitment

---

1997 Kyoto Protocol to the United Nations Framework Convention on Climate Change

Annex B

Party Quantified Emission Limitation or Reduction Commitment (percentage of base year [1990] or period)

Australia 108	Liechtenstein 92
Austria 92	Lithuania[a] 92
Belgium 92	Luxembourg 92
Bulgaria[a] 92	Monaco 92
Canada 94	Netherlands 92
Croatia[a] 95	New Zealand 100
Czech Republic[a] 92	Norway 101
Denmark 92	Poland[a] 94
Estonia[a] 92	Portugal 92
European Community 92	Romania[a] 92
Finland 92	Russian Federation[a] 100
France 92	Slovakia[a] 92
Germany 92	Slovenia[a] 92
Greece 92	Spain 92
Hungary[a] 94	Sweden 92
Iceland 110	Switzerland 92
Ireland 92	Ukraine[a] 100
Italy 92	United Kingdom of Great Britain and
Japan 94	Northern Ireland 92
Latvia[a] 92	United States of America 93

[a] Countries that are undergoing the process of transition to a market economy (these parties have the option of selecting a base year other than 1990).

---

period shall be used to meet the commitments in this Article of each Party included in Annex I." Although the protocol has approved the enhancement of sinks to meet the emissions reduction obligations of Annex I parties under Article 3, the specific details of how sinks credits will accrue has been left for future negotiation.

The third option for Annex I parties to meet their obligations under Article 3 is the emissions trading opportunities that were proposed by the United States and are outlined in Article 17. This market-based approach will allow Annex I parties to buy and sell emissions credits through a system modeled on the sulfur dioxide emissions trading program found in the 1990 amendments to the U.S. Clean Air Act. The specific rules concerning how the trading system will function (for example, how will the initial credits be allocated?) and who will manage the trades (the World Bank?) have been left to future negotiations.

The joint implementation program that had been approved by the parties at COP 1 was modified and made its way into the Kyoto Protocol in

1997 Kyoto Protocol to the United Nations Framework Convention on Climate Change

Article 2.1.a

1. Each Party included in Annex I, in achieving its quantified emission limitation and reduction commitments under Article 3, in order to promote sustainable development, shall:

(a) Implement and/or further elaborate policies and measures in accordance with its national circumstances, such as:

(i)   Enhancement of energy efficiency in relevant sectors of the national economy;

(ii)   Protection and enhancement of sinks and reservoirs of greenhouse gases not controlled by the Montreal Protocol, taking into account its commitments under relevant international environmental agreements; promotion of sustainable forest management practices, afforestation and reforestation;

(iii)   Promotion of sustainable forms of agriculture in light of climate change considerations;

(iv)   Research on, and promotion, development and increased use of, new and renewable forms of energy, of carbon dioxide sequestration technologies and of advanced and innovative environmentally sound technologies;

(v)   Progressive reduction or phasing out of market imperfections, fiscal incentives, tax and duty exemptions and subsidies in all greenhouse gas emitting sectors that run counter to the objective of the Convention and application of market instruments;

(vi)   Encouragement of appropriate reforms in relevant sectors aimed at promoting policies and measures which limit or reduce emissions of greenhouse gases not controlled by the Montreal Protocol;

(vii)   Measures to limit and/or reduce emissions of greenhouse gases not controlled by the Montreal Protocol in the transport sector;

(viii)   Limitation and/or reduction of methane emissions through recovery and use in waste management, as well as in the production, transport and distribution of energy.

Article 6. This fourth option allows Annex I parties to earn credit for projects that lower emissions in other Annex I countries. For example, the government of Japan has entered into an agreement to convert coal-fired electricity plants to natural gas in the Russian Far East. The lower emissions that will result from this fuel-switching project will accrue to Japan to help meet its obligations under Article 3. The original focus of the "activities implemented jointly" approved at COP 1 was to generate credit for Annex I projects in non–Annex I countries. This variation now forms the basis of the fifth option.

The fifth and final option is based on the "Clean Development Mechanism" (CDM) established under Article 12. Proposed in the AGBM by the Brazilian delegation, the CDM allows Annex I parties to earn credits for lowering emissions in non–Annex I countries.[58] That is, for example, the United States could earn emissions reduction credits for transferring energy-efficient technologies to China. Again, the details of how such credits would accrue and which organization would have oversight over the CDM was left to future negotiations by the parties in Kyoto.

Finally, on the question of which gases would be controlled under the protocol, the parties agreed to a "basket" of six gases in two groups: carbon dioxide, methane, and nitrous oxide in one group, and perfluorocarbons, hydrofluorocarbons, and sulfur hexafluoride in the other.

Annex I parties must use 1990 as the base year for meeting their emissions reduction obligations with the gases listed in the first group above. For the second group, Annex I parties may select either 1990 or 1995 as the base year. Most important, the protocol makes no requirement that any or all of these gases be controlled. Annex I parties are free to decide which gas, or combination of gases, will be controlled to meet their differentiated targets under Article 3.

COP 4, Buenos Aires (November 2–13, 1998)

It is important to recognize that COP 3 and the Kyoto Protocol represent just the beginning of an ongoing process that will include many more important milestones in the development of the FCCC and its related agreements. The parties met again in Buenos Aires in November 1998 at COP 4. All the precedent-setting features of the Kyoto Protocol were under negotiation in Argentina, in the form of a work program that established a timetable for agreement on all of the final details of the protocol. The parties are now committed to completing all of the work on the remaining details of the protocol by COP 6 to be held in 2000.[59] Other important events that occurred during COP 4 include the signing of the Kyoto Protocol by the United States on November 12, 1998, and the decision by Argentina to become the first non–Annex I party to voluntarily accept obligations to reduce greenhouse gas emissions. Kazakhstan also announced that it would consider joining Annex I and accept emissions reduction obligations as part of Annex B of the protocol. Finally, the parties agreed to meet in Amman, Jordan for COP 5 in October–November 1999.

There was a convergence of opinion between climate change policymakers and scientists as to the limited success of COP 3 and the adoption of the Kyoto Protocol. Ambassador Stuart Eizenstat, the chief U.S. negotiator in Kyoto, testified in February 1998 before the Senate Foreign Relations Committee that the protocol represents a historic first step in an ongoing process to deal with climate change.[60] Professor Bert Bolin, the former chairman of the IPCC, wrote in a leading scientific journal that, even with the emissions controls established by the protocol, atmospheric concentrations of carbon dioxide will increase by about 29 ppmv between 1990 and 2010 (from 363 to 382 ppmv).[61] By his calculations, if all Annex I parties failed to meet their full obligations under Article 3, and actually increased their carbon dioxide emissions 20 percent by 2010, atmospheric concentrations would increase only 1 to 1.5 ppmv higher than the full compliance scenario described above. Still, Bolin echoed Ambassador Eizenstat's remark when he referred to the protocol as "an important first step."

The protocol represents much more than an important milestone in the ongoing United Nations climate change negotiations. An attempt to control the climate system of Earth is, in effect, the future cornerstone of the international community's effort to develop policy responses to global environmental change. The FCCC and the Kyoto Protocol are planetary management responses that support the recognition that humans are now a global force on Earth. In the words of a distinguished group of scientists: "[H]umanity's dominance of Earth means that we cannot escape responsibility for managing the planet. Our activities are causing rapid, novel, and substantial changes to Earth's ecosystems."[62]

Notes

1. "Kyoto Protocol to the United Nations Framework Convention on Climate Change," FCCC/CP/1997/L.7/Add.1, December 10, 1997 (http://www.unfccc.de); "United Nations Framework Convention on Climate Change" (hereafter, FCCC), A/AC.237/18 (Part II)/Add.1, May 15, 1992 (http://www.unfccc.de); United Nations General Assembly Resolutions 44/228 (1989), 43/53 (1988), 44/207 (1989), 45/212 (1990), 46/169 (1991), 44/206 (1989), 44/172 (1989), http:// www.un.org.
2. FCCC, Article 2.
3. The Alliance of Small Island States includes a group of developing nations that are all low-lying archipelagoes and, as a result, susceptible to rising sea levels. This voting bloc includes, for example, the governments of the Bahamas, Kiribati, Maldives, and the Seychelles.
4. On the 1972 United Nations Conference on the Human Environment, held in Stockholm, Sweden, see Lynton K. Caldwell, *International Environmental Policy,* 3d ed. (Durham, N.C.: Duke University Press, 1996).
5. For an excellent overview of climate change science, see Steven P. Hamberg et al., *Common Questions about Climate Change* (Geneva: UNEP and WMO, 1997), http://www.gcrio.org/ipcc/qa/cover.html.
6. Bert Bolin, "The Kyoto Negotiations on Climate Change: A Science Perspective," *Science,* January 16, 1998, 330–331.
7. IPCC Working Group II, "Summary for Policy-Makers," in *Climate Change 1995, Impacts, Adaptations, and Mitigation of Climate Change: Scientific-Technical Analyses* (Cambridge: Cambridge University Press, 1996).
8. On the history and procedure of the IPCC, see Bert Bolin, "The Intergovernmental Panel on Climate Change," *Earthquest,* summer 1990, 1–4.
9. IPCC, *Climate Change* (Cambridge: Cambridge University Press, 1990); IPCC, *Climate Change 1995: The Second Assessment Report,* 3 vols. (Cambridge: Cambridge University Press, 1996).
10. IPCC Working Group I, "Summary for Policymakers," in *Climate Change 1995: The Science of Climate Change* (Cambridge: Cambridge University Press, 1996), 4–5.
11. See Bolin, "The Kyoto Negotiations on Climate Change," n. 7.
12. See IPCC Working Group II, "Summary for Policy-Makers."
13. On General Circulation Models, see Stephen H. Schneider, "Introduction to Climate Modeling," in *Climate System Modeling,* ed. Kevin E. Trenberth (Cambridge: Cambridge University Press, 1992).

14. See Warren M. Washington, "Climate-model Responses to Increased CO_2 and Other Greenhouse Gases," in Trenberth, *Climate System Modeling*, 645–647.
15. Jonathan Patz, Paul R. Epstein, and Thomas A. Burke, "Global Climate Change and Emerging Infectious Diseases," *Journal of the American Medical Association*, January 17, 1996.
16. Ibid., 217.
17. William H. Calvin, "The Great Climate Flip-flop," *Atlantic Monthly*, January 1998.
18. For an account of the International Geophysical Year and the development of climate change science, see Jonathan Weiner, *The Next One Hundred Years* (New York: Bantam Books, 1990), 30–31.
19. Roger Revelle and Hans Seuss, "Carbon Dioxide Exchange between Atmosphere and Ocean and the Question of an Increase in Atmospheric CO_2 during the Past Decades," *Tellus* 9 (1957): 18–27.
20. See Weiner, *The Next One Hundred Years*, chap. 3.
21. Daniel Bodansky, "Prologue to the Climate Change Convention," in *Negotiating Climate Change*, ed. Irving M. Mintzer and J. A. Leonard (Cambridge: Cambridge University Press, 1994).
22. Ibid., 48.
23. See Bolin, "The Intergovernmental Panel on Climate Change," 1–4.
24. See IPCC, *Climate Change 1995: The Second Assessment Report*.
25. IPCC Working Group III, *Climate Change 1995*: Economic and Social Dimensions of Climate Change (Cambridge: Cambridge University Press, 1996).
26. E. Masood, "Climate Panel Confirms Human Role in Warming, Fights Off Oil States," *Nature* 378 (1995): 524.
27. John P. Holdren et al., *Scientists' Statement on Global Climatic Disruption* (Washington, D.C.: Ozone Action, 1997), http://www.ozone.org.
28. Ibid.
29. White House, June 26, 1997 (http://www.whitehouse.gov).
30. Ibid.
31. FCCC, Article 2.
32. Mathew Paterson, *Global Warming and Global Politics* (New York: Routledge, 1996), 33–34.
33. "Proceedings of the World Conference on the Changing Atmosphere: Implications for Global Security, Toronto, June 27–30, 1988," WMO doc. 710, 1989.
34. United Nations General Assembly Resolution 44/207 (1989).
35. For a complete account of the events surrounding the negotiations on the "United Nations Framework Convention on Climate Change," see Bodansky, "Prologue to the Climate Change Convention."
36. Jill Jager and Howard L. Ferguson, eds., *Proceedings of the Second World Climate Conference* (Cambridge: Cambridge University Press, 1991).
37. Also known as the Earth Summit, the conference was held in Rio de Janeiro, Brazil, in June 1992. See Michael Grubb et al., *The Earth Summit Agreements: A Guide and Assessment* (London: Earthscan, 1993).
38. See Bodansky, "Prologue to the Climate Change Convention."
39. For the full text of the 1985 Vienna "Convention for the Protection of the Ozone Layer," see Michael R. Molitor, *International Environmental Law: Primary Materials* (Cambridge, Mass.: Kluwer Law International, 1991), 451–464.
40. Ibid., 480–502.
41. For a complete list of all Annex I parties, see FCCC, A/AC.237/18 (Part II)/Add.1, May 15, 1992 (http://www.unfccc.de).
42. White House, *The Climate Change Action Plan*, October 1993.
43. For a complete account of all the FCCC Conferences of the Parties, see http://www.iisd.ca/linkages/climate/climate.html. The drop in emissions of greenhouse gases in the United Kingdom and Germany was due to policy decisions unrelated to climate change. The United Kingdom had decided to move away from coal

and to make use of the natural gas flowing from its North Sea fields. Germany had made enormous investments in phasing out inefficient and dirty coal-fired steam power plants in the former East Germany.

44. On "joint implementation" see L. D. Danny Harvey and Elizabeth J. Bush, "Joint Implementation: An Effective Strategy for Combating Global Warming?" *Environment,* October 1997, 14–20, 36–44.

45. "Sinks" are natural processes in the climate system where, for example, carbon dioxide is removed from the atmosphere. The planting of young trees is one means of enhancing sinks to remove carbon dioxide from the atmosphere through photosynthesis. At issue during the AGBM negotiations was whether parties could get credit for lowering their emissions through the enhancement of natural sinks processes.

46. See n. 3.

47. The Global Climate Coalition (GCC) includes numerous American companies that are members of, among others, the American Petroleum Institute, the Western Fuels Association, the American Automobile Manufacturers Association, and the Chemical Manufacturers Association. The GCC was established to coordinate U.S. industry opposition to the United Nations climate change negotiations.

48. "Kyoto Protocol to the United Nations Framework Convention on Climate Change," final draft by the Chairman of the Committee of the Whole, December 10, 1997, FCCC/CP/1997/CRP.6.

49. An American company, Ocean Farming, Inc., has entered into an agreement with the government of the Marshall Islands to conduct iron fertilization projects within their territorial waters. These types of sinks enhancement projects are not, however, approved under the Kyoto Protocol as a means of achieving emissions reductions by Annex I parties. See Steve Nadis, "Fertilizing the Sea," *Scientific American,* April 1998, 33.

50. FCCC, Article 2.

51. See FCCC, Article 7.

52. Ibid., Article 8.

53. Ibid., Article 9.

54. Ibid., Article 10.

55. Ibid., Article 11.

56. Ibid., Article 12.

57. See the "Kyoto Protocol," Article 23.

58. Joint implementation can occur between Annex B countries (FCCC Annex I parties; see the "Kyoto Protocol," Article 6) or between Annex B and non–Annex B countries through the Clean Development Mechanism ("Kyoto Protocol," Article 12).

59. FCCC Conference of the Parties, fourth session, "Plan of Action, Draft decision proposed by the President of the Conference", U.N. Doc. FCCC/CP/1998/L.23, 14 November, 1998. http://www.unfccc.de. A complete and detailed summary of the COP 4 proceedings can be found in the "Earth Negotiations Bulletin" at http://www.iisd.ca/linkages.

60. Statement of Stuart E. Eizenstat, Under Secretary of State, before the Senate Foreign Relations Committee, 105th Cong., 2d sess., February 11, 1998.

61. See Bolin, "The Kyoto Negotiations on Climate Change."

62. Peter M. Vitousek et al., "Human Domination of Earth's Ecosystems," *Science,* July 25, 1997, 494–499.

11

Lapsed Leadership:
U.S. International Environmental Policy Since Rio

Robert L. Paarlberg

As in other areas, the leadership of the United States is essential in global environmental affairs. If the United States decides to take a lead, a strengthening of international environmental policy becomes possible. If the United States fails to lead or resists the leadership of other nations, paralysis scts in. In this chapter we ask why the U.S. government has failed to provide international environmental policy leadership in two critical areas: biodiversity protection and climate change.

The United States boasts a strong record of environmental policy action at home, where cooperation with foreign governments is not necessary and where most of the benefits of policy action are realized exclusively by Americans rather than being shared with foreigners. In its national environmental policies, the United States has consistently set a high standard. As of 1996, hazardous wastes were generally disposed of in an environmentally sound manner; 64 percent of the population was served by secondary sewage treatment; lead emissions had decreased 84 percent since 1984; sulfur dioxide emissions had been dropping since the late 1970s; and more than 10 percent of total U.S. land was designated as reserves, managed reserves, sanctuaries, parks, protected landscapes, and monuments.[1] The United States has also managed effective international leadership on some important issues. In stratospheric ozone protection, vigorous U.S. leadership was at various stages critical to the successful completion of the 1987 Montreal Protocol and the subsequent London agreements to control and eliminate production of chlorofluorocarbons (CFCs).[2]

Since the early 1990s, however, effective U.S. international environmental policy leadership has lapsed. This change was first evident at the 1992 United Nations Conference on Environment and Development, popularly called the Earth Summit, in Rio de Janeiro. President George Bush stood virtually alone among the leaders of the industrial world by refusing to accept the stronger climate change policy—the limiting of carbon dioxide emissions to 1990 levels by 2000—that the European Union (EU) was backing. He also refused to sign the newly negotiated international Convention on Biodiversity (CBD). Bush's performance at Rio was so harshly criticized by candidates Bill Clinton and Al Gore in the 1992 presidential election campaign that when they emerged victorious, it was natural to expect that U.S. leadership in these two areas would be restored.

Since 1993, however, despite strong efforts by the Clinton-Gore administration, the U.S. government has remained a laggard rather than a leader in both biodiversity and climate change. In the area of biodiversity protection, the Clinton-Gore administration fulfilled its pledge to sign the CBD in 1993, but the U.S. Senate has not approved the convention, obliging the United States to participate only as an "observer" to the convention's activities. By 1997, 169 sovereign nations around the world had signed and ratified the CBD, but the United States still had not. Likewise, in climate change policy, the Clinton-Gore administration formally endorsed the Rio emissions stabilization goal in 1993, but then failed to secure from Congress the energy tax that was necessary to attain that goal, and in 1997 the United States was once again rated "absolute last" among twenty industrial nations in efforts to reduce carbon dioxide emissions.[3]

In this chapter we first review the history of the lapses of U.S. leadership concerning climate change and biodiversity and then seek to explain them. We conclude that despite some superficial similarity, these cases are substantially different. Lagging U.S. leadership on climate change policy is the result of several powerful political factors, including strong domestic opposition from both industry and organized labor, a still-weak scientific consensus on the gains that might come from action, plus an unsolved international cooperation problem. Compared to stratospheric ozone protection, these barriers to action are stronger across the board in climate change policy. In the area of biodiversity protection, however, these barriers to action have been relatively weak, and faltering U.S. leadership must be explained in other ways.

The analysis that follows underscores the difficulty of taking policy action on international environmental problems in the United States. It is rare to see the executive branch and Congress engaged at the same time in the pursuit of the same international environmental policy objective. In the exceptional case of CFCs, all of the most important political forces and factors needed for effective U.S. leadership action fell into place. For climate change and biodiversity, albeit for different reasons, a more typical pattern of interbranch division has blocked effective action.

Weakened U.S. Policy on Biodiversity and Climate Change

President Bush's refusal to undertake firm international commitments on climate change and biodiversity drew intense criticism from U.S. environmental activists and Democratic leaders in Congress, including Senator Gore. Bush held back in 1992 despite an extraordinary plea for greater flexibility from William K. Reilly, who was the head of the Environmental Protection Agency (EPA) and the leader of the U.S. delegation in Rio. This foot-dragging was a surprise as well as a disappointment to the environmental community. Bush had earlier promised the American people he would be "the environmental president," and initially he had lived up to this promise by promoting the strong 1990 Clean Air Act. Yet by 1992, partly in response to the start of an economic recession, he had abandoned his environmental policy agenda both at home and abroad and yielded to the anti-regulatory preferences of his so-called Competitiveness Council, a cabinet-level agency headed by Vice President Dan Quayle. The council weakened U.S. environmental policy during the final years of the Bush administration by giving private companies a direct political channel through which they could seek relief from regulations of all kinds.

Clinton and Gore attacked Bush for backsliding on environmental policy at Rio. In the official manifesto of their 1992 presidential campaign, a book entitled *Putting People First,* they wrote, "The world faces a crisis because of global climate change, ozone depletion, and unsustainable population growth. These developments threaten our fundamental interests—and we must fight them at a global level. America must lead the world, not follow."[4] In his 1993 book, *Earth in the Balance,* Gore wrote, "The Earth Summit was a success for the world as a whole, but it was a serious setback for our nation. At a crucial moment in history, when the rest of the world was requesting and eagerly expecting American leadership—not to mention vision—our nation found itself embarrassed and isolated."[5]

The election of Clinton and Gore seemed at first to guarantee a return of environmental policy leadership and activism. One of President Clinton's first actions was to abolish the Competitiveness Council and replace it with the White House Office of Environmental Policy, designed to ensure that environmental activists would now have representation at the White House. Carol Browner, Gore's former chief legislative aide in the Senate, became the EPA administrator, and Bruce Babbitt, a committed environmentalist, became secretary of the interior. High-level positions throughout the executive branch, including the Department of State, were given to former environmental activists from organizations such as the World Resources Institute, the Wilderness Society, the National Audubon Society, and the Sierra Club.

This new executive branch team set out quickly to make amends for Bush's Rio performance. On Earth Day 1993 President Clinton confirmed his intent to sign the CBD. He also agreed to accept quantitative targets for reducing U.S. greenhouse gas emissions and promised a detailed plan for meeting those emissions reductions targets by the end of the summer. Clinton's designated undersecretary of state for global affairs, Timothy Wirth, at this point announced to the United Nations that U.S. environmental policies had "sharply changed" since the Bush administration. The United States would now "publicly resume the leadership the world expects."[6]

This was a brave start by the executive branch, but Clinton and Gore quickly encountered opposition from Congress. Even before the first year of the new administration was over, and despite the fact that both houses of Congress were still under Democratic Party control, U.S. international environmental policy leadership again faltered.

The Convention on Biological Diversity

In June 1993 President Clinton formally carried out his promise to sign the CBD. But when he submitted it to the Senate for approval in November 1993, he met resistance. Despite solid Democratic control of Congress in 1993 and 1994, the Senate failed to approve the treaty, leaving U.S. formal participation in limbo. As of 1998, the Senate—under Republican control—still had not approved the CBD, even though the governments of 169 other countries around the world had done so. On the issue of biodiversity, six years after Rio, the United States was once again standing alone.

Senate failure to approve the CBD was not a trivial lapse. It forced the U.S. government to attend annual meetings of the Conference of the Parties to the convention not as an official party but as an "observer." The lack of official status weakened U.S. influence at a critical period in the life of the new CBD. The official parties have begun to negotiate legally binding protocols on issues of commercial and practical importance to the U.S. biotechnology industry such as biosafety and the transboundary movement of living modified organisms. The lack of U.S. participation in official CBD activities jeopardizes U.S. trade interests in biotech products, places at risk future U.S. access to genetic materials from source countries in the developing world, and diminishes what could be a valuable international sharing of U.S. expertise on wildlife preservation (where U.S. systems are state of the art) and on biodiversity reporting and review procedures.[7]

Why did the U.S. Senate refuse to approve the CBD? In 1993 the Clinton administration did all that should have been required to gain Senate cooperation. It first secured a formal endorsement for approval from the representatives of leading U.S. biotechnology and pharmaceutical industries. These industries were originally skeptical toward the CBD, but decided in 1993 to offer an endorsement in part because they had begun to understand the perils of having the United States remain on the outside. For example, after Bush had declined to sign the CBD, Venezuela had retaliated by halting any new agreements with U.S. scientific institutions interested in gathering biological materials from Venezuelan forests.[8] Industry also went along because the new Clinton administration promised to add some unilateral "interpretations" to the convention, to be contained in the formal letter of submittal that the State Department was to send to the Senate. These Clinton administration side agreements with industry did not please the most extreme elements of the U.S. environmental community, but were widely acknowledged as the price needed to ensure the Senate's cooperation. By the time Clinton submitted the CBD in November 1993, it was officially supported by a broad coalition of private companies, environmental and developmental nongovernmental organizations, scientific groups, and academic institutions. Acknowledging this broad base of domestic support, the Senate Committee on Foreign Relations promptly endorsed the convention in a bipartisan 16–3 vote.

Then the process came to a halt. No floor vote on approval was taken in 1993, 1994, or since. Senate Majority Leader George Mitchell, D-Maine, decided not to schedule a floor vote in 1993 or 1994 once it became clear that the two-thirds needed to approve a treaty was not yet there. It requires only a minority of one-third plus one (thirty-four senators) to block a treaty, and by late 1993 a total of thirty-five senators—all Republicans—had made clear they opposed the CBD.

They claimed various reasons for their opposition. Some said the text was too binding on congressional prerogatives; for example, it might constrain future options to amend the U.S. Endangered Species Act. Others said the text was too vague and ambiguous, a bit like the original 1973 Convention on International Trade in Endangered Species (CITES). The CBD was initially just a framework convention that encouraged governments to take certain actions, but did not require them to achieve particular goals or funding levels. Others stated that the CBD was not needed because CITES was doing fine. Some based their opposition on worries about possible constraints on U.S. businesses and agriculture. They dismissed Clinton's unilateral "interpretations" as not binding on the convention's other signatories and noted that the leadership of the American Farm Bureau Federation also opposed the CBD. Some were opposed, apparently on principle, to any treaty that would strengthen the role of any non-U.S. multilateral decision-making forum. Apparently, some were even opposed because of popular anxieties, generated by a privately financed fringe campaign launched by associates of Lyndon LaRouche, depicting the CBD as inspired by paganism and nature worship and a first step toward an authoritarian world government.[9]

Some senators feared the financial obligations that might be incurred if the CBD were approved; the CBD's Article 20 stated that the developed country parties "shall provide new and additional financial resources to enable developing country Parties to meet the agreed full incremental costs to them of implementing measures which fulfill the obligations of this Convention." What exactly would constitute an incremental cost was not defined in the CBD text. Article 21 seemed to leave the construction of a financial mechanism and specific financial obligations to the Conference of Parties, but, at the insistence of the developed countries, the Global Environment Facility, a mechanism more securely controlled by the donors, was designated as an interim venue for handling project financing. Still, in 1993, at a time of tight U.S. budget constraints and collapsing congressional interest in open-ended foreign assistance programs for the developing world, the uncertain financial arrangements were cited as a concern.

Beneath the surface of these various arguments, pure partisanship was clearly at work in the 1993–1994 defeat of the CBD. The Republican minority in Congress at that time was using party line voting to block the agenda of the new Democratic president. Not a single House Republican voted for the president's 1993 budget plan, and unified Republican opposition also undercut his 1993–1994 health care plan.[10] In this partisan atmosphere, it was relatively easy for the Senate minority leader, Bob Dole, R-Kan., a presidential aspirant for 1996, to find the thirty-four Republican senators needed to block the CBD.[11]

Senate inaction on the CBD did not oblige the U.S. government to abdicate completely a leadership role in the area of protecting biological diversity. The United States is party to CITES and in 1994 launched the International Coral Reef Initiative to promote the protection, sustainable management, and monitoring of coral reefs and related ecosystems such as mangroves and sea grasses. U.S. partners in this effort include Australia, France, Jamaica, Japan, the Philippines, and the United Kingdom. In some other biological conservation issue areas, however, the United States remained as much a laggard as on the CBD. The fifteen countries of the European Union (EU) plus Canada and several developing nations, including Malaysia and Indonesia, favored a legally binding convention protecting the world's forests, but the United States, joined by Brazil and some other forest-exploiting developing nations, remained opposed.[12]

Climate Change

U.S. performance also fell far short of the original Clinton administration promise in climate change policy. During the 1992 campaign, Clinton and Gore criticized President Bush for failing to embrace the quantified policy objectives proposed by the EU (a limiting of carbon dioxide emissions to 1990 levels by 2000), and they promised to embrace this goal as national policy, if elected. President Clinton formally adopted the emissions limit goal in April 1993 and won praise for having restored the United States to a position of international leadership on climate change policy.[13]

Almost immediately, however, Clinton began to encounter difficulties. In 1993 he failed to secure from Congress the energy tax needed to meet his new emissions limitation commitment and was forced to rely on less effective voluntary measures. By the time of the 1995 Berlin climate change conference, U.S. officials had to admit that domestic emissions were still going up and the president's pledge would not be fulfilled. Undaunted, U.S. negotiators nonetheless went on to embrace a technically ambitious goal of putting a fixed cap on international greenhouse gas emissions.[14] Congress, however, was not comfortable with this approach, and for the next year and a half the president equivocated both on how tight the cap should be and when it should come into effect. In the summer of 1997, the Senate passed a 95–0 resolution telling the Clinton administration not to enter into any binding international agreement on climate change that failed to discipline the greenhouse gas emissions of developing countries. When Clinton's negotiators at the December 1997 Kyoto conference disregarded the Senate and entered into such an agreement, a complete impasse ensued. Knowing what the outcome would be, Clinton did not submit the agreement for Senate approval and hinted he might not do so until developing country participation was secured. In the meantime, Republicans in Congress insisted that so long as the agreement had not been approved, no U.S. policy steps should be taken toward its implementation.

The pivotal moment in this floundering U.S. performance on climate change policy came with Clinton's failure in 1993 to secure congressional support for the BTU tax he had requested as part of his first year deficit reduction plan. This energy tax proposal was presented to Congress more as a deficit reduction policy than as an environmental initiative, and its failure reflected congressional resistance to any new taxes, not just skepticism on the climate change hypothesis. Still, environmentalists inside the Clinton administration took the energy tax defeat as a serious setback. They had originally pushed the president to ask for a more narrowly based "carbon tax" on the burning of fossil fuels such as coal and petroleum. Gore strongly supported the carbon tax idea with climate change goals in mind, but Clinton decided that a pure carbon tax would never be enacted by Congress because it would hit coal-producing states such as West Virginia and coal-using states in the Middle West too hard. He decided instead to propose a more broadly based tax on all energy sources (the so-called BTU tax), while adding some environmental content at the margins by placing surcharges on energy generated from fossil fuel sources.

Congress rejected even this compromise proposal when it was harshly criticized not only by Republicans but also by Democrats who thought Clinton had promised the middle class a tax cut in the 1992 campaign, not a tax increase. The BTU tax proposal also still angered the coal industry, which argued that it should be excused from the surcharges because of the burdens it was already bearing under the 1990 Clean Air Act. When Clinton gave in to this coal industry demand, he then angered representatives from states that produce oil as well as those with heavy home heating oil consumption, who also wanted an exemption. Debate over the measure degenerated into a contest over who would get an exemption and who would not. In the end, Clinton withdrew the BTU tax proposal altogether, replacing it with a far more modest (and environmentally insignificant) 4.3 cent per gallon increase in the 14.1 cent per gallon federal tax on gasoline.

Coming so early in the term, the BTU tax defeat left Clinton with no obvious way to fulfill his earlier pledge to reduce U.S. greenhouse gas emissions. He had promised in his first year to devise a policy for reaching the goal of 1990 levels by 2000, but the administration's Climate Change Action Plan (CCAP), proposed in October 1993, was only a weak set of voluntary measures. The CCAP consisted largely of two new government-industry partnerships, to be known as Climate Challenge and Climate Wise Companies. These were voluntary programs run by the Department of Energy (rather than EPA), designed to entice utilities and other U.S. companies into negotiating domestic emissions reduction agreements with the government, in return for a mix of technical assistance and public recognition. The total cost to taxpayers was a modest $1.9 billion over six years. The CCAP included no revived proposal for an energy tax, no new international negotiations initiatives, and not even a tightening of CAFE (corporate average fuel efficiency) standards for automobiles, despite Clinton's 1992 campaign pledge to do so.

Environmental groups were properly suspicious of the voluntary approach and of the administration's optimistic projections of what that approach might achieve. In April 1994 the Natural Resources Defense Council charged that the Clinton plan would achieve only about one-third of the emissions reductions it promised. This charge of inadequacy proved accurate; in the spring of 1995, on the eve of the Berlin climate change conference, Tim Wirth, who was heading the U.S. delegation, admitted that the United States would probably fall short of the emissions stabilization pledge by a wide margin.[15]

A core of strong climate change policy advocates inside the Clinton administration was embarrassed by this lagging performance and upped the ante in July 1996 by announcing at a conference in Geneva that the United States now favored "legally binding" greenhouse gas emissions standards. This was a surprising step because, just one month earlier, senior State Department officials had reassured skeptics in Congress that the administration did not intend to make any new "quantitative commitments" on climate change. When the new negotiating position was revealed, U.S. business groups protested immediately.[16] Congress likewise signaled its displeasure. In June 1997 Sen. Robert Byrd, D-W.Va., introduced Senate Resolution 98, which called on the Clinton administration not to agree to any binding international treaty on climate change that did not simultaneously bind developing countries such as China, India, or Mexico. Within a month Byrd's resolution had sixty-two Senate cosponsors, and by late summer the measure passed the Senate by a 95–0 vote.

Some of those who voted for this measure genuinely wanted the strong participation of developing nations in a tough international climate change agreement, but most were planning to use the anticipated refusal of these countries to participate as a convenient excuse for opposing the Clinton administration's binding limits approach. In hopes of appeasing Congress, the administration proposed an "evolution" measure that would require developing country parties to the treaty to adopt quantitative greenhouse gas emissions obligations by 2005 (based on "agreed criteria" not yet spelled out). This compromise failed when it proved not strong enough to impress Congress, but still too strong for most developing countries.

The administration's performance at the December 1997 Kyoto summit widened this domestic split with Congress and deepened the paralysis. Clinton's negotiators sought to lure developing countries into a binding limits agreement by offering a cut in U.S. greenhouse gas emissions larger than anything previously discussed. The United States offered to cut to 7 percent *below* 1990 emissions levels by the years 2008 to 2012. This tactic failed when the developing countries, led by China, still refused to accept any emissions reduction obligations.[17] The result was the worst of both worlds: a promised U.S. cut larger than Congress was ready for, without the guarantee of developing country participation that Congress had warned would be necessary.

Congressional criticism of this outcome was instantaneous. House Speaker Newt Gingrich called the treaty a "surrender" and an "outrage." He said, "It is profoundly wrong that approximately 134 countries were allowed to vote on a treaty by which they will not be bound." Sen. Chuck Hagel, R-Neb., who had been in Kyoto, said flatly, "There is no way, if the president signs this, that the vote in the United States Senate will even be close. We will kill this bill." Sen. James Inhofe, R-Okla., called the treaty a "political, economic and national security fiasco" and said it would never be ratified by the Senate in any form. Sen. Richard Lugar, R-Ind., said the president "hasn't even begun to make the case on climate change. And now he has to explain how the U.S. negotiators botched it in Kyoto." Even some liberal Democrats criticized the agreement. Sen. John Kerry, D-Mass., who was also in Kyoto, said, "What we have here is not ratifiable in the Senate in my judgment."[18]

The Clinton administration responded with procedural evasion: it opted to postpone submitting the treaty for approval, promising it would first seek guarantees of developing country participation. In February 1998 Undersecretary of State Stuart Eizenstat, who had led the U.S. delegation in Kyoto, promised the Senate Foreign Relations Committee a "full-court diplomatic press" not only to persuade major developing countries to adhere to the pact but also to secure the stronger "emissions trading" rules Clinton had championed as the least painful path toward U.S. treaty compliance. Yet the likelihood of securing these objectives was low, and senior White House officials admitted, off the record, that the treaty might not be ready for submission to the Senate any time during the remainder of Clinton's term in office.[19]

The practical outcome for U.S. climate change policy is likely to be a continued lack of domestic discipline and continued growth in greenhouse gas emissions. Members of Congress hostile to the Kyoto agreement warned the Clinton administration not to undertake any steps and not to appropriate any funds to implement the agreement until it has been submitted to the Senate and approved. Even if the agreement were approved, it would be a poor device for imposing timely domestic disciplines on the United States because compliance would not be measured until the years 2008–2012, more than two presidential terms after Clinton is scheduled to leave office.

The U.S. ability to comply is suspect, even assuming eventual ratification. U.S. greenhouse gas emissions have continued to rise rather than fall throughout the first six years of the Clinton-Gore administration. When the Kyoto agreement was negotiated, U.S. greenhouse gas emissions were 10 percent above 1990 levels and projected to rise to 13 percent above those levels by 2000, having increased at an undisciplined 3.4 percent annual rate in 1996 alone.[20] This poor track record inspires little confidence that the Clinton administration's promise of a 7 percent cut from 1990 levels in 2008 to 2012 can be met. Because emissions are likely to continue increasing in the near term, as much as a 30 percent cut would be needed to meet treaty requirements by the time compliance becomes mandatory in 2008 to 2012.[21]

While promising ambitious cuts ten years in the future to an international audience in Kyoto, the Clinton administration has been unwilling, since 1993, to reconsider the practical policy steps at home—either fuel taxes or fuel rationing—that will be needed to secure the cuts. When President Clinton was asked at a White House–sponsored climate change policy symposium in October 1997 why he was not at least proposing a carbon tax as part of U.S. climate change policy, his response was fatalistic: "[That] would be a grand gesture, but it would not happen."[22] The president was no doubt alluding to the fact that only 23 percent of the American people at the time supported taxes on energy.[23] On rationing, the administration was equally evasive. It championed "tradable permits" as a low-pain approach to greenhouse gas emissions cuts, but never sufficiently emphasized that some form of highly intrusive fossil fuel rationing (the creation of emissions "permits") would have to be enacted by Congress as an essential feature of such a scheme. The U.S. administration, therefore, could be accused by its critics at home and abroad of first failing to meet a modest emissions reduction goal for 2000, of covering up that failure by claiming it planned to meet a far more ambitious goal for the years 2008–2012, and of then taking no tangible policy steps in the direction of reaching this goal, yet all the while blaming developing countries (hardly the source of the greenhouse gas emissions problem) for creating the impasse.

Explaining Weak U.S. Leadership on Biodiversity and Climate Change

Past studies of U.S. international environmental policy have implicitly identified a wide range of possible explanations for weak rather than strong international leadership. Among these explanations are industry or labor opposition at home due to projected burdens on the domestic economy, a lack of scientific consensus regarding the nature or magnitude of the environmental threat, and poor prospects for international cooperation. In the case of the 1987 Montreal Protocol to protect stratospheric ozone, the United States was able to take an effective lead once these potential blocking factors, where they existed, had been overcome. In this section we first consider how and why these potential blocking factors have not been overcome in the case of climate change policy. Then we ask why, for international biodiversity policy, U.S. leadership has continued to falter even though the blocking factors mostly have been overcome.

Climate Change: Easily Explained Failure

The U.S. failure to lead on climate change policy has multiple causes: domestic opposition from labor and industry, weak science, and unsolved international cooperation problems. Comparisons to the Montreal Protocol example are instructive. For all the reasons that strong leadership on stratospheric ozone was possible between 1986 and 1991, so far it has been impossible on climate change.

Private industry in the United States supported both the 1987 Montreal Protocol that cut CFC production by 50 percent and the subsequent London agreements that promised a complete ban on CFCs. As early as August 1986, the Alliance for Responsible CFC Policy, a prominent business-based group, had endorsed international controls on CFC growth, and the leading U.S. producer, DuPont, went even further and backed international controls on overall levels of CFC production. DuPont was motivated partly by its early lead in the search for CFC substitutes, giving it an advantage over its competition from an international agreement limiting CFC use.[24]

In contrast, private industry in the United States has strongly opposed domestic or international controls on greenhouse gas emissions. In 1993, when Clinton proposed his BTU tax, the coal, petroleum, and public utilities industries mounted a strong resistance. Organized industry opposition prior to the Kyoto conference in 1997 took the form of a $13 million ad campaign sponsored by private energy-linked companies. The ads became a factor in strengthening congressional resistance to the administration's preference for binding emissions limits. The leading corporate voice against a strong policy on this occasion was the Global Climate Change Coalition, a consortium of coal, oil, and automobile companies and utilities (originally spun out of the National Association of Manufacturers in 1989) that fought hard against binding treaty limits. Parallel to this umbrella lobby effort was the more narrow Coalition for Vehicle Choice, a Washington-based group financed by the U.S. auto industry, which spent the two years leading up to Kyoto convincing small business, labor, and local civic groups throughout the United States that a treaty limiting emissions would be "bad for America." This coalition persuaded 1,300 such groups to sign a 1997 ad to that effect and published the list of signatories in the *Washington Post*.

Corporate money was also used effectively to generate "studies" that frightened voters and members of Congress about the costs of tighter greenhouse gas emissions limits. The Global Climate Change Coalition released a study late in 1997 purporting to show that cumulative losses to the U.S. economy from a climate treaty could amount to $30,000 by each American household in the years 2000–2020. The Center for Energy and Economic Development, a group with a $4 million annual budget sponsored by the coal industry, targeted business and civic groups in eleven states with a similar message.[25]

The controversial promises made by Clinton's negotiating team in Kyoto prompted industry opponents into a further round of action. In April 1998 representatives of large oil companies, trade associations, and conservative policy research organizations, working through the Washington offices of the American Petroleum Institute, drafted a plan to spend $5 million over the next two years to "maximize the impact of scientific views consistent with ours"—in other words, views skeptical of the idea of human-induced climate change. The group planned to focus its efforts on Congress, the media, and other influential audiences.

Some smaller segments of U.S. industry have agreed to support greenhouse gas emissions limits, most notably the U.S. Business Council for Sustainable Industry, a group that includes the natural gas industry, which would see its share of the fossil fuel market grow under a tighter emissions regime. The insurance industry is also favorably inclined toward tighter emissions controls, hoping for protection against claim settlements that might accompany sea level rise or violent weather fluctuations if a warming-induced climate change were to occur. On balance, however, private industry in the United States has been a consistent opponent of more stringent climate change policies.

In contrast to its stand on ozone protection, organized labor in the United States is also opposed to tighter climate change policies. Organized labor took little interest in the Montreal Protocol, because so few jobs of any kind—let alone union jobs—were linked to CFC production. Even for DuPont, the largest U.S. producer of CFCs, revenues from CFC production were only about 2 percent of total corporate revenues. On climate change policy, however, labor opposition has become a significant factor; the potentially vulnerable United Mine Workers spent $1.5 million in 1996 and 1997 to block a strong treaty. Other labor groups fear that substantially higher fuel costs due to climate change policy would slow economic growth and harm workers. Private estimates tend to bear out these fears. Immediately following the Kyoto summit, Yale economist William Nordhaus estimated that reaching the summit's goals in the United States might require a doubling of the wholesale price of crude oil, coal, and natural gas, which would work through the economy to produce the equivalent of a $2,000 per year increase, per American household, in outlays for gasoline and heat. Even official U.S. Department of Energy estimates allude to additional costs for middle class workers, in the form of significant job cuts in a number of energy sensitive U.S. industries, including aluminum, cement, chemicals, oil, paper, and steel.[26] Fuel- and fertilizer-dependent agricultural workers also would be hurt. Labor's lack of support for the Clinton administration's position on climate change was underscored immediately following the Kyoto conference when House Democratic Leader Richard Gephardt of Missouri, a labor ally with a populist economic philosophy (and a potential challenger to Gore for the Democratic presidential nomination in 2000), declined to offer any view at all on the treaty.

Another contrast to the ozone example is apparent when we consider the importance of a strong international scientific consensus in backing U.S. environmental policy leadership. In the case of controlling CFCs, U.S. support (including corporate support) for the Montreal Protocol in 1987 and the subsequent London agreements rested on a sturdy scientific foundation. By 1987 massive ozone loss had been measured by NASA-sponsored high-altitude aircraft examining the stratosphere over the Antarctic, and the link between ozone loss and CFCs became impossible to deny. In addition, atmospheric and medical scientists were able to draw direct, quantifiable links between ozone loss, increases in surface UV radiation, and increased skin cancer.[27]

The scientific consensus regarding human-induced climate change is not yet this good. In Chapter 10 of this volume, Michael R. Molitor quotes an assertion President Clinton made in June 1997 that the science of climate change had become "clear and compelling." Relative to the significant economic cost of taking action to reduce greenhouse gas emissions, however, this scientific consensus was not yet strong enough.

Atmospheric concentrations of greenhouse gasses can be measured with confidence, as can recent changes in global average temperature, but quantifying the impact of a changed greenhouse gas concentration on temperature remains controversial. Computer model estimations of this impact must rest on a number of sensitive assumptions about Earth's rotation, surface friction at sea level, the uncertain movement of carbon between the atmosphere and the ocean, plus rainfall and cloud formation, as naturally occurring water vapor is also a greenhouse gas. Until recently, the modeling techniques used to generate estimates of future temperature rise were not even capable of depicting the present global climate, without fudging. Also, as these techniques have improved, their projections of future warming and sea level rise have grown more modest rather than more severe. In its December 1995 Second Assessment Report, the Intergovernmental Panel on Climate Change (IPCC) actually scaled back its projections of global warming significantly, compared to an earlier 1990 report. Instead of a 3.5–8 degree Celsius warming by 2050, the report estimated only a 1.8–6.3 degree warming by 2100. The report included a strong statement—"the balance of evidence suggests that there is a discernible human influence on the climate"—that was given great play at the time by the environmental community. But the IPCC was subsequently criticized by a former president of the National Academy of Sciences for alleged alterations made in this statement *after* it had received formal approval from the panel's scientific board of advisers.[28]

A more recent scientific challenge to the theory of human-induced climate change is a hypothesis that links climate cycles to solar radiation cycles. Actual changes in Earth temperatures appear to correlate more strongly with changes in solar radiation, as measured historically through sunspot counts or more recently through radiance-measuring satellites, than with changes in human-generated greenhouse gas concentrations. This solar hypothesis emerged just prior to the Kyoto conference, complicating the task of scientific consensus building.[29]

A final contrast between the Montreal Protocol case and climate change lies in the problematic area of international cooperation. In the case of stratospheric ozone protection, international cooperation was a problem that could be solved because production of CFCs was concentrated within a relatively small number of wealthy industrial countries—half the world total was in the United States in the 1970s—and because the proposed limits on CFC production had little projected impact on the welfare of those countries or on the future economic growth potential of the developing countries. For greenhouse gas emissions, securing international support for effective action is far more daunting. A number of European countries, led by Germany and Britain, are ready to join an international effort to reduce greenhouse gas emissions. Germany can afford to make stringent reductions from a 1990 baseline because of a massive shutdown of dirty industries in the eastern half of the country that was undertaken for other reasons, and Britain because of a switch already made since 1990 from burning dirty coal to North Sea natural gas. Yet among most developing countries, other than the small island states threatened by sea level rise, willingness to sacrifice to reduce greenhouse gas emissions is close to nonexistent.

Greenhouse gas emissions in developing countries are growing rapidly enough to constitute a significant policy problem, but will not surpass industrial country emissions overall for another twenty or thirty years, and until then developing country leaders will have reason not to feel responsible for the problem. Their attitude was summed up at the Kyoto meetings by Mark Mwandosya of Tanzania, chair of the developing country caucus: "Very many of us are struggling to attain a decent standard of living for our peoples, and yet we are constantly told that we must share in the effort to reduce emissions so that industrialized countries can continue to enjoy the benefits of their wasteful life style."[30] On a per capita basis, human activity in the United States today still puts into the atmosphere roughly ten times as much carbon dioxide as human activity in China. Persuading the governments of Brazil, China, India, or Mexico to compromise their hopes of rapid industrial development to help the already wealthy countries reduce greenhouse gas emissions is a problem in international cooperation that has not yet been solved.

Negotiating a firm treaty guarantee in advance of significant developing country emissions discipline is so unlikely that other means to proceed ought to be considered. One option is to soften the trade-off between reduced fossil fuel use and income growth in today's poor countries by investing in technological innovations that are less fossil fuel dependent. One of the best ways to trigger these investments would be to increase fuel prices unilaterally in the United States, rather than waiting to act until an enforceable international agreement has been negotiated. In some cases it makes sense to postpone unilateral action until international cooperation has been assured; in this case, as in many others, unilateral U.S. action at home is the form of leadership most needed abroad.[31] Even among other industrial countries, the United States should feel an international obligation to act first, because it releases twice as much carbon dioxide per capita as Germany, Japan, or Russia and almost three times as much as Italy.

A domestic tax on fossil fuels would almost certainly be rejected by Congress if presented as part of a larger tax increase plan, as in 1993. In 1998, however, the federal budget ran a surplus, making it easier to propose that any new tax on fossil fuels be fully offset with parallel tax *cuts* in other politically sensitive areas, such as federal taxes on income or capital gains. In this less-constrained fiscal environment, cash compensation could even be offered to those, such as coal miners, most adversely affected by a fossil fuels tax. A unilateral, revenue-neutral tax reform of this kind would be the most efficient way to generate, through energy price incentives in the market place, the innovative investments that are needed in more efficient fossil fuel burning technologies, in safe nuclear power, and in the most important renewable forms of energy, such as wind, geothermal, and solar. The international payoff from these investments would be new energy technologies ready for sale or transfer to countries such as China, India, or Mexico. Perhaps only by taking timely unilateral action of this kind at home can the United States make it possible for poorer nations to escape from their dependency on fossil fuels for affordable industrial development.

A revenue-neutral fossil fuel tax at home might also be the natural prelude to more formal international cooperation. An agreement with other governments to tax fossil fuel use at home (and to keep the revenue at home) would be easier to negotiate and enforce than the binding emissions limits pushed by U.S. negotiators at Kyoto.[32] The binding emissions approach, as Thomas Schelling has noted, requires the unprecedented creation and allocation of hundreds of billions of dollars worth of global property rights. It requires that all the world's governments will "calmly sit down and divide up rights in perpetuity worth more than a trillion dollars."[33] By comparison, an international agreement to impose domestic fossil fuel taxes would be much simpler to negotiate. In this sense, by embracing the binding limits approach, the Clinton administration made an already difficult task of global cooperation on climate change even more difficult.

Biodiversity: Partisanship, Senate Rules, and Weak Connections to Human Health and Welfare

Explaining the weakness of U.S. leadership in international biodiversity protection presents a more challenging analytic problem. The Senate's refusal to approve the Convention on Biodiversity cannot be blamed either on industry or labor opposition, or on an inadequate scientific consensus regarding the importance of biodiversity protection, or on any international cooperation problems. A different dynamic had to be at work.

Neither industry nor labor opposition was behind the Senate's 1993–1994 failure to approve the CBD. Industry opposition was an important factor when President Bush refused to sign the CBD at Rio in 1992, but by 1993 a broad-based coalition of U.S. biotechnology and pharmaceutical companies had received sufficient assurances from President Clinton (in the form of unilateral U.S. "interpretations" to the convention) to announce public support for ratification. The willingness of the private sector to support international cooperation in this area was not surprising: U.S. multinational biotech and pharmaceutical companies have a significant stake in open trade and global genetic prospecting, which makes them more internationalist in outlook than some other industrial leaders and conspicuously more internationalist than some traditional, sovereignty-minded U.S. senators. Organized labor likewise has presented no obstacle to CBD ratification. The American Farm Bureau Federation opposed the convention when approval was blocked the first time, but has not been active in its opposition since that time.

Nor was lack of scientific consensus regarding biodiversity the main problem. The senators who blocked CBD approval did not base their dissent on lack of a scientific consensus regarding species loss or on doubts regarding the potential value of genetic resource protection. It would have been difficult for them to do so because by 1993 the CBD was strongly endorsed by many scientific groups and academic institutions.[34] Scientists may disagree about the magnitude of the biodiversity protection problem, but not about its human causes or its potential irreversibility. Nor is lack of support from other governments abroad an explanation for the Senate's failure to approve the CBD because the United States stood virtually alone in its refusal. By 1997, 169 other governments around the world had already signed and ratified.

Several other explanations also can be rejected. One is the assertion that Senate treaty-approval rules will always get in the way of U.S. environmental leadership abroad. A second is that Congress will always block initiatives taken by the executive branch. The biodiversity and climate change cases presented here seem to conform to these two generalizations, but the stratospheric ozone case refutes both.

In the case of the Montreal Protocol on CFCs, Congress was anything but a blocking agent. To the contrary, pressures from Congress (then under Democratic Party control) pushed the Reagan and Bush administrations toward a stronger agreement than some in the executive branch favored. Nor was a two-thirds Senate vote for the treaty an impediment. In March 1988, only a few months after the completion of the international negotiations, the U.S. Senate approved the Montreal Protocol, 83–0. In American politics, there is no safe generalization stating that the executive branch will always take the lead in international environmental matters. In the early 1980s, Congress wanted a more aggressive stance, while the Reagan administration, especially during its first term, attempted to roll back environmental regulations at home and abroad.

The influence of political parties is a possible explanation. Pure partisanship clearly played a role in the biodiversity vote; all thirty-five of the senators opposed to the convention in 1993 were Republicans. To what extent does the stronger environmentalism of Democrats versus Republicans explain the fluctuating strength or weakness of U.S. international environmental policy leadership? When Congress was under Democratic control in the 1980s, it took the lead in pushing reluctant Republican presidents to do more. Then when the presidency came under Democratic control in 1993, the executive branch took the lead, only to be blocked after the 1994 election by a Congress controlled by Republicans.

There is no denying the obvious differences that exist between most Republicans and most Democrats on environmental policy. In the 104th Congress (1995–1996) Republican committee chairs in the House received on average only a 12.4 rating (on a scale from 0–100) from the League of

Conservation Voters. By contrast, Democratic committee chairs in the 103d Congress (1993–1994) had received a 73.3 rating from the LCV.[35] Yet this party-based explanation cannot be determining in the case of either biodiversity or climate change because U.S. leadership faltered on both of these issues in the 1993–1994 period, when both the executive branch and Congress were controlled by Democrats. Partisanship was also not in evidence in the case of the Montreal Protocol, which was negotiated by a Republican administration and approved unanimously by the Senate.

For climate change policy, prior to the December 1997 meeting in Kyoto, congressional skepticism toward the binding emissions limits approach was essentially nonpartisan: the Senate resolution warning against exclusion of developing countries passed 95–0. Some of the fiercest policy debates prior to Kyoto actually took place among Democrats in Congress and also within Clinton's executive branch. Top Clinton appointees responsible for the performance of the U.S. economy, such as Treasury Secretary Robert Rubin and Undersecretary Lawrence Summers, argued against tight binding limits on greenhouse gas emissions. In terms of presidential politics, the most dramatic political contest over the Kyoto agreement developed between Gore and Gephardt, potential rivals for the Democratic nomination in 2000.

For the CBD, there was more clearly a straight partisan flavor to the original Senate opposition. Yet something less tangible also blocked Senate action on this issue. It is inherently difficult to rally domestic political support for the CBD partly because the issue is presented as one of protecting nonhuman species (in contrast to both stratospheric ozone and climate change) and partly because the nonhuman species Americans care most about are already protected by other measures. A strong domestic endangered species act protects the animals U.S. voters care most about at home, and many of the species that attract human sympathies abroad are seen to be protected under CITES. Most of the additional species the CBD might protect would be plants or insects, living in settings for the most part distant from and unfamiliar to U.S. voters.

The gains to human health and survival that might come from preserving biodiversity abroad may be undeniable in the long run, but they are not as compelling in the short run as preserving stratospheric ozone (for every 1 percent loss of ozone, UV radiation at the Earth's surface increases by about 2 percent, and the incidence of skin cancers by more than 2 percent). The argument for biodiversity protection in tropical countries is a noble one, in part because it goes beyond the short-term good of the human species alone, but this has not helped the issue gain a critical mass of domestic political support.

Conclusion

This analysis of lagging U.S. leadership on international environmental policy points to a complex conclusion. We find several different reasons for the recent failure of the U.S. government to provide leadership on biodiversity protection and climate change. The short-term material interests of organized domestic industry and labor groups, plus a scientific consensus not yet strong enough to override these domestic interests, plus an essentially unsolved problem of international cooperation and burden sharing, all combined to produce policy paralysis on climate change. In the case of biodiversity protection, another set of forces weakened policy. Industry and labor were not opposed, the scientific consensus was strong, and international cooperation was assured, but Senate approval of the CBD did not happen. It was actively blocked by the forces of partisanship in the U.S. Senate, taking advantage of the two-thirds rule for approval of a treaty, and passively by the relative indifference of the political audience to the somewhat obscure nonmaterial issues at stake.

One larger conclusion we might draw is that U.S. international environmental politics is not so different from other kinds of politics. Advocacy by organized groups stressing short-term material interests will tend to dominate the debate, and Congress, more often than the executive branch, will get the last word. This is a political process that can, on occasion, sustain successful U.S. environmental leadership abroad, as in the stratospheric ozone protection case. But just as often it will make that sort of outward-oriented leadership difficult.

Nevertheless, other forms of leadership can be pursued. Strong domestic environmental policy actions within the United States (on clean air or species protection, for example) can provide a model for governments contemplating parallel measures abroad. Technological innovations, such as improved toxic waste disposal or less dangerous farm chemicals, brought about by tight U.S. domestic environmental regulations, can later be extended to users abroad. To deal with climate change, a unilateral, revenue-neutral tax on fossil fuel use would not require any international negotiations at all, but could do more than any international agreement to reduce greenhouse gas emissions in the United States and eventually in poor countries as well. An appreciation for the international environmental gains that might come through less direct paths such as these could help to offset the weakness of U.S. leadership through more traditional means.

Notes

1. Organization for Economic Cooperation and Development, *OECD Environmental Performance Reviews: United States* (Paris: Organization for Economic Cooperation and Development, 1996).

2. Edward A. Parson, "Protecting the Ozone Layer," in *Institutions for the Earth,* ed. Peter M. Haas, Robert O. Keohane, and Marc A. Levy (Cambridge: MIT Press, 1993), 27–73.

3. The rating is by the World Wildlife Fund (WWF). The WWF scorecard rated nations in four areas: fulfillment of the 1992 Rio pledge on stabilization, support for significant reductions in carbon-dioxide emissions, per capita carbon-dioxide emissions, and gross national carbon-dioxide emissions. The United States was the only country to receive a failing grade on all four. The United States is the single largest

emitter of CO_2, accounting for nearly 22 percent of the world's total, and was also top on the list of per capita emissions. "Spotlight Story," *Greenwire*, February 28, 1997, 3.

4. Bill Clinton and Al Gore, *Putting People First: How We Can All Change America* (New York: Times Books, 1992), 94.

5. Al Gore, *Earth in the Balance: Ecology and the Human Spirit* (New York: Plume, 1993), xiii.

6. William K. Stevens, "Gore Promises U.S. Leadership on Sustainable Development Path," *New York Times*, June 15, 1993, C4.

7. Kal Raustiala and David G. Victor, "The Future of the Convention on Biological Diversity," *Environment* 4 (May 1996): 42.

8. Ibid.

9. This explanation was later offered, in frustration, by Tim Wirth. "Address to the National Conference of the Ecological Society of America," Salt Lake City, Utah, August 1, 1995.

10. On free trade in 1993 and 1994—for example, the North American Free Trade Agreement and the General Agreement on Tariffs and Trade—Republicans in Congress did support Clinton, but only because here Clinton was completing initiatives launched earlier by Presidents Reagan and Bush.

11. The CBD was not the only international treaty favored by the Clinton administration that was blocked in this fashion by the Republican Senate minority in 1993 and 1994. Another was the Convention on the Elimination of All Forms of Discrimination Against Women, a treaty that would establish an international "bill of rights for women." The Senate Foreign Relations Committee voted in favor of the treaty in 1994, but the full Senate never approved it.

12. Paul Lewis, "5 Years After Earth Summit, U.N. Seeks to Fill In Gaps," *New York Times*, April 7, 1997, A3.

13. See, for example, Gregg Easterbrook, "From Uncle Smoke to Mr. Clean," *New York Times*, August 13, 1993, A13.

14. See Chapter 10.

15. Steven Greenhouse, "Officials Say U.S. Is Unlikely to Meet Clean-Air Goal for 2000," *New York Times*, March 30, 1995, A6.

16. Christopher Douglass and Murray Weidenbaum, "The Quiet Reversal of U.S. Global Climate Change Policy," *Contemporary Issues Series* 83 (St. Louis: Center for the Study of American Business, Washington University, 1996).

17. See Chapter 10.

18. James Bennet, "Warm Globe, Hot Politics," *New York Times*, December 11, 1997, A1.

19. "Clinton Insists on Third World Emissions Role," *New York Times*, December 12, 1997, A16.

20. John H. Cushman Jr., "U.S. Says Its Greenhouse Gas Emissions Are at Highest Rate in Years," *New York Times*, October 21, 1997, A22.

21. John H. Cushman Jr., "Whether It Creates Jobs or Joblessness, the Agreement Will Affect Everyone," *New York Times*, December 12, 1997, A16.

22. John J. Fialka, "Clinton Expects Developing Nations to Cooperate on Global Warming Pact," *Wall Street Journal*, October 7, 1997, A2.

23. Willett Kempton, "How the Public Views Climate Change," *Environment* 39 (November 1997): 12–21.

24. Parson, "Protecting the Ozone Layer," 41.

25. John J. Fialka, "Clinton's Effort to Curb Global Warming Draws Some Business Support, but It May Be Too Late," *Wall Street Journal*, October 22, 1997, A24.

26. Christina Duff, "Accord May Cool U.S. Economy, Experts Warn," *Wall Street Journal*, December 11, 1997, A2.

27. Parson, "Protecting the Ozone Layer," 32.

28. One scientist-approved statement deleted from the final report said, "None of the studies cited above has shown clear evidence that we can attribute the observed

changes to the specific cause of increased greenhouse gasses." For a critical discussion of these alterations, see Douglass and Weidenbaum, "The Quiet Reversal," 6.

29. Soon after the Kyoto conference, Princeton University Press published a 262-page book on the science of global warming by geoscientist S. George Philander, which did not refute (or even mention) the solar radiation hypothesis, but raised another possible challenge to the climate change hypothesis: the possibility that terrestrial reactions to greenhouse gas buildups, for example, more plant growth, could serve as a natural stabilizer keeping the earth's temperature within a moderate range. See S. George Philander, *The Uncertain Science of Global Warming* (Princeton: Princeton University Press, 1998).

30. William K. Stevens, "Greenhouse Gas Issue: Haggling Over Fairness," *New York Times*, November 30, 1997, 6.

31. For a more general argument stressing the role unilateralism can play in promoting global environmental protection, see Robert Paarlberg, *Leadership Abroad Begins at Home: U.S. Foreign Economic Policy After the Cold War* (Washington, D.C.: Brookings, 1995).

32. For a brief discussion of this option, see Richard N. Cooper, "Toward a Real Global Warming Treaty," *Foreign Affairs*, March/April 1998, 66–79.

33. Thomas C. Schelling, "The Cost of Combating Global Warming," *Foreign Affairs*, November/December 1997, 8–14.

34. "Congress Fails to Ratify Treaty to Protect the World's Biological Diversity," *International Environmental Reporter*, October 19, 1994, 845.

35. LCV ratings are based on percentage of key votes considered "pro-environmental action" rather than "anti-environmental action" and are compiled here from the LCV's National Environmental Scorecard.

12

The Dutch National Plan for Sustainable Society

Duncan Liefferink

The Netherlands—boasting an average 370 consumers and almost 150 cars per square kilometer, heavy industrial activity, and highly intensive agriculture—is one of the most heavily polluted countries in the world. At the same time, it has a certain reputation as a forerunner in the field of environmental policy. This may seem a contradiction. It can be argued, though, that it was the very seriousness of environmental pollution in the Netherlands that brought about comparatively far-reaching policy efforts. It is perhaps more surprising that this reputation is to a large extent built on a policy plan. The 1989 National Environmental Policy Plan (NEPP), rather than concrete policy performance, is the basis of the Netherlands' reputation as an environmentally progressive country. Foreign observers denote the NEPP as "perhaps the most serious attempt to integrate environmental concerns into the full range of public policy" and "the world's first comprehensive national plan for a sustainable economy."[1] As we will see below, the NEPP indeed contains a number of innovative impulses for a radical transformation, an "ecological modernization" of society. But it still is a program for further action.

In order to understand the full significance of the NEPP, it is necessary to investigate how the NEPP is rooted in the Dutch political system and how it relates to earlier environmental plans and policies. This is the focus of the next section, where it is shown that the NEPP approach is as much a culmination of earlier trends and initiatives as a revolutionary new start. The third section will examine the follow-up and implementation of the NEPP. Very much in line with the Dutch planning tradition, the NEPP led to a host of other documents that elaborated aspects of, monitored, or updated the original plan. These documents include the NEPP-Plus of 1990, the second NEPP in 1993, and the third NEPP in 1998. But to what extent have these documents actually been put into practice? It would appear that a considerable gap still remains between the high ambitions of the NEPP and practical implementation.

Apart from giving direction to the recent development of domestic environmental policy in the Netherlands, the NEPP approach has also had a certain impact abroad, both inside and outside Europe. Soon after the publication of the NEPP, it came to be seen as one of the first and most eloquent expressions of a new way of thinking in environmental policy. In fact, the first sentences of the preface of the NEPP unequivocally refer to its ambition to put into practice the goals of sustainable development, as formulated in particular by the World Commission on Environment and Development (also known as the Brundtland Commission) and published as *Our Common Future* (the Brundtland Report).[2] The NEPP thus anticipates and works out many elements of Agenda 21 as it was adopted more than three years later at the United Nations Conference on Environment and Development (UNCED), held in Rio de Janeiro in June 1992. This may explain why the plan could act as a source of inspiration for the elaboration of similar ideas in other countries as well as at the level of the European Union (EU). The discussion of the international impact of the NEPP in the penultimate section of this chapter will enable us to put its allegedly "unique" and "exemplary" character in perspective. To what extent, then, is the reputation of the NEPP justified? In the final section we will come back to this question.

History and Content of the
1989 National Environmental Policy Plan

The NEPP did not, of course, come like a bolt from the blue. It was preceded by almost two decades of environmental policy development. Since the beginning of the 1970s an extensive system of environmental laws and policies had been set in place.[3] Many gaps and shortcomings still existed, some of which were intended to be tackled by the NEPP, but there can be little doubt that by 1989 the environment had become an established policy sector in the Netherlands. Two features of the Dutch political system appear to me to be crucial for the understanding of the context in which the NEPP emerged.

Some Core Features of the Dutch Political System

The first of these features is the basically consensual style of Dutch policymaking. In the first half of this century and particularly in the period after the Second World War, Dutch politics was characterized by consultation and consensus at the elite level. Top representatives of interest groups (industry, farmers, and the like) were closely involved in those sectors of policymaking that were directly relevant to them. In exchange for influence on the content of policies, they committed themselves to the decisions made and played an active role in their implementation. An important precondition for this system to work was a relatively homogeneous and to some extent passive society, with strong trust in top-level political leaders. The rapid economic growth in the postwar period no doubt added to the success of what the political scientist Arend Lijphart in his classical study called the "politics of accommodation."[4] Policymaking by consultation and consensus among elites was not unique for the Netherlands. Similar systems existed in several other countries, particularly in the northwestern part of Europe, and can be drawn together under the theoretical notion of corporatism.[5] Typical for the Dutch corporatist system was its strongly confessional coloring. Society was to a large extent organized along religious lines, and decision making took place among the top-level representatives of the Protestant, Catholic, and "neutral" (that is, socialist and liberal) "pillars." During the 1960s and 1970s, the pillarized structure of society started to erode, and as a consequence the influence of elites decreased and policy conflicts were fought out more openly.[6] Generally speaking, however, a style of negotiation and compromise continued to be a central characteristic of Dutch political culture.

A second characteristic of the Dutch political system is the major role of planning. In 1945, for instance, the Central Planning Bureau (CPB) was established to offer guidance to the reconstruction of the country after the Second World War. Although the idea of economic planning in the strict sense of the word was given up after the 1950s, the CPB's economic fore-casts still play an important role in the preparation of socioeconomic policy in the Netherlands. In the postwar period, spatial planning was governed by the so-called National Plan, an instrument that had in fact been inherited from the period of the German occupation. In the 1960s, the area of spatial planning was considerably decentralized, but planning at the local, provin-cial, and state levels remained the principal policy instrument.[7] In almost all other policy fields, furthermore, government plans have become important tools for agenda setting and policy formulation. With the exception of spa-tial planning, where other procedures apply, such plans are not strictly binding, but as comprehensive policy proposals they can acquire considerable political weight.

The Development of Dutch Environmental Policy

As in many other industrial countries, environmental problems started to be recognized as an area for public policy during the 1960s. In 1971 the first Environment Ministry, the predecessor of the present Ministry of Housing, Physical Planning, and Environment (Volkshuisvesting, Ruimtelijke Ordening en Milieubeheer, VROM), was established. Not totally unexpected, one of the first achievements of the new ministry was the publication of a policy program. The Urgency Memorandum coupled a sur-prisingly profound analysis of the causes and effects of environmental degra-dation with an ambitious package of proposed measures.[8] It was estimated that within five to ten years the most urgent problems could be solved and an end to the further increase (usually referred to as a "standstill") of envi-ronmental pollution could be reached. With the benefit of hindsight, it is easy to say that this was a fairly optimistic view. In its first decade, the min-istry spent much of its time and energy on developing new administrative structures and asserting its place among the other, more established policy interests. Yet, a number of basic environmental laws were adopted, each cov-ering a different sector or "compartment" of environmental policy, such as water pollution, waste, or noise.[9]

The problems inherent in this approach became apparent about 1980. The abundance of "compartmental" plans and policies had led to a fragmentation of the policy field. Coordination between the different compartments was poor, entailing the risk of shifting the environmental burden, for instance, from the atmosphere to water or soil. Firms had to deal with several types of licenses under the various compartmental laws, often following different procedures. It was recognized that this situation was not efficient and, in the end, not effective either. Coordination with other policy fields, moreover, was still problematic, not least because relations with other government departments continued to be frosty.

The Immediate Predecessors of the NEPP

Whereas some of the procedural problems could be alleviated relatively easily by the gradual introduction of the General Environmental Provisions Act of 1980, the lack of coordination both inside the policy field and with other policy areas called for a more fundamental rethinking of environmental policymaking. And indeed, the first steps taken to that end were made in the form of a series of policy plans. In 1984 the first so-called Indicative Multi-Year Programme for the Environment (IMP) was published.[10] It set out general policy lines for the entire environmental field for the period 1985–1989. Policies regarding the effects of environmental problems, for one part, were built around a number of themes, such as acidification or eutrophication, which encompassed all relevant aspects of the former compartments. For another part, policies focused on distinct sources of environmental pollution, referred to as target groups—for example, agriculture, industry, and households (consumers). For each of these target groups, tailored policy packages had to be developed, preferably in close cooperation with the target groups themselves. The key concept behind the source-oriented policy "track" was that of the "internalization" (*verinnerlijking*) of responsibility for the environment. By paying attention to the needs and wishes of the target groups and actively involving them in the formulation of policies, polluters were supposed to develop a sensitivity for the environmental impact of their behavior. This should eventually lead to a situation where environmental responsibility is a normal element of daily practice.[11]

Although the word *internalization* as such quite rapidly faded away in the public debate about environmental policy in the Netherlands, the concept is crucial for an understanding of the NEPP and the development of Dutch environmental policy up to the present day. The reason for the great influence of the idea and the way it was worked out by the minister of the environment, Pieter Winsemius, was probably that it touched two different areas at the same time. On the one hand, the focus on coherent policies for different categories of polluters was a response to the problem of fragmentation. Not only could the shifting of problems from one environmental compartment to another be more easily avoided, but by directly cooperating with target groups such as transport or agriculture, the Ministry of the Environment was in fact effectively penetrating the "natural" domains of other government departments as well. The fact that this was basically accepted by the target groups, on the other hand, was related to the way cooperation was put into practice. As a former business consultant and prominent member of the Dutch liberal-conservative party (Volkspartij voor Vrijheid en Democratie, VVD), Winsemius had an open ear for industry's complaints about the complexity and inflexibility of environmental regulation and its wish to better take into account the balance between costs and benefits of policy measures. For that reason, he was prepared to go quite far in discussing alternative policy options and time paths with industry. As will be shown in more detail below, this may be reminiscent of the old politics of accommodation. The approach did not necessarily lead to formal regulation, moreover, but agreement could be made in a covenant between the state and the relevant branch organizations. The new approach thus had some deregulatory traits and seemed to renew the somewhat halfhearted attempts of the first half of the 1980s to deregulate environmental policy.[12]

The 1989 NEPP

Almost as Johann Sebastian Bach did not invent polyphonic music but elevated it to a state of unthought-of perfection, the NEPP of 1989 brought the way of thinking initiated in the IMPs to full maturity. Procedurally speaking, the first NEPP was the crown on the new integrated environmental planning system.[13] It encompassed the entire policy field and was signed not only by the minister of the environment but also by his colleagues responsible for the Ministries of Economic Affairs (or Industry), Agriculture, and Transport and Public Works. It was to be updated in annual "Environment Programs" and fully renewed every four years. Implementation was to be monitored biannually by the National Institute of Public Health and the Environment (Rijksinstituut voor Volksgezondheid en Milieu, RIVM).

From a substantive point of view, the distinctive feature of the NEPP is that it attempts to underpin its policy approach with the help of a comprehensive analysis of the mechanisms of environmental deterioration, an element reminiscent of the 1971 Urgency Memorandum. In this analysis, which is in fact a form of general systems theory, the natural environment is seen as both a reservoir or pool of raw materials and a sink for waste products.[14] Both functions of the environment are connected by substance flows. In present-day society, according to the NEPP, "leaks" from the economic substance cycle go beyond the carrying capacity of the environment and lead to the "roll-off" of environmental costs to other geographical scale levels, to other groups in society, or to future generations. Policies directed toward sustainable development, therefore, should primarily be aimed at separating the economic substance cycle from substance flows in the ecological subsystem through more efficient use and reuse of raw materials. In addition to that, particularly as long as substance cycles have not yet sufficiently been closed, the external effects of the economic substance cycle must be controlled.

As a logical consequence of this analysis, the emphasis in the NEPP is on source-oriented measures. The NEPP distinguishes three types. So far, environmental policy had been dominated by *emission-oriented measures,* end-of-pipe technology that reduces emissions without changing processes of production and consumption as such. In the short and medium term, the NEPP argued, these types of measures will continue to be needed. Basically, however, add-on technology is at odds with the idea of sustainable development because it does not lead to the closure of substance cycles. Instead, these measures often require even more raw materials and more energy. In the longer term, therefore, a shift has to be made to *structure-oriented measures.* These entail the fundamental transformation of processes of production and consumption. At certain places in the NEPP, the structure-oriented strategy is somewhat restrictively equated with basically technical, process-integrated measures, but elsewhere it is made clear that changes in consumer behavior are also seen as part of it.[15] Finally, the possibility of *volume-oriented measures* is mentioned, that is, the (imposed) reduction of the amount of raw materials used and products made. From a socioeconomic point of view this is clearly a kill or cure remedy, which should be reserved for exceptional cases where no further delay can be accepted.

Based on the general analysis in the first part, the second part of the NEPP lays out more concrete policy strategies. Targets for the year 2000 are formulated for eight environmental themes: climate change, acidification, eutrophication, diffusion of substances, disposal of waste, disturbance, dehydration, and squandering. In this list, "diffusion of substances" entails the spreading of various hazardous substances, such as heavy metals, pesticides, and radioactive materials, posing risks to humans and ecosystems. The theme of disturbance deals with the nuisance caused by noise and odor as well as industrial risks. "Squandering" refers to the need to improve the management of natural resources and to close substance cycles. The targets specified for the eight themes in turn lead to proposing more than 200 concrete policy actions. Many of those aim at specific target groups, of which the NEPP has nine (agriculture, traffic and transport, industry and refineries, gas and electricity supply, building trade, consumers and retail trade, environmental trade, research and education, and societal organizations). The organization of this part of the NEPP thus basically follows the approach developed in the earlier IMPs. What is more remarkable here, and what strikes most when first reading the NEPP, is the ambitiousness of the policy targets. For many substances, emissions reductions of 70 to 90 percent are the goal in 2000, relative to different base years in the 1980s. This applies to "bulk pollutants" such as sulphur, nitrogen, and phosphorus relevant to acidification and eutrophication, as well as to various organic compounds, metals, and metalloids. For carbon dioxide (CO_2) an (at first sight) more modest target is set, amounting to the stabilization of 1989–1990 emissions in 2000. An overview of the NEPP targets as well as the contributions of the target groups to the various themes is given in Table 12-1.

With regard to the instruments to reach those targets, the NEPP is not very explicit. In a short section on instruments, it is somewhat surprisingly stated that "to influence behavior, the preference will continue to be for phys-

Table 12-1 Overview of NEPP Targets and Contributions of Targets Groups

Theme	Overall targets for 2000 (unless otherwise indicated)	Contribution of target groups (1995)					
		Agriculture	Traffic and transport	Industry and refineries	Gas and electricity	Building trade	Consumers and retail
Climate change	3–5% reduction of CO_2 emissions relative to 1989–1990	x	x	x	x		x
Acidification	Deposition of 2400 acid equivalents/hectares (1,400 eq./ha on forests in 2010), i.e., 70–90% reduction of emissions of SO_2, NO_x, NH_3, and VOC relative to 1980[a]	x	x	x			
Eutrophication	Balance between input and output of phosphorus and nitrogen in water and soil, i.e., 70–90% reduction of emissions relative to 1985	x		x			x
Diffusion	50–70% reduction of emissions of certain toxic substances (pesticides, heavy metals)	x	x	x			x
Disposal of waste	10% waste prevention and 55% reuse of products and materials			x		x	x
Disturbance	Standstill of noise nuisance at 1985 level, less than 12% of people affected by odor, risk of major accident of 10^{-6} per year per installation		x	x			x

| Dehydration | Standstill of dehydrated area; later tightened to −25% | | x |

Sources: Data from "National Environmental Policy Plan: To Choose or to Lose," Second Chamber, sess. 1988–1989, 21137, nos. 1–2 (English version); "National Environmental Policy Plan Plus," Second Chamber, sess. 1989–1990, 21137, nos. 20–21 (English version); *Nationaal Milieubeleidsplan 3* (The Hague: Ministerie van Volkshuisvesting, Ruimtelijke Ordening en Milieubeheer, 1998).

Note: The table summarizes the overall goals of the NEPP (as revised in the NEPP-Plus) and indicates which target groups had in 1995 a share of more than 10 percent in the respective themes. The theme of squandering has been omitted from this table as it does not entail quantified targets and pertains to all target groups. The target groups of environmental trade, research and education and societal organisation have been omitted because they are not primarily sources of environmental problems.

[a] SO_2 = sulfur dioxide; NO_x = nitrogen oxide; NH_3 = ammonia; VOC = volatile organic compounds.

ical regulation with the establishment of source-oriented standards."[16] At first sight, the NEPP as a whole speaks another language. The document is imbued with the idea of consultation and cooperation with the target groups, and thus it prepared the ground for the veritable explosion of voluntary agreements in the environment field in the 1990s. Looking more closely, however, it should be noted that in practice environmental agreements seldom stand alone. They are often linked to "harder" policy instruments—for instance, to legal obligations of a more general kind, or to licensing procedures.[17] Economic instruments, such as environmental taxes, finally, play a very limited role in the NEPP. Apart from one important and in fact highly successful levy in the field of water pollution, economic instruments have never aroused much enthusiasm in the Netherlands, and attempts to assign a larger role to them in the NEPP were halted in view of their supposed effect on the collective tax burden and the competitiveness of Dutch industry.[18] Skepticism about the use of economic instruments was also expressed by the man who can be regarded as the spiritual father of the NEPP approach, Pieter Winsemius.[19]

The Reception of the NEPP

The making of the NEPP gave rise to serious controversies not only between the ministries involved in the process but also between the parties in the governing coalition. Shortly before the publication of the plan in May 1989 this even led to the fall of the government. Some of these political complications can be related to more general political problems between and inside the governing parties, which will not be discussed here.[20] Others, however, were due to an unusually high level of public and political attention to environmental problems that had emerged in the months before publication.

In 1988 a "state of the environment" report was published by the RIVM. It was designed as a background study for the NEPP and carried the pregnant title *Concern for Tomorrow*.[21] The report showed that without a radical change of processes of production and consumption, a serious further deterioration of environmental quality could be expected. *Concern for Tomorrow* conveyed a sense of urgency that had not been seen since the publication of the *Limits to Growth* report to the Club of Rome in 1972.[22] This sense was further heightened by Queen Beatrix's personal Christmas Message, which was in 1988 entirely devoted to the environment. Although the image of entire Dutch families assembled around the radio at 1 p.m., Christmas Day, may at first remind one of Woody Allen's *Radio Days*, the impact of these royal messages, owing to their broad reach and the moral status the queen still has in the Netherlands, should not be underestimated.

As might be expected, the first reactions from societal groups on the NEPP were divided.[23] Industry and the agricultural community generally welcomed the cooperative approach of the NEPP but warned against imposing too high costs on firms in view of the open and export-oriented character of the Dutch economy. Environmental organizations criticized the

NEPP for not questioning the basic premise of economic growth. Many were bewildered, furthermore, by the plain conclusion in the NEPP that the interim target of a 70 to 80 percent reduction of acidifying substances in 2000 would protect no more than 20 percent of the Dutch forests.[24] While some commentators focused on the fate of the remaining 80 percent of the forests, others stressed the word *interim*, which implied that further measures were needed after 2000. Perhaps most significantly, the NEPP was generally not received as overly ambitious or unrealistic. For instance, the Social-Economic Council (Sociaal-Economische Raad, SER), a high-level corporatist-type institution consisting of representatives from employers, workers, and the government, emphasized that a fundamental change in the behavior of producers and consumers was necessary to create a more sustainable society. The NEPP, according to the council, was only a first step toward this end.[25]

Follow-up and Achievements of the NEPP

With its 258 pages, the NEPP looks comprehensive, but several aspects of it had to be further worked out in specific plans and memoranda. The NEPP announced no less than twenty-seven such documents for 1989–1990.[26] I do not intend to discuss all of them here. Instead, I will restrict myself to a brief review of the major revisions of the NEPP, the so-called NEPP-Plus of 1990 and the second and third NEPPs of 1993 and 1998, respectively. After that I will turn to the achievements of the NEPP approach in practice and highlight some of the most serious remaining problems. The section will be concluded with an evaluation of the NEPP approach in more theoretical terms and some perspectives for the future.

Major Follow-up Plans

If not the fundamental cause, the NEPP was the immediate reason for the fall of the government in May 1989. In view of that, it was only natural that environmental issues played an important role in the election campaign. Prime Minister Ruud Lubbers, for instance, surprised all parties concerned (including probably his own party) by proposing a reduction of CO_2 emissions by 8 percent in the following cabinet period (1989/1990–1994). The new government, again headed by Lubbers but now consisting of Christian Democrats and Social Democrats, took office in November 1989. It soon made clear that the 8 percent commitment was to be understood in relation to the projected 2 percent annual growth in emissions rather than to 1990 levels.[27] Lubbers's firm language was thus reduced to reaching the stabilization target some years earlier than originally proposed in the NEPP.

The history of the CO_2 target is exemplary for what happened to the NEPP as a whole. The new Social Democratic minister of the environment, Hans Alders, started by announcing an ambitious tightening of the NEPP. When the so-called NEPP-Plus was finally published in June 1990, however, much of the momentum had already been lost and the document contained little more than a slight acceleration of some of the NEPP measures, notably in the fields of air pollution and waste management. The target of a standstill for CO_2 emissions in 1994, for instance, was confirmed and a 3 to 5 percent reduction target for 2000, relative to 1990, was added.[28]

The second NEPP, published in December 1993, is more substantial than the NEPP-Plus.[29] Its main function being that of "keeping the process going," it largely follows the lines of the 1989 NEPP, but it elaborates on certain issues that had been relatively underdeveloped in the earlier document. There is, for instance, a stronger focus on implementation and on the need to strengthen international efforts in order to increase policy effectiveness. At the same time, the opportunities to develop such "active environmental diplomacy" are assessed in a more realistic way.[30]

The third NEPP was issued in February 1998.[31] On the basis of the observation that the emissions of many substances (but not all, see below) had decreased during the 1990s and thus a "decoupling" from economic growth had been achieved, the third NEPP claims that environmental policy is now shifting away from "cleaning-up" or sanitation to a new phase of environmental and resource management. Also in this phase, the report stresses, the generally successful cooperation with target groups will be continued. The most notable innovation in the third NEPP is the projected gradual increase in emphasis on economic and particularly fiscal instruments. A few months before the third NEPP, a plan was presented by the government, proposing a major tax reform in the beginning of the next century, including an increase of taxes on energy and other environmental resources and fiscal stimulation of environmentally friendly processes and products.[32]

Achievements and Persistent Problems

Setting aside for a moment the question of the effect of the NEPP on environmental quality, the approach initiated by the IMPs of the mid-1980s and culminating in the 1989 NEPP has in any case led to a dramatic change in the strategies and instruments of Dutch environmental policy. In the 1970s and 1980s the policy field was dominated by a combination of laws and permits. During the late 1980s and the 1990s, the emphasis rapidly shifted from direct regulation to negotiation and voluntary agreements between the state and private actors. Between 1985 and 1997, about 100 environmental covenants were concluded. About half of these aim at improving energy efficiency in almost all sectors of the Dutch economy. The others deal with various other environmental issues, ranging from the environmental impact of an entire industrial sector to one specific product or substance.[33] Whereas those in the latter group are signed on behalf of the government by the Ministry of the Environment, the so-called Long-Term Agreements on energy efficiency improvement are signed by the Ministry of Economic Affairs. Although the coordination of Dutch climate policy rests with the Environment Ministry, energy policy as such is the domain of the

Ministry of Economic Affairs. In this particular case, this situation did not lead to conflicts, as the Ministry of Economic Affairs appeared to be even more eager than the Environment Ministry to replace the old "command-and-control" policy with voluntary agreements.[34]

The NEPP approach was put into practice not only in the form of covenants with industry, however. Another notable example of a strategy directed toward "internalization" and consensus that emerged in the wake of the NEPP is the so-called region-oriented environmental policy. For historical reasons, the fields of physical planning, water management, and nature protection used to be strongly divided among different policy levels and policy agencies. Particularly in practical policymaking in local and regional contexts, this often led to serious problems of coordination. The aim of the region-oriented approach as instigated by the Ministry of the Environment was to better integrate the environmental aspects of these three policy fields within designated regions. As such, the region-oriented approach can be put on a par with the source-oriented and effect-oriented "tracks" of environmental policy, first introduced in the IMPs of the mid-1980s. The strategy that was followed consisted of extensive consensus-seeking processes involving several government departments, regional and local authorities, and a wide variety of private interests, such as farmers, industry, recreation, and environmental organizations. These processes were supposed to result in an improved understanding between the parties involved, more adequate definitions of the problems at stake, and, it was hoped, the generation of policy solutions. In most of the regions where the approach was applied, the outcomes were laid down in a commonly endorsed, nonbinding action plan, in fact a kind of regional covenant. From a more strategic point of view, the region-oriented approach—like the target group approach discussed earlier—may be interpreted as a tool used by the Ministry of the Environment to penetrate issue areas so far dominated by other departments. Research by Van Tatenhove suggests that the region-oriented approach has indeed contributed to the establishment of closer and in fact more friendly relations with the Ministry of Agriculture, the first ministry in charge of the management of rural areas and nature protection.[35]

What did all this bring in terms of environment quality in the Netherlands? Unfortunately, it is extremely difficult to establish exact causal relationships between specific policy measures and the state of the environment. Some insight may be gained, however, by checking if trends in emission and pollution figures have actually changed since the start of the NEPP approach (see Table 12-2). The third NEPP, the *1997 Environmental Balance*, and the fourth follow-up report to *Concern for Tomorrow*, the latter two published by the RIVM in mid-1997, show that the emissions of most pollutants declined over the last couple of years. Carbon dioxide emissions form the major exception to this trend. They increased by 7 percent between 1990 and 1996, making the achievement of the minus 3 to 5 percent target for 2000, mentioned in the NEPP-Plus, highly unlikely. With present policy, according to the RIVM, emissions of most other substances will also start to increase again after the decade between 2000 and 2010, owing to the growth in production volume. As a consequence, emissions in 2020 are likely to be generally lower than 1995 levels but higher than the current policy targets for 2000 or 2010. The most serious excessive emissions are expected for CO_2, nitrogen oxides (NO_x), ammonia (NH_3), and nutrients (nitrate and phosphate). The RIVM report points out, furthermore, that most success has been achieved so far in industry and less so in agriculture. Private consumers are identified as a group particularly hard to reach for policymakers.[36]

An Assessment of the NEPP Approach

The NEPP approach has been interpreted by some theorists as a paradigmatic case of the political program of ecological modernization. Mainstream environmental policy as it was built up in most industrial countries during the past decades focused on measures to mitigate the effects of environmental degradation and on the installation of end-of-pipe technology. Traditionally, this approach has been contrasted with the radical program of de-industrialization, a partial or even total rejection of technological rationality, and a return to small-scale production and consumption. The program of ecological modernization is to be regarded as a third way out of the dilemma of environmental disruption, still relying on modern technological—in fact often "high-tech"—solutions, but at the same time transforming the entire process of production and consumption in such a way that its environmental impact is minimized. Characteristic for this approach, according to the sociologists Gert Spaargaren and Arthur Mol, is an emphasis on "clean technology, economic valuation of environmental resources, alteration of production and consumption styles, prevention, and monitoring of compounds through the production-consumption cycles."[37] In environmental policymaking, this takes the form of a shift away from "command-and-control" to a new generation of policies. That may include dialogue and cooperation as well as market-oriented instruments, notably "green" taxes. Due among other things to the influential Brundtland Report, ideas that can be associated with ecological modernization have gained widespread support.[38] The Dutch NEPP translated these ideas into a concrete set of policy measures. The detailed and consistent elaboration of the leading ideas of a synergy between economy and ecology, a common responsibility for environmental protection and a basic partnership between the state and polluting sectors may explain the lively foreign interest in the NEPP.

Apart from being one of the first and most convincing expressions of the program of ecological modernization, however, it is important to note that the NEPP approach is at the same time deeply embedded in Dutch political tradition. In the environmental field, "internalization" and the target group strategy no doubt constituted an innovation in comparison with the more legalistic approach of the 1970s and early 1980s, but the model of negotiation and consensus as such is anything but new in the Netherlands. A substantial

Table 12-2 Overview of Original NEPP Targets and Achievements in 1995–1996

Theme	Overall targets for 2000 (unless otherwise indicated)	Achieved 1995–1996 (as indicated)
Climate change	3–5% reduction of CO_2 emissions relative to 1989–1990	1990–1996: 7% increase of CO_2 emissions
Acidification	Deposition of 2,400 acid equivalents/hectares per year (1,400 eq./ha.yr on forests in 2010), i.e., 70–90% reduction of emissions of SO_2, NO_x, NH_3, and VOC relative to 1980[a]	1990–1996: 28% reduction of acid deposition (1996: approx. 4,000 acid eq./ha.yr); remaining bottlenecks are NO_x and NH_3 emissions
Eutrophication	Balance between input and output of phosphorus and nitrogen in water and soil, i.e., 70–90% reduction of emissions relative to 1985	1985–1995: approx. 50% reduction of emission of nutrients from industry; appr. 20% for emissions from agriculture
Diffusion	50–70% reduction of emissions of certain toxic substances (pesticides, heavy metals)	Emission reductions for most substances on or ahead of schedule, but problems remain for specific heavy metals and organic substances.
Disposal of waste	10% waste prevention and 55% reuse of products and materials	1995–1996: re-use 72% (NEPP 3 target: 80% in 2010); "decoupling" of economic growth and waste production, partly due to structural effects
Disturbance	Standstill of noise nuisance at 1985 level, less than 12% of people affected by odor, risk of major accident of 10^{-6} per year per installation	Remaining bottlenecks particularly in the field of noise nuisance (new targets will be set in 1999)
Dehydration	Standstill of dehydrated area; later tightened to −25%	Reduction of dehydrated area some years behind schedule

Sources: Data from *Nationaal Milieubeleidsplan 3* (The Hague: Ministerie van Volkshuisvesting, Ruimtelijke Ordening en Milieubeheer, 1998); Rijksinstituut voor Volksgezondheid en Milieu, *Nationale Milieuverkenning 4, 1997–2020* and *Milieubalans '97. Het Nederlandse milieu verklaard* (Alphen aan den Rijn: Samsom H. D. Tjeenk Willink, 1997).

[a] SO_2 = sulfur dioxide; NO_x = nitrogen oxide; NH_3 = ammonia; VOC = volatile organic compounds.

influence by private actors on the content of policies in exchange for a serious commitment to the outcome of the decision process and active participation in the implementation of policies is a core feature of the NEPP approach and in fact contains elements of the old corporatist politics of accommodation. Besides the obvious fact that the target groups in environmental negotiations are no longer organized along confessional lines, the crucial difference is probably the openness of the process and the role of peak-level associations in relation to their members. Whereas in traditional corporatism the game is played between the government and a small and closed circle of high-level representatives from private interest organizations, relations between public and private actors in environmental target group negotiations are less fixed. Some environmental covenants, for instance, were signed by the government and only one branch association, while in others several, possibly even competing, organizations were involved. In some cases, moreover, environmental and consumer organizations participated in the earlier phases of the process. It is an interesting question if and in which form these relations will stabilize in the future. On the one hand, negotiations are now, more than before, usually limited to those parties most directly involved, excluding environmental and consumer organizations.[39] On the other hand, with the maturation of the target group approach one might expect industry to respond by better coordinating its input into the process, but this does not always appear to be the case. A case in point is the 1997 revision of the covenant on packaging and packaging waste. While the original agreement was signed in 1991 by the minister of the environment and the chairman of an umbrella organization representing the entire packaging chain, the second covenant was split into six parts, involving more specific branch associations. At least partly, this change can be ascribed to the inability of the umbrella organization to hold together the divergent interests of producers of raw materials, manufacturers, retailers, and recyclers.[40] It is too early to argue, in other words, that with the NEPP approach the environmental policy field is "returning" to the corporatist roots of the Dutch political system, after the more contentious period of the 1970s and early 1980s. It seems likely, however, that the seed of the NEPP approach would not have caught on so rapidly without the fertile soil of the basically consensual political culture in the Netherlands. As will be discussed in the next section, this insight is particularly relevant in relation to attempts to transpose the approach to other contexts.

In short, the NEPP approach can be seen as a consensual variant of the program of ecological modernization, strongly rooted in Dutch political culture and paying relatively little attention to the more market-oriented side of ecological modernization, notably the use of economic instruments.[41] After a decade of experience with the approach initiated by the IMPs and culminating in the 1989 NEPP, how can we evaluate the experiment? To what extent does the NEPP approach really carry with it the potential to put a society on the track toward a more sustainable society? On the one hand, as we have seen, industry in particular has performed relatively well during the past years. Emissions of many substances have been reduced in absolute terms and will be further reduced in the near future. As target group negotiations and environmental covenants have in practice been directed primarily toward industrial sectors, these encouraging results should most likely be credited to the NEPP approach. They seem to indicate that cooperation and consensus—and perhaps even internalization—does work. On the other hand, the projections of the RIVM for the more distant future should be taken seriously. They point to two major deficiencies in the present NEPP approach: the apparent difficulties in going beyond the level of advanced technology-based measures to a more structural transformation of the economy, and the problems with reaching target groups other than industry, notably consumers.

The inability of the NEPP approach to bring about more profound changes of processes of production and consumption is most acute in relation to the issue of climate change. In our industrial society, which is so strongly based on the use of fossil fuels, technological measures to reduce CO_2 emissions in most cases do not even keep up with the pace of economic growth. But also for other substances, as the RIVM reports show, technological solutions will in the longer term be overtaken by the sheer growth of the volume of production. The 1989 NEPP also recognizes this dilemma when it points out that, besides emission-oriented measures, volume-oriented and particularly structure-oriented measures are needed. In practice, however, the NEPP approach does not appear to work here. Although the gradual shift to a more service-oriented economy can also be observed in the Netherlands, the Dutch economy still relies heavily on a number of input-intensive sectors, such as the chemical industry and refineries, intensive agriculture, and goods transport. So far, there has been a great reluctance even to start a debate about a fundamental restructuring of these sectors. A government memorandum on the environment and the economy, published jointly by the ministers of the environment and economic affairs in 1997, was supposed to address this issue; they largely evaded it, however, by focusing on more limited proposals benefiting both the environment and the economy, so-called "win-win" options.[42] Also in cases where fundamental choices between environment and economy have to be made, the consensual NEPP approach often turns out to fail and old conflicts between the Ministry of the Environment and other government departments, notably Economic Affairs and Transport, reappear. Recent examples include a number of large infrastructural projects, such as the expansion of Schiphol international airport near Amsterdam. The partnership envisaged by the NEPP seems to have evolved mainly in relation to the Ministry of Agriculture. An outbreak of swine fever in the beginning of 1997, moreover, decisively added to the pressure for environmental reasons on this ministry to substantially reform the intensive livestock industry in the Netherlands. Farmers' organizations, however, strongly opposed the ministry's proposal to cut down pig-breeding by 25 percent.

If little support for more far-reaching, structure-oriented measures can be found even inside the government, it is no surprise that such measures are hardly addressed in negotiations with the target groups. The NEPP approach may have been successful in identifying and developing opportunities for energy saving and the improvement of processes that are also profitable from a business point of view, but it seems to reach its limit when pollution prevention does not immediately pay. For that reason, the Social Democratic Party suggested in its program for the 1998 elections to work toward a second generation of environmental covenants. Such agreements, while carrying on the basic philosophy of the NEPP, should aim at radical innovation, particularly in those sectors that most heavily burden the environment, and thus bring industry an essential step further on the way to sustainable development.[43] For this proposal to be successful, a (further) intensification of the corporatist traits of the target group approach would probably be required. Firm agreements with organizations covering large sectors would be needed, as well as the willingness and the power of those organizations to take far-reaching, possibly painful measures. Considering the difficulties encountered in implementing the NEPP already at this moment, however, putting the approach in a higher gear, as it were, may be questionable as a realistic option. Even with internalization, in the end, turkeys are not likely to vote for Christmas.

The second important shortcoming of the NEPP approach relates to the target group of consumers, including consumers as car drivers. Because consumers are numerous, diverse, and not well organized, they are not suitable parties to voluntary agreements. The second and third NEPPs recognize the problem and identify consumers—along with many small- and medium-sized enterprises—as a crucial but "not easily accessible" target group for policies. It is pointed out in particular that they often "contend with a lack of insight into the environmental consequences of their behavior."[44] One solution is to provide better information so that consumers will develop a sense of environmental responsibility, for instance, through television campaigns or green labels for environmentally friendly products. As Albert Weale rightly argues, it is particularly in relation to consumers that the character of internalization as a moral appeal comes to the fore.[45] One may either hail or reject this aspect of the NEPP approach on ideological grounds, but there can be little doubt that it will take a long time before this kind of appeal to civil society will bear the fruit of an actual change of behavior (if at all). In view of this, a gradual shift to more financial incentives to consumers may be envisaged. While the energy tax for small energy users of 1996 may be regarded as only a modest step in this direction, it should be noted that the projected major tax reform, referred to above, is increasingly seen as an opportunity to introduce "green" elements in the tax system. Economic instruments are by no means incompatible with the program of ecological modernization, but as we have seen, the emphasis in the NEPP approach has so far been on the alternative route of negotiation, persuasion, and consensus.

The International Impact of the NEPP Approach

The NEPP approach and particularly its centerpiece, the 1989 NEPP, attracted much attention not only from scholars but also from policymakers in other countries. This was due to the qualities of the plan, no doubt, but also to its support by the Dutch government. In the following we will briefly examine these efforts, their backgrounds, and their results.

The most conspicuous example of the "export" of the NEPP is the EU's Fifth Environmental Action Programme.[46] It was prepared by the European Commission in the early 1990s and adopted by the Council of Ministers in February 1993. Although not strictly binding, the program is supposed to guide policy development until 2000. It cannot escape notice that the Fifth Action Programme, like the NEPP, is built around themes and target groups, but the similarity goes further than that. Particularly, the ideas of shared responsibility and partnership, not only between different levels of governance but also between public and private actors, is suggestive of the NEPP. A broadening of the range of instruments is suggested. In relation to the target group of industry, the importance of dialogue, covenants, and self-regulation is stressed. As the political scientist Annica Kronsell has shown, many of the key participants in the network preparing the Fifth Action Programme were Dutch. The fact that the EU's director-general for the environment at the time, the Dutchman Laurens-Jan Brinkhorst, preferred the program to be developed by a group not too closely linked to the European Commission even made the way free for appointing a Dutch civil servant as one of the lead authors.[47] Despite the ambitions relating to policy processes and instruments, probably the main achievement of the Fifth Action Programme lies in its comprehensive view of environmental problems. The systematic treatment of themes and target groups puts issues on the agenda that had been neglected at the EU level and provides a basis for establishing links with other policies, such as transport or agriculture. The mid-term review of the Fifth Action Programme suggests, however, that elaboration of the ideas of shared responsibility and partnership has so far hardly evolved beyond the stage of study and debate.[48] The use of voluntary agreements at the EU level, for instance, is hampered not only by legal restrictions but also by the basically noncorporatist character of public-private relations in Brussels, expressing itself, among other things, in a decentralized organization of many industrial sectors.[49]

Aside from the EU, the NEPP approach was propagated to a large number of individual countries, ranging from China and economies-in-transition like Latvia and Hungary to Western industrial countries like Austria. In the United States, contacts were established both at the federal level and at the state level, for instance, in New Jersey and North Dakota. In most cases, workshops and training were organized in the respective countries, or delegations were received in The Hague. The challenge in these sessions was to work out the core idea of developing comprehensive solutions for polluting sectors on the basis of a dialogue with all parties involved in accordance with local circumstances. In many countries much effort still had to be put into establishing more effective working relations between departments within the government. This is in fact a step preceding negotiations with business and reminds one of the period of the IMPs of the mid-1980s in the

Netherlands. The Ministry of the Environment found that three factors were particularly important for a more or less successful adaptation of the NEPP approach.[50] First, the constitutional context should not be too complicated. In federal systems, the division of powers between different levels of government—often going hand in hand with a somewhat legalistic system of checks and balances—may inhibit the process. This applies to the United States and Germany, for instance, but also to the EU. Second, without a certain degree of trust among all actors involved, both public and private, an open dialogue turned out to be difficult to achieve. This may explain difficulties particularly in some of the central and eastern European countries. Third, in order to act as a discussion partner for the government, business and civil society should be sufficiently organized in the form of branch associations and nongovernmental organizations. The latter two factors refer to a consensual, corporatist policy culture as an important (though of course not sufficient) condition for an NEPP-like approach. The Dutch efforts, in sum, did not lead to a large number of NEPP clones all over the world. They were rather intended to help other countries in finding their own ways to solve the complex problems of integrated environmental policy and planning. For this purpose the NEPP, as one of the first and most radical attempts to put the Brundtland Report into practice, could quite successfully be presented as a source of inspiration. The plan could thus become a notable force in the dissemination and elaboration of the ideas of ecological modernization.

While in bilateral relations focusing, for instance, on the transfer of technology the ecological and economic benefits for both parties are quite clear, what did the Dutch see as the purpose of exporting environmental management concepts? One may assume that an element of complacency and the parsonical ambition to act as a model for the rest of the world played a role, but at the same time there was a clear perception of self-interest behind the Dutch efforts. In the first place, in view of the transboundary transport of pollutants, it was obvious that firm policies abroad were needed simply to achieve the ambitious domestic environmental targets.[51] Second, it was recognized that the relatively costly measures of the NEPP could lead to competitive disadvantages for Dutch industry. It was argued that, beside directly propagating strict standards in international negotiations, supporting the build-up of effective environmental management systems in other countries might help in a more indirect way to lay the foundations for similarly demanding measures to be taken abroad.[52] Following this philosophy and almost as if to illustrate the Dutch consensus model, business actively contributed to the export of the NEPP approach. The Dutch federation of industry, for instance, many times joined the ministerial teams delegated to international workshops on the NEPP.[53]

Conclusion

In the beginning of this chapter, the question was raised why and how a policy *plan* could acquire such a central place in the evolution as well as the international reputation of Dutch environmental policy. At the end of the day, the NEPP as such is indeed nothing more than a set of concepts and intentions for the development of a more sustainable society. The power of such concepts should not be underestimated, however. As we have seen, the ideas of the NEPP were in fact quite successfully used by the Dutch Ministry of the Environment as strategic tools to strengthen the position of environmental policy against other interests. These concepts were also the basis for the export of the NEPP to other countries and the EU. At the same time, the approach developed in the NEPP fueled practical policymaking. Within the Dutch political context, the idea of partnership, negotiation, and consensus between the government and polluting sectors led to a level of technological reduction and prevention measures that would probably not have been reached with traditional regulation. Even within this specific context, however, the NEPP strategy seems to draw near to its limits. The coming years may turn out to be crucial to finding out if the consensual approach will be sufficiently robust to accomplish the next steps toward sustainable development or if other means will be needed to bring about the fundamental transformation of production and consumption at which the NEPP is eventually aiming.

Notes

1. Albert Weale, *The New Politics of Pollution* (Manchester, England: Manchester University Press, 1992), 125; David Wallace, *Environmental Policy and Industrial Innovation: Strategies in Europe, the U.S., and Japan* (London: Earthscan and the Royal Institute of International Affairs, 1995), 44.
2. World Commission on Environment and Development (WCED), *Our Common Future* (New York: Oxford University Press, 1987).
3. For a general discussion of Dutch environmental policy, covering both history and organizational features, see Duncan Liefferink, "The Netherlands: A Net Exporter of Environmental Policy Concepts," in *European Environmental Policy: The Pioneers*, ed. Mikael Skou Andersen and Duncan Liefferink (Manchester, England: Manchester University Press, 1997), 210–250.
4. Arend Lijphart, *The Politics of Accommodation: Pluralism and Democracy in the Netherlands* (Berkeley: University of California Press, 1968).
5. Philippe C. Schmitter, "Still the Century of Corporatism?" *Review of Politics* 36 (1974): 85–131. For an excellent introduction into corporatist theory, see P. J. Williamson, *Corporatism in Perspective: An Introductory Guide to Corporatist Theory* (London: Sage, 1989). Sometimes corporatism in liberal democracies is referred to as neo-corporatism to distinguish it from earlier normative forms of corporatism and from corporatism in totalitarian regimes.
6. See Jan van Putten, "Policy Styles in the Netherlands: Negotiation and Conflict," in *Policy Styles in Western Europe*, ed. Jeremy Richardson (London: George Allen and Unwin, 1982), 168–196.
7. Jan Tinbergen, "The Development of the Planning Idea," *Planning and Development in the Netherlands* 5, no. 2 (1971): 103–110; James Goodear Abert, *Economic Policy and Planning in the Netherlands, 1950–1965* (New Haven: Yale University Press, 1969); Th. G. Drupsteen, *Ruimtelijk bestuursrecht. Deel 1: Ruimtelijke Ordening en Volkshuisvesting* (Alphen aan den Rijn: Samsom, 1983), 29–34.
8. "Urgentienota Milieuhygiëne" (Urgency memorandum on environmental hygiene), Tweede Kamer 1971–1972, 11906, nos. 1–2.

9. For a detailed analysis of the institutionalization of Dutch environmental policy, see Jan van Tatenhove, *Milieubeleid onder dak. Beleidsvoeringsprocessen in het Nederlandse milieubeleid in de periode 1970–1990; nader uitgewerkt voor de Gelderse Vallei,* Wageningen Studies in Sociology, no. 35 (Wageningen: Wageningen Agricultural University, 1993), chap. 2; Pieter Leroy, "De ontwikkeling van het milieubeleid en de milieubeleidstheorie," in *Milieubeleid, een beleidswetenschappelijke inleiding,* ed. Pieter Glasbergen, 4th. ed. (The Hague: VUGA, 1994), 35–58.

10. "Indicatief Meerjaren Programma Milieubeheer 1985–1989" (Indicative multi-year program for the environment), Tweede Kamer 1984–1985, 18602, nos. 1–2. See also "Indicatief Meerjaren Programma Milieubeheer 1986–1990," Tweede Kamer 1985–1986, 19204, nos. 1–2.

11. The ideas behind "internalization" have probably been worded best by the inventor of the concept: Pieter Winsemius, *Gast in eigen huis* (Alphen aan den Rijn: Samsom H. D. Tjeenk Willink, 1986). For a more profound analysis of the politics of "internalization" than space allows here, see Kees Le Blansch, *Milieuzorg in bedrijven. Overheidssturing in het perspectief van de verinnerlijkingsbeleidslijn* (Amsterdam: Thesis Publishers, 1996).

12. For a discussion of these attempts, see Kenneth Hanf, "Deregulation as Regulatory Reform: The Case of Environmental Policy in the Netherlands," *European Journal of Political Research* 17 (1989): 193–207.

13. "National Environmental Policy Plan: To Choose or to Lose," Second Chamber, sess. 1988–1989, 21137, nos. 1–2 (English version; hereafter "NEPP").

14. Weale, *The New Politics of Pollution,* 128.

15. "NEPP," 102 and 115–118.

16. Ibid., 124.

17. See Duncan Liefferink and Arthur P. J. Mol, "Voluntary Agreements as a Form of Deregulation? The Dutch Experience," in *Deregulation in the European Union: Environmental Perspectives,* ed. Ute Collier (London: Routledge, 1998): 181–197.

18. Jan van der Straaten, "The Dutch National Environmental Policy Plan: To Choose or to Lose," *Environmental Politics* 1 (spring 1992): 59–60; see also Duncan Liefferink, "New Environmental Policy Instruments in the Netherlands," in *New Instruments for Environmental Protection in the EU,* ed. Jonathan Golub (London: Routledge, 1998), 85–105.

19. Winsemius, *Gast in eigen huis,* 97–98.

20. For a detailed account of the strategies of the Ministry of Housing, Physical Planning, and Environment and the political complications during the preparation of the NEPP, see Weale, *The New Politics of Pollution,* 139–145.

21. Rijksinstituut voor Volksgezondheid en Milieuhygiëne (RIVM), *Zorgen voor morgen. Nationale Milieuverkenning, 1985–2010* (Concern for tomorrow. State of the Dutch environment, 1985–2010) (Alphen aan den Rijn: Samsom H. D. Tjeenk Willink, 1988).

22. Dennis L. Meadows, Donella H. Meadows, Jørgen Randers, and William W. Behrens III, *The Limits to Growth* (New York: Universe Books, 1972). The report to the Club of Rome was particularly well received in the Netherlands; see, for instance, Maurits Groen, *Naar een duurzaam Nederland* (The Hague: SDU, 1988).

23. See E. C. van Ierland, A. P. J. Mol, and A. Klapwijk, eds., *Milieubeleid in Nederland. Reacties op het Nationaal Milieubeleidsplan* (Leiden: Stenfert Kroese, 1989).

24. "NEPP," 133.

25. Sociaal-Economische Raad (SER; Social Economic Council), *Advies Nationaal Milieubeleidsplan* (Advice on the NEPP), no. 89/17 (The Hague: SER, 1989).

26. "NEPP," 243.

27. Ute Collier, *Energy and Environment in the European Union: The Challenge of Integration* (Aldershot, England: Avebury, 1994), 126.

28. "National Environmental Policy Plan Plus," Second Chamber, sess. 1989–1990, 21137, nos. 20–21 (English version).

29. "Nationaal Milieubeleidsplan 2. Milieu als maatstaf," Tweede Kamer 1993–1994, 23560, nos. 1–2.
30. For a more detailed discussion of the international aspect of the NEPPs, see Liefferink, *The Netherlands*, 232–234.
31. *Nationaal Milieubeleidsplan 3* (The Hague: Ministerie van Volkshuisvesting, Ruimtelijke Ordening en Milieubeheer, 1998).
32. "Belastingen in de 21e eeuw" (Taxes in the twenty-first century), Tweede Kamer 1997–1998, 25810, nos 1–2; see also *Nationaal Milieubeleidsplan 3*, 367–383.
33. See the inventory in J. H. G. van den Broek and M. P. H. Korten, *Milieu—en energieconvenanten in Nederland* (Deventer: W. E. J. Tjeenk Willink, 1997).
34. See "Nota Energiebesparing. Beleidsplan energiebesparing en stromingsbronnen" (Memorandum on energy conservation. Policy plan for energy conservation and renewable energy), Tweede Kamer 1989–1990, 21570, nos. 1–2, particularly at 35–39. In this document, issued simultaneously with the NEPP-Plus, the Ministry of Economic Affairs had already presented the idea of voluntary agreements with industry as a full-fledged alternative to direct regulation.
35. Van Tatenhove, *Milieubeleid onder dak;* Jaap Frouws and Jan van Tatenhove, "Agriculture, Environment and the State: The Development of Agro-Environmental Policy-making in the Netherlands," *Sociologia Ruralis* 33, no. 2 (1993): 220–239; Liefferink, "New Environmental Policy Instruments."
36. Rijksinstituut voor Volksgezondheid en Milieu (RIVM), *Nationale Milieuverkenning 4, 1997–2020* (State of the Dutch environment no. 4, 1997–2020), (Alphen aan den Rijn: Samsom H. D. Tjeenk Willink, 1997); RIVM, *Milieubalans '97. Het Nederlandse milieu verklaard* (Environmental balance 1997. The Dutch environment explained) (Alphen aan den Rijn: Samsom H. D. Tjeenk Willink, 1997).
37. Gert Spaargaren and Arthur P. J. Mol, "Sociology, Environment, and Modernity: Ecological Modernization as a Theory of Social Change," *Society and Natural Resources* 5, no. 4 (1992): 338–339; Martin Jänicke, "Über ökologische und politische Modernisierungen," *Zeitschrift für Umweltpolitik* no. 2 (1993): 159–175; Maarten A. Hajer, *The Politics of Environmental Discourse: Ecological Modernization and the Policy Process* (Oxford: Clarendon Press, 1995); Arthur P. J. Mol, *The Refinement of Production: Ecological Modernization Theory and the Chemical Industry* (Utrecht: International Books, 1995).
38. WCED, *Our Common Future.* See, for example, Albert Weale, "Ecological Modernisation and the Integration of European Environmental Policy," in *European Integration and Environmental Policy*, ed. J. D. Liefferink, P. D. Lowe, and A. P. J. Mol (London: Belhaven Press, 1993), 196–216.
39. Van den Broek and Korten, *Milieu—en energieconvenanten in Nederland*, 17.
40. Preliminary finding of an EU-funded research project entitled Joint Environmental Policy-Making: New Interactive Approaches in the EU and Selected Member States, carried out by the Universities of Wageningen (The Netherlands), Aarhus (Denmark), and Salzburg (Austria). It should be added, however, that the role of the umbrella organization Stichting Verpakking en Milieu (SVM) was also weakened by the 1994 EU directive on packaging and packaging waste, which interfered with the Dutch consensus approach; see Markus Haverland, "Convergence of National Governance under European Integration? The Case of Packaging Waste" (paper presented at the summer symposium "The Innovation of Environmental Policy," Bologna, July 21–25, 1997).
41. For further discussion of this point, see Liefferink, "New Environmental Policy Instruments."
42. "Milieu en economie" (Environment and economy), Tweede Kamer 1996–1997, 25405, no. 1.
43. Partij van de Arbeid, *Een wereld te winnen. Ontwerp verkiezingsprogramma 1998–2002* (A world to be won. Draft election program 1998–2002), October 1997; see also Jacqueline Cramer and Ab Stevels, "Kabinet kiest niet echt voor milieu"

(Cabinet does not really choose in favor of the environment), *NRC-Handelsblad,* September 9, 1997.

44. "Nationaal Milieubeleidsplan 2," 43. See also Gert Spaargaren, "The Ecological Modernization of Production and Consumption: Essays in Environmental Sociology" (Ph.D. diss., Wageningen Agricultural University, 1997), esp. 121–125.

45. Weale, *The New Politics of Pollution,* 150–151.

46. "Towards Sustainability: Environmental Action Programme, 1993–2000," *Official Journal of the European Communities,* C 138, May 17, 1993.

47. Annica Kronsell, "Policy Innovation in the Garbage Can: The EU's Fifth Environmental Action Programme," in *The Innovation of EU Environmental Policy,* ed. Duncan Liefferink and Mikael Skou Andersen (Oslo: Scandinavian University Press, 1997), 111–132; Duncan Liefferink and Mikael Skou Andersen, "Strategies of the 'Green' Member States in EU Environmental Policy Making," *Journal of European Public Policy* 5, no. 2 (1998): 254–270.

48. *Progress Report on the Implementation of the European Community Programme of Policy and Action in Relation to the Environment and Sustainable Development* (Brussels: European Commission, 1995); *Proposal for a Decision of the European Parliament and the Council on the Review of the European Community Programme of Policy and Action in Relation to the Environment and Sustainable Development "Towards Sustainability"* (Brussels: European Commission, 1995).

49. *Communication from the Commission to the Council and the European Parliament on Voluntary Agreements* (Brussels: European Commission, 1996); Wolfgang Streeck and Philippe C. Schmitter, "From National Corporatism to Transnational Pluralism: Organized Interests in the Single European Market," *Politics and Society* 19, no. 2 (1991): 133–164.

50. Interview with P. E. de Jongh, former project leader of the NEPP and former Deputy Director-General at the Ministry of the Environment, The Hague, October 23, 1997.

51. "NEPP," 181–186; "Nationaal Milieubeleidsplan 2," 58–70.

52. For a detailed analysis of the motivations behind the Dutch positions in EU acidification policy, for instance, see Duncan Liefferink, *Environment and the Nation State: The Netherlands, the European Union, and Acid Rain* (Manchester, England: Manchester University Press, 1996).

53. Interview with de Jongh.

13

Democracy and Nuclear Power in the Czech Republic

Regina S. Axelrod

How could it have happened that we let ourselves be led too far by the old totalitarian megalomania? Why with Temelin did we proceed on a steep slope at whose foot everything is different, not only the relationship with the environment, but also the relationship between the citizen and the state? How could we miss the juncture from which a road led to savings, sustainable development and to an uninhabitable country?

Petr Pithart, former prime minister, Czech Republic,
and current chair of Senate, translated from *Listy* 5, 1994,
by Mirka Jehlickova

Private property, rational prices and individual responsibility are more important for environmental protection than the activities of governments, legislators and of environmental organizations.

Vaclav Klaus, former prime minister, Czech Republic,
"Quality of Life, Environment and Systemic Changes,"
Address to the International Geographic Union Congress,
Prague, August 22, 1994

This chapter explores the construction of the one-thousand megawatt Temelin nuclear power plant in the Czech Republic. The chapter not only provides an opportunity for examining the extent to which sustainable development policy is being addressed in a former Soviet bloc country but also offers insights into the problems of building democratic institutions in such a country. In 1989 the Iron Curtain fell and communism as it was known ended in central and eastern Europe, but the transition to democracy and a market economy has been more complex than most westerners anticipated.

The Czech Republic is in the first group of candidates in central and eastern Europe to join both the European Union (EU) and the North Atlantic Treaty Organization (NATO). In December 1997 the Czech Republic, Estonia, Hungary, Poland, and Slovenia were invited to begin negotiations for EU accession. The Czech Republic has already begun to harmonize its environmental and energy legislation with the EU as a prerequisite for membership. The ability of the Czech Republic to develop the necessary democratic attributes familiar to western Europe is also a necessary prerequisite. The adoption of the *acquis communautaire*—the body of European Community law—will make it more difficult for the nations of central and eastern Europe to join the EU because of the huge financial investment necessary to meet EU standards.

Austria, a non-nuclear state, has consistently and aggressively opposed the construction of the Temelin nuclear plant. Temelin is approximately fifty miles from its border, and the Austrians have made the proximity an issue in the Czech accession proceedings. Other states such as Germany, which closed its Russian-made nuclear plants in the eastern part of the country, also have a stake in the future of Temelin.

The Czech experience with nuclear power is a test case that will affect the viability and future marketability of nuclear power in central and eastern Europe. The upgrading of the Temelin nuclear power plant was part of a G-7 (Canada, France, Germany, Italy, Japan, the United Kingdom, and the United States) commitment to take action in response to the legacy of unsafe Russian-built nuclear power plants. The Chernobyl accident in the Ukraine is a constant reminder of the danger to human life and the environment. The European Bank for Reconstruction and Development (EBRD) refused to fund the completion of two nuclear power plants in the Ukraine until it shut down the remaining units at Chernobyl. Countries such as Bulgaria, Hungary, and Slovakia must now decide if they wish to have a nuclear future or to close existing plants and not build any more.[1] The international community also has a stake in the outcome as there is intense competition among American and European nuclear engineering companies for contracts to upgrade and complete nuclear plants in the region.

Energy Policy in Central and Eastern Europe

Building large nuclear power plants to produce electricity was consistent with the communist vision of progress of the former Soviet Union. Throughout central and eastern Europe, energy-intensive industries were supported by cheap energy: the higher the energy intensity, the greater the inefficiency in the use of energy, and the higher the energy demand for a given level of output. According to 1996 statistics from the Ministry of Environment, Czech energy intensity was much higher than that in western Organization for Economic Cooperation and Development (OECD) countries and one-third higher than that of the United States. The Stalinist model required maximum production levels. Economic incentives encouraged increased energy consumption.[2] The energy sector used between 30 percent and 50 percent of total industrial investment.[3] The results were distorted economies and overdependency on low energy prices.

Central and east European countries paid a high price to the former Soviet Union for their energy. They needed oil and natural gas and, while the price paid was less than the market price, these nations in return sold goods to the former Soviet Union at less than market prices. The former Soviet

Union controlled the natural gas and oil pipelines and could close them without notice. This power was a type of blackmail, and the regimes in central and eastern Europe took the threat seriously. They could not risk the political instability that could result from a cutoff of oil. Since 1990 these states have actively sought ways to free themselves from energy sources from the former Soviet Union.

The soft brown coal with high sulfur content used in many countries of central and eastern Europe is a source of severe air pollution. The crude mining practices, larger plant size, and absence of desulfurization equipment have led to a catastrophic situation in northern Bohemia in the Czech Republic, an area termed the Black Triangle that extends to the German and Polish borders. Children have been forced to stay home from school because the air is too dangerous to breathe, and cars have been banned from city centers. In the winter, there is permanent smog. The substitution of nuclear power for coal, thereby reducing harmful air emissions, has been argued by some to be beneficial to the environment.

The Eastern Movement of Nuclear Power

Nuclear power advocates saw the opportunity and accepted the challenge. The former Soviet Union, with compliance or agreement from the states of central and eastern Europe, had planned dozens of nuclear power plants for the region. Skoda, a Czech company, was named the prime contractor. The success of the Temelin project would now give the Czech electric utility Ceske energeticke zavody (CEZ) and Skoda a future in the modernization of these partially completed plants throughout the area.

The former Soviet Union's monopoly over nuclear reactors in central and eastern Europe has left enormous problems. The reactors are considered to be poorly engineered, lacking many of the safety features mandatory in the West. To restore public confidence in the safety and reliability of nuclear power, foreign assistance was sought to improve safety through the upgrading or closing of these plants located in Bulgaria, the Czech Republic, Hungary, Lithuania, Slovakia, and the Ukraine.

A G-7 summit held in July 1992 focused on the safety of these plants, especially in view of the 1986 Chernobyl disaster. The industrialized states wanted many of them closed, and an emergency plan was developed. "A longer term goal of the assistance program is to shut down the most dangerous nuclear power reactors and replace them with alternative energy sources."[4] Almost $1 billion was pledged from the EU, the International Atomic Energy Agency (IAEA), the Organization for Economic Cooperation and Development, the European Bank for Reconstruction and Development, and individual states to develop alternative energy sources and energy efficiency programs. The EU earmarked 4.5 million ECU (European currency units*) in 1990, 3.5 million ECU in 1991, and 20 million ECU in

---

* At the time, 1 ECU equaled approximately U.S. $1.30.

1992 to update regulations and improve safety and off-site preparedness. However, as these funds promised new life to the nuclear industry in the form of orders for new equipment, instrumentation and control systems, and nuclear waste storage facilities, the focus shifted to temporarily increasing the safety of the plants instead of closing them. Although a few plants have been taken off-line since the collapse of communism, a vast new market benefiting suppliers of nuclear technology has emerged.[5]

One of the major problems encountered by the nuclear industry is grafting western technology onto Russian-designed reactors. Temelin is to be the first such redesign project on a Russian VVER one-thousand megawatt plant. Skeptics are concerned that Russian reactor containment designs can not be properly retrofitted. A 1993 IAEA study of the VVER 440 and 230 reactor models concluded that the containment structure could not withstand a primary circuit pipe breach.[6] The cooling systems are also inadequate, and the reactors are prone to metal fatigue. Even more recent versions, for example the 213 model, did not meet western safety standards.

The nuclear industry consulted with Russian nuclear engineers to facilitate western financing of new projects. The irony is that the nuclear industry in the West found itself in the awkward position of supporting for use in eastern Europe a technology it had criticized only a few years earlier. Plant designs considered too dangerous for the West are still in use in central and eastern Europe. However, Germany closed a former East German VVER 440/213 plant and canceled upgrading a VVER 1000 plant because the government considered them too expensive and problematic to upgrade safely.

The nuclear industry has nevertheless taken steps to move eastward in Europe and to Asia. Nathaniel Woodson, president of Westinghouse, said, "We believe we bring solutions to Central and Eastern Europe and will continue to try to grow our service business outside the U.S. and set new standards in the U.S."[7] Originally, the anticipated market in central and eastern Europe was not new plant construction but upgrading existing Russian-designed plants. But the strategy is changing, and the nuclear industry is now poised to develop a new generation of nuclear power reactors if financing can be found.

Sustainable Development and the Environment

The most widely used definition of sustainable development is "development that meets the needs of the present without compromising the ability of future generations to meet their own needs."[8] It was popularized by the 1987 UN Brundtland Commission report, *Our Common Future* (see Chapter 1).

From Communism to a Free Market

The swift transition from a centralized economy run by an economic and technocratic elite to one based on free market principles and pluralism has been uncertain and painful. The demise of central planning left a vacuum in policy direction. Decisions about energy production, supply, and consumption were made in the absence of environmental criteria. "The application of Marxist ideology in practice led to environmental devastation in all Communist countries but its low point was probably reached in the Czech Republic." [9]

Under communism, environmentalists were labeled right wing because they were accused of trying to destroy socialist dreams by imposing costly demands on the government. After 1992 they were branded left wing extremists trying to ruin the free market economy by advocating a role for the state in protecting the environment.

One major difference between western democracies and communist systems and states undergoing political transformation is that in the West the public has more opportunities to influence policymaking. Opening up the decision-making process facilitates public discussion of issues. Greater public participation encourages problems to surface and solutions to be considered early in the decision-making process. A sustainable development program that included the environmental impact of energy usage could call on the expertise of interest groups, nongovernmental organizations (NGOs), and the general public and result not only in better decisions but also popular support for these decisions.

Embracing Sustainable Development

The first postcommunist government of Czechoslovakia (which split into the Czech Republic and Slovakia in 1993) enthusiastically developed policies consistent with principles of sustainable development. Environmental issues had been part of the pre-1989 opposition, and some of the dissidents held government positions. Bedrich Moldan, the Czech environmental minister—the Czech and Slovak Republics had their own environment ministers—instituted a Green Parliament, which was a forum for environmental interest groups to discuss and recommend environmental proposals. The period was full of optimism and a sense of mission. Influenced by the Brundtland Commission, the new government issued a report, "Concept of State Ecological Policy" (also known as "The Rainbow Program"), which called for the integration of the environment into all policy sectors. Air and water pollution, solid waste disposal, and the cleanup of highly contaminated areas were given priority. [10]

During that period a proposal was also made for an environmental code of ethics for business that was endorsed by many companies. It proposed the rational use of natural resources, the internalization of environmental costs, and the establishment of a Czech environmental protection agency. An eco-tax was proposed on fossil fuels; the money collected would be used to clean up contaminated areas such as northern Bohemia. [11] The overall strategy was to use economic and financial instruments to change the behavior of the polluters rather than relying on end-of-the-pipe solutions. The national-level

Federal Committee for the Environment wanted to make environmental recovery a central concern in the shift to a market economy. Its chair, Josef Vavrousek, raised his committee's activity to the international arena by hosting a pan-European EU-sponsored conference on the environment at Dobris Castle in 1991. The conference produced a notable EU report on the state of Europe's environment, called the "Dobris Assessment," in 1995. Additional conferences followed.

All this changed following the elections of 1992, which brought a new Czech government headed by Vaclav Klaus to power. The Federal Committee was dismantled, and the Czech Environment Ministry became demoralized while losing political clout. The ministry's dedicated environmentalists were replaced by party stalwarts. There were no monitoring systems or inspection programs to follow up and enforce legislation. Other issues such as crime, inflation, and the Czech-Slovak split replaced the environment on the government agenda, although a majority of people still believed environmental problems were urgent.[12]

The Klaus government ignored the work of the earlier government, focusing instead on free market rationalizations for ignoring the environment. During the preparation of the "State Environmental Policy" document in 1995, Prime Minister Klaus refused even to allow the term "sustainable development" to be used. A ministry official explained that the term was dropped for domestic political reasons, because support of the concept could be perceived as a way for socialists to return to greater state-directed activity.[13] But Klaus wanted to limit any government responsibility for environmental matters. References were made throughout the plan to the economic transformation and the appropriate role for the state now that ownership relations were changed. The document stated, "The Czech Republic's environmental policy is conceived as a dynamic approach which will facilitate identifying ecologically, economically, socially and politically optimal policies as opposed to establishing an inflexible system which could hamper economic development and lead to State control."[14] The government's perspective was that environmental problems would be solved in the marketplace and that it was the environmentalists who were the problem.[15] The optimal level of pollution was proclaimed to be whatever was socially acceptable. However, there were few mechanisms for the public to register its preferences, making it impossible to ascertain what the optimal level was.

After 1992 NGOs no longer had access to the Environment Ministry, and relations became strained. In fact, some environmental groups discovered they were on a list of extremist NGOs (including skinheads and anarchists) put together by the Security Information Services. The suspected intention was to discredit them and deny them the opportunity to address the public. The government explained it was an unofficial list, but the environmentalists insisted that their names be removed. In June 1997, the list was given to the police, but the police soon apologized and said that the responsible person would be punished. Many of these environmental activists were pre-1989 dissidents, but were now labeled enemies of the state.

Perhaps the reason that there was a diminished level of interest in environmental issues was that there was a "lack of social basis for the pursuit of advanced environmental policies typical of the first two years of the 1990s."[16] Czech scholar Petr Jehlicka maintains that the lack of public involvement and information provided by the media and government, as well as the absence of an educated and economically secure middle class, were important factors affecting the public perception that environmental concern meant no more than reducing pollution.[17]

The 1995 State Environment Policy document referred to the Temelin nuclear facility as a remedy to the air pollution from coal burning units. It also projected that the Czech Republic will achieve a level of environmental quality comparable to the countries of western Europe by the year 2005, an unrealistic expectation given the state of the environment and the level of administrative infrastructure, resources, and expertise necessary to realize that goal.

Energy Policy

The government had said it would retire coal burning plants when Temelin came on-line. However, these plants will still be needed as backup when Temelin is off-line for maintenance and repairs. The closing of coal burning plants also has the unpopular prospect of increasing unemployment. The Ministry of Industry and Trade has not prepared an energy plan since 1992, although its public statements describe a free market orientation.[18] Its only policy has been to offer subsidies to encourage switching to home electric heating, which has the unfortunate consequence of increasing consumption of electricity.

The Road to Temelin

The Decision to Upgrade

The Temelin nuclear facility was approved in 1978, and in 1981 Czechoslovakia received the designs from the former Soviet Union. Construction started in 1986. It was part of a massive project to build four one-thousand megawatt reactors designed in the former Soviet Union at Temelin, with others to be located throughout Czechoslovakia. Because of the Chernobyl accident, construction was suspended in 1989 pending a review of the reactor design. The government was under pressure to take action due to general concern about the safety of Russian-designed reactors. The plan was scaled back in 1990 for political reasons: for example, the government wanted to use the opportunity to build ties to the West; the Russians could not deliver the designs on schedule; and environmental problems surfaced. Petr Pithart, the first postcommunist prime minister of the Czech Republic, complained that information essential to making a decision about the plant's future was missing. Pithart reduced the number of reactors from four to two and tried to initiate a public debate, but he left the final decision to the next government. In spring 1992 new data were released showing that energy consumption would not increase substantially from 1989 to 2005. It could have been used to show that Temelin was unnecessary, but the Klaus government led by the Ministry of Industry and Trade favored Temelin. Not even Parliament could initiate a public discussion of the issue.

A 1990 analysis by the International Atomic Energy Agency found design flaws in the VVER 1000 and recommended changes, for example replacement of the instrumentation and control systems and fuel assembly. In fall 1992 CEZ and Westinghouse signed letters of intent for supplying nuclear fuel and replacing the instrumentation and control systems subject to U.S. Export Import Bank (Exim Bank) loan guarantees. Halliburton NUS, an American company, completed a probabilistic safety assessment that examined issues such as commercial policy and personnel issues.

In March 1993 CEZ awarded the contract to Westinghouse after two rounds of bidding. Controversy erupted over the bidding process in 1996 when it was revealed that information may have been leaked to Westinghouse about the bids of its competitors, allowing it to enter a second bid that was just under the next lowest bid.[19]

The U.S. Role

U.S. support for Westinghouse's bid to upgrade Temelin was critical. There was intense lobbying by Westinghouse to get the Exim Bank to approve the loan guarantees in support of a seventeen-bank consortium headed by Citibank. For Westinghouse, the goal was to replace Russia as the supplier of nuclear fuel and provide the instrumentation and control systems. CEZ and the Czech Ministry of Industry and Trade told the United States that the Temelin project could lead to additional upgrading contracts. According to U.S. officials, without the support of the Exim Bank, Westinghouse would not have won the contract because other bidders had the support of their governments. The United States told the Czech government that if Westinghouse won the contract, it would encourage increased cooperation between the United States and Czech firms in nuclear and other industries.[20] After the Exim Bank gave preliminary approval in September 1991, the U.S. Embassy in Prague assured Czech officials that Westinghouse would have access to competitive financing through the bank for the instrumentation and control systems and the specially designed nuclear fuel assembly. It is clear that both the Czechs and the Americans were interested in making the deal.

At the request of the Exim Bank, the National Security Council began an interagency review of the reactor design and the technical ability of the Czech regulatory authorities to ascertain compliance with U.S. environmental policy. However, the unified procedures established for interagency review of projects were not triggered because the exports for Temelin did not include "the entire nuclear reactor or nuclear steam supply system."[21] An environmental impact assessment on the redesigned Temelin project was therefore never performed.

The Exim Bank's nuclear engineer reviewed the project to assess safety, environmental risks, and feasibility. To learn about Soviet reactors, he relied on U.S. Department of Energy (DOE) reports, IAEA analyses, Czech officials in Prague and Temelin, and a DOE study of VVER reactors. However, officials at IAEA and DOE deny that "any such assessment had actually been made."[22]

The Nuclear Regulatory Commission (NRC) did not perform its own evaluation of the reactor design but still lent its support. It was alleged by Temelin opponents that its cautious report was rewritten to obtain the approval of Vice President Al Gore. Moreover, the Exim Bank consultations with Czech officials were frustrating because the information requested was not freely forthcoming. One bank official complained, "It is absolutely unacceptable to have a situation where we don't get a document or are not otherwise informed of something because we didn't ask exactly the 'right' question in the 'right way.' "[23] Nevertheless, in March 1994 the Exim Bank's board of directors approved the loan.

Because of lobbying by American and Czech environmental NGOs as well as by Austria in both the U.S. Congress and the Czech Republic, Congress decided to investigate the project. By then, more than 1 million Austrians had signed a petition protesting the loan. The Austrian government had offered to pay the Czech government to switch from nuclear power to natural gas at Temelin. It had also asked that an environmental impact assessment with public comment, or at least a preliminary safety review, be made, which would be the procedure if the reactors were located in Cuba or Mexico. Thirty-two members of the U.S. Congress sent a letter to Kenneth Brody, the Exim Bank chairman, strongly recommending that Temelin be required to meet western health and safety standards as a condition for the loan guarantee.[24]

The House Energy and Commerce Committee began an investigation into the Exim Bank decision in March 1994. Congress expressed concern about potential liability in case of a nuclear accident as well as the potential costs of more projects to upgrade Russian plants with American tax dollars. Committee chairman John Dingell was concerned about an information gap, "because the Russians refused to relinquish the documentation with design specifications of the Temelin plant."[25] Dingell requested all communications among the Exim Bank, the Czech Republic, the DOE, the NRC, and Westinghouse concerning safety and cost. He wanted data on the whole project, not just Westinghouse's role; but the Czech government was unwilling to produce any documents, for example, about the internal organization of CEZ.[26]

A General Accounting Office (GAO) study was carried out at the request of Dingell's committee. But by the time the report was ready, a new Republican-led Congress was in place, and Representative Dingell had lost his position as chairman of the Energy and Commerce Committee. The

GAO report offered no recommendations about upgrading Temelin. It found the Exim Bank's analysis and actions in reviewing Temelin to be "reasonable." It stated, "U.S. officials strongly supported industry's participation in the Temelin project and worked with Westinghouse and the Czech government to help bring about the acceptance of a U.S. firm for the project."[27] The new committee chairman had no interest in pursuing the matter of safety at Temelin any further.

Exim Bank officials recommended that in the future "unified nuclear procedures"—which require extensive analysis and an environmental assessment—should be applied to the export of major parts of nuclear power plants with the participation of relevant U.S. agencies. "The fact that there will be many more nuclear upgrades in the future supports the need for environmental review. . . . In Temelin, there was no procedure and we had to exert a lot of effort to push the other agencies to deal with the issue."[28] The bank said that it would change its internal procedures to address environmental concerns about the components of nuclear plants that do not fall under the State Department's unified nuclear procedures.

On December 3, 1996, the Exim loan guarantee for the consortium was signed at the U.S. Embassy in Prague. Rep. Joseph Kennedy, D-Mass., had tried (unsuccessfully) to get a last-minute reversal from the Exim Bank.[29] But the project had support in the United States, from former president Bush to Vice President Gore, the NRC, the DOE, and the State Department, on grounds that it benefited American competitiveness.

Problems at Temelin

The many delays in the construction of Temelin contributed to an escalation of costs. In 1992 the price tag was estimated at 68 billion Czech crowns (Kc) with half already spent. The projected cost rose to 85 billion Kc in 1996 and 98.5 billion Kc in 1998, exceeding the financial break-even point established by CEZ and potentially discouraging investors.

Westinghouse asked for increased compensation, claiming it underestimated its charges due to safety and design changes, salary increases, and prolonged labor contracts.[30] CEZ blamed Westinghouse for insisting on two thousand design changes. Temelin is now in its sixth major round of changes.

CEZ also blamed Skoda for raising prices, but it had no choice but to pay. Other delays had to do with coordinating suppliers and work schedules. CEZ admitted that experts had underestimated the work needed to upgrade the Russian design to meet western standards.[31] A summary of administrative, safety, and technical problems is given in the box.

The opening of Temelin is long overdue. In 1989 it was discovered that less construction than officially claimed had actually been completed. The start-up date moved from 1992 to 1994, 1995, and 1997. As of 1998 it was again extended to 2000.

There was little public discussion surrounding the decision to resume construction of Temelin. Two groups, Hnuti Duha (Rainbow Movement)

Summary of Administrative, Safety, and Technical Problems at the Temelin Plant

1. Lack of adequate documentation from the Russians necessitating redrawing of designs.
2. Safety goals not well defined. Too many suggestions and insufficient standards to assess degree of change necessary.
3. CEZ underestimated magnitude and complexity of integrating western and Russian technology.
4. Westinghouse had no incentive for timely completion.
5. Inadequate communication and coordination of activities on site and with Westinghouse Pittsburgh headquarters.
6. Russian and American cables were incompatible, requiring total replacement.
7. Russian and American safety codes differed.
8. Russian and American assumptions about equipment capability differed.
9. Westinghouse designs lacked level of detail familiar to Czech workers.
10. Absence of plans for long-term storage of nuclear waste.
11. Westinghouse misplaced two nuclear fuel rods that were found in the airport.
12. State Office of Nuclear Safety inspections revealed some noncompliance with safety standards.
13. Tritium will be released in the Vltava River, which supplies drinking water to Prague.

and the South Bohemian Mothers Against Temelin, however, developed a substantial presence. A newer group, the Within Sight of the Temelin Nuclear Power Plant Civic Association, has tried to arouse interest in the local community.

Numerous protests against the Temelin plant occurred in the 1990s, especially on the anniversary of the Chernobyl accident. In 1995 former prime minister Pithart was among the demonstrators, and in 1996 the deputy chair of the Parliament, Petra Buzkova, joined the protest. Groups such as Children of the Earth, Citizens Against Temelin, and Greenpeace often cooperate. The Austrian Green Party, accompanied by citizens from Germany, Denmark, and Austria, also held demonstrations. Petitions were presented to the government with no official response.

Austria has a strong interest in the plant because of Temelin's close proximity to its border. Low-level radiation and the risk of major accidents make location of nuclear power plants a transboundary issue. Austria began lobbying Washington in the early 1990s. The Greens in Austria have been vocal in their opposition, gaining political party support. They would like the Austrian government to make the decommissioning of Czech nuclear plants a condition for EU membership. The provincial governor (*Landeshaupt-*

mann) of Upper Austria has tried to arouse public awareness of the dangers of nuclear power and supports antinuclear groups.

The Provincial Assembly of Upper Austria recommended that the Austrian government propose to the EU the conversion of Temelin to gas or steam, offering an Austrian loan to pay for it. It also established a fund to finance activities to stop Temelin construction, as well as studies on energy conservation and consumption forecasting. Austrians claim that it would be too expensive to bring Temelin into compliance with EU nuclear standards, making the plant unprofitable. Austria has stationed a permanent representative in Prague to channel information about safety and cost to the Czech and Austrian governments.

The Tide Turns

An unusual opportunity to discuss and assess energy policy began in January 1998 following the defeat of the Klaus government in parliament. In a ministerial meeting of the interim government, appointed by President Vaclav Havel, questions were raised about the continued postponement of Temelin and its increasing cost. Martin Bursik, the environment minister, asked that an energy policy concept be prepared consistent with the law requiring an environmental impact assessment. The Ministry of Industry and Trade agreed to present two scenarios—one with increased coal mining and the other with limits to coal but increased energy imports. Environmentalists proposed a third option that included the closing of Temelin. There were three public hearings with participation of the Czech Senate, environmental NGOs, business groups, CEZ, and the general public. Both the press and television increased coverage of Temelin, focusing on cost and continuing safety problems. Alternatives were debated publicly for the first time.

It is significant that an issue hidden from public scrutiny by prior governments has emerged in the public arena. The Ministry of Industry and Trade report issued in June 1998, however, reaffirmed plans for the completion of Temelin and discounted the outside analysis it had commissioned, which was more favorable to conservation and renewable energy. It appears that the Social Democratic Party—which won the largest number of votes in the June 1998 elections—is just as committed to the completion of Temelin as the Klaus government. Nevertheless, it formed a commission in October 1998 to study the situation further. Chaired by Deputy Prime Minister Pavel Mertlick, the commission included representatives from the Ministries of Industry and Trade, Environment, and Finance; the OECD; the EU Commission; and the IAEA. While it will examine only fiscal and contractual issues associated with Temelin, focusing on the competitiveness of Temelin, Miloš Kuzvart, the environment minister, hopes to introduce questions concerning reactor safety and the cost of the total nuclear fuel cycle.

Government and Regulation

The Czech government has been under pressure to revise the way it has conducted business since 1989. The legacy of past practices lingers especially when learning takes place "on the job." Many from the old communist elites found ways to stay on in local government and in managerial positions in the new privatized economy.

From 1992 to 1996 the government was preoccupied with the economy and other matters such as education, judicial reform, and privatization. The transformation to a market economy was supposed to be completed by 1996. Former prime minister Klaus convinced the public that the Czech Republic was well on its way to becoming a partner equal to its western neighbors. It joined the OECD in 1995 and was then first in line for EU and NATO membership. It was disappointing when, in 1997, the currency lost value, banks failed, inflation increased, unemployment grew, and the International Monetary Fund asked that remedial measures be taken. Klaus was a firm believer in leaving the market alone and in taking minimal action to intervene in environmental matters.

The government is a coalition, and the leadership of ministries is assigned to political parties according to electoral results. Ministers are not necessarily expert in their area of responsibility, which makes reaching consensus on decisions difficult. The first Environment Ministry was enthusiastic about its mission, compared to later ministries, which produced few new initiatives. The Environment Ministry under Klaus had little influence, but since 1997 it has improved relations with NGOs, giving them more opportunities to present information and analyses.

Regulating industry, specifically the energy industry, is a new task for the Czech government. With little experience in promulgating and enforcing regulations and resistance by those being regulated, the record is poor. The Ministry of Industry and Trade oversees CEZ, but CEZ is primarily state-owned, and there is little incentive to exercise vigorous oversight. Under communism, the party/state was both owner and regulator. Checks and balances were absent because theoretically all parties had similar interests. The administration of the system of fines for environmental pollution prior to 1989 illustrates the lack of interest in enforcing government laws and rules. Penalties were most often waived or, if not, they were so low that paying the fine was more cost-effective than correcting the problem. "National Committees" responsible for administering the fines were notorious for forgiving them. There was little incentive to observe laws and regulations.[32] The Environment Inspectorate established in 1992 to exercise oversight over potential polluters has had few resources and powers to do the job.

In February 1998 CEZ shareholders asked that the roles of managing director and chairman of the CEZ board be separated and that members of the supervisory and management boards be changed. The Ministry of Industry and Trade, which is the majority shareholder, now has a representative on the CEZ board along with the CEZ director. The supervisory board members were reduced to six from eleven. The goal is to increase state control of CEZ and oversight over Temelin construction.

EU Membership as a Force for Change

The prospect of becoming a full partner in the EU has been a catalyst for change in the Czech Republic. As part of the accession process, it will have to demonstrate that it has adopted Community legislation. Environmental and energy legislation may be the most difficult to implement. Although there will be financial burdens for which EU programs can cover only a small portion, there will also be advantages for the countries of central and eastern Europe, such as trade and business opportunities, and greater political security and stability. A few specific areas are worth noting:

- Sustainable development has become an integral component of EU policy. The Czech Republic will have to incorporate the concept into its environmental and energy programs and planning.
- Although the EU has been unable to agree on a nuclear energy policy, it has adopted standards for worker health and exposure to ionizing radiation. The nuclear plants at Temelin and Dukovany must be brought up to EU and international safety standards.
- Energy pricing must now be competitive, consistent with EU policy. Price subsidies, an obstacle to competitiveness and conservation of energy, must be eliminated. The Czech government must undertake legislative reform and encourage energy-saving technology. According to Deputy Energy Minister Miroslav Tvrznik, Czech policies are out of line with EU directives. "Only the expanded support of effective energy use and the development of alternative sources of energy in the Czech Republic can help us reach a comparable level of energy source utilization."[33]
- Access to documents and the transparency of decision making must be improved. A freedom of information act proposed in 1992 has still not been passed. However, in June 1998 an environmental right-to-know act was passed. Access to environmental information is essential for public input into government policymaking.
- More than one hundred environmental regulations have been issued in the Czech Republic, half of them since 1989. However, most need better implementation. Existing legislation in the field of chemicals and water is inadequate.

Building Democracy and Environmental Protection Through Public Participation

When democratic attributes such as public participation are compared across the countries of central and eastern Europe, similar deficiencies may be traced to the influence of Soviet political and bureaucratic structures and patterns of interaction. Nevertheless, one must keep in mind that these states have distinctive histories and cultures that temper the Soviet influence. Much of the reluctance to participate directly in politics can be traced to the dearth of real opportunities for public involvement prior to 1989. While bodies such as the National Committees theoretically involved the public in local administration, there was also an absence of electoral competition and public input.[34] Most decisional authority flowed downward. The "highly centralized structure of the state itself" was constraining.[35] In fact, individuals were punished if they challenged or questioned government decisions. The public was discouraged from making demands on their leaders because the state, in theory, provided for their needs. There were no means to link people to their leaders other than through the Communist Party.

The public therefore lacked experience in civic life, including membership in intermediary organizations such as NGOs and political parties. Information was the property of the technical elites, and criticism was denied to citizens. General apathy and passiveness were characteristic of public behavior. Most people acted content because they did not believe anything could be changed.

Some experts on central and eastern Europe, such as scholars Keith Crawford and Petor Sztompka, point out the difficulty of changing this political culture.[36] Since the political transformation of 1989, the average Czech has been preoccupied with economic issues. Membership in political parties or NGOs is still low; political parties are still considered a dirty business.[37] The problem is how political efficacy can be created so that the public has the resources and motivation to play an active role in the policy-making process. Unfortunately, there is still a reluctance to seek information or challenge authorities, risking adverse consequences for nothing. In sum, it should not be surprising that the level of public participation in the Czech Republic remains low. The political culture did not support public opinion formation in the past, and citizens withdrew from public life.

Accountability

The hierarchical government structure originating in the Austro-Hungarian empire and reinforced under communist rule not only discouraged public participation but also influenced bureaucratic behavior. Bureaucrats were not regarded as public servants but as servants of the state. Bureaucratic accountability meant that no one took responsibility.[38] Administrators could be severely disciplined, even at the local level, for a small deviation, so a poor decision that did not have the intended result could be costly for the decision maker. Administrators disliked taking decisions for which they might be blamed and held accountable. Therefore, most orders were passed orally, with no written record. The reluctance to take responsibility for actions was typical of the communist legacy and is a continuing problem.

Accessibility of Information

Since 1989 people have been encouraged to take responsibility for themselves, yet the policy-making process does not provide sufficient opportunities to make decisions about their future. People are hesitant about becoming involved in problems that they do not believe they can solve. For example, citizens feel they are not sufficiently expert to assess the wisdom of building a nuclear plant. A poll done by the Institute for Public Opinion Research in Prague in 1993 and 1995 showed that a majority of people trusted the government to make the right decision on nuclear power.[39] (Those under twenty-nine and over sixty were more distrustful than the other age groups.) Ironically, 65 percent also agreed with demonstrators supporting environment protection! Because most information is still controlled by the government, it is difficult to make independent judgments without countervailing facts. Even some academic elites do not feel qualified to have an opinion about nuclear power because it is outside their particular expertise.

Another study of attitudes in central Europe reported that the Czech people believe they are not given alternatives but only short-term facts, and they are dissatisfied with the amount and quality of information. These attitudes are consistent throughout Hungary, Poland, Russia, Slovakia, and the Ukraine.[40] Without information, the public is precluded from playing a role in shaping issues and defining the government agenda. Authorities may be threatened by the potential creation of alternative centers of power that challenge bureaucratic decisions. Without an active political culture, bureaucratic expertise remains a valuable tool for keeping the public at a distance.

The few avenues for public input to policymaking are inadequate. There is a legal requirement to conduct environmental impact assessments, but the period for public comment is very short. Citizens are excluded from participating in the critical early stages of decision making.[41] Permits for nuclear power plant construction are approved at the district level, but the central government appoints the head of the district, and the citizens cannot veto this official's decisions. From the government's perspective, public participation slows decision making. This attitude reinforces the reluctance of the public to learn about issues, especially technically complex issues such as nuclear power. Because people generally do not believe they can influence decisions, they are not persistent in pursuing information about issues. In general, people do not challenge the authorities, but accept government decisions. They lack interest in public life and avoid political conflict.

The media could have a role in providing public input, but so far have proved timid. The implementation of freedom of information laws has been slow. Most newspapers report events but do no investigative stories. They report government actions with little analysis or background, tending instead to present different ideological interpretations of the same events. Journalists may fear embarrassing the government. Television gives ample opportunity for political talk, but too often interviewers do not ask probing questions.

Government officials use the opportunity to talk to the public without debating each other on issues.

The Relationship Between Czech Political Culture and Temelin

Political culture involves attitudes, values, and beliefs toward political institutions and practices. The Czech political culture described in the previous section influenced policymaking at Temelin as follows:

- The low level of information about nuclear power contributed to the belief that it was safe. Some residents near the Dukovany nuclear power plant do not respond to alarms because they say they can not see any pollution. The public has been unable to challenge government pronouncements about safety at the Temelin plant. The public is unaware of alternative energy resources that would be compatible with sustainable development while reducing air pollution in northern Bohemia. Information could be used as a formidable tool to shape public opinion and encourage public interest and debate.
- The media often discredit NGOs and protest activity, giving minimum coverage to their activities. Television showed foreigners at a Temelin demonstration to raise questions about its legitimacy. The media need to challenge public officials more and break through the barriers limiting the flow of information. In spring 1998, for example, the future of Temelin was finally explored on television with discussion from representatives of government ministries, CEZ, and other experts.
- The lack of public debate leaves decision making to special stakeholders, such as bureaucrats. Public activity is considered an impediment to government decisions. More opportunities for public oversight could result in better decisions as problems surface. Even the Parliament never debated the decision to complete Temelin. The lack of communication among members of Parliament, NGOs, scientists, researchers, professional associations, and bureaucrats inhibits sharing of information among groups and, consequently, the development of a civil society.
- Local governments were not involved in the licensing process for Temelin. Communities were denied an opportunity for public discussion even after requests were made to the central government. Local authorities' opinions were not considered. The decision to grant a construction license was approved by the state office, which evaluated only the building plans and not the environmental impact of the plant.
- The lack of individual responsibility within the organization's decision-making hierarchy contributed to delays at Temelin. Difficulties in obtaining clearance or approval on highly technical issues poten-

tially can compromise safety levels if decisions are made under pressure and without proper oversight.

- Administrative practices and rules were loosely enforced. There is a poor history of monitoring and implementing environmental legislation. Nuclear energy technology requires a high level of safety and low levels of risk and uncertainty, with a decision structure that provides for extensive monitoring, oversight, and redundancy.
- Because discussion of the decision to continue construction of Temelin was suppressed, with government officials refusing to engage in open debate, the potential for latent conflict remains. "There existed no legitimate alternative political grouping able to offer a fresh approach to dealing with a particular problem such as the environment, and the leadership was thus trapped and prevented from seeking solutions to the worsening ecological situation."[42] The NGOs are weak, with low membership and few resources. Except for the Rainbow Movement, most have dropped Temelin from their agendas.
- Temelin was consistent with the practice of building grandiose projects, which symbolically reinforced loyalty to the state. However, if Temelin turns into an unprofitable financial liability without public debate to legitimize the decision to continue construction, it could become the center of a future political conflict. In 1998 an opportunity emerged to broaden discussion that could legitimize the decision over Temelin's future.
- The attitude that there is an objective nonpolitical solution to Temelin that is best made by experts ignores the political aspects of a conflict. It is as if the truth was waiting to be found by a divine expert. According to this view, the public should not have a role in decision making on a technical issue, and the government should not ask them. Among some decision makers there is no understanding that participants to any conflict have particular biases and that any decision will reflect those biases as well as the objective analysis.

With all this said, it is also true that Czech political culture is undergoing a transformation. Many Czechs want closer ties with western Europe. The adjustment will not be easy; beliefs and attitudes that worked well in the past are slow to change. According to East European scholar Klaus von Beyme, the peaceful revolution of 1989 led by "intellectuals and their followers" did not transform political systems.[43] There is still a lack of trust between authorities, accompanied by a low level of political efficacy. As people become more familiar with democratic forms of political activity they will begin to challenge existing bureaucratic/technocratic elites.

Concepts like "sustainability" are new to the Czech Republic. But the issue is not just the difference between a communist system or a free market system—serious environmental problems such as air pollution plague both economic systems, and both discount these problems in their decision making. Sustainability requires group or collective action with a concern for the public interest; it is future oriented. Sustainable development can succeed only if the public recognizes its importance and learns to participate more fully in the political process. Public participation transfers legitimacy to sustainability. But the discredited planning legacy of the past may also have to be revitalized and reinvigorated to develop environmental policies consistent with the principle of sustainability. Planning and public input can be compatible, but this requires an educated and informed public willing to make the investment. The challenge for the Czech government is to develop energy policy that is consistent with sustainable environmental goals in a democracy that includes a greater role for the public through a variety of participatory mechanisms.

A public debate finally began in 1998. There was an opportunity for the public to engage in the political discussion of the problems associated with nuclear power as well as coal burning from a long-term perspective. Comprehensive review and planning could produce an energy policy with a diverse mix of sources, including renewable energy and conservation.

The interim nonpartisan government appointed in January 1998 began a policy review process involving more participants and more comprehensive analysis. Just how extensive the debate is throughout the Czech Republic depends on the willingness of governments such as the coalition government established under the leadership of Social Democrat prime minister Miloš Zeman in July 1998 to establish mechanisms for broad public participation and transparency. However, it does not appear that the policy toward Temelin will be changed even after this brief period of public debate; the Social Democrat minister of industry and trade announced the continuation of construction, rejecting further analysis of cost-effectiveness and safety and in October 1998, without informing other ministers, proposed building more nuclear plants. The development of an energy policy compatible with sustainable development is still in the future.

Former prime minister Pithart summarized the dilemma: "The construction of Temelin does not only change our attitude to energy saving, nature, and our health; it changes the whole social, economic, and political climate. With Temelin producing energy on a large scale, we are closer to a centralized, strong state and further away from regions, municipalities, and from citizens. . . . With Temelin, 'small is beautiful' is not valid, the statement which is valid says 'huge is also powerful.'"[44]

Notes

This chapter is based on work supported by the National Science Foundation under Grant No. SBR-9708180. Any opinions, findings, and conclusions or recommendations expressed in this chapter are the author's and do not reflect the views of the National Science Foundation. The author wishes to thank Petr Jehlicka for his helpful and insightful comments on this chapter and Stanislava Hybnerova for her enthusiastic support for the project.

1. *Financial Times*, February 27, 1997.
2. For a discussion of energy policy in central and eastern Europe, see Peter Rutland, "Energy Rich, Energy Poor," *Transition* III, No. 9 (1996): 5; and John M. Kramer, "Energy and the Environment in Eastern Europe," in *To Breathe Free*, Joan DeBardeleben, ed. (Washington, D.C.: Woodrow Wilson Center, 1991), 57–79.
3. Janusz Cofala, "Energy Reform in Central and Eastern Europe," *Energy Policy* XXII (1994): 486.
4. "Nuclear Safety: International Assistance Efforts to Make Soviet Designed Nuclear Reactors Safer," General Accounting Office, *Report to Congressional Requesters*, GAO/RECD, 94–234, September 1994, 1.
5. Colin Woodard, "Western Vendors Move East," *Transition* 17 (November 1995): 24.
6. Ibid.
7. *Nucleonics Week*, December 14, 1995, 4.
8. World Commission on Environment and Development, *Our Common Future* (London and Oxford: Oxford University Press, 1987), 43.
9. Petr Jehlicka and Jan Kara, "Ups and Downs of Czech Environmental Awareness and Policy: Identifying Trends and Influences," in *Protecting the Periphery: Environmental Policy in Peripheral Regions of the European Union*, ed. Susan Baker, Kay Milton, and Steven Yearly (London: Frank Cass, 1994), 154. See also Barbara Jancar-Webster, "Environmental Politics in Eastern Europe in the 1980s," in *To Breathe Free*, 25–56; and Andrew Tickle and Ian Welsh, eds., *Environment and Society in Eastern Europe* (New York: Longman, 1998).
10. Richard Andrews, "Environmental Policy in the Czech and Slovak Republics," in *Environment and Democratic Transition: Policy and Politics in Central and Eastern Europe*, ed. Anna Vari and Pal Tamas (Dordrecht: Kluwer Academic Publishers, 1995), 28.
11. Ibid., 31.
12. "Status of National Environmental Action Programs in Central and Eastern Europe," *Country Reports* (Szentendre, Hungary: Regional Environmental Center, May 1995), 43.
13. Brian Slocock, "Paradoxes of Environmental Policy in Eastern Europe: The Dynamics of Policy-making in the Czech Republic," *Environmental Politics* V (autumn 1996): 513.
14. "State Environmental Policy." Document approved by the Government of the Czech Republic, Ministry of the Environment, August 23, 1995.
15. For an excellent discussion of environmental policy in the Czech Republic, see Bedrich Moldan, "Czech Republic," in *The Environmental Challenge for Central European Economies in Transition*, ed. Jurg Klarer and Bedrich Moldan (West Sussex: Wiley, 1998), 107–130.
16. Petr Jehlicka, "The Development of Czech Environmental Policy in the 1990s: A Sociological Account" (paper presented at the Summer Symposium of the University of Bologna, July 1997), 14.
17. Ibid., 12–14.
18. "Energy Policy of the Czech Republic," draft, Ministry of Industry and Trade, April 24, 1996, 2.
19. Czech News Agency (CTK), May 11, 1996; and *Prague Post*, June 5, 1996.
20. "Nuclear Safety: U.S. Assistance to Upgrade Soviet-Designed Nuclear Reactors in the Czech Republic," Report to the Ranking Minority Member, Committee on Commerce, House of Representatives, GAO, June 1995, 4–5.
21. Ibid., 7.
22. S. Jacob Scherr and David Schwarzbach, "Turning Points," *Amicus Journal* (winter 1995): 14.
23. "Nuclear Safety," 11.
24. *East European Reporter*, March 25, 1994.
25. *The Energy Daily*, March 17, 1994.

26. *Nucleonics Week,* March 17, 1994, 3.
27. "Nuclear Safety," 1.
28. Ibid., 12.
29. *Prague Post,* December 18, 1996.
30. *Prague Post,* January 14, 1998.
31. *Nucleonics Week,* August 24, 1995.
32. For an excellent description of environment policy administration, see Andrews, "Environmental Policy in the Czech and Slovak Republics," 5–48.
33. "An Interview with M. Tvrznik, Deputy Minister at the Ministry of Industry and Trade," *Energy,* English Supplement, June 1997, 5.
34. Kenneth Davy, "The Czech and Slovak Republics," in *Local Government in Eastern Europe: Democracy at the Grassroots,* ed. Andrew Coulson (Lyme, N.H.: Edward Elgar, 1995), 41.
35. Adam Fagin and Petr Jehlicka, "Sustainable Development in the Czech Republic: A Doomed Process?" *Environmental Politics* VII (spring 1998): 119.
36. Keith Crawford, *East Central European Politics Today* (New York: St. Martin's Press, 1996); and Piotr Sztompka, "The Intangibles of the Transition to Democracy," *Studies in Comparative Communism* 24, No. 3 (1991).
37. Z. Vajdova, "Politicka kultura lokalnich politickych elit: srovnani ceskeho a vychodonemeckeho mesta," (Political Culture of Local Poltical Elites: A Comparison of Czech and East German Cities), Working Papers, Institute of Sociology, Academy of Sciences of the Czech Republic, 97:3, 1997, 38.
38. Jehlicka and Kara, "Ups and Downs of Czech Environmental Awareness and Policy," 156.
39. Czech News Agency (CTK), November 29, 1995.
40. "Security for Europe Project," Final Report, Center for Foreign Policy Development, Thomas J. Watson Institute for International Studies, Brown University, December 1993.
41. Fagin and Jehlicka, "Sustainable Development in the Czech Republic," 120.
42. Adam Fagin, "Environment and Transition in the Czech Republic," *Environmental Politics* III (autumn 1994): 481.
43. Klaus von Beyme, *Transition to Democracy in Eastern Europe* (New York: St. Martin's Press, 1996), 41.
44. *Listy* 5 (1994).

14

The Three Gorges Dam and the Issue of Sustainable Development in China

Lawrence R. Sullivan

A ccording to the International Union for the Conservation of Nature and the World Commission on Environment and Development (WCED), known as the Brundtland Commission, sustainable development is "development which meets the needs of the present without compromising the ability of future generations to meet their own needs. Sustainable development implies handing down to successive generations not only man-made wealth but also natural wealth (soils, water, plants, and animals) in adequate amounts to ensure continuing improvements in the quality of life."[1] Of critical importance to sustainable development is a concern for land usage and the need for popular input into developmental decisions. Land is a nonrenewable resource and is ultimately a limiting factor to sustained development over generations. The same is true for popular input: no plan, it is argued, is sustainable if it does not meet the basic needs of the people living in a region or the society as a whole and if there is no meaningful participation by affected peoples in the basic decision making that shapes major developmental projects, such as the Three Gorges Dam in the People's Republic of China (PRC). In addition, the specific social and cultural context in which any plan for development is undertaken is crucial to determine its sustainability. Any strategy of economic development that is not based on consideration of these factors—strategies that waste valuable land resources and that are formulated in a political vacuum by a self-appointed elite with little or no consideration of the impact of development plans on the local population—will ultimately prove to be unsustainable and become an enormous burden on society's resources and a threat to political stability.[2]

This chapter examines the various controversies that have involved the Three Gorges Dam in regard to the overall compatibility of this project with the goals and parameters of sustainable development. Specifically, it will summarize the contending positions of dam supporters and opponents in China over two key components of the sustainable development model mentioned above: land usage and popular input. To be sure, in China's media this has been a one-sided debate, since the government will allow only "positive reporting" about the dam. Despite such authoritarian strictures—which at first glance violate the concept of popular input—dam critics in and outside the Chinese government have made their views known. *Yangtze! Yangtze!*, which was originally published in China by Guizhou Province People's Publishing House, circulated for several years among the hydropower community in China and was instrumental in mobilizing opposition to the Three Gorges Dam in the late 1980s when the National People's Congress (NPC) refused to back the project. Dai Qing's most recent compilation of articles (some of which were written under pseudonyms by individuals working on the project), entitled *The River Dragon Has Come!*, could not be published in China, but mimeographed copies are apparently available even on the dam construction site in Sandouping, Hubei Province.[3] More important, Dai Qing suggests that the issue of the dam is still very controversial and the subject of considerable discussion among the elite in the Chinese Communist Party (CCP) and government, largely because of its ballooning costs and the fear of social unrest in the region.[4]

Sustainable development is an issue highly relevant to China's current economic and social conditions. Several years of rapid (and often uncontrolled) economic development since economic reforms were introduced in 1978, preceded by decades of nearly equal rapid growth under the centralized state planning system inherited from the Soviet Union, have left the country with economic, demographic, and, especially, environmental problems. Many people in and outside the country believe that these problems require immediate attention and a shift in economic strategies that incorporates the basic principles of sustainable development.[5] Problems that have brought the issue of sustainable development to the forefront of current Chinese thinking include:

- Rapid depletion of land resources through conversion of agricultural lands into industrial and commercial use.
- Growing pollution of air and water and the increase in other forms of pollution resulting from high levels of energy use, especially the burning of coal, by outworn industries from the Soviet-style planning era and from an increased per capita consumption, especially the increasing numbers of cars and trucks that are causing a growth in demand for oil close to 15 percent per year.
- Degradation of soil, forests, and grasslands and increased soil erosion because of mismanagement and long-term government inattention to the agricultural sector.
- The continued impact of China's huge population—1.2 billion—on every facet of the country's development.[6]

In addition, sustainable development has been an increasingly important issue in U.S.-China relations, so much so that it was a major topic of trips to the PRC by the former U.S. Department of Energy secretary Hazel O'Leary in February 1995 and more recently by Vice President Albert Gore in the spring of 1997. Joint projects, such as the Ussuri River Watershed Land Use project, have become an increasing focus of current American and Chinese exchanges in both the government and private sectors. Such projects are of great concern to China's neighbors in East Asia, such as Korea and Japan, which are most directly affected by the PRC's environmental excesses.[7]

The Three Gorges Dam and Sustainable Development

International advocates of hydropower have long argued that hydro-electric dams are a perfect example of "renewable" or sustainable development, largely because of the use of water as their fuel and the fact that dams employ technologies that are non-greenhouse gas-emitting.[8] It has even been suggested that industrial countries should meet their obligations to limit greenhouse gas emissions under the UN's framework climate convention by helping to pay for hydropower dams in developing countries.[9] In China's case, hydropower development has been put on the fast track by the PRC government as a way, in part, to stem the country's enormous dependence on coal and to avoid substantial increases in oil imports. Since 1978, when economic reforms in China began, the growth in China's gross domestic product has expanded by more than 9 percent a year, and with it demand for energy has increased as well. In the present Ninth Five Year Plan (1996–2000), China plans to increase annual electricity capacity by about 20 gigawatts per year, which is roughly equivalent to adding a major power station every two to three weeks.[10] Although energy intensity (a measure of energy consumed per unit of economic output) has been dropping in China since 1977, the PRC still remains one of the most energy-intensive economies in the world.[11] In addition, the country is highly dependent on coal for its energy supply with more than 1.4 billion tons burned every year, much of which is high in sulfur and a major source of environmental pollution, especially in the southwest. Since China is averse to meeting its growing energy needs by becoming a major oil importer and considering the rather small-scale use of nuclear power and natural gas, reducing the heavy reliance on coal can come only by dramatically increasing the contribution of hydropower to the total production of electricity.[12] Current plans in China thus call for hydropower to increase gradually from the present 25 percent contribution to national electrical generating capacity to 30 percent by the year 2000.[13] Several major hydropower projects are now undergoing construction in China and are touted as solutions to China's energy and agricultural needs consistent with the basic guidelines of sustainable development.[14]

Proponents of the Three Gorges Dam in and outside the Chinese government emphasize the dam's enormous installed capacity of electrical generation, which is currently listed as 18,000 megawatts (18 gigawatts). When completed in 2009, the dam will provide 85 billion kilowatt hours of electricity, approximately 10 percent of the country's total capacity as of 1993, thereby eliminating the annual burning of 40 million to 50 million tons of coal in steam power plants and significantly reducing air pollution in the Yangtze River basin.[15] In addition, the dam is officially advertised as providing long-term solutions to the perennial problems of flooding on the Yangtze, which have caused the loss of tens of thousands of lives over the past century and periodic losses in agricultural and industrial production. The 1931 flood, for instance, caused 140,000 deaths, while in 1954 nearly 30,000 people were killed in floods that also disrupted the entire economy of the region for more than 100 days. Summer 1998 witnessed another severe flood throughout the Yangtze Valley, though reported deaths were less than 5,000, most due to landslides.[16] Although construction of the Three Gorges Dam will cause the loss of 30,000 hectares of river valley land in a rich orange-growing region, the Chinese government argues that the economic benefits outweigh the costs and that the local environment is being protected by increased reforestation projects and the establishment of environmental monitoring systems. The economic benefits include the decrease in shipping costs on the river by upward of 40 percent and the ability of 10,000-ton ships to ply the smooth waters of the reservoir to inland cities, most notably Chongqing, Sichuan. In addition, the dam will serve as a magnet for investment, especially in industry, in a region that has lagged behind the rest of the country. Finally, in line with the importance of popular input, the government emphasizes the role of the NPC—the highest lawmaking body in China—in approving the dam by a vote in 1992 of 1,767 in favor, 177 opposed, and 644 abstentions. Relocation of the 1.3 million to 1.9 million people in the proposed reservoir area is under way. These people, the government claims, support the dam with great national pride, especially those who live in the small towns and cities along the river and who are being moved to newly constructed apartments and into industrial jobs.[17] In cities such as Badong, Sichuan, site of Chinese munitions production in the 1960s, the construction of a new town to make way for the floodwaters is being carried out in conjunction with a major conversion of its military industries to civilian production. And while some of the majestic scenery of the Three Gorges will undoubtedly be reduced, the Chinese government emphasizes that the waters will rise only 97 meters up the gorges' walls, thereby preventing the loss of this site for future generations. Three Gorges, in short, is touted as sustainable development in action.

Sustainable Development or Degradation?

The view that the Three Gorges Dam comports with sustainable development is not, however, endorsed by all interested parties in and outside of China. In its decision in 1995 against financing U.S. companies interested in winning contracts for Three Gorges, the U.S. Export-Import Bank cited several factors that suggested that the current design of the dam would not meet the basic goals of sustainable development because of adverse effects on water quality in the proposed 400-mile reservoir, and deleterious effects of the project on ecological resources, endangered species, and cultural antiquities.[18] In addition, some Chinese scientists, engineers, and ecologists have also attacked the project for these and other negative effects of the dam.[19] According to Dai Qing, a former journalist and leading dam critic, the Three Gorges Dam is an example not of "sustainable development," but of "uncontrolled development" because of its egregious environmental and social impacts and spiraling costs.[20] Contrary to the optimistic and benign effects of the dam propounded by its supporters, especially former premier Li Peng, Dai argues that the dam will cause "long-term upheaval and damage" to the surrounding environment and the local population that will affect the region and country for several generations.[21] Throughout the planning and initial stages of construction, a realistic appraisal of the project's impact on the region's environment—land, water, and air—have been systematically understated and ignored by the "red specialists" (*hongse zhuanjia*, the engineers and bureaucrats who have pushed this project for years) whom Dai accuses of pushing the project for political and bureaucratic reasons. Moreover, despite the decision of the NPC—which itself came after virtually no debate among the body's delegates—popular input into the project by residents in the river valley has, Dai charges, been systematically ignored and vocal critics of the dam have been arrested or otherwise silenced by a government policy that allows only "positive reporting" about the dam.[22] If sustainable development means a concern for maintaining the integrity of ecological systems and involving the local population that will be affected in a process that meets their social and economic needs, the Three Gorges Dam does not qualify. And if sustainable development is the model for future approaches to interactions between humans and their environment, then Three Gorges is a relic of the past, that is, of the old Soviet-style economic planning system with its emphasis on "grandiose" engineering projects that are supported by huge bureaucracies and political elites who are more interested in national pride and political bombast than sustainable development.[23] To the extent that Three Gorges will destroy the Yangtze River system and damage its estuaries and extinguish local species while significantly eroding the living standards of local residents, it will compromise the ability of future generations to meet their needs—the very antithesis of sustainable development.[24]

The controversy over the Three Gorges Dam must, of course, be interpreted within the larger context of China's overall energy policy. Although official statements and decisions by the Chinese government have emphasized the importance of energy conservation in recent years, advocates of the dam and other major electrical-generating projects in China believe that China's energy needs require full-speed ahead on these projects if the country's rapid economic growth is to be continued. Critics of the project both in the PRC and abroad, however, believe that despite some progress and much official rhetoric on energy conservation, the Chinese should look to solutions of their energy needs not in the form of such huge projects as the Three Gorges Dam but, rather, in more small-scale and perhaps less grandiose energy-saving efforts. Consider the problem of highly inefficient medium and small-scale industrial boilers in China that burn coal and are based on designs and production methods typical of those used in developed countries before 1950. If the operating efficiency levels of boilers in China were brought into line with standards in the developed world, current coal consumption in China could be reduced by about 70 million tons per annum (20 percent more than the amount slated to be saved by a fully operational Three Gorges Dam).[25] The enormity of waste in Chinese energy consumption, especially in the industrial sector, is so great that funds should be shifted from huge, potentially destructive projects like Three Gorges into a variety of energy-saving projects.

Land Usage and Pollution

In the 1930s, the Chinese sociologist Fei Xiaotong observed that in the Yangtze Valley "honor, ambition, devotion, and social approval are all linked up with the land."[26] As long as a farmer owned his land, he felt secure; it was his flesh and blood. Thus, any issue involving land usage—especially loss of land by the cultivator—is of major importance in Chinese politics. In the case of the construction of the Three Gorges Dam, it is generally agreed that approximately 30,000 hectares of arable land now under intense cultivation will be lost to the reservoir and approximately one-half of the projected 1.3 million to 1.9 million people who will be relocated because of the dam will be farmers. In a country where on average 400,000 hectares of land are lost to industrial and commercial usage every year, the 30,000 hectare figure is not particularly significant in the larger picture. Yet within the proposed reservoir region, the displacement of farmers and the question of their future livelihood is perhaps the major social and political issue surrounding the construction of the dam, especially since much of the inundated farmland is prime agricultural property along the river that is now used for high-yielding production of oranges and other cash crops. Whether adequate barren land exists in the region for relocation by the affected farmers is the heart of the issue: supporters of the dam suggest that surplus lands exist and can be readily converted to agricultural use without having to relocate farmers at great distance from their current homes; dam critics scoff at such optimistic scenarios and, instead, suggest that the Yangtze Valley region is already suffering from population pressure on the land and that proposed sites for agricultural relocation—away from the river and up nearby mountainsides—are largely marginal lands with minimal productive capacity and on terrain with a gradient slope greater than 25 degrees. Under current Chinese law, slopes of that gradient cannot be subject to cultivation. Moreover, dam critics argue that taking cultivation higher up on the mountain slopes will increase deforestation and soil erosion, thereby worsening the siltation flow into the Yangtze and increasing the danger of floods—the very problem that the dam is supposed to solve.[27]

Population resettlement for large hydropower projects, such as Three Gorges, is also a very sensitive issue in China, largely because of the disastrous long-term effects of resettlement from previous construction projects. China has approximately 10.2 million people who are officially labeled as "reservoir relocatees" (*shuiku yimin*). That number includes both those who were forced to move since the mid-1950s and their descendants in the new resettlement communities.[28] The fact is that resettled populations have been left considerably poorer than before they were moved. In 1989, 70 percent of the relocatees were "living in extreme poverty," usually without access to adequate land and often in substandard "temporary" housing. The Xin'an River

Power Station, which was constructed during the late 1950s in Zhejiang Province and involved the relocation of more than 300,000 people and the inundation of 21,000 hectares of land, had a severe impact on the local agricultural (and industrial) economy. Two of the most affected counties—Chun'an and Lin'an, near the city of Hangzhou—saw such substantial reductions in grain production that they shifted from a surplus-producing region to a grain deficient one as rural relocatees were forced to rely on 0.02 hectares of land per capita; 60 percent of the people living in Chun'an County had an annual per capita income of less than 200 yuan ($25).[29] By 1986, many of the relocatees had still not been fully compensated for the loss of their land, housing, and personal effects. In another case, that of the Three Gate Gorge Dam (*sanmenxia*) constructed on the middle reaches of the Yellow River in the late 1950s and early 1960s in Henan Province, destitute relocatees from Shanxi Province—the reservoir site west of Henan—fought for years to return to their farmland that had never been submerged because the project had been scaled back to avoid flooding the city of Xi'an.[30] Twenty thousand hectares of land were retrieved by the original owners, but only after major street demonstrations and pitched battles between relocatees and army production units that had taken over the land in the relocatees' absence.

In response to these previous experiences, the Chinese government in the case of the Three Gorges project has officially adopted a policy of "Developmental Resettlement," a comprehensive plan that includes lump-sum reimbursement for lands lost to inundation, rural resettlement, township and factory relocation, personnel training, and other issues pertinent to relocation.[31] For the rural population in the region who will lose most of the 30,000 hectares of land, the plan is to keep the relocatees in the area by "moving them back from the river and settling them in nearby areas up the mountains." One official involved in relocation, Li Boning, has argued that there are abundant natural resources in the area, including upward of 1.3 million hectares of undeveloped land in the nearby counties and municipalities where people will be resettled.[32] Citing infra-red photos of land resources in the area, Li insists that, unlike past resettlement efforts, local farmers who are willing to move into these barren land areas will receive sufficient land to prevent substantial losses of income, which, local polls show, rural relocatees fully expect to occur.[33] Trial resettlement projects carried out over the past five years, Li emphasized, have shown that there will be no need to employ migrants in other areas and that developmental resettlement is a new innovation and an important reform in the approach to resettlement.[34]

Dam critics scoff at these kinds of official estimates of available land in the region and criticize the potential income-producing potential of resettled farmers as overly optimistic. They charge that, as in similar large-scale projects in the past, the government is trying to lure farmers into "voluntarily" resettling on land that, in reality, will be extremely difficult to cultivate. These farmers, critics say, will be forced to resettle for a second and third time as a result of rapid deterioration of marginal farmland and inadequate water resources for irrigation and residential use.[35] The Three Gorges region is already overpopulated and suffers from excessive cultivation with little surplus land available for resettlement and bleak prospects for relocatees to achieve per capita income comparable to their present levels.[36] As one investigation in the area revealed: "All of the arable land above the future submersion line is on mountain slopes and is scattered throughout the region."[37] Since China's Water and Soil Protection Act prohibits cultivation not only of land with a gradient slope of 25 degrees or more but also of areas that have already lost more than 30 percent of their vegetative cover, very little of the 1.3 million hectares cited by Li Boning could be legally subject to cultivation. Since the number of rural relocatees is greater than the government's official figure (900,000 according to dam critics versus 320,000 by the government's count), it is estimated that relocatees will receive substantially less land (estimated to be in total from 0.03 to 0.06 hectares per capita) than promised by authorities.[38] In order to reach official goals of land allocation, entire swaths of mountainsides would have to be illegally filled with relocatees whose land would be very difficult and costly to convert to high-yielding grain and cash crop soil. One estimate presented the frightening scenario that to convert each 0.06 hectare of land in the mountains would "require 140 explosive charges . . . 1.12 billion such charges [for all the land slated for reclamation] or 15,000 explosions a day for twenty 20 years!"[39] Since much of the land free from inundation is above 600 meters, farmers who now rely on cash crop production, especially oranges, will see their incomes plummet because such crops cannot be raised at such high altitudes.[40] In Badong County, the most underdeveloped region in the Three Gorges Valley, Tujia minority peoples have been moved up the mountains to where there is little arable land, increasing soil erosion, and little hope of sustenance. And while local officials are scrambling for outside industrial investment to provide jobs and alternative sources of production, the large investment flows and new employment promised by "Developmental Resettlement" have simply not been forthcoming.[41]

In short, dam supporters and critics paint diametrically opposed pictures of the consequences of the Three Gorges Dam on land usage in the region. The former suggest that the availability of barren, surplus land in the region will make the transition to farming on mountainsides rather easy; the latter suggest that overcultivation of the area is already in evidence and that the prospects for farmers in the region under the new policy of "Developmental Resettlement" is no less bleak than in previous water control projects. Rather than "moving back from the river and settling in nearby areas up the mountains," relocated farmers, it is feared, will join the army of "floating laborers" who travel throughout the country searching for work, or, worse, they will refuse to move from below the submersion line, setting up a confrontation with the government and its local police forces.[42]

Dam supporters and critics have also sparred over the issue of altered land usage and its impact on pollution. Supporters, such as Li Boning, suggest that with "strict planning procedures and quality control standards in place," opening new lands up the mountainsides to grain and citrus fruit tree production will have a minimal impact on soil erosion and water quality. "This is not a case of unplanned and haphazard development of barren lands," Li Boning insists. Indeed, Li even argues that opening the land to development will actually stem erosion and deforestation by the construction of stone wall terraces on the mountainsides that, he suggests, will actually improve soil retention. "The same is true where grasses and trees were planted to help in soil conservation."[43]

Again, critics present a totally different picture, one that suggests the dam project will bring considerable harm to the region's environment through more intensified land usage. Since rural relocatees will, in all likelihood, be forced to cultivate lands exceeding 25 degrees gradient, this will add to the already severe problem of deforestation in the region with concomitant increases in degradation of vegetative cover, soil erosion, and river siltation.[44] Along with the pollution that will come from the inundation of old factories along the river and increased investment in highly polluting village and township enterprises that already contribute to the 16.6 billion tons of wastewater that flow into the Yangtze annually, a dramatic drop in the Yangtze's water quality will likely occur.[45] And since direct administrative authority over environmental protection work in the dam area has been given to the Three Gorges Project Development Corporation—the very organization charged with building the dam—it is unlikely that environmental and pollution issues will have much impact on the project.

Population Relocation and Popular Input

A perennial feature of dam and hydropower construction in China during the Mao years (1949–1976) was the total lack of any popular input on the national or regional level from the Chinese people into these major construction decisions that profoundly affected their lives. As one study of past dam-building practices noted, "all a particular leader had to do was point his finger at a certain place and a decision would be made to build a dam between one mountain and another."[46] In the case of the Three Gorges Dam, the Chinese government has given lip service to the idea of popular input into the project but without any real effort, especially at the local level, to meet the standards established under the sustainable development framework. The result has been a widespread resignation by future relocatees to their fate and a general feeling that on such major projects the interests and views of the locals count for little. As one villager commented: "We will not survive, but we can't do anything about it. . . . The nation says to move. We will see what happens when the waters come."[47]

To the extent that there was any popular input into the decision to build the Three Gorges Dam, it came in the 1992 vote by the National People's Congress. Although this traditionally rubber-stamp body has in recent years exhibited some life in bringing the major issues confronting China up for discussion and even debate, the decision on the dam was very perfunctory.[48]

No open debate was allowed—indeed, efforts to discuss the issue prior to the vote by some informed delegates were met with a cutoff of microphones—and the general consensus was that the real decision to go ahead with the dam had already been made by the highest organs of the Chinese Communist Party in accord with "Deng Xiaoping's support."[49] Since then the government has been most concerned with deploying adequate police and other resources in the region to stifle dissent and to crush any incipient movement on the part of dam critics to mobilize popular opposition among the local affected populations. In May 1992, 179 people were arrested in the rural county of Kaixian, Wanxian Prefecture in Sichuan Province for allegedly belonging to the Democratic Youth Party. They were accused of "counter-revolutionary activities aimed at sabotaging the policy of opening and reform and at disrupting the smooth progress of the Three Gorges project."[50] In the last five years, considerable emphasis has been given to strengthening security by reorganizing public and state security units in the region and deploying units of the People's Armed Police to confront what the government admits is "growing outrage among resettlers toward the government, resulting in resistance to resettlement and interference with the construction of the Three Gorges project."[51] Throughout the region, local police and militia forces have been ordered to "resolutely uphold the policy of speed and severity in striking blows at crimes and criminals that sabotage Three Gorges construction and relocation."[52] In such an atmosphere, most locals, especially resettled farmers, have accepted their fate and realize that overt resistance is futile.

In the eyes of the red specialists, local residents, especially farmers, are hopelessly mired in narrow, partisan interests and should, therefore, have no role in affecting decisions on a project of such enormous national importance. In this sense, China is far from accepting the basic principle of "sustainable development" that argues for "reflecting the needs of the people living in the region." Such an approach would only strengthen regional forces in China and undermine the national goals that the Three Gorges Dam is slated to meet, especially in providing the central government with continued control over China's electrical grid. The result is that local and regional leaders in the party and government apparatus have found their political positions severely constrained by the political dynamics of the project. While some leaders have been condemned by their local constituencies for failing to strive for a fair deal and for selling out local interests, others have been punished politically and legally for challenging aspects of the project.[53] In the meantime, major political resources at the local level have been invested in setting up the bureaucratic and propaganda network—neighborhood committees, billboards, local ads, radio and TV broadcasts—for creating "positive support" by the locals for the project while keeping all visible signs of dissent out of the press.[54] This, in turn, has been combined with heavy doses of nationalism linked to the project's completion: "The successful construction of this project can show the world that the Chinese people have aspirations and the ability to do a good job in this project which has become the focus of world attention," Li Peng has proclaimed on several occasions.[55] But for Dai Qing this approach is all part of an effort to shore up the old central-planning bureaucratic structure and suppress the recent trend of democratization in Chinese society and politics: Three Gorges, she claims, is "a product of political authoritarianism and of a command economy. Many important people have been kept silent about this highly politicized project because their positions in the Communist Party do not depend on their merit, but on how much they are favored by the leaders."[56]

In contrast to the government's heavy-handed, security conscious approach to controlling the social and political situation in the Three Gorges region, proposals have been aired for a more politically responsible approach to implementing the project. The Chinese government should, it is argued, learn from past mistakes committed during previous large-scale projects and institute more consultative practices that might help diffuse local resentment and resistance. According to two journalists who have visited the region and conducted in-depth interviews: "Listening to the opinions of the masses will lessen their suffering and help prevent 'rebellions' by tens of thousands of people. It can also help reduce the costs of resettlement for the state. Regular meetings should be convened," they argue further, "where representatives of the relocatees can voice their views on problems with reimbursement, and the difficulties they are having maintaining their standards of living and work." These two journalists also advocate that more visits by central government personnel to the site be organized on a less orchestrated basis and that China's national representative political institutions—namely, the various people's congresses and political consultative bodies that have recently shown more willingness to take independent stands on national and local political issues—should also send delegations and help monitor resettlement sites after people have been moved. Unfortunately, since it is well known that "the offices overseeing resettlement work have little real power and the accounting and auditing systems in China are unsound," the benefits from such increased monitoring are questionable, especially for such a high priority project as the Three Gorges Dam in which individual leaders like Li Peng have invested so much prestige.[57] In short, if China is to avoid the widespread resentment among resettlers that followed previous large-scale projects and led to considerable social unrest, the old authoritarian approach must be replaced by a more "democratic spirit" that gives the interests of the local population greater legitimacy and can begin to bring China's practices more in line with the principles of sustainable development.[58]

Continuing the Debate

The two issues of land usage and popular input central to sustainable development are both evident in the case of the Three Gorges project. On the question of land usage, dam supporters and critics differ over critical *technical* issues of how much, if any, barren land is available in the region for development and whether farmers currently cultivating the rich river bottom land can equal their present income levels by shifting cash crop production to mountain slopes. Differences also exist over whether the resettlement of large numbers of farmers on the mountain slopes will exacerbate or only marginally affect the region's environment, specifically the water quality of the river, which has already suffered from industrial and residential sources of pollution. In this sense, the debate on land usage is occurring within the framework of sustainable development that both parties ostensibly accept, though with radically different conclusions about the impact of the dam project. While dam supporters push for construction of the Three Gorges Dam in line with current specifications, critics advocate construction of a series of small and medium-size dams on the Yangtze tributaries, or, at a minimum, a reduction in the height of the Three Gorges Dam from 185 to 160 meters, which, they argue, would mean the inundation of less arable land, would require far fewer people to be relocated, and would involve less risky engineering.[59]

On the issue of popular input, however, the Chinese government makes no pretense that Three Gorges should be based on the principle of "listening to the people," especially those living in the affected region. In the ideology of development that still shapes the worldview of the red specialists who control the various state bureaucracies involved in such massive construction projects in China, local interests are considered excessively narrow, an obstacle to the macroeconomic and political goals that these projects serve. Political institutions in the region have not, therefore, been arranged to solicit local opinion and incorporate local needs so much as to lead a massive propaganda campaign that is aimed at convincing the locals that the project is inevitable and will add to national glory. To the extent that adherence to basic principles of sustainable development, such as considering the "specific social and cultural context in which the plan will be implemented," obstructs the construction project, they have been summarily dismissed by the Chinese government. Sufficient police and legal forces have, moreover, been deployed to make sure that local agitators cannot gain the upper hand and that demonstrations, such as those that have slowed the Narmada River project in India, do not occur in the Three Gorges area.[60] And where members of the Communist Party and local governments have paid more attention to local needs than to the interests of the dam, their careers have been threatened or even ended by the central authorities in Beijing.[61] By this political measure of sustainable development, at least, the Three Gorges Dam is already showing severe cracks.

Notes

1. World Commission on Environment and Development (WCED), *Our Common Future* (Oxford: Oxford University Press, 1987) and Y. K. Alagh and D. T. Buch, "The Sardar Sarovar Project and Sustainable Development," *Toward Sustainable Development: Struggling over India's Narmada River,* ed. William F. Fisher (Armonk, N.Y.: Sharpe, 1995), 291.
2. The definition of "sustainable development" employed here is currently applied in the "Report on the Ussuri River Watershed Land Use Project," which involves the gov-

ernments of China and Russia, Ecologically Sustainable Development, Inc., and the National Committee on U.S.-China Relations. See *Notes from the National Committee* (New York: National Committee on U.S.-China Relations, 1997), 7–8.

3. A slightly different version of the book, entitled *Whose Yangtze? [Sheide Changjiang?]*, ed. Dai Qing and Xu Weijia, was published in Hong Kong by Oxford University Press, 1996.

4. Two of China's top leaders, President and CCP General Secretary Jiang Zemin and the economic czar and current premier Zhu Rongji, have expressed little support for the dam, although Jiang did officiate at the formal diversion of the Yangtze River at the Sandouping dam site on November 8, 1997—an event Zhu Rongji failed to attend. The major supporter of the dam is the former premier Li Peng. During one visitation to the dam site, Qiao Shi, a Politburo member, expressed considerable concern about the quality of construction at the project, but he was unceremoniously dropped from the CCP leadership at the September 1997 Fifteenth Party Congress. Xinhua (New China News Agency), November 12, 1995, and Xinhua, June 19, 1996.

5. China's monumental environmental problems are explored in Vaclav Smil, *Environmental Problems in China: Estimates of Economic Costs*, East-West Center Special Reports, no. 5 (Honolulu: University of Hawaii, 1996), and Vaclav Smil, *China's Environmental Crisis: An Inquiry into the Limits of National Development* (Armonk, N.Y.: Sharpe, 1993). The impact of Soviet development on the Russian ecology and society is reported in *Ecocide in the USSR*, ed. Murray Feshbach and Alfred Friendly Jr. (New York: Basic Books, 1992).

6. The concept of sustainable development gained support in China in the 1994 "Agenda 21" document and in the recently promulgated Ninth Five Year Plan (1996–2000). The Fifteenth Chinese Communist Party Congress, held in September 1997, also stated that China must implement sustainable development strategies. There is, however, evident confusion in China over "sustainable" versus "sustained" development as Chinese leaders often employ the latter, interpreting it simply as long-term and rapid economic growth, which remains the number one priority of the national leadership. Christiane Beuermann, "China and Climate Change," in *International Politics of Climate Change: Key Issues and Critical Actors*, ed. Gunnar Fermann (Stockholm: Scandinavian University Press, 1997), 228.

7. In a report entitled *China–U.S. Relations in the Twenty-First Century: Fostering Cooperation, Preventing Conflict* (New York: Columbia University, 1996), the American Assembly, Columbia University, urged China's participation in the U.S.-Asian Environmental Partnership. Other joint efforts relevant to sustainable development include the "Energy Efficiency and Renewable Energy Protocol" agreement signed in February 1995 by the U.S. Department of Energy and the Chinese State Science and Technology Commission. China is judged as having a substantial capacity for collaborating with foreign institutions and participating in the international scientific community concerned with global environmental issues, yet the country remains adamantly opposed to making commitments to greenhouse gas emissions reduction targets and timetables. Beuermann, "China and Climate Change," 224, 232.

8. J. A. Veltrop, "Water, Dams, and Hydropower in the Coming Decades," *International Water Power and Dam Construction* 43, no. 6 (1991): 37–46; Thomas Russo, "Making Hydropower Sustainable," *Fortnightly* 133 (January 1995): 14–19.

9. Tim Jackson, "Joint Implementation and Cost-Effectiveness under the Framework Convention on Climate Change," *Energy Policy* 23, no. 2 (1995): 117.

10. "Status Report/China Energy and Efficiency—Information Page," February 1998, 1 (http://www.oit.doe.gov/ International/China.htm).

11. Since the early 1980s, the Chinese economy has grown by about 126 percent, whereas energy consumption increased by only 61 percent. "Status Report/China Energy and Efficiency." Overall energy efficiency in China, however, is about 32 percent, 10 percent lower than developed countries in the world, while GDP per unit of

energy consumption is about one-half to one-third of that of developed countries. See "Li Peng's China Energy Speech," a summary of an article published in *People's Daily,* May 30, 1997 (http://www.pnl.gov/china/lipeng.htm).

12. In 1993, China became a net oil importer for the first time when total imports jumped by 29 percent in value. This led Chinese officials to backtrack on oil pricing reforms and to impose a temporary import ban in 1994. In regard to natural gas, China has proven reserves of 1.3 trillion cubic meters, but extracting and using this resource has been slow. China has installed 2.1 gigawatts of nuclear power, but this accounts for only 1 percent of the national capacity for electricity generation. Another 6.6 gigawatts capacity will be added by 2005 and provide 2 percent of capacity. "Li Peng's China Energy Speech."

13. In 1994, China generated 926 billion kilowatt-hours of electricity, 19 percent of which came from hydropower. By the year 2020, China will become the world's largest emitter of carbon dioxide gases even with its turn to greater reliance on hydro, nuclear, and alternative sources of energy. *China Statistical Yearbook, 1996* (Beijing: Tongji Chubanshe [Tongji Publishing House]), 203–207, and Beuermann, "China and Climate Change," 215, 230.

14. After the Three Gorges Dam, the second largest project in China is the Xiaolangdi Dam undergoing construction on the Yellow River. Unlike the Three Gorges, it involves irrigation and is slated to increase crop yields on about 2 million hectares of land and improve the labor productivity of about 4.5 million farmers, whose incomes are expected to rise by 33 percent in Henan and 12 percent in nearby Shandong. For this and other reasons, Xiaolangdi, unlike Three Gorges, has received funding from the World Bank. Tony Walker, "Virtuous Dam Rises on Yellow River," *Financial Times,* May 2, 1997.

15. For official Chinese statements on the Three Gorges, see China Yangtze Three Gorges Project Development Corporation, *The Three Gorges Project,* June 1996, and Zhu Rulan et al., "The Three Gorges Project: Key to the Development of the Yangtze River," *Civil Engineering Practice* (Journal of the Boston Society of Civil Engineers Section/ASCE) 12 (spring/summer 1997): 39–72. For statements of support by U.S. companies with potential commercial involvement in the project, see, for instance, *A Project to Save Lives and Benefit a Nation,* issued by J. M. Voith Inc.

16. "Raging Yangtze Kills 2,000," Associated Press, Beijing, August 6, 1998.

17. Nineteen cities and 326 villages are slated for partial or full inundation by the dam once it is completed in 2009.

18. "Statement of the Board of Directors of the Export-Import Bank of the United States," Martin A. Kamarck, President and Chairman, May 30, 1996, and Samuel R. Berger, White House, "Memorandum for [former] Chairman and President, Mr. Kenneth D. Brody, Export-Import Bank of the United States, Three Gorges Project in PRC," September 22, 1995. Current specifications for the Three Gorges Dam call for a dam crest of 185 meters, dam length of 2,000 meters, normal pool level of 175 meters, total storage capacity of 39.3 billion cubic meters, and flood control storage of 22.1 billion cubic meters.

19. William Wanli Huang, "The Gigantic Yangtze Three Gorges Dam Must Never Be Built," and "The Limited Benefits of Flood Control: An Interview with Lu Qinkan," *Civil Engineering Practice* 12 (spring/summer 1997): 93–98 and 99–103, respectively. The former is the most senior hydrologist in China and has opposed the Three Gorges since the 1950s. The latter was deputy chief engineer in China's Ministry of Water Resources and Electric Power; in 1988 he refused to sign the leading group's assessment for the Three Gorges project.

20. Dai Qing, "The Three Gorges Project and Sustainable Development in China," John R. Freeman Lecture, Massachusetts Institute of Technology, April 16, 1996, *Civil Engineering Practice* 12 (spring/summer 1997): 79–92. The cost of the dam was initially set at $6 billion and is now estimated to be $25 billion when completed in 2009. Some critics, however, argue that the cost will reach $75 billion.

21. Dai Qing, "The Three Gorges Project: A Symbol of Uncontrolled Development in the Late Twentieth Century," in *The River Dragon Has Come! The Three Gorges Dam and the Fate of China's Yangtze River and Its People*, ed. John Thibodeau and Philip Williams, trans. Yi Ming (Armonk, N.Y.: Sharpe, 1997).

22. Debate and questions about the project by dam critics were summarily cut off by the NPC chair, Wan Li. Dai Qing, *Yangtze! Yangtze! Debate over the Three Gorges Project*, ed. Patricia Adams and John Thibodeau, trans. Yi Ming (Toronto: Probe International, 1994), 113.

23. In the case of the Three Gorges, the major bureaucratic backers are the Ministry of Water Resources and the Yangtze Valley Planning Office, each of which employs tens of thousands of people and maintains control over huge construction gangs. Both evidently see the Three Gorges as part of a concerted effort by Beijing to break the emerging provincial-level control of China's power-generating capacity under the economic reforms. Michel Oksenberg and Kenneth Lieberthal, *Policy-Making in China: Leaders, Structures, and Processes* (Princeton: Princeton University Press, 1988), chap. 6.

24. A major critic of hydropower throughout the world has made this argument for all big dams, which he believes violate the fundamental principles of sustainable development. Patrick McCully, *Silenced Rivers: The Ecology and Politics of Large Dams* (London: Zed Books, 1997), 140. Species endangered by the Three Gorges Dam include the Chinese river dolphin, the Yangtze River sturgeon, and the Siberian crane.

25. See "Project Title: China: Efficient Industrial Boilers," Proposal to the World Bank Global Environmental Trust Fund (http://www.worldbank.org/htm/def).

26. Fei Xiaotong, *Peasant Life in China: A Field Study of Country Life in the Yangtze Valley* (New York: Dutton, 1939), 181.

27. Estimates of the annual flow of rock and earth into the Yangtze range from 40 million to 640 million tons. Vaclav Smil, *The Bad Earth: Environmental Degradation in China* (Armonk, N.Y.: Sharpe, 1984), 87.

28. Jun Jing, "Rural Resettlement: Past Lessons for the Three Gorges Project," *China Journal*, July 1997, 65–92. Professor Jing has carried out extensive research in China among "reservoir relocatees," especially in the remote Gansu Province.

29. Mou Mo and Cai Wenmei, "Review of the History of Population Resettlement in the Xin'an River Power Station Project," in Thibodeau and Williams, *The River Dragon Has Come!*, 104–123, and Jun Jing, "Rural Resettlement."

30. Leng Meng, "The Massive Population Resettlement on the Yellow River" (Huanghe dayimin), *Chinese Writers* (Zhongguo zuojia) (1996), 60–92, translated in *Chinese Studies in Sociology and Anthropology* (Armonk, N.Y.: Sharpe, forthcoming).

31. Li Boning (a major figure in charge of resettlement in the Three Gorges region), "General Plan for Population Resettlement" and "Opinions and Recommendations on the Three Gorges Project," in Thibodeau and Williams, *The River Dragon Has Come!*, 40–50, and Dai Qing, *Yangtze! Yangtze!*, 89–106.

32. Li Boning, "General Plan for Population Resettlement," 42.

33. Forty-two percent of farmers in one village polled expect "drastic reductions" in income despite government promises to the contrary. Ding Qigang, "What Are the Three Gorges Resettlers Thinking?" in Thibodeau and Williams, *The River Dragon Has Come!*, 70–89.

34. According to an independent survey recently conducted in the Three Gorges region, "the resettlement program . . . has been plagued by inadequate compensation and a shortage of new jobs and farmland for people being relocated." Eric Eckholm, "Relocations for China Dam Are Found to Lag," *New York Times*, March 12, 1998.

35. This pattern of optimistic forecasts by government officials and the bleak realities that confront resettled farmers after resettlement has occurred in the case of several hydrostation projects in China, such as the Liujiaxia dam in Gansu Province. Jun Jing, "Rural Resettlement." For similar experiences among dam "oustees" in India, see Fisher, *Toward Sustainable Development*.

36. Qi Ren (pseudonym), "Is Developmental Resettlement Possible?" in Thibodeau and Williams, *The River Dragon Has Come!*, 50–62.
37. Ibid., 59.
38. Ibid., 59–60. This author also describes the Three Gorges region as "very mountainous, [where] land is [already] scarce, and population density is high" (57).
39. Ibid., 60 and 61.
40. This has led some local farmers to convert their lands to a new crop—opium. Richard Hayman, "Epilogue," in Thibodeau and Williams, *The River Dragon Has Come!*, 177–190.
41. By 1991, prospects for major industrial employment in Badong and other areas were downplayed by government officials, who shifted their concerns to relocating farmers to new barren land. Jun Jing, "Rural Resettlement," and Eckholm, "Relocations for China Dam Are Found to Lag."
42. Around 100 million people now compose this army of "floating laborers."
43. Li Boning, "General Plan for Resettlement," in Thibodeau and Williams, *The River Dragon Has Come!*, 45.
44. In the 1950s, 20 percent of the Three Gorges area was forested, but by the 1990s this had been reduced to 10 percent with concomitant increases in landslides and sediment flow into the Yangtze. Chen Guojie, "The Environmental Impacts of Resettlement in the Three Gorges," in Thibodeau and Williams, *The River Dragon Has Come!*, 63–69.
45. Jin Hui, "Water Pollution in the Three Gorges Reservoir," in Thibodeau and Williams, *The River Dragon Has Come!*, 160–170. Mercury, cadmium, chromium, arsenic, phenol, lead, and cyanide are contained in the wastewater that now flows into the Yangtze.
46. Shui Fu, "A Profile of Dams in China," in Thibodeau and Williams, *The River Dragon Has Come!*, 20–21.
47. Quoted in Hayman, "Epilogue," 180.
48. The role of the NPC and the impact of reforms on its institutional configuration is analyzed in Kevin O'Brien, *Reform without Liberalization: China's National People's Congress and the Politics of Institutional Change* (Cambridge: Cambridge University Press, 1990).
49. Dai Qing, *Yangtze! Yangtze!*, 107–117. Dai Qing argues that in backing the dam, Deng Xiaoping made the project virtually unassailable in party councils. Dai Qing, "The Three Gorges Project: A Symbol of Uncontrolled Development," 13.
50. Quoted in Human Rights Watch/Asia, from a report by Human Rights Watch, *The Three Gorges Dam in China: Forced Resettlement, Suppression of Dissent and Labor Rights Concerns*, February 1995, 7:10.
51. Qing Heng, Li Jan, Hu Tiheng, and Liu Xinyu (cadres of the public security bureau in Wanxian, county), "Public Safety and Security in the Three Gorges Area," internal government document acquired by Human Rights Watch/Asia.
52. Human Rights Watch/Asia *The Three Gorges Dam in China.*
53. This was apparently the case with Sichuan's first party secretary, who has vehemently opposed the project. As a result, the city of Chongqing—the largest municipality in the country, with 14 million people—was separated from Sichuan and granted province-level status. All its political leaders, some of whom were arrested on charges of corruption, were replaced with appointees from Beijing. Interviews, Sichuan sources and Hayman, "Epilogue," 187.
54. A major critic of the dam lost his post at the *Yangtze River Daily*, a local newspaper.
55. Xinhua, April 2, 1993, and AFP (Agence France-Presse), November 9, 1997.
56. Dai Qing, "The Three Gorges Project and Sustainable Development in China," 91.
57. Mou Mo and Cai Wenmei, "Review of the History of Population Resettlement," 123.
58. Resentment over past projects was so great that Dai Qing noted her fears in 1989 during the pro-democracy demonstrations that dispossessed reservoir refugees would

descend on China's cities and cause chaos. During the Cultural Revolution, the top official in charge of resettlement was assassinated. Dai Qing, *Yangtze! Yangtze!*, 130. Perhaps the best example of local interests being sacrificed in the project is that much housing under construction in Chongqing and other areas is too expensive for the locals and has been bought up by outsiders.

59. Alternate plans for the Three Gorges project call for twenty-six separate hydro stations on tributaries with a total generating capacity equivalent to the promised output of Three Gorges, and at less cost and disruption of the environment. Dai Qing, "The Three Gorges Project and Sustainable Development in China," 89. For a report on the risky practices occurring at the Three Gorges Dam site and the "cavalier" attitude of Chinese engineers, see Leonard S. Sklar and Am L. Luers (Sklar-Luers and Associates), "Report on a Site Visit to the Three Gorges Dam, Yangtze River, Hubei Province, China," October 17–18, 1997, available on Internet from "owner-irn-three-gorges@igc.org" (November 11, 1997).

60. Protests in China erupted among relocatees in Hubei in March 1994. *Eastern Express*, Hong Kong, March 4, 1994, 9, reprinted in *FBIS-China,* March 9, 1994, 60. Popular mobilization against the Narmada Dam in India is vividly recounted in Fisher, *Toward Sustainable Development.*

61. Although he still survives, the party secretary of Sichuan drew considerable fire when he personally traveled to Beijing to complain about the embezzlement and corruption of resettlement funds. Interview, Sichuan source.

15

Mining, Environmental Protection, and Sustainable Development in Indonesia

Richard O. Miller

In *Our Common Future*, the World Commission on Environment and Development (the Brundtland Commission) defined sustainable development as "development that meets the needs of the present without compromising the ability of future generations to meet their own needs."[1] Since the Brundtland Commission brought the concept of sustainable development to wider attention, much discussion has centered on its precise meaning and its utility as a source of policy guidance or inspiration. The proliferation of definitions means that to some, "[s]ustainable development has become devalued to a point where . . . it is now just a cliché."[2]

For many countries eager to raise their standard of living and increase economic growth, "sustainable development" as defined by the Brundtland Commission seems to imply a low rate of economic growth that inhibits their ability to develop their energy and mineral resources. Mining is an extractive enterprise. The resources that it exploits are nonrenewable. Many citizens in developing countries do not view mining as an enterprise in which these resources are extracted at a "sustainable" rate. Instead, mining sustains development, contributing to economic growth, enlarging the technological base, and promoting industrial development.

Throughout the world, mining has become increasingly recognized as a potential "engine of development," providing jobs, expanding technological capacity, and generating national income. At the same time, and in many cases belatedly, mining's potential for causing substantial and long-term environmental damage is being viewed with alarm.[3]

The resources exploited by mining are nonrenewable—mineral deposits are limited, and ore bodies are finite. However, the resources that are affected by mining are renewable—water, land, and plant and animal life.

Many countries, including the United States, have sad legacies from unregulated or poorly regulated mining. Appalachian streams that are acidic, western rivers and tributaries that are sterile, and scarred and unproductive lands in the Midwest that are only notable as chronicles of environmental destruction are eloquent examples of what can occur when minerals are exploited without regard to environmental impacts on other resources.

Many developing countries regard the mineral resources they possess as a potential engine of development—providing the investment, infrastructure, and capital to promote other nation-building activities. Given the fact that most developing countries with mineral resources have opted to exploit them, the dilemma for mining and for environmental protection becomes how to extract mineral resources economically and in a way that promotes, rather than impedes, long-term development.

Indonesia, one of the most dynamic economies in all of Asia during the 1980s and much of the 1990s, is a useful example of the difficult problems that are faced by countries that have concluded that mineral development is a vital component of future growth. Well aware of the benefits that development can bring, Indonesia also recognizes that such development can significantly affect the prospects for long term-growth, particularly when it affects the integrity of the country's ecosystems.

The fourth most populous country in the world, and the largest predominantly Muslim state, Indonesia contains some of the most diverse populations and cultures of any developing country. Its history and culture are a rich layering of Hindu and Buddhist, Muslim and Christian religions and Asian, Indic, indigenous, and colonial influences. Long valued for their exotic woods, textiles, and spices, the "Spice Islands" of history now draw interest from metropolitan nations because of the variety and richness of their natural and mineral resources. Indonesia's tropical hardwood stands are the largest outside of the Amazon rain forest and shelter rare and endangered species while providing sustenance for traditional cultures and lifeways throughout an archipelago that numbers in excess of 13,000 islands and stretches across three time zones. The forest resources of Indonesia represent over half of the tropical forest in Asia.

Indonesia also enjoys significant mineral resources, and mineral development has played a major role in the nation's economic history. Tin mining began in the early eighteenth century, coal mining was undertaken in the mid-nineteenth century, and gold, copper, nickel, as well as many industrial minerals, are actively mined. Since the late 1960s, offshore petroleum reserves also have been developed and provided much of the capital that supported economic diversification and growth during the 1970s and early 1980s.

The purpose of this chapter is to describe the mining sector's role in development and social change in Indonesia and its contribution to promoting or retarding sustainable development. A major focus of this chapter is the implementation of environmental policy in a developing country such as Indonesia. The scholar Dwight Y. King has suggested that actual policy implementation is often difficult in developing countries because they lack the institutional infrastructure and other resources needed to translate generalized policy effectively into specific actions needed for successful implementation.[4] Thus, many developing countries have laudable objectives for environmental protection and management and can point to elaborate legislative enactments and regulatory schemes. However, these do not necessarily lead to environmental protection on the ground.

Since the late 1980s, the mining sector has occupied an important position in the overall development scheme of the Indonesian government. As the Ministry of Mines and Energy's Coal Policy Draft Strategic Plan points out, coal mining will provide "a competitive and reliable source of energy for domestic [and] fiscal revenue through generation of taxes, duties, royalties and levies." [5] Development of all types of minerals has expanded considerably since the late 1970s. As a result of the reforms of the banking sector and easing of foreign investment restrictions, the structure of the mining industry has also changed. Formerly, mines were either state owned or were joint ventures between private companies and the Indonesian government. Joint ventures between private foreign firms and Indonesian firms are now permitted, and participation in the mining sector by foreign firms has increased significantly.

The world's largest known gold deposit is being mined in Irian Jaya and gold, copper, and molybdenum mining development and exploration activities are being pursued in many areas of Indonesia. Along with major deposits of valuable ores, Indonesia has the ninth largest coal reserves in the world, approaching 36 billion tons.[6] These reserves are being actively developed to support the planned expansion of the country's electric power industry and, to a lesser extent, to serve as a source of foreign exchange. During the 1970s and early 1980s much of Indonesia's economic development was financed by the expansion of petroleum production. Coal reserves are expected to play an equally significant role in the future. Bituminous coal production has increased from 10.9 metric tons in 1990 to 41.8 metric tons in 1995.[7] Most of the new coal mining activity is in the form of foreign/domestic joint ventures that have been initiated over the last few years. Most new coal mining activity is on the island of Kalimantan, where forty-five new operations are under way. While much of this coal will be directed to domestic power production, there is a strong export market for Indonesian coal in Southeast Asia.

According to the World Bank, the development of these and other resources over the past three decades has led to a reduction in poverty and helped Indonesia to be counted among those countries whose economic development and continued growth seems assured. The World Bank noted, "Sustained rapid growth has allowed living standards to improve significantly, with a 4.5% annual increase in per capita income since 1970."[8] The Bank also cited another report, which found that "over the past two decades Indonesia has had the highest annual average reduction in the incidence of poverty of all the countries studied."[9]

The considerable progress being made in the alleviation of poverty and the transformation to a modern industrial economy has not come without cost. The World Bank report cited above also notes that Indonesia's rapid growth has had significant impacts upon the natural environment. "[T]he pace and pattern of development have led to growing concern about the sustainable use of natural resources (land, forests, water and energy) and the social and economic costs of urban and industrial pollution." [10] In its drive to industrialize and exploit its rich resources, Indonesia has experienced extensive damage to many of its ecosystems and the resource values that they contain. Mining is among the many activities that are now affecting the ecosystems of Indonesia. The rapid expansion of the mining sector is part of an array of challenges to the institutional capacity of the government to achieve environmental protection.

Mining, the Environment, and Development

While most industries affect the environment, perhaps none is so visible in its effects and potentially so dramatic in its consequences for the environment as mining. Mining brings to any developmental context a host of pressures that strain the capacity of institutions to mitigate environmental impacts and manage social change. At the same time, mining activity also brings a set of benefits, which can act to strengthen public institutions, improve the lives of large segments of the population, and dramatically affect the fabric of local communities.

Mining's Potential Environmental Impacts

As mentioned earlier, mining is an extractive activity that affects other resources. Environmental problems from mining include the effects on land and topsoil resources where vegetation and habitat are destroyed during the mining process, and effects on water quality—discharges from mining operations can add to siltation, release heavy metals and other toxics into water systems, destroy streamflows, and damage aquifers. Where disturbed land is not adequately reclaimed or reclamation is not completed on a timely basis, erosion and permanent loss of topsoil can occur, with concomitant damage to soil productivity, habitat, and water quality. Where naturally occurring recovery processes are not effective or where they are slow, mining damage can be virtually permanent. Lost topsoil takes land out of productive use; where water flows through mined areas, becomes acid, and then discharges into streams, it destroys fisheries; where abandoned mine wastes leach toxic chemicals into ground water, they threaten community water supplies. In the United States, there are areas where this kind of environmental damage is still evident from mining that took place half a century ago. Efforts to reclaim these lands are very costly. Where water treatment is required, remediation can mean expensive cleanups and perpetual treatment.

In Indonesia, mining activity confronts several challenges. The climate of Indonesia is equatorial, with heavy rainfall, ranging from two to four meters per year, punctuated with brief dusty dry seasons. These monsoon conditions make mining more difficult and, equally important, can make land reclamation objectives harder to achieve, since heavy rainfall can cause rapid erosion and sedimentation—washing away replantings and hampering the revegetation effort. Dry seasons, when they are prolonged, as was the case in 1997 and 1998, bring increased danger from brush and forest fires. Forest fires or fires that originate as the result of land clearing can ignite surface coal outcrops, which can become a health and safety hazard that is difficult and expensive to eliminate.

Topography also complicates mining activity. Steep slopes and areas of seismic instability in Indonesia mean that practices of disposal of spoil and tailings must be very carefully designed and implemented. The isolation of many mines increases development and production costs and also adds to the costs and effort required of the government to make regular inspections and ensure sustained environmental compliance.

Mining and Industrial Development

While the potential environmental impacts are significant, mining can also have consequences that developing countries find attractive. Modern mining brings an advanced technology to a country. Often regarded as a technologically backward sector, the international mining industry has undergone major advances since the late 1960s that have led to pronounced increases in the capacity of mines, their productivity, and environmental restoration capability. This transformation has made mining a capital- rather than a labor-intensive industry, where sophisticated machinery is used to extract minerals on a large scale. Although no longer demanding large supplies of labor, mining can work to upgrade local labor forces, providing them with new technical skills. Mining activities also create a demand for support services that can have a high technical and scientific component. Analytical laboratories, equipment supply and maintenance, and a well-functioning business infrastructure are required to support modern mining. These activities are complementary to a large number of other business and manufacturing operations and may have an extensive technical multiplier effect.

Reclamation of mined lands is an element of mining that brings technical applications to bear on environmental problems that are not unique to mining. Forestry and construction are activities that also can disturb lands. Mining reclamation technology can be transferred into these sectors, with beneficial results. The physical support infrastructure necessary for mining— roads, bridges, loading facilities, housing, and transportation sites such as ports and landing areas—can become the beginnings of expanded infrastructure for development.

Mining not only requires a substantial capital investment; it requires long-term commitments of human and material resources. A typical mine can be in operation for twenty to forty years. This means that its production and its effects, both positive and negative, can be considered in government planning decisions for a long time, offering the possibility of long-term investments in an area and possibly offering a source of economic stability for generations.

Indonesia's Structure for Environmental Protection

Indonesia's efforts to manage the social and environmental problems associated with mining activity have been long-standing, dating back to the colonial era. Laws developed for regulating mining following the departure of the Dutch in 1949 were vague and directed more to ensuring that the post-colonial regime obtained revenue from mineral development. Thus, from the beginning of the modern epoch the Indonesian government recognized the revenue-generating capacity of mining and gave it priority. Revenues from mineral extraction—petroleum, gold, tin, and coal—were all expected to contribute to financing development projects. Revenue, however, was not the only focus. Early post-colonial laws, such as the Law on the Basic Provisions of Mining and Its Implementing Regulations of 1967, provide significant authority to government officials responsible for protecting the environment and ensuring that mining companies comply with the terms of the agreements developed as part of the mineral exploitation process.

At the present time, Indonesia's approach to environmental protection is fairly typical of most developing countries. Protection of the environment emerged as a political issue during the 1970s, and environmental policy was established through a framework of laws and regulations over the next decade. This structure has been expanded and supplemented over the years. Regulations have been developed along sectoral or commodity lines by the ministries responsible for the activity or commodity. Typically, they focus on the management of the activity or the exploitation of the commodity.

The early laws and their implementing regulations have been buttressed by additional legislation dealing directly with environmental protection and supplemented by regulatory decrees. The legal and regulatory scheme for environmental protection has been gradually articulated so that all activities and commodities are included. Indeed, many of the concepts relating to environmental management and many of the tools for ensuring effective environmental protection through regulation that are found in the United States and western Europe are in place in Indonesia.

The basic statute establishing environmental management and protection policy for Indonesia is Act No. 4 of 1982.[11] This act establishes basic rights and obligations and also creates a conceptual framework that incorporates very progressive ideas concerning the importance of ecosystems, the concept of carrying capacity, and the recognition of the government's obligation "[t]o cultivate and develop the public's awareness of its responsibility in the management of the living environment."[12] Act No. 4 also continues a policy established by earlier legislation, which designated as government property all mineral resources within Indonesia. This provides the government a substantial degree of control over resource development and exploitation.

Under the 1982 law, the government's ability to regulate and to control environmental impacts is quite sweeping. National policy requires that "[t]he utilization of man-made resources which affect the livelihood of the general public shall be regulated by the State for the maximum welfare of the people." The national government has the authority to "regulate the allocation, development, use, reuse, recycling, provision, management and supervision of resources [and] regulate legal actions and legal relations between persons and/or other legal subjects pertaining to resources."[13]

Regarding mining, the law continues and makes more explicit earlier references regarding damages to the environment. Article 20 states, "Whosoever damages and/or pollutes the living environment is liable for payment of compensation to victims whose rights to a good and healthy living environment have been violated." And, especially important for mining, it declares, "Whosoever damages and/or pollutes the living environment is liable for payment to the State of the costs of the restoration of the living environment."

This "polluter pays" principle means that mine operators have a legal obligation to pay for any environmental damage they cause. If they fail to do so, the government can step in and reclaim the land and pursue the company for damages. A recently issued decree from the Ministry of Mines and Energy requiring financial guarantees (bonding) from mine operators provides an additional mechanism to ensure that obligations to reclaim land are fulfilled.[14]

Article 22 of the act also establishes a system of fines and penalties for the commission of willful or negligent acts that cause environmental damage.[15] Article 16 establishes the requirement that any planned activity that is "considered likely to have a significant impact on the environment must be accompanied with an analysis of environmental impact, carried out according to government regulations."[16] In the accompanying elucidation of the act's provisions, the broad outlines of an environmental assessment process are established. The impact assessment must consider the impacts of the proposed activity on a wide range of social and natural resources values. Additional guidelines regarding the determination of significant impacts were issued by the Ministry of Population and Environment in 1987.[17]

This basic framework was supplemented by Government Regulation No. 29 of 1986, which developed an environmental impact assessment process (Analisis Mengenai Dampak Lingkungan, or AMDAL).[18] This regulation provides substantial guidance to project or development proponents regarding the nature of the analysis and documents to be submitted for review by the government. The regulation established AMDAL commissions within each ministry to assess environmental impacts of proposed activities that fall within the ministries' areas of responsibility.

In addition, institutional capacity for environmental management was strengthened by the creation of the Environmental Impact Management Agency (BAPEDAL) in 1990. In 1993, BAPEDAL issued Government Regulation No. 51 regarding environmental impact assessment, which revoked and modified earlier decrees dealing with impact assessment. It established requirements for the scoping document known as the Terms of Reference, which essentially describes baseline environmental conditions and how the proposed action may affect these conditions. It also clarified the relationship between environmental impact statements, environmental management plans, and environmental monitoring plans. The fundamental goal of this series of regulations was to make environmental impact assessments and the process for conducting them an integral part of the determination of a proposed project's feasibility. Rather than focusing on the economic or technical issues associated with a project, the Terms of Reference attempts to predict the effects of the activity on the environment. It also establishes categories of phenomena that should be studied, including climate, physiography, biology, and hydrology, as well as social aspects such as effects on demography, culture, and economics.

Importantly, Article 10 of this regulation requires that AMDAL reviewing commissions issue a decision on the environmental impact statement within forty-five days of its submission. Absent any action by the commission within the specified time limits, the submission shall be considered as having been approved.

Primary responsibility for the management and development of Indonesia's mineral and energy resources rests with the Ministry of Mines and Energy. The ministry has supplemented the general mining laws with specific regulations and decrees, including ministry-specific decrees for implementing the environmental statutes and decrees discussed earlier.

The Implementation Record

King and the political scientist Andrew MacIntyre have observed that although large-scale policies or prescriptions can be developed, their implementation at the local level is far less certain. According to MacIntyre, the limitations of Indonesian institutions to implement change below the national level relate primarily to economic management; the same may be true of the capacity of Indonesian institutions to implement policy effectively at the on-the-ground level of environmental management.

At this time, a reasonably comprehensive regulatory and enforcement scheme is in place for managing the environmental effects of mining. It is broad in scope, and establishes a process whereby decision makers can make judgments regarding the environmental impacts from proposed mineral development. Explanatory notes and preambles that accompany legislation and regulations link mining and environmental protection to sustainable and socially optimal development. However, the real test of the effectiveness of regulatory policy is the impact of that policy on the ground.

The specific requirements for firms to submit the information used by the government to determine the technical adequacy of environmental management plans—Indonesia's "regulatory infrastructure"—are vague and lack important details. The information used by government officials to determine the degree of compliance with environmental requirements is also often incomplete and imprecise. Thus, government decision makers are often confronted with mining proposals that describe only in a general way what activities are planned, when they are scheduled, and where they will be located. This means that site-specific impacts are difficult to predict and analyze. Environmental performance standards are often couched in general terms, which makes determination of compliance difficult and subject to dispute.

A major difference between this and the U.S. scheme for regulating surface coal mining is the degree of specificity of the information requirements. The United States requires detailed information, which imposes a significant collection and analysis burden on both mine operators and the reviewing agency authority. Such detail enables the regulatory authority to make precise judgments about the feasibility of mining and whether mine operators can meet environmental protection standards. It should be noted that this elaborate regulatory structure has not developed quickly, and its contours did not go uncontested. The existing American regulatory program for surface coal mining was first promulgated in 1978. Many aspects of it were challenged in the courts and some parts of the program still await final legal action.

The scholar Carl H. Petrich observed that, in contrast, there has been little in the way of legal interpretation and activism relating to Indonesia's environmental protection scheme. Indonesian culture tends to avoid overt conflict, preferring the development of an informal consensus on policy choices. This societal preference is expressed in the 1982 law, which "stipulated that all disputing sides settle their conflicts through negotiations or mediation before a legal settlement in court is sought."[19]

This cultural predilection for consensus, while damping down conflict, also tends to limit the range of options that can be taken to enforce environmental laws. Penalty systems may indeed be in place, but their use is limited. No mine has ever been closed down as a result of failure to adhere to environmental protection requirements.

Staffing constraints within the Ministry of Mines and Energy add to the difficulty of effective enforcement. The ministry has an inspection cadre of approximately 100 inspectors responsible for inspecting more than 260 mines scattered throughout an archipelago that stretches nearly 2,300 miles and contains some of the world's most difficult and challenging terrain and climate conditions, with very few roads for easy access to mine sites. Mines are required to be inspected every six months, an inspection rate that is in sharp contrast to the U.S. requirement of a partial inspection at least once per month and a complete inspection every three months. Increase in mining activity has led to a concomitant increase in the submission of mining proposals for approval by the ministry and the ministerial-level AMDAL commission established to review and approve the plans. These documents resemble the Environmental Impact Statements that often accompany project proposals for mining activities on federal lands in the United States. They are lengthy, with extensive citations regarding flora and fauna, climate, hydrology, and related resources, and include methods and technologies for mitigating environmental impacts.

However, their capacity to serve as an inspection platform for enforcement is limited. The degree of detail in the typical proposal does not often permit a reviewer to relate discrete activities to specific geographic locations on a map. This can create significant problems for enforcement. For example, without precise geographic information, it is difficult to determine whether a company is operating within the boundaries of the designated area. Without specific design and engineering standards for such important components of a mining operation as sedimentation ponds, it is difficult to determine whether they are constructed so that they have the storage capacity needed to meet the goal of preventing suspended solids from running off the mine site.

Regulatory specificity does not develop overnight. Often, the detailed requirements are elaborated in a series of regulatory refinements. If one looks at the evolution of the Indonesian regulatory scheme, it is evident that every new decree contains a greater decree of specificity than the previous one. A good example of this is the requirement for financial guarantees. This requirement, intended to ensure that some land could be reclaimed in the event a company ceased mining due to bankruptcy, had been a general feature of early post-colonial mining laws. Over the years, the decrees implementing this requirement have become more detailed. The most recent iteration, issued in 1996, contains very specific financial requirements for financial guarantees to ensure reclamation.

However, in addition to the problems created by inadequate technical review capacity, the previously mentioned forty-five day limit for review of proposals is widely regarded as unrealistic and contributing to cursory reviews. While this time limit may be extended at the request of the commission if it determines that additional information is needed, the limitation can act as a "temporal hammer," precluding effective review of environmental information and the measures proposed by mine operators to protect the environment. As proposals increase in scope and complexity, this problem is certain to be aggravated.

Along with the increase in the scale of the proposals that are being presented to the AMDAL commissions, the sheer number of proposals is likely to continue to grow. Confronted with an increasing number of complex proposals, it would appear that absent a substantial infusion of technical review capacity to the AMDAL staffs, the only possible solution for improving reviews would be to stretch out the review process.

How does the already overtasked bureaucracy cope with the increase in workload? The ministry is well aware of the projected increase in mining activity and is attempting to respond to it. In addition to the new decrees issued or under development, the training of inspectors and analytical cadres has increased, and greater technical capability is being developed. Efforts are also under way to improve and reorganize the technical expertise available to the AMDAL commissions. This may include some restructuring as well as additional training in the analysis of environmental information.

Effective mining regulation does not occur on command. Any industry must learn to implement new requirements in its operations. Both the government and industry have learning curves when regulatory regimes are imposed or are significantly expanded. During the past two years, industry and the ministry have begun to focus more on the environmental consequences of mining operations. Decrees have been issued by the ministry that make the mine technical manager at a specific mine site responsible for environmental matters, including compliance. However, while this expanded authority at the mine site is promising, it is not at all clear that this new role is being effectively discharged.

All mining activity takes place in the context of Indonesian bureaucracy and politics. It is no secret that Indonesia has a high incidence of official corruption, both petty and on a truly grand scale.[20] Part of this is due to the low salaries of the bureaucracy, which provide incentives for venality. At the upper levels of government, high-ranking officials or members of their families are often included as "partners" or retained as "consultants" in joint ventures. Members of former president Suharto's family have a labyrinth of interests in all phases of economic activity in Indonesia, and this extends to the mining industry. This pattern of connection and obligation may restrain efforts to ensure compliance at some mines.

The Role of Large Companies in Achieving Environmental Protection

Indonesia has its own mining association, similar to those in the United States, which acts as a voice for the industry and serves as an informal sounding board for government policy initiatives that affect its members. In keeping with Indonesian cultural norms, policy relating to mining activities is developed through consensus building. The regulatory development process in the United States—with its proposed rulemakings, public comment period, and issuance of final rules, often as a prelude to litigation—is not found in Indonesia. Important draft decrees are informally reviewed by industry, and perspectives are obtained and incorporated to the extent needed to build a consensus on a specific regulation.[21]

Where industry is more likely to make its influence directly felt is in the obtaining of permits for mining and development. Typically, mining decisions are made easier when the Indonesian partner in the joint venture, and/or consultants hired to lend assistance to the project are well connected to the upper reaches of the government. A recent example of the excesses that can occur under these conditions is the Bre-X gold scandal. This combination of cloak-and-dagger and low comedy involved the Canadian mining exploration firm of Bre-X and a reported find of an enormous gold deposit in Kalimantan, Indonesia. Bre-X stock was the object of intense market speculation following announcements of a gold find that increased in size with every press release. Competitors for the prize scrambled to hire Suharto family members as "consultants" to their companies in an effort to influence government decisions on exploration and development permits. The company went bankrupt and investors lost millions of dollars when it became known that the exploration samples were salted. The reported "suicide" of the lead geologist for the company only added to the mystery.[22]

However, it is not easy to determine how or whether this directly translates into increased threats to the environment. Environmental information presented during the AMDAL review process would generally seem to meet existing requirements for scope and detail; the requirements themselves and their lack of specificity may be more important in determining the quality of environmental analysis and decision making. Scarce resources, particularly analytical staff within the government, make careful analysis of impacts more difficult to accomplish, particularly within the time frames for review established by the AMDAL process.

Environmental protection relies upon a structured regulatory scheme, employing various methods such as inspection and enforcement to achieve compliance. All of this rests upon the tacit assumption that when the standards are adhered to, the result will be some desired level of environmental protection.

Indonesia has a regulatory scheme in place, and inspection and enforcement efforts are made to achieve compliance. The overall level of compliance with the regulatory scheme is highly variable for many companies. However, this observation must be followed by the question of "compliance with what?" As noted, existing standards are often vague, and design and construction requirements, maintenance, and environmental management schedules are ill defined or absent. The level of "compliance" with these standards may indeed be high. However, vague standards make it difficult for regulatory authorities to measure actual environmental protection achieved. Under these conditions, it is hard to provide a definitive answer to the simple question: Are the regulatory prescriptions working?

Large mining companies compete in an environment of international markets, in which a premium is placed on efficiency and prices are continually under pressure.[23] Strong incentives for operational efficiency and maximum economic recovery of the resource exist in countries that have stringent environmental requirements that are uniformly enforced. Economically efficient mining tends to be less environmentally damaging than less efficient mining using outdated technologies. Methods of smelting and washing used by large companies tend to be more technologically and environmentally sophisticated. Such processes tend to be "closed systems," with substantial recycling of chemicals and water used in the extraction process.

On-the-ground observation suggests that large foreign firms do a better job of mine planning, achieve a higher level of environmental protection, and cause less long-term damage to the environment than do firms operating under older agreements or those that are state-run enterprises. Most large foreign firms have mining operations in countries in which environmental controls are strict and effectively enforced. The technology for compliance is substantially transferable, and large firms know how to mine without excessive environmental damage.

Operations that create the most severe environmental impacts are not those of large foreign companies that have been investing recently in mining operations in Indonesia. Although mines that under earlier policies were conducted as state enterprises have been gradually supplanted by new ventures and operational arrangements made possible by the investment reforms of the 1980s, state-owned mines continue to be operated. Visits to these mines and inspection of their operations indicate that they are not managed as efficiently as mines operating undxer the newer arrangements. State-owned mines tend to be operated with old equipment, have low relative rates of resource extraction, and neglect environmental protection and remediation.

While conducted on a lesser scale, it would appear that another source of threats to the environment may come from smaller mine operators, who are more difficult to regulate and who use mining practices that pose significant risks to the environment. Smaller operators also often suffer from poor capitalization, and as regulatory requirements increase, they may sacrifice whatever environmental protection they now achieve to remain economically viable. Indonesia also must contend with the environmental impacts of its substantial numbers of illegal mines. In illicit gold mining in Indonesia the extraction process usually makes use of mercury. The expended mercury, an extremely hazardous heavy metal, is often discharged into waters after separation from the gold. In addition, illegal mining creates extensive soil erosion and destroys habitats; the disturbed land with its lasting scars is never reclaimed. Because of their small size and the rugged geography of many areas in Indonesia, illegal mining operations are very difficult to control, and the environmental damage they cause is hard to contain. While it is not possible to judge with accuracy the degree of environmental harm that stems directly from illegal mining, it does seem likely that locally it may cause significant cumulative environmental damage.

Mining and Sustainable Development

Mining in Indonesia faces major technical difficulties. Current mining practices by many companies are not always adequate. Inefficient mining practices and poor reclamation mean that "[r]ivers used for human drinking water and food supplies are contaminated, carrying their load of soil, coal dust and heavy metals downstream, degrading wetlands, mangrove swamps, shallow seas and valuable fisheries." [24]

A closely related issue is how mining can be done so that nearby communities can be sustained. The intrusion of mining activities—the social and economic changes and dislocations that it can bring—are well known and are usefully addressed as a problem of sustainable development. Measures for the mitigation of the social and economic impacts of mining must be in place and effective if mining is to operate in a way that will allow local communities to continue to function. Working with nongovernmental organizations (NGOs) is an important component of effective mitigation, but in Indonesia progress in this area has been very uneven on the part of both industry and the government. NGOs are present in Indonesia and often have a presence in local communities; however, most observers would likely conclude that their ability to raise the level of environmental protection is constrained and their success limited. The former leadership in Indonesia was suspicious of NGOs and often worked to make them ineffective.

In regard to overall threats to the Indonesian environment, it may be that actual and potential harm to the environment is caused more by poor regulation of its forest resources, fisheries, and air quality than by mining. This seems to be the World Bank's conclusion in its report *Indonesia: Environment and Development*.

Mining: A Temporary Use or Long-Term Threat

In arguing for a national regulatory scheme for coal mining in the United States, advocates for a national act charged that, absent national legislation, individual states would compete with one another for mining activity through inadequate regulatory regimes and lax enforcement. Environmental groups expressed concern that without a national statute, state regulators would join one another in a "race to the bottom," where the low bidder would receive the bulk of industry interest. To some extent, there may be a similar concern at the international level. There is no reason to anticipate that the results of competition among developing countries for mining projects will be dramatically different from those that troubled environmental and citizens' groups in the United States.

Another challenge confronting regulatory institutions in Indonesia and elsewhere is that mining activity is expanding, and with limited investment capital, companies are selecting mining projects in which the potential return is greatest. As eastern Europe and the former Soviet Union are opened up to expanded mineral development, the limited amount of investment capital will be available for allocation to increasingly large numbers of potential investment projects. Faced with competition from other countries, some may initiate a bidding war for mineral development and participate in a race to the bottom, reflected in lowered environmental protection requirements and lax enforcement as a way to make their mineral resources appear more economically attractive.

At the same time, mining companies must go where the resources are, and it appears that some of the most significant mineral resources to be found anywhere are in Indonesia. It would seem clear that regulatory requirements for environmental protection, so long as they do not create undue economic burdens, would not act to inhibit mineral development activities in Indonesia. Most large mining companies are active in countries with sophisticated regulatory schemes and effective requirements for environmental management and protection. Thus, operating in a developing country does not routinely impose an unfamiliar set of requirements. The new environmental management challenges that are present are largely those associated with operating in locales where conditions are dramatically different from those previously experienced. Given the worldwide growth of mining activity, unfamiliar environments are becoming increasingly rare, and technologies for managing environmental impacts in exotic venues are being continually developed.

For mining to contribute to sustainable development, the most fundamental concern for policymakers should be the degree to which mining is regarded and conducted as a temporary use of the land. Where mining is viewed as a temporary use, reclamation can restore land to its former productivity or to other beneficial uses. Where mining is permitted to be the final use of the land, a debased and squalid resource that is a continuing source of environmental pollution is the legacy for future generations.

In developing countries like Indonesia, achieving the goal of environmental protection will, as elsewhere, depend on the degree to which the environmentally protective policies articulated at the national level are reflected in actual implementation and compliance. Carefully regulated mining is certainly compatible with and supportive of the concept of sustainable development. At the same time, considerable demands will be made on all developing countries to mobilize their mineral resources. Nations that are confronted with the challenges of burgeoning populations, rising expectations, and the active interest of large foreign firms may choose to regard mining primarily as a way to sustain development rather than as a means to achieve sustainable development. Such a choice made under what Peter Savage called the "logic of haste" that pressures for development impose may have local environmental consequences whose cumulative effects may render hollow grand national policies for environmental protection and conservation.[25]

Notes

The views expressed are the author's and may not necessarily reflect the views of the Office of Surface Mining or of the Department of the Interior.

1. World Commission on Environment and Development (Brundtland Commission) *Our Common Future* (London: Oxford University Press, 1987).
2. Johan Holmberg and Richard Sandbrook, "Sustainable Development: What Is to Be Done," in *Making Development Sustainable: Redefining Institutions, Policy, and Economics,* ed. Johan Holmberg (Cambridge: IUCN Publications Services, 1992; distributed in U.S. by Island Press, Washington, D.C.), 20.
3. Bharat B. Dhar and D. N. Thakur, *Mining and Environment: Proceedings of the First World Mining Environment Congress* (Brookfield, Vt.: A. A. Balkema, 1996).
4. Dwight Y. King, "Bureaucracy and Implementation of Complex Tasks in Rapidly Developing States: Evidence from Indonesia," *Journal of Comparative and International Development* 30 (winter 1995/96): 78–92; Andrew MacIntyre, "Politics and the Reorientation of Economic Policy in Indonesia," in *The Dynamics of Economic Policy Reform in South East Asia and the South West Pacific,* ed. Andrew MacIntyre and K. Jaya Suruja (Singapore: Oxford University Press, 1992).
5. Directorate General of Mines, "Proposals for a National Coal Policy," Ministry of Mines and Energy, Jakarta, Indonesia, 1996, 9.
6. National Mining Association, *International Coal,* 6th ed. (Washington, D.C.: National Mining Association, 1996).
7. Ibid.
8. World Bank, *Indonesia: Environment and Development* (Washington, D.C.: International Bank for Reconstruction and Development [World Bank], 1995), 5.
9. Quoted in ibid.

10. Ibid., 9.
11. Republic of Indonesia, *Act No. 4 of 1982 Concerning Basic Provisions for the Management of the Living Environment.*
12. Ibid., Art. 9.
13. Ibid., Art. 10.
14. Ibid., Art. 20.
15. Ibid., Art. 22.
16. Ibid., Art. 16.
17. Republic of Indonesia, State Minister of Population and Environment, Decree No. KEP-491/MENKLH/6/1987 (June 1987).
18. Republic of Indonesia, Government regulation No. 29, 1986, pertaining to Analisis Mengenai Dampak Lingkungan (AMDAL).
19. Carl H. Petrich, "The Applicability of the U.S. NEPA Experience to Indonesia's Environmental Management Challenge" (paper presented at DOEME Workshop II, Jakarta, Indonesia, no date).
20. Adam Swarz, *A Nation in Waiting: Indonesia in the 1990's* (Boulder, Colo.: Westview Press, 1994), chap. 6.
21. Kadar Wiryanto, Ministry of Mines and Energy, interview by Richard Miller, Jakarta, Indonesia, April 1997.
22. Diane Francis, *Bre-X: The Inside Story* (Toronto: Key Porter, 1997).
23. Craig Andrews, "Mining Investment Promotion: A View from the Private Sector," *Natural Resources Forum,* February 1991.
24. Michael Hamilton, "Improving Mining and Environmental Policy in Indonesia," *Land and Water* 41 (July/August 1997): 42.
25. Peter Savage, "Temporal Perspectives in Development Administration," in *Temporal Dimensions of Development Administration,* ed. Dwight Waldo (Durham, N.C.: Duke University Press, 1970), 31.

Index

population growth and, 166
women, poverty and, 165
Quantified emission limitation and reduction obligation (QELRO)
 AGBM proposals, 224
 Kyoto Protocol commitments, 230
Quayle, Dan, 238

Radical environmental NGOs, 61, 62
Rainbow Movement, Czech Republic, 283, 288–289
Ramakrishna, Kilaparti, 24n15
Ramsey, Ross, 208n43
Randers, Jørgen, 49n17, 276n22
Raustiala, Kal, 25n34, 154n2, 254nn7, 8
Realist school of international relations, 2, 53
Regimes. *See* International regimes
Regulatory competition
 environmental, 193–195
 European Union, 77
 failures in, 207n23
 Indonesian mining and, 330
Reilly, William K., 197, 207n30, 237
Renner, Michael, 48n1, 185nn9, 11, 186nn28, 30, 31, 32, 33, 34, 35, 37
Repeat players, treaty compliance and, 143–144
Repetto, Robert, 181–182, 188nn94, 95
Research, environmental NGOs', 67
Revelle, Roger, 218, 221, 234n19
Revesz, Richard L., 206n19
Rhodes, Carolyn, 94n12
Richardson, Dick, 25n21
Richardson, Jeremy J., 94n12, 95n16, 96n41
Rio + 5, New York (1997), 2
Rio Declaration on Environment and Development, 10, 158
 Bush refusal to sign, 236
 international law integration and, 126
 Principle 2, 15
 Principle 10, 20
Ripa di Meana, Carlo, 89–90
Rittberger, Volker, 24n8
River Dragon Has Come!, The, 301
RIVM. *See* National Institute of Public Health and the Environment
Roberts, Adam, 49n12
Roderick, Peter, 151, 154nn2, 12, 155nn24, 25
Rogers, Adam, 185n2
Roman law doctrine limiting sovereignty, 15
Roodman, David Malin, 188nn88, 90
Rosenau, James, 114n6
Rosenbaum, Walter A., 60, 71n17
Ross, Michael, 189n106
Rowlands, Ian H., 24nn8, 19, 25n38
Rubin, Robert, 252
Ruggie, John Gerard, 25n26
Rule supervisory IGOs, 56
Runge, C. Ford, 209n47

Russia. *See* Soviet Union, former
Russo, Thomas, 312n8
Rutland, Peter, 298n2

Sage, Colin, 24n17
Sanctions, trade, 140–141, 152
Sandbrook, Richard, 331n2
Sands, Philippe, 16, 25nn28, 36, 134–135n3, 135nn7, 9, 10, 136nn17, 21, 26, 33, 155nn24, 25
Savage, Peter, 331, 332n25
Sbragia, Alberta, 96n41
Schelling, Thomas C., 250, 255n33
Scherr, S. Jacob, 298n22
Schloming, Gordon C., 70n2
Schmidheiny, Stephan, 207n35
Schmitter, Philippe C., 275n5, 278n49
Schneider, Stephen H., 233n13
Schreurs, Miranda A., 26n41, 94n1
Schumann, Robert, 73
Schwab, Robert M., 206–207n19
Schwarzbach, David, 298n22
Science
 CFC control, 247–248
 climate change, 212–218
 economic costs of greenhouse gas emission reductions and, 248
Scientists' Statement on Global Climatic Disruption (1997), 219–220
Secondary legislation, IGOs and, 122
Second Assessment Report, IPCC, socioeconomic analyses of, 219
Second Best, Theory of, 207n24
Second World Climate Conference, Ministerial Declaration of, 222
Self-reporting, treaty compliance and, 147
Serafy, Sarah El, 206n13
Seuss, Hans, 218, 221, 234n19
Shackleton, Michael, 94n8
Shui Fu, 315n46
Sikkink, Kathryn, 24n16, 25n27
Silent Spring, 57
Simmons, P. J., 205n3
Simms, Andrew, 71n16
Singh, Jyoti Shankar, 186n51
Single European Act of 1987, 74
Sinks, climate change, 224, 232, 235nn45, 49
Sitarz, Daniel, 185n2, 185n3
Sklar, Leonard S., 316n59
Skoda (Temelin contractor), 281, 288
Skogh, Gören, 155n22
Skolnikoff, Eugene B., 25n34, 154n2
Slaughter, Anne-Marie, 114n10
Sloan, Blaine, 49n29
Slocock, Brian, 298
Smil, Vaclav, 312n5, 314n27
Smith, Fred L., 71n32
Social Democratic Party
 Netherlands, 272
 Czech Republic, 290